VOLUME 580

MARCH 2002

THE ANNALS

of The American Academy *of* Political
and Social Science

ALAN W. HESTON, *Editor*

EARLY ADULTHOOD IN CROSS-NATIONAL PERSPECTIVE

CABRINI COLLEGE LIBRARY
610 King of Prussia Road
Radnor, PA 19087

Ⓢ Sage Publications   *THOUSAND OAKS   LONDON   NEW DELHI*

S0-BSB-079

#49056349

H
I
.A4
V.580

The American Academy of Political and Social Science

c/o Fels Center of Government, University of Pennsylvania, 3814 Walnut Street,
Philadelphia, PA 19104; (215) 746-6500; (215) 898-1202 (fax); www.1891.org

Board of Directors
LAWRENCE W. SHERMAN, *President*
KATHLEEN HALL JAMIESON, *Chair*

ELIJAH ANDERSON
STEPHEN B. BURBANK
HENRY LOUIS GATES, JR.
FREDERICK HELDRING
RICHARD D. LAMBERT
JANICE FANNING MADDEN

SARA MILLER McCUNE
MARY ANN MEYERS
KLAUS NAUDÉ
LOUIS H. POLLAK
JAROSLAV PELIKAN

Editors, THE ANNALS

ALAN W. HESTON, *Editor*
JENNIFER WARREN, *Managing Editor*

RICHARD D. LAMBERT, *Editor Emeritus*
DARLENE WOLTMAN, *Business Manager*
RENOS NEOPHYTOU, *Deputy Business Manager*

Origin and Purpose. The Academy was organized December 14, 1889, to promote the progress of political and social science, especially through publications and meetings. The Academy does not take sides in controverted questions, but seeks to gather and present reliable information to assist the public in forming an intelligent and accurate judgment.

Meetings. The Academy occasionally holds a meeting in the spring extending over two days.

Publications. THE ANNALS of the American Academy of Political and Social Science is the bimonthly publication of The Academy. Each issue contains articles on some prominent social or political problem, written at the invitation of the editors. Also, monographs are published from time to time, numbers of which are distributed to pertinent professional organizations. These volumes constitute important reference works on the topics with which they deal, and they are extensively cited by authorities throughout the United States and abroad. The papers presented at the meetings of The Academy are included in THE ANNALS.

Membership. Each member of The Academy receives THE ANNALS and may attend the meetings of The Academy. Membership is open only to individuals. Annual dues: $65.00 for the regular paperbound edition (clothbound, $100.00). For members outside the U.S.A., add $24.00 for shipping of your subscription. Members may also purchase single issues of THE ANNALS for $20.00 each (clothbound, $28.00).

Subscriptions. THE ANNALS of the American Academy of Political and Social Science (ISSN 0002-7162) is published six times annually—in January, March, May, July, September, and November—by Sage Publications, 2455 Teller Road, Thousand Oaks, CA 91320. Telephone: (800) 818-SAGE (7243) and (805) 499-9774; FAX/Order line: (805) 375-1700. Copyright © 2002 by the American Academy of Political and Social Science. Institutions may subscribe to THE ANNALS at the annual rate: $420.00 (clothbound, $475.00). Add $24.00 per year for subscriptions outside the U.S.A. Institutional rates for single issues: $81.00 each (clothbound, $91.00).

Periodicals postage paid at Thousand Oaks, California, and at additional mailing offices.

Single issues of THE ANNALS may be obtained by individuals who are not members of The Academy for $32.00 each (clothbound, $42.00). Single issues of THE ANNALS have proven to be excellent supplementary texts for classroom use. Direct inquiries regarding adoptions to THE ANNALS c/o Sage Publications (address below).

All correspondence concerning membership in The Academy, dues renewals, inquiries about membership status, and/or purchase of single issues of THE ANNALS should be sent to THE ANNALS c/o Sage Publications, 2455 Teller Road, Thousand Oaks, CA 91320. Telephone: (800) 818-SAGE (7243) and (805) 499-9774; FAX/Order line: (805) 375-1700. *Please note that orders under $30 must be prepaid.* Sage affiliates in London and India will assist institutional subscribers abroad with regard to orders, claims, and inquiries for both subscriptions and single issues.

Printed on recycled, acid-free paper

THE ANNALS

© 2002 *by* The American Academy *of* Political *and* Social Science

All rights reserved. No part of this volume may be reproduced or utilized in any form or by any means, electronic or mechanical, including photocopying, recording, or by any information storage and retrieval system, without permission in writing from the publisher. All inquiries for reproduction or permission should be sent to Sage Publications, 2455 Teller Road, Thousand Oaks, CA 91320.

Editorial Office: Fels Center of Government, University of Pennsylvania, 3814 Walnut Street, Philadelphia, PA 19104-6197.

For information about membership* (individuals only) and subscriptions (institutions), address:

SAGE PUBLICATIONS
2455 Teller Road
Thousand Oaks, CA 91320

Sage Production Staff: BARBARA CORRIGAN, SCOTT SPRINGER, and ROSE TYLAK

From India and South Asia, write to:
SAGE PUBLICATIONS INDIA Pvt. Ltd
P.O. Box 4215
New Delhi 110 048
INDIA

From Europe, the Middle East, and Africa, write to:
SAGE PUBLICATIONS LTD
6 Bonhill Street
London EC2A 4PU
UNITED KINGDOM

*Please note that members of The Academy receive THE ANNALS with their membership.
International Standard Serial Number ISSN 0002-7162
International Standard Book Number ISBN 0-7619-2690-9 (Vol. 580, 2002 paper)
International Standard Book Number ISBN 0-7619-2689-5 (Vol. 580, 2002 cloth)
Manufactured in the United States of America. First printing, January 2002.

The articles appearing in THE ANNALS are abstracted or indexed in *Academic Abstracts, Academic Search, America: History and Life, Asia Pacific Database, Book Review Index, CAB Abstracts Database, Central Asia: Abstracts & Index, Communication Abstracts, Corporate ResourceNET, Criminal Justice Abstracts, Current Citations Express, Current Contents: Social & Behavioral Sciences, e-JEL, EconLit, Expanded Academic Index, Guide to Social Science & Religion in Periodical Literature, Health Business FullTEXT, HealthSTAR FullTEXT, Historical Abstracts, International Bibliography of the Social Sciences, International Political Science Abstracts, ISI Basic Social Sciences Index, Journal of Economic Literature on CD, LEXIS-NEXIS, MasterFILE FullTEXT, Middle East: Abstracts & Index, North Africa: Abstracts & Index, PAIS International, Periodical Abstracts, Political Science Abstracts, Sage Public Administration Abstracts, Social Science Source, Social Sciences Citation Index, Social Sciences Index Full Text, Social Services Abstracts, Social Work Abstracts, Sociological Abstracts, Southeast Asia: Abstracts & Index, Standard Periodical Directory (SPD), TOPICsearch, Wilson OmniFile V,* and *Wilson Social Sciences Index/Abstracts,* and are available on microfilm from University Microfilms, Ann Arbor, Michigan.

Information about membership rates, institutional subscriptions, and back issue prices may be found on the facing page.

Advertising. Current rates and specifications may be obtained by writing to THE ANNALS Advertising and Promotion Manager at the Thousand Oaks office (address above).

Claims. Claims for undelivered copies must be made no later than six months following month of publication. The publisher will supply missing copies when losses have been sustained in transit and when the reserve stock will permit.

Change of Address. Six weeks' advance notice must be given when notifying of change of address to ensure proper identification. Please specify name of journal. **POSTMASTER:** Send address changes to: THE ANNALS of the American Academy of Political and Social Science, c/o Sage Publications, 2455 Teller Road, Thousand Oaks, CA 91320.

THE ANNALS

of The American Academy *of* Political
and Social Science

ALAN W. HESTON, *Editor*

---------------- **FORTHCOMING**----------------

GLOBALIZATION AND DEMOCRACY
Special Editors: Ronaldo Munck
and Barry Gills
Volume 581   May 2002

CROSS-NATIONAL DRUG POLICY
Special Editors: Robert MacCoun
and Peter Reuter
Volume 582   July 2002

ALTERNATIVE MEDICINE
Special Editors: Helen Scheehan
and Barry Brenton
Volume 583   September 2002

See page 2 for information on Academy membership and
purchase of single volumes of **The Annals.**

CONTENTS

'est in the cultural, social, and economic forces that shape the life
ᴄᴏᴜ_ and establish critical life transitions can be traced back to the seminal
ideas of Karl Mannheim (1923). Building on Mannheim's work, in the middle
part of the past century, Matilda Riley and her colleagues under the aegis of
the Social Science Research Council published a monumental review of theory and research on aging. This volume drew on research concepts and tools
from demography, cultural studies, developmental psychology, sociology, and
history. It explored the meaning of age for individuals and social systems and
laid out an agenda of research on the cultural meaning of age, the social organization of age groupings, and the biological change that accompanies aging,
helping to found the field of social gerontology. It established age as a fundamental pillar for analyzing individual and social change in the behavioral sciences. The most recent effort to expand the interdisciplinary work was spear-
headed by Reed Larson who has organized an interdisciplinary team of
researchers to review comparative research on adolescent development
(Larson 2002).

Over the past half century, notable progress has occurred in refining theory about age-related phenomena as well as developing the tools to examine
aging as an individual process and how social systems respond to the aging of
populations (Buchmann 1989; Coleman 1961; Elder 1974; Ryder 1965). The
meaning of age has been unpacked by cultural historians and contemporary
ethnographers; biological and psychological advances have illuminated the
physical and interpersonal components of development from fetal age to old
age; and demographers and sociologists have made strides in understanding
the ramifications of both period and cohort effects.

Despite the immense achievements in the second half of the twentieth century, we are still a long way from realizing the vision of C. Wright Mills who,
drawing on Mannheim's work, argued that understanding social change
required investigating the minute points of the intersections of biography
and history within society (Mills 1959, ch. 9; see also Mills 2000). Nowhere is
the gap between the vision and the reality more evident than in comparative
and historical research on the organization of the life course—the subject of
this issue. Our theories purporting to explain the organization of the life
course have not been up to the task of reconciling cross-national differences,
and our methodological tools for investigating differences within and across
societies are still crude. This set of articles on the similarities and differences
in the transition to adulthood in nations with advanced economies poses a
series of fascinating puzzles that when solved will illuminate both our understanding of historical change and personal development in early adulthood.
The two final articles in this issue advance our understanding of the wide differences that are displayed in the preceding articles.

The transition to adulthood has interested cultural anthropologists, sociologists, and demographers for many decades. Developmental psychologists—long interested in childhood, adolescence, and changes in later life—have also begun to appreciate the observations of Erik Erikson (1963): that important, even essential, processes occur in this period of life. In part, interest has grown as the boundaries of adolescence were extended beyond the teen years (Furstenberg 2000). *Youth*, a term more familiar to chroniclers of the nineteenth century, seemed a more appropriate term to describe the growing ranks of semiautonomous young people who inhabit the period of life from the late teen years to the early thirties (Kett 1977). Early adulthood has become an amorphous band rather than a sharp transition.

Many of the articles in this issue address the question of why adolescence, as a life stage, no longer serves as a prelude to full adulthood. The postindustrial economy that began to take form in the final third of the twentieth century dramatically altered the established life course pattern that had been in place during the transformation from agrarian economic systems to industrial ones. The highly compressed and tightly organized transition from adolescence to early adulthood, which prevailed during the middle decades of the twentieth century, came to an abrupt end in the 1960s in most Western nations (Buchmann 1989; Kohli 1985; Modell, Furstenberg, and Hershberg 1976; Winsborough 1979). In short order, the age of full-time employment was deferred in favor of an extended period of education for a much greater share of the population between ages eighteen and twenty-two. These changes came more rapidly in some countries than in others, as is attested to by several articles in this issue. The prolongation of education and full-time employment had profound changes on other events in the early part of adulthood. Most notably, they wrecked havoc on the orderly progression to marriage and parenthood that characterized the baby boom era in the past century.

It is far easier to describe this broad and relatively uniform change in Western societies than to explain the wide variation that occurred in how different nations reshaped the transition to adulthood. Or perhaps we should say adult *transitions*. That there are deep and profound differences within the West in the early part of adulthood cannot be contested if readers consider the array of evidence presented in this issue. However, it is equally clear that no simple scheme for explaining the social organization of early adulthood seems to account for the diverse patterns described in many of the articles.

As Thomas D. Cook and Frank F. Furstenberg Jr. point out in their article, the countries look remarkably similar at age fifteen: virtually no one has left school, established an independent household, assumed a full-time job, formed a union, or begun childbearing. And they are almost as similar again at age thirty-five, by which time a vast majority of adults in every nation have negotiated all of the transitions. However, during the two decades between these ages, youth in many countries are likely to experience early adulthood in quite varied ways. The paths to adulthood in Italy, Sweden, Germany, and the United States (to take a few examples) eventually converge, but along the way it is very differently arranged and must feel very dissimilar to those negotiating the twists and turns as well as those who observe the transition events. How are we to make sense of these differences?

The most refined theoretical work on the problem of why variation occurs has been advanced by Esping-Andersen (1990), who identified distinct economic and policy regimes that emerged from historical and cultural differences among nations in response to industrialization. These constellations, many suspect, should have some impact on regulating the flow of individuals into the labor force and hence the shaping of adult transitions. However, Esping-Andersen's typology of capitalist and welfare states requires some refinement if it is to map on well to many of the aspects of adult transitions that are described in the articles contained in this issue, as Breen and Buchmann point out in the concluding article. Breen and Buchmann present an intriguing scheme for understanding the disparate country-level differences.

This project was conceived during 1997-1998, when the coeditors of this issue participated in a yearlong seminar that focused on this problem at the Center for Advanced Study in the Behavioral Sciences (CASBS) under the sponsorship of the Carnegie Foundation. Carnegie had supported an earlier initiative to examine the transition into adolescence, producing a series of volumes that summarized the results of a decade-long effort to map what is known about early adolescence (Carnegie Council on Adolescent Development 1995). We set out to extend this approach to the transition from adolescence to adulthood. It became quickly apparent that the agenda had to be pared down to a more modest scale if only because very little research had been carried out in the fields of developmental psychology, history, and sociology on adult transitions. Much of the work that has been done in this field has been carried out by social demographers and, to a lesser extent, economists, who have tracked entrance into the labor force.

We decided that a reasonable starting point was to examine historical and cross-national data on the transitions that had long interested demographers: departure from school, entrance into the labor force, setting up an independent household, union formation, and childbearing. No one, up to then, had comprehensively investigated what was known about these transitions across time and across nations with advanced economies. We later expanded our purview to include comparative data on the health and well-being of young adults. (In the past several years, under the leadership of Reed Larson, a committee from the Society for Research on Adolescence has done a superb review of the existing literature with special attention to the developmental processes that take place during adolescence and early adulthood.)

Oddly enough, we discovered more data than analysis existed. Over the past several decades, international research teams had begun to collaborate in a number of efforts involving the collection of comparable data from a number of nations on one or another domains of adult life such as education and labor force participation, problem behaviors, or time use. The earliest of these studies, such as the time use surveys, now have accumulated several waves of information, permitting historical analysis. However, little or no effort had been devoted to investigating how these various domains are packaged together in different nations or what could be loosely thought of as the social organization of early adulthood. (For an exception, see the work of Karl Ulrich Mayer forthcoming.)

So our small seminar decided that our task for the year would be to identify the major data sets on which comparative and historical analysis could be carried out and to organize a team of researchers to prepare descriptive papers on the extant data. With additional assistance from the Foundation for Child Development and the MacArthur Foundation, we were able to commission a series of papers, most of which have been included in this issue. Our aim was then to look across the data sets to discover what could be learned about the causes and consequences of different "regimes" of the transition to adulthood. Our intention was to reveal how the timing, order, and relation of the adult transitions and related behaviors of individuals in the age group eighteen to thirty-four had changed over time. A second objective was to explore how different nations had organized this part of the life course.

Whenever possible, we endeavored to involve authors who were already intimately familiar with the data that they were examining. The guidelines for analysis were hammered out in a working conference in 1998. Our goal was first and foremost to describe what could be learned about the transition to adulthood and its accompanying patterns of behavior from each data set. We confined ourselves primarily to the countries with developed economic systems, though we allowed latitude, depending on the data source and domain of interest, to include nations that might be of comparative interest such as the eastern bloc of European countries. Finally, we strongly encouraged the authors to identify groupings of nations that appeared to share the same regime of adult transitions. Whenever the data permitted, we urged the authors to examine historical change in patterns of adult transitions or behavior associated with early adulthood. While these guidelines appear relatively simple and straightforward, we discovered that they were not so easily implemented in practice.

Secondary analysis of this sort is no task for the fainthearted. Formidable obstacles lie in the path of conducting cross-national data collection even when it is undertaken by researchers who already possess some familiarity with the data sets, as was true for most of the authors in this issue. We will not dwell at length on the political problems that some authors encountered in gaining access to the data sources. Nonetheless, this barrier to secondary analysis of cross-national data sets cannot completely be ignored. It created serious problems for some authors, who found themselves in lengthy negotiations with individual researchers in different countries who held the rights to data that sometimes had been collected decades earlier. No statute of limitation exists in most countries on the time it takes for data to enter the public domain. Clearly, the advent of the Web has helped to make country-level data more widely available, but it has not necessarily liberated data sets from investigators who display little enthusiasm for sharing their data with unknown researchers across the Atlantic.

Access was not the only problem our authors faced in assembling extant data. Several authors were forced to piece together data from different countries because the information had never been properly documented or harmonized. Many of the collaborative studies that had been undertaken over the years involved little actual sharing or exchange of data by national researchers. Data isolated in local archives introduced a set of vexing problems of reconciling seemingly similar surveys. In all the data sets examined in this issue, we rely on information that was intended to be comparable if not identical. Getting closer to the data itself, analysts discovered that sampling design varied in seemingly minor ways that might have large effects. Time diaries were collected in different seasons, the labor force was defined differently, or some such variation. Completion rates ranged from highly respectable to abysmal, vitiating country-level comparisons. And coding schemes were not always followed uniformly, or investigators decided to improvise or elaborate on a set of codes that had not been commonly agreed on. Thus, comparative data is hardly ever completely comparable.

It remains for authors in this issue to adjust for the incomparable features of the data and interpret country-level differences with some caution. Even data collected over time fall prey to variations in research design as investigators invariably try to correct for prior deficiencies and in so doing render comparisons hazardous. More recently, studies such as the Luxembourg Survey and the Family and Fertility Surveys were designed explicitly for use of the international research community. While not free of these concerns, they are designed to minimize them.

Beyond these "merely" methodological problems lies a set of phenomenological concerns that vexes even the most hardened comparative researchers. If, for example, the meaning of marriage differs across nations, it is even less certain what counts as suicide, drunken driving, or leisure time across nations where seemingly objective terms are transformed by varying cultural interpretations. These issues are by no means unique to cross-national research; they bedevil census studies and surveys within nations. However, the problems of interpreting "real" differences are surely magnified when national and cultural boundaries are crossed. So much so that the display of factual data as is presented in this issue must be subjected to both methodological and cultural scrutiny.

For this very reason, two of the participants in the seminar at CASBS, Cook and Furstenberg, along with two international authorities on early adulthood, Marlis Buchmann and Richard Breen, arranged an international meeting to discuss earlier drafts of the articles included in this issue. Annually, the Johann Jacobs Foundation hosts a conference in Marbach, Germany, devoted to topics related to youth and youth policy. In the fall of 1999, some thirty scholars met at Marbach to discuss and interpret the country-level differences of six exemplar countries: Britain, France, Germany, the Netherlands, Sweden, and the United States. These countries were selected for both theoretical and practical reasons.

As Cook and Furstenberg explain in their article reprising highlights of the Marbach meeting, the organizers aimed to select countries that seemed to reflect distinctively different regional, historical, and cultural patterns, or policy and political responses to early adult transitions—what we earlier referred to as different regimes of early adulthood. Our aim was to subject these national specimens to a more thoroughgoing analysis by cultural historians; specialists of youth behavior in sociology, economics, or demography; and policy experts representing the eight nations. On a practical level, our choices of countries were dictated to some extent by the availability of such country experts.

The results of the Marbach meeting were illuminating. We knew more when we left than we did before we arrived—more than a trivial accomplishment for any international meeting—but the conference also confirmed what we suspected when we discussed the findings at an earlier meeting of the paper writers the preceding spring. Country-level differences in the transition to adulthood could not easily be accounted for by historical, cultural, economic, political, or sociological circumstances. Instead, some patterns seemed attributable to particular historical events, cultural differences, policy and political responses to youth problems, or more general economic and social policies. National experts used all of these categories of explanations, often in particular and unique combinations, to account for the demographic and sociological descriptions of their countries. But it was clear that no single overarching theory such as the one advanced by Esping-Andersen (1990) could do justice to the varied set of results that emerged. Breen and Buchmann, in the final article, revisit the data and show how it can be organized into a common theoretical framework.

Readers of the articles, no doubt, will have more to add, and that is one of the main purposes of this issue: to stimulate theoretical and empirical examinations of the transition to adulthood that provide a more parsimonious and satisfying explanation of country-level differences. Without better theory and methods, we cannot even hope to take cross-national comparison beyond the largely Western world represented in this issue. And we cannot expect to understand, much less anticipate, the historical changes now occurring in both economically advanced and economically developing nations. So this issue represents only a down payment on a larger effort that will require both more and better data as well as analysis that blends cultural and political history with common features of social change that have been occurring in countries with advanced economies such as the growth of higher education, the development of new technologies, and the increasing premium put on gender equality.

Clearly, we learned that distinctive differences in the transition to adulthood do exist. That much we can document in the articles describing the different demographic and social behaviors that constitute adult transitions and their sequelae. Many of the contrasts in demographic events are most extreme between Northern and Southern Europe where the timing of full-time employment, household departure, marriage, and childbearing vary by as much as five or more years. Our explanations of these behaviors, however, are inadequate and far too particularistic to satisfy most social scientists. Simply chalking these differences up to cultural constructions or policy supports does not take us very far in understanding how life course arrangements are structured or how they change when conditions dictate. Readers of this issue will occasionally sense the frustration of the authors in accounting for the differences; nonetheless, we believe these differences lay the groundwork for developing better data and a more comprehensive theory of the conditions that alter the cultural and social construction of this stage of life. Nonetheless, as Breen and Buchmann demonstrate, it is possible to gain theoretical leverage by looking at cross-cultural institutional differences that structure the education system and labor market. These systems, in turn, have powerful implications for the ways that young people experience the transition to adulthood.

But there are real limitations to going beyond the description provided in this issue. Further advances require integrating data sets pertaining to different domains of adult transitions. For example, we have made significant strides yet in relating the timing and sequencing of important demographic events with contextual information about educational and training systems, the labor market, and the cultural expectations associated with early adulthood, much less the data about time use or mortality and morbidity. Until these sorts of data are assembled in an integrated data set, we cannot expect to make more headway in comparative research. This kind of international collaboration is not easily organized because the funding is largely sponsored by national or at best regional interests. Or we might say that global social science, in contrast with the global economy, is occurring at a snail's pace.

Without international sponsorship, it is unlikely that many of the methodological problems mentioned earlier can be surmounted. Some promising developments are occurring as European countries have begun to collect and analyze comparable data across the nations in the European Common Market. It is remarkable how few efforts have occurred to do the same in North America, where Canadian and American researchers have not exploited the natural experiment created by two very different policy regimes governing support for youth living side by side. And of course, the comparison with Mexico is equally tempting for similar reasons.

In large measure, the barriers to such comparisons have to do with the organization and funding of research as well as the absence of an academic community that traverses national boundaries. While these boundaries are breaking down to some extent in Europe, they remain virtually intact in North America.

It is easier to imagine the benefits of comparative analysis across the Anglo nations as well. Clearly, Patrick Heuveline and Manuel Eisner, in their respective articles, show that certain early adult patterns exhibiting antisocial and aggressive behavior are remarkably clustered in English-speaking countries. Why this is so remains largely a mystery and a tempting challenge for researchers and historians to explore. However, to our knowledge, there is little or no research that pulls together data that might permit more careful investigation of differences and similarities across the Anglo countries. It would be naive to believe that similarities among the Anglo nations can be traced to any single explanation, but the sources of aggressive and antisocial behavior is an inviting topic for future research.

We suspect that the future of comparative research on this topic will involve some integration of qualitative studies, quantitative surveys, and analysis of census and administrative data. Qualitative research would greatly help in understanding how young people construe early adulthood and interpret what they are doing. The surveys often impose cultural uniformity in response categories that may ignore particularities that lie beneath the surface. Missing the ways that experience is misaligned across national boundaries is, after all, what we are most interested in.

That the nature of early adulthood is changing across the Western world and elsewhere as well is not debated. But the way that the pressures for change are mediated and modified at the national level requires subtle examination by knowledgeable observers. The Marbach conference demonstrated the value of this exchange at the same time that it revealed how limited are our theories of how social change in the life actually plays out—the minute points of the intersections of biography and history that Mills wrote about nearly a half century ago.

Although the picture we can assemble is only partial, it does reveal that adulthood is less easily definable and less easily attained than it was in the middle part of the past century when the old industrial economy began to transform into one requiring different skills, more education, and a mastery of new technology. The fact that countries are managing this transformation quite differently does not mean that the new economic era has not posed similar problems for young adults in becoming incorporated in the larger society. Clearly, one of the by-products of educational extension is later family formation and perhaps more fluid family arrangements than in the recent past. However, as Fussell points out in her article, this accommodation introduces a new set of unsettling concerns such as population replacement or the stability of childcare institutions. Young adults reacting individually, as Mannheim noted nearly a century ago, create cohort changes that ripple across society, forcing institutions to adapt or malfunction.

The inability to provide school-to-work mechanisms in some countries and the strains on the apprentice system in others are resulting from changes in the labor market that is unable to absorb unskilled workers and anticipate changes in labor demand. The growth of the university as "a parking lot," providing time for youth who otherwise would not be employed or employable is another manifestation of the poor articulation between the educational system and the new economy. The inability of most young adults to assume stable employment if not stable career trajectories has powerful effects on marriage and childbearing. Along with the growing expectation of gender equality, cohabitation has become a way of testing commitment and, in some societies, an alternative to making premature commitments. Childbearing is inevitably deferred when children both are an expression of family commitment and require a steady flow of resources.

The demographic changes extend the period of growing up and push the youth stage to ages that were once unimaginable. But if the early part of the life course is becoming more protracted, so too is the latter part as lifestyles and medical advances extend the older years. Squeezed in between are the middle years that curiously provide more of an imagined contrast to the period of growing up or growing old than a distinctive stage. In fact, in many advanced societies, there is reason to suspect that the middle years are characterized by greater demands created by helping to manage longer spells of dependent youth while caring for a greater number of elderly kin.

This issue only begins to address the fascinating questions of how the rearrangement of the life course is playing out in the psychological, economic health, and social adjustment of the various age groupings. There are many theoretical reasons to believe that the freedom accompanying early adulthood may come at a cost for individuals and society. As Durkheim (1951) so compellingly argued more than a century ago, lack of social regulation resulting from the absence of institutional engagement and institutional control places stress on individuals and fosters anomie in societies. High rates of problem behavior are characteristic of youth outside of family, educational systems, the military, or the labor force. Incorporation into these systems promotes health and reduces risk-taking behaviors.

Policies that engage young people in school, work, civic life, and family are far more accessible in some nations than others. While neither Heuveline nor Eisner is able to test the link between institutional involvement and problem behavior, their findings cry out for a more direct examination of the social integration of young adults and the consequences for civic and social behavior.

This points again to the need to develop more holistic and integrated data sets that allow us to look at both macro-level policies and economic conditions as well as institutional arrangements, patterns of adult transitions, and individual development in the young adult years. It was our original dream to provide such an integrated data set—like many dreams, one larger than we could have imagined when this research undertaking began. If this issue pushes that dream closer to reality, then we think readers will judge it to be a great success.

FRANK F. FURSTENBERG Jr.
THOMAS D. COOK
ROBERT SAMPSON
GAIL SLAP

References

Buchmann, Marlis. 1989. *The script of life in modern society: Entry into adulthood in a changing world*. Chicago: University of Chicago Press.

Carnegie Council on Adolescent Development. 1995. *Great transitions: Preparing adolescents for a new century*. New York: Carnegie.

Coleman, James S., with John W. C. Johnstone and Kurt Jonassohn. 1961. *The adolescent society*. Westport, CT: Greenwood.

Durkheim, E. 1951. *Suicide, a study in ecology*. Glencoe, IL: Free Press.

Elder, Glen H. 1974. *Children of the great depression*. Chicago: University of Chicago Press.

Erikson, Erik H. 1963. *Childhood and society*. New York: Norton.

Esping-Andersen, G. 1990. *The three worlds of welfare capitalism*. Princeton, NJ: Princeton University Press.

Furstenberg, Frank F. 2000. The sociology of adolescence and youth in the 1990s: A critical commentary. *Journal of Marriage and the Family* 62:896-910.

Kett, Joseph. 1977. *Rites of passage: Adolescence in America*. New York: Basic Books.

Kohli, Martin. 1985. The world we forgot: A historical review of the life course. In *Later life: The social psychology of aging*, edited by Victor W. Marshall, 271-303. Beverly Hills, CA: Sage.

Larson, Reed, ed. 2002. *Adolescence in the Twenty-First Century* 12 (1).

Mannheim, Karl. 1952 [1923]. The problem of the generations. In *Essays on the sociology of knowledge*. London: Routledge and Kegan Paul.

Mayer, Karl Ulrich. Forthcoming. The paradox of global social changes and national path dependencies: Life course patterns in advanced societies. In *Inclusions / Exclusions*, edited by A. E. Woodward and Martin Kohli.

Mills, C. W. 1959. *Sociological imagination*. New York: Oxford University Press.

———. 2000. *Sociological imagination*, with a new afterward by Todd Gitlin. New York: Oxford University Press.

Modell, John, Frank F. Furstenberg, and Theodor Hershberg. 1976. Social change and transitions to adulthood in historical perspective. *Journal of Family History* 1 (1): 7-32.

Riley, Matilda White, Marilyn Johnson, and Anne Foner. 1972. *Aging and society, vol. 3: A sociology of age stratification*. New York: Russell Sage.

Ryder, Norman B. 1965. The cohort as a concept in the study of social change. *American Sociological Review* 30:843-61.

Winsborough, Halliman. 1979. Changes in the transition to adulthood. In *Aging from birth to death: Interdisciplinary perspective*, edited by Mathilda W. Riley, 137-52. Boulder, CO: Westview.

ANNALS, *AAPSS*, **580**, March 2002

The Transition to
Adulthood in Aging Societies

By ELIZABETH FUSSELL

ABSTRACT: Population aging and the delay in family formation that are occurring in industrialized countries are intimately related. Young adults are spending more of their early twenties attending school and focusing on employment, and they are postponing marriage and childbearing until their late twenties and early thirties. In sum, they are having fewer children later in life, and in doing so, they contribute to the aging of the population. Some argue that population aging results in lower public and private investments in children and greater public expenditures on the elderly. In this article, the author reviews evidence for this argument and concludes that population aging does not necessarily result in lesser investment in children and youth. Instead, our new demographic condition demands a renegotiation of the public intergenerational contract between age groups.

Elizabeth Fussell is an assistant professor in the sociology department of Tulane University. Her teaching and research specializations are demography, migration, youth, and sociology of the family. She received her doctorate from the University of Wisconsin–Madison in 1998.

E CONOMICALLY developed countries face two interrelated demographic trends that will shape our collective future. The first trend is known as the second demographic transition in which delayed age at marriage, increased prevalence of cohabiting unions, and more frequent divorce result in low fertility overall and proportionately more nonmarital fertility (Lesthaeghe 1995). The second trend is population aging in which the elderly population is growing faster than the youthful population. These two trends are intimately tied together. As young people delay or forgo forming families and fewer children are added to the population, the median age of the population rises. The consequences of this dynamic process of family change and population aging have only begun to be observed. The focus of attention has mainly been on the problem of economically providing for the growing population older than age 65 (Davis, Bernstam, and Ricardo-Campbell 1986; National Research Council 2001). Only a few researchers have asked what the consequences of population aging will be for children and youth (Preston 1984; Fussell 2002).

In the first demographic transition in Europe and the countries settled by Europeans, fertility and mortality rates shifted from high to low levels. During this transition, marriage norms suppressed the average number of births women experienced by delaying the age at marriage until men achieved economic independence and stigmatizing nonmarital fertility (Coale and Watkins 1986). In the second demographic transition,

the relationship between marriage and fertility has weakened. Marriage is more optional as greater emphasis is put on the quality of the marital relationship rather than the ability of marriage partners to fulfill functional roles. This change is associated with more nonmarital births, a late age at marriage, an increase in the practice of premarital cohabitation, and more frequent divorce (Cherlin 1992; Lesthaeghe 1995). As a result of these changes, the traditional family of two opposite-sex parents and their biological offspring is no longer as normative. Varied family forms, including single parents, cohabiting parents, same-sex parents, and stepparent families are increasingly common. One demographic consequence of these changes is that birth rates are at an all-time low.

Low fertility is of concern primarily because it causes population aging. The age of a national population is mainly determined by the fertility of that nation, but "the death rate determines what the average birth rate in the long run must be" for the population to reproduce itself but not explode or implode (Coale 1964, 57). In economically developed countries, most deaths occur relatively late in life, and they are balanced by a similar number of births. Thus, the median age of the population is relatively old, and population growth rates are close to zero. An older population age structure demands that a relatively smaller labor force support the relatively larger elder population. Preston (1984) asserted that this has contributed to diminishing public and private investments in children. Thus, sustaining an old population depends on maintaining a labor force that can be productive enough to reproduce and support children and youth and assist in supporting the retired population. This article examines the young adult life course in industrialized countries undergoing the second demographic transition. In doing so, it opens a discussion about how these countries might invest in youth in an attempt to ameliorate the problems associated with an older population age structure.

DATA

The data used in this analysis come from a variety of published demographic sources assembled in the United States Census Bureau's (2001) International Database (IDB). The IDB contains the most recently available demographic data for all countries and areas. These include rates of population growth, age distributions, age-specific fertility and mortality rates, marital status, and economic activity broken down by age and sex. I have included industrialized nations having complete data for the 1990s. These data are supplemented with data on education from the United Nations Educational, Scientific, and Cultural Organization and migration from the Organization for Economic Cooperation and Development.

THEORIES OF LATER AND LESS CHILDBEARING

In European countries undergoing the first demographic transition,

marriage and childbearing often occurred in the mid-twenties, after most young men achieved economic independence. In the twentieth century, the timing of age at first marriage for men and women[1] declined from the mid-twenties in the 1900s to the early twenties during the marriage boom after World War II but then began to increase again (Cherlin 1992; Hajnal 1953). Modell, Furstenberg, and Hershberg (1976) showed that between 1880 and 1970 in the United States, the age congruity of family and economic transitions increased—in other words, movement into family roles followed movement into economic roles more closely in 1970 than in 1880. Rindfuss (1991) also found that transitions into economic and family roles are typically concentrated in the early twenties for the graduating high school class of 1972 in the United States. This concentration of life course events was stressful and generally unsustainable. Since the 1970s, we have seen a growing separation in time between the age at which young people enter into economic roles and when they move into family roles. What has caused young men and women to delay entering into family roles?

Easterlin (1987) offered an explanation for later and less childbearing based on intergenerational income ratios. He proposed that young adults delay childbearing until they have achieved levels of economic well-being similar to those they experienced as children. Those who grew up in modest conditions will achieve the necessary level of well-being early and thus begin childbearing earlier and have more children than those who grew up in relatively better-off times. This explains why the small depression era birth cohort had more children earlier during the post–World War II period, while the large baby boom generation delayed childbearing until the mid-1980s through the 1990s. However, this cyclical explanation does not explain the long-run decline in fertility.

Changes in women's economic roles better explain changes in marriage and fertility patterns over the length of the century. As women achieved higher levels of education and entered the labor force in greater numbers, they had fewer children. In economic terms, when women had more employment options, the opportunity costs of having many children exceeded women's earnings on average. This view of fertility decline posits that men and women behave as rational economic actors and maximize their marriage and fertility choices according to their labor market opportunities (Becker 1981; Oppenheimer 1988; Chafetz and Hagan 1996). However, this explanation is also weakened by the fact that fertility began to decline long before women's entry into the nondomestic economy.

Lesthaeghe (1995) argued that economic explanations are not sufficient to explain changes in family formation patterns. He argued that the long-run secular declines in fertility are not well explained by intergenerational income ratios and only partially explained by changes in women's labor force participation. In the second demographic transition, ideational and attitudinal changes,

such as increased antiauthoritarian sentiment, the strengthening of market orientation, the need for self-fulfillment and recognition, belief in the symmetry of gender roles, and increased tolerance of deviance created the social context necessary for the acceptance and diffusion of non-traditional family formation patterns. Furthermore, once these ideational changes spread throughout society, it is impossible for people to revert to previous ways of thinking and behaving.

These theories suggest that the economic circumstances of young families, the labor force participation of women, and changes in ideology, particularly gender ideology, have all played a role in fertility decline. In the next section of the article, I show how a new dynamic of increasing time spent in school and less stable employment in advanced industrial countries have altered the early life course of the majority of young adults in these countries, a change that undoubtedly impacted their family formation patterns as well.

LONGER EDUCATION,
LESS STABLE EMPLOYMENT,
AND LATER FAMILY FORMATION

In the last half of the twentieth century, the spread of secondary education has fundamentally shaped the young adult life course by occupying most of young adults' time in their teen years. In most countries, nearly all adolescents attend secondary school until the mandatory age, which ranges from fourteen to eighteen[2] (see Table 1). The Organization for Economic Cooperation and

TABLE 1

NET ENROLLMENT RATES IN ALL PUBLIC AND PRIVATE FULL-TIME SECONDARY EDUCATION, ARRANGED IN DESCENDING ORDER FOR AGE SEVENTEEN, IN 1992

Country	Age							
	14	15	16	17	18	19	20	21
Belgium	98.9	98.7	97.2	93.6	49.8	25.1	10.6	4.4
Germany (FTFR)	93.9	93.1	95.3	92.8	82.3	55	29.3	16
Netherlands	98.7	99.0	97.3	90.8	67.9	42.3	25.4	14.7
France	94.3	94.1	92.1	87.2	58.6	34	12	3.1
Sweden	99.7	95.6	89.2	87	59.6	11.5	2.7	1.7
Norway	99.4	99.3	92.8	86.6	77.2	34.6	17.6	11.9
Finland	99.8	99.8	94.5	85.8	79.7	26.8	16.5	15.3
Switzerland	98.3	95.8	85.2	82	74.2	48.9	20.6	8.2
Poland		81.6	85.1	81.6	49.8	17.3	5.8	
Denmark	93.4	97.8	92.4	80.1	68.9	48.4	28.3	16.3
Canada	99.8	98.7	96.3	72	36.9	11.1	14	
United States	98.7	95.7	91.4	72	20.6	5.8	1.7	0.6
Ireland	97.6	94.3	87.5	70.2	33.1	11.5	7	3.6
Spain	100.4	91	75.6	66.9	35.5	20.7	17.2	10.6
New Zealand	98.9	96.7	87.8	65.7	20.8	5.9	2.4	1.7
Greece	94.2	86.1	88.4	62.1	19.4	10.5	4.7	3.1
Australia	97.5	92	78.7	58.8	14.2	2.8	3.3	
United Kingdom	99.6	98.9	75.3	55.3	18.7	4.3	1.9	1.2
Hungary	88.7	84.4	75.2	45.4	12.2	3.9	1.4	
Czech Republic	106.4	90.2	86.9	39.4				
Russia	95.1	59.6	47.7	8.4	0.1			

SOURCE: Organization for Economic Cooperation and Development (1995a).
NOTE: FTFR = Former Territory of the Federal Republic of Germany.

Development ([OECD] 1995) concluded that current school enrollment rates "suggest that universal secondary education is on the horizon" in western Europe and Scandinavia, where more than 80 percent of seventeen-year-olds were currently enrolled in school in 1992. The numbers also look promising for the group of English-speaking countries (the United Kingdom, the United States, Canada, Australia, and New Zealand) and southern European countries although the enrollment rates at age seventeen are slightly lower, ranging from 55 to 72 percent. In contrast, the eastern European countries have both lower age limits for compulsory education and lower enrollment rates at all ages. However, even while a larger proportion of teens are in school, their smaller birth cohorts are diminishing the demand for secondary education.

Today, the challenge facing industrialized countries is to improve the quality of the labor force and increase their earning ability (OECD 1998). Expanding tertiary education to a greater proportion of the population is one means for increasing human capital stocks. OECD found that during the 1990s, the expected number of years an individual spent attending school rose significantly and there was an expansion of

TABLE 2

NET ENROLLMENT RATES IN ALL PUBLIC AND PRIVATE FULL-TIME
TERTIARY EDUCATION (UNIVERSITY AND NONUNIVERSITY)
ARRANGED IN DESCENDING ORDER BY AGE EIGHTEEN, IN 1992

Country	Age							
	17	18	19	20	21	22	23	24
United States	3.3	33.8	36.7	31.3	27.8	19.2	12.0	8.0
Belgium	0.7	27.8	36.0	34.4	27.2	18.5	10.9	6.1
Canada	9.4	23.9	35.9	33.6	28.4	21.4	14.3	9.6
Greece		25.6	34.2	20.9	15.8	8.1	6.0	3.7
France	1.9	20.1	30.8	34.6	30.4	22.8	15.7	10.1
Ireland	6.8	24.5	27.6	22.6	15.8	9.7	5.6	3.6
Australia	15.2	29.1	27.4	20.4	13.6	9.0	6.3	4.6
New Zealand	1.5	19.7	24.9	22.9	17.9	11.2	6.7	4.5
Spain	0.3	18.3	24.0	25.5	23.4	21.3	16.5	12.6
Netherlands	1.6	10.9	19.9	23.6	24	21.4	17.6	12.6
United Kingdom	1.4	14.9	19.6	17.6	12.5	7.2	4.4	3.1
Czech Republic		17.0	14.4	12.4	12.4	9.6	1.4	
Norway		0.5	14.0	19.3	21.4	21.9	19.9	16.2
Poland		0.7	13.6	17.6	15.1	13.2	11.4	8.3
Austria		5.8	12.8	16.1	16.7	16.3	16.2	15.3
Finland	0.5	2.2	12.8	17.9	25.1	27.3	24.8	21.5
Sweden		1.1	12.8	13.9	14.4	14.5	13.7	12.4
Hungary		6.0	10.3	11.5	10	7.8	5.4	3.1
Russia	18.7	17.8	7.7	2.8	1.5	0.9	0.5	0.3
Germany (FTFR)	0.6	1.7	6.1	12	15.1	16.5	17.2	17.3
Denmark		0.5	5.0	13	18.5	21.4	21.7	20.3
Switzerland	0.2	1.0	3.9	9.0	12.4	12.8	12.0	10.6

SOURCE: Organization for Economic Cooperation and Development (1995a).
NOTE: FTFR = Former Territory of the Federal Republic of Germany.

education to include more people outside of the traditional school ages in European member countries. This expansion of tertiary education is not uniform across countries (see Table 2). The English-speaking countries and most of the western and southern European countries show high enrollments concentrated in the traditional ages of tertiary education (seventeen to twenty-one). The eastern European and Scandinavian countries, however, have lower enrollment rates overall, peaking at later ages. Clearly, higher education occupies some young adults' time,

but it is not the only productive activity in which they are engaged.

Young adults also increase their human capital through early experimental or trial labor force participation. Among industrialized countries, there are different systems for channeling youth into occupations. In western and northern Europe, few teenagers work while attending school and combine the two only to a limited degree in their early and late twenties. In many of these countries, general and vocational education is organized in schools, so students do not enter into formal employment until completing their education. In the Anglo-Saxon countries, some youth receive on the job training in part-time or seasonal employment, but there are relatively few programs that channel them into jobs (Arum and Shavit 1995). In the central European countries of Austria, Germany, and Switzerland, the vocational and educational training system tracks students from school into work. But these programs are part of the old industrial structure and are not responsive enough to changes in labor demand, especially as information and communication technology changes production processes and consequently labor demand (Heinz 2000; Wyn and Dwyer 2000). Nevertheless, some combination of school and work during adolescence is likely to be helpful in managing the school-to-work transition.

In some countries, school and employment compete for adolescents' time, and in others, they more easily combine. Table 3 shows the proportion of each age group in various combinations of education and employment for countries included in the OECD (1998) Education Database.[3] Teenagers in English-speaking countries have the greatest proportions combining education and employment, though usually this is done through informal arrangements. Formal work-study programs are undertaken by large proportions of fifteen- to nineteen-year-olds in Austria, Germany, and Switzerland. In contrast, Belgium, the Czech Republic, Finland,[4] France, Greece, Italy, Spain, and Sweden have the largest proportions of fifteen- to ninteen-year-olds

exclusively in school. These groupings of countries cluster around distinct educational systems and perhaps cultural values regarding the combination of work and school. By age twenty-five to twenty-nine, most young adults (about 60 percent in Switzerland and Spain and up to 87.7 percent in the Czech Republic) are in the labor force and out of education. But what are their circumstances in today's labor markets?

Instability in employment is an acknowledged feature of employment in economies restructuring from manufacturing to services. Growing numbers of jobs are now part-time instead of full-time, particularly for low-skill workers (Wyn and Dwyer 2000). Hand in hand with this shift is the widening wage gap between the highest and the lowest paid workers as the new economy jobs in high technology or finance sectors are highly remunerated while wages in old industrial economy jobs stay the same (Levy 1998; Western and Healy 1999; Morris and Western 1999). Furthermore, there is more job changing early in the career, and unemployment spells last longer than they did for earlier cohorts, again a sign of the effects of the new flexible economy in which employers' commitment to workers is low (Bernhardt, Morris, Handcock, and Scott 2001). Employment conditions in the United States and Europe differ since strong welfare states and industrial relations institutions in Europe make for more unemployment but higher wages, while the less regulated U.S. labor markets experi-

(text continues on p. 26)

TABLE 3

EDUCATION AND WORK STATUS OF THE YOUTH POPULATION,
BY AGE GROUP, FOR 1996 (IN PERCENTAGES)

Country and Age Group	Work-Study Program	In Education				Not in Education			
		Employed	Unemployed	Not in Labor Force	Subtotal	Employed	Unemployed	Not in Labor Force	Subtotal
Australia									
Fifteen to nineteen	m	29.4	6.0	38.6	74.0	17.2	6.0	2.8	26.0
Twenty to twenty-four	m	19.8	2.4	9.3	31.5	53.4	7.5	7.6	68.5
Twenty-five to twenty-nine	m	11.2	0.8	2.8	14.8	64.5	5.7	14.9	85.2
Austria									
Fifteen to nineteen	25.3	1.0	0.5	53.1	79.9	13.7	1.9	4.5	20.1
Twenty to twenty-four	3.3	5.9	0.7	20.6	30.6	58.9	3.7	6.9	69.4
Twenty-five to twenty-nine	1.1	6.7	0.4	7.1	15.4	72.1	4.0	8.5	84.6
Belgium									
Fifteen to nineteen	1.5	0.7	0.2	85.4	87.8	3.3	1.6	7.3	12.2
Twenty to twenty-four	0.7	2.5	0.9	35.2	39.3	42.5	10.4	7.9	60.7
Twenty-five to twenty-nine	0.3	3.7	0.5	2.6	7.0	75.0	8.9	9.1	93.0
Canada									
Fifteen to nineteen	m	26.2	5.0	51.9	83.0	8.9	3.7	4.4	17.0
Twenty to twenty-four	m	16.4	1.5	19.9	37.7	43.7	9.3	9.2	62.3
Twenty-five to twenty-nine	m	6.6	0.5	5.2	12.3	67.0	8.7	12.1	87.7
Czech Republic									
Fifteen to nineteen	m	2.3	0.1	67.9	70.4	17.2	3.1	9.3	29.6
Twenty to twenty-four	m	0.8	0.1	13.7	14.6	72.4	3.0	10.0	85.4
Twenty-five to twenty-nine	m	0.3	n	1.0	1.3	84.2	3.5	11.0	98.7
Finland									
Fifteen to nineteen	n	8.7	13.2	62.7	84.5	10.0	3.2	2.3	15.5
Twenty to twenty-four	0.2	12.0	9.8	26.1	48.1	32.8	12.4	6.6	51.9
Twenty-five to twenty-nine	0.1	9.0	2.9	7.6	19.7	62.9	8.3	9.1	80.3

(continued)

TABLE 3 Continued

Country and Age Group	Work-Study Program	In Education				Not in Education			
		Employed	Unemployed	Not in Labor Force	Subtotal	Employed	Unemployed	Not in Labor Force	Subtotal
France									
Fifteen to nineteen	5.3	0.4	0.1	90.2	96.1	1.1	1.6	1.3	3.9
Twenty to twenty-four	4.8	3.1	0.7	42.4	50.9	31.5	12.6	4.9	49.1
Twenty-five to twenty-nine	1.6	3.9	0.5	5.0	11.0	66.7	13.2	9.1	89.0
Germany									
Fifteen to nineteen	20.8	1.8	0.7	67.2	90.5	5.8	1.6	2.0	9.5
Twenty to twenty-four	8.9	3.6	0.2	19.4	32.0	52.9	6.8	8.2	68.0
Twenty-five to twenty-nine	1.1	3.9	0.2	8.5	13.7	68.7	6.6	11.0	86.3
Greece									
Fifteen to nineteen	0.3	0.6	0.9	78.5	80.4	8.7	5.9	5.1	19.6
Twenty to twenty-four	0.2	1.4	1.6	27.1	30.3	42.0	16.5	11.1	69.7
Twenty-five to twenty-nine	n	1.1	0.6	3.0	4.6	65.7	13.0	16.7	95.4
Italy									
Fifteen to nineteen	m	0.6	0.7	70.7	72.0	11.8	6.3	9.9	28.0
Twenty to twenty-four	m	1.0	1.6	29.3	32.0	34.2	16.6	17.3	68.0
Twenty-five to twenty-nine	m	1.3	0.8	10.7	12.7	56.4	12.2	18.6	87.3
Spain									
Fifteen to nineteen	0.2	1.6	2.7	69.0	73.5	13.0	9.1	4.4	26.5
Twenty to twenty-four	0.1	4.3	5.5	34.0	43.9	33.4	17.6	5.0	56.1
Twenty-five to twenty-nine	n	4.9	4.4	6.9	16.2	53.0	19.3	11.5	83.8
Sweden									
Fifteen to nineteen	m	12.5	3.3	70.6	86.5	6.1	1.8	5.6	13.5
Twenty to twenty-four	m	7.8	4.8	26.9	39.6	42.1	8.8	9.5	60.4
Twenty-five to twenty-nine	m	8.0	2.5	9.2	19.6	66.2	7.8	6.3	80.4

Switzerland									
Fifteen to nineteen	32.3	12.4	(1.4)	46.1	92.3	4.3	(0.9)	(2.5)	7.7
Twenty to twenty-four	9.2	20.9	(1.4)	15.3	46.7	46.6	(2.4)	(4.3)	53.3
Twenty-five to twenty-nine	1.0	22.4	(0.8)	4.2	28.3	57.0	5.3	9.4	71.7
United Kingdom									
Sixteen to nineteen	8.1	25.3	3.9	32.6	69.9	17.9	7.2	5.0	30.1
Twenty to twenty-four	2.7	11.4	1.2	12.3	27.6	53.8	8.5	10.1	72.4
Twenty-five to twenty-nine	1.1	8.7	0.8	3.0	13.6	65.6	6.9	13.9	86.4
United States									
Fifteen to nineteen	m	25.9	4.3	51.4	81.6	10.1	2.8	5.5	18.4
Twenty to twenty-four	m	19.3	1.1	12.2	32.5	51.2	5.5	10.8	67.5
Twenty-five to twenty-nine	m	8.6	0.4	2.9	11.9	71.5	4.1	12.5	88.1

SOURCE: Organization for Economic Cooperation and Development (1998, Table D1.1).
NOTES: m = missing; n = not available. Numbers in parentheses indicate that low numbers contributed to high sampling variability.

25

TABLE 4
ECONOMICALLY ACTIVE POPULATION, BY AGE AND SEX (IN PERCENTAGES)

Country	Year	Age Group—Men			Age Group—Women		
		15-19	20-24	25-29	15-19	20-24	25-29
Czech Republic	1991	34.6	88.0	96.3	35.4	88.3	98.0
Australia	1995	58.5	87.8	93.3	60.3	78.0	68.0
New Zealand	1997	58.0	85.2	91.3	56.5	70.6	66.1
Denmark	1996	72.8	84.4	90.3	67.0	76.5	80.1
Switzerland	1990	56.0	83.8	93.9	49.2	80.4	71.4
United Kingdom	1996	63.9	83.6	93.2	59.6	70.3	72.2
Lithuania	1996	27.6	82.7	89.4	20.0	71.1	83.4
United States	1996	53.2	82.5	92.9	51.3	71.3	75.8
Netherlands	1996	52.5	79.8	92.7	50.5	79.0	79.6
Romania	1996	35.2	78.2	91.6	26.0	61.6	76.6
Germany	1996	34.4	77.3	85.4	26.4	67.7	74.0
Norway	1996	42.2	76.0	88.4	41.8	68.0	77.1
Ireland	1996	23.9	74.7	92.1	17.9	67.4	77.6
Russia	1996	17.3	74.3	81.9	17.3	66.3	70.3
Estonia	1995	21.7	73.8	91.5	18.5	52.7	68.9
Austria	1996	52.3	73.6	87.7	35.4	71.4	79.7
Hungary	1996	17.7	72.9	90.7	12.9	49.3	53.5
Poland	1996	16.0	72.7	93.2	10.6	57.7	71.1
Finland	1996	30.7	70.9	87.9	22.5	56.0	75.5
Greece	1995	17.1	70.6	94.3	17.1	50.0	70.8
Portugal	1996	27.2	69.2	90.2	19.7	57.3	81.2
Luxembourg	1996	15.4	66.6	91.3	13.8	60.5	69.0
Sweden	1996	24.2	66.1	85.7	27.4	60.1	79.1
Canada[a]	1996		63.5	90.4		59.5	77.5
Spain	1996	26.6	63.2	88.2	21.8	56.6	73.9
Belgium	1995	8.6	60.2	93.0	5.0	54.9	81.6
France	1996	9.4	58.0	92.2	5.3	48.6	81.4
Italy	1996	22.0	57.3	81.5	17.5	47.9	60.4

SOURCE: United States Census Bureau (2001).
a. ages 15-24 are combined.

ence less unemployment and much lower wages at the bottom of the wage scale. In these ways, workers have borne the brunt of economic restructuring.

Regional differences in the pace of entry into the labor force for young men and women reflect differences in the ease with which youth find employment in labor markets with varying degrees of regulation and labor demand. By age twenty to twenty-four, the majority of men and women in all countries are economically active (see Table 4). However, the percentage of young men who are economically active is highest among English-speaking countries, with relatively unregulated markets and weak unemployment programs. The percentages of twenty- to twenty-four-year-old men in the labor market are similar for eastern and western European countries, with the southern European countries having the lowest percentages economically active at this age. This is due in part to the mutual exclusiveness of work and school in these countries, but it may also be due to weaker demand for labor. By age twenty-five to twenty-nine, more than 90 percent of young men are economically active in all countries but a few with either generous welfare states (Germany, Sweden, Austria, Finland, Norway) or weak labor demand (Italy, Russia, Spain, Lithuania). Women's economic participation, being less normative, is shaped by both labor demand and policies and cultural norms regarding the combination of work and family. It is notable, however, that by age twenty to twenty-four, more than 60 percent of women in the English-speaking countries, western Europe, and Scandinavia are economically active. In contrast, only 48 to 58 percent of women in this age group in eastern and southern European countries are economically active. While it is difficult to make generalizations from this data, they point out the countries in which the transition into employment is most difficult for young adults.

Youth face particular challenges as the newest entrants into the labor market. In a comparison of OECD countries, Gaude (1997) found that in absolute terms, youth (age fifteen to nineteen) unemployment rates vary more according to economic conditions than do adult rates, increasing more in recessions and always remaining higher than unemployment for other age groups. This reflects the fact that youth are less likely to be hired and are the first laid off during a recession. But youth unemployment rates have also risen in spite of the fact that increased

educational participation and the diminished size of youth cohorts in these countries have lessened the supply of labor for entry-level positions (O'Higgins 1997). The difficult employment conditions youth face— both the well-known instability of being last hired, first fired and the instability of employment in the new regime of flexible employment relations—are important structural conditions underlying the delay in entry into family responsibilities.

Historically, and perhaps only to a slightly lesser extent today, economic independence for men was one of the central norms regulating entry into marriage in western Europe (Coale and Watkins 1986). The rule of primogeniture and the practice of the circulation of servants, in which young adults apprenticed in a craftsman's home or worked as house servants or field laborers, reinforced the value that youth must be economically independent before marrying and establishing an independent household (Hajnal 1982). In contrast, joint households in which young married couples lived with parents or other relatives were more normative in eastern and southern European regions. This system posed fewer economic constraints on marriage, and hence marriage was earlier and more prevalent in eastern and southern than in western and northern Europe (Hajnal 1965). Hajnal drew a line from St. Petersburg, Russia, to Trieste, Italy, to show the geographic boundaries of the eastern and western European marriage systems.

Contemporary research shows that this division persists though

TABLE 5

PERCENTAGE OF SINGLE MEN BY AGE GROUPS

Country	Year	>15	15-19	15-24	20-24	25-29	25-39	30-34	35-39	40-44	40-49	45-49
Hungary	1990	5.6[a]	NA		**33.2**	11.8		7.1	5.1	3.8		3.1
Russia	1989	19.6[b]	96.4		59.5	**20.8**		10.5	6.8	4.7		3.7
Lithuania	1989	23.0[b]	96.9		65.8	**22.2**		11.5	8.5	6.6		5.6
Estonia	1989	23.1	97.0		64.8	**24.3**		13.1	9.9	8.7		7.6
Romania	1992	26.1	98.1		69.7	**29.6**		15.9	10.2	6.9		5.2
Poland	1990	27.1	99.4		77.1	**34.0**		17.9	11.7	8.3		7.2
Belgium	1995	29.5	99.8		89.9	52.5		**28.1**	17.0	11.4		8.7
Canada	1991	29.8	98.7		81.6	**45.7**		24.2	14.8	9.8		7.6
United States	1995	31.0	98.7		80.7	51.0		**28.2**	20.3	14.0		8.1
Australia	1991	33.1	97.4		86.9	52.5		**27.8**	15.8	10.1		8.1
Italy	1991	34.3	99.1		93.9	63		**30.9**	17.4	11.8		9.8
New Zealand	1991	34.9	99.6		90.3	55.6		**28.4**	15.1	9.2		7.3
Germany	1991	42.7		93.7			**36.4**				9.5	
Portugal	1991	43.5		90.4			**22.3**				5.0	
Luxembourg	1991	43.7		94.0			**33.9**				9.7	
Greece	1991	44.5		95.5			**34.9**				6.4	
United Kingdom	1991	45.0		93.5			**33.7**				9.9	
Austria	1991	45.8		93.2			**37.2**				10.2	
Netherlands	1991	47.0		96.2			**9.3**				9.3	
Spain	1991	48.4		95.3			**34.3**				10.4	
France	1991	48.9		95.7			**36.2**				10.9	
Denmark	1991	49.1		97.4			**12.7**				8.1	
Norway	1991	49.3[c]		77.4			**43.7**				11.1	
Finland	1991	49.6		96.2			**44.1**				15.3	
Sweden	1991	50.7		97.8			55.3				**17.9**	
Ireland	1996	58.5[d]	99.8		97.2	72.5		**37.4**	22.2	17.4		16.2
Switzerland	1991	81.1		95.1			**38.2**				10.5	

SOURCE: United States Census Bureau (2001).

NOTES: None of these countries enumerate nonmarital unions as marriages. Numbers in bold indicate the age group by which 50 percent of men are married. NA = not applicable.

a. Includes only those age twenty and older.
b. Includes only those age sixteen and older.
c. Includes only those age fifteen to seventy-nine.
d. Includes all ages (zero and older).

with some modifications: marriage is still early and frequent in eastern Europe and later and less prevalent in western and northern Europe and now in some areas of southern Europe (Sardon 1993; Monnier and Rychtarikova 1992). The English-speaking countries of the New World have followed most closely the marriage norms of the United Kingdom. These regional patterns are seen in the age-specific percentage remaining single for men and women (see Tables 5 and 6). For both men and women, the lowest proportions single for all ages and the earliest ages at

TABLE 6

PERCENTAGE OF SINGLE WOMEN BY AGE GROUPS

Country	Year	>15	15-19	15-24	20-24	25-29	25-39	30-34	35-39	40-44	40-49	45-49
Hungary	1990	11.1[a]			54.8	**25.6**		15.1	11.6	9.3		7.6
Russia	1989	13.2[b]	85.9		**33.5**	12.0		6.9	5.3	4.5		3.5
Estonia	1989	16.6[b]	90.3		**40.4**	16.3		10.1	7.4	6.7		6.7
Romania	1992	17.1	88.0		**39.6**	13.3		6.7	4.9	3.9		3.4
Poland	1990	19.0	96.0		**47.9**	15.9		9.0	6.9	6.0		5.0
Belgium	1995	22.0	98.4		**74.4**	34.4		17.7	10.8	7.3		5.3
Canada	1991	23.2	95.6		64.6	**29.7**		16.3	10.7	7.9		6.4
United States	1995	23.5	96.1		66.8	**35.3**		19.0	12.6	8.7		6.1
Slovenia	1991	25.2	97.9		66.1	**29.6**		15.2	10.9	8.9		7.7
Australia	1991	25.8	96.4		73.8	**34.9**		17.4	9.9	6.4		5.0
Italy	1991	26.5	96.9		77.2	**39.1**		17.8	11.2	8.2		7.5
New Zealand	1991	28.2	98.9		77.6	**39.2**		19.6	10.1	6.1		4.8
Germany	1991	34.3		83.9			**22.1**				5.6	
Greece	1991	35.7		78.7			**15.8**				5.4	
Luxembourg	1991	36.7		84.0			**22.1**				7.0	
Austria	1991	37.8		84.3			**24.8**				7.9	
Portugal	1991	37.9		78.6			**15.2**				7.0	
United Kingdom	1991	37.9		85.8			**23.1**				5.7	
Switzerland	1991	39.1		87.3			**26.6**				9.2	
Netherlands	1991	40		88.8			**25.8**				6.0	
Denmark	1991	40.7		93.4			**36.8**				6.6	
Finland	1991	41.7		90.9			**31.3**				10.5	
Spain	1991	42.1		87.9			**23.2**				8.3	
Sweden	1991	42.3		93.8			**41.0**				11.1	
Lithuania	1989	42.4	56.7		**31.2**	16.1		9.9	7.1	5.1		5.3
Ireland	1996	51.7[c]	99.7		93.4	58.5		**26.9**	15.7	11.9		10.1
France	1991	52.3		88.9			**26.1**				8.4	
Norway	1991	41.4[d]		91.8			**28.8**				6.2	

SOURCE: United States Census Bureau (2001).

NOTES: None of these countries enumerate nonmarital unions as marriages. Numbers in bold indicate the age group by which 50 percent of men are married.

a. Includes only those age twenty and older.
b. Includes only those age sixteen and older.
c. Includes all ages (zero and older).
d. Includes only those age fifteen to seventy-nine.

which the proportion single falls below 50 percent are found in eastern Europe, then the English-speaking countries, followed by southern Europe and lastly western Europe and Scandinavia.

Although marriage was typically the institution in which childbearing occurred historically, variations on this pattern have emerged in recent years. In the aggregate, the peak ages of childbearing follow the

TABLE 7

AGE-SPECIFIC FERTILITY AND TOTAL FERTILITY RATES (PER 1,000)

Country	\multicolumn{7}{c}{Age Group}	Total Fertility Rate
	15-19	20-24	25-29	30-34	35-39	40-44	45-49	
United States	62.1	116.3	118.4	79.3	31.8	5.9	0.2	2.07
New Zealand	27.3	86.5	130.6	91.7	30.2	4.3	0.3	1.85
Sweden	9.0	70.5	132.5	103	43.7	7.5	0.3	1.83
Australia	23.8	91.3	137.8	79.5	24.9	4.5	0.4	1.81
Ireland	15.2	43.8	104	125.8	59.0	12.6	0.7	1.81
Norway	13.6	73.5	128.1	95.9	36.9	5.5	0.2	1.77
United Kingdom	23.4	77.1	111.7	87.7	36.1	7.0	0.3	1.71
Finland	9.1	61.7	121.1	97.7	38.6	7.7	0.4	1.68
Canada	24.3	71.1	112.8	85.8	30.7	4.8	0.2	1.65
Denmark	8.1	58.3	126.2	94.2	33.2	4.6	0.1	1.62
France	7.0	55.7	124	90.3	36.5	7.6	0.4	1.61
Luxembourg	10.3	69.2	113.9	86.1	30.1	3.4	0.0	1.57
Belgium	10.5	67.2	125.7	69.7	20.8	3.2	0.2	1.49
Netherlands	4.1	32.4	95.6	114.7	44.1	6.2	0.3	1.49
Switzerland	3.8	42.9	104.5	98.1	36.7	5.8	0.2	1.46
Lithuania	38.8	112.6	82.0	37.7	15.7	3.3	0.3	1.45
Poland	20.6	103.7	91.5	47.6	21.1	5.3	0.3	1.45
Hungary	29.9	101.8	96.7	45.4	15.6	2.8	0.1	1.45
Austria	16.6	73.4	97.9	60.3	22.3	3.9	0.2	1.37
Russia	44.6	111.9	67.2	30.5	10.6	2.2	0.1	1.34
Portugal	19.8	69.7	94.4	57.8	20.9	4.9	0.3	1.34
Greece	14.0	69.8	90.5	58.8	22.8	4.8	0.4	1.30
Czech Republic	24.9	102.2	81.3	35.2	10.6	1.7	0.1	1.28
Estonia	34.9	97.7	72.1	34.3	13.6	2.9	0.1	1.28
Romania	39.6	103.3	69.2	27.7	10.4	2.9	0.2	1.27
Germany	10.4	52.8	88.2	70.7	26.2	4.6	0.2	1.26
Spain	9.1	35.9	90.9	78.9	28.4	5.2	0.3	1.24
Italy	7.1	46.9	87.0	69.5	29.5	5.6	0.3	1.22

SOURCE: United States Census Bureau (2001).
NOTE: All figures are projected for 1999.

timing of marriage quite closely; however, the total fertility rates follow a distinct pattern. Total fertility rates are highest in the English-speaking and Scandinavian countries, followed by western Europe, and then the eastern and southern European countries (see Table 7). This inconsistency may be due in part to differences in patterns of fertility within marriage. For example, while marriage and childbearing usually happen quite early in the life course in eastern European countries, childbearing generally stops early as well. In southern European countries, both marriage and parenthood occur later in the life course, but they share a pattern of low fertility with eastern Europe. In Scandinavia, where cohabitation often takes the place of marriage and more children are born within cohabiting relationships, the relationship between marriage and childbearing is weakest. In the English-speaking countries and western Europe, the relationship between marriage and childbearing is weakening but still relatively strong, with both marriage and childbearing occurring later in the life course. By having fewer children later in life, regardless of the arrangement in which it occurs, individuals contribute to the aging of the population.

But perhaps an older population is simply the unintended, but acceptable, consequence of a more individualized and satisfying life course? For those who spend more time in school and find themselves on an improving occupational and earnings trajectory, this may be true. However, for those who experience an unstable school-to-work transition and have difficulty gaining a foothold in the labor market, their early life ambitions may be frustrated. Insofar as either trajectory prevents young adults from achieving their family goals, this may be an unacceptable tradeoff.

There is evidence that a substantial number of young adults are postponing their family because of unstable employment early in life. Oppenheimer and her colleagues (1997) found that in the United States, men's instability in their early occupational trajectories is an important reason for their later ages at marriage. This is particularly so for those with less education and for African American men who face labor market discrimination and are often geographically mismatched with employment (Lichter, McLaughlin, and Landry 1992). Men's economic circumstances also

affect the timing of women's marriage since men's ability to earn is often viewed as a prerequisite to marriage (Smock and Manning 1997; Liefbroer and Corijn 1999). Clearly, for some, unstable early labor market experiences contribute to the delay in entry into marriage and childbearing.

Given that the advanced industrial economies are all restructuring toward more flexible and less stable employment regimes, improving the economic circumstances of young men and women should be a policy goal. Indeed, embedded in the goal of smoothing the transition into economic independence for young adults is the solution to some of the major problems associated with population aging. By creating a more productive, though proportionately smaller, labor force and ensuring the reproduction of the population, the retired population can be more easily supported, and the pace of population aging may be slowed.

SUSTAINING AN
OLD POPULATION

An older population age structure is a certain feature of our current demographic regime. The lower fertility rates and longer life expectancies achieved today are demographic success stories that are the basis for our older age structure. This population age structure is likely to persist since low fertility maintains or reduces the size of each subsequent birth cohort. Put simply, in a population with sustained replacement-level (2.1 births per woman) or below-replacement-level fertility,

TABLE 8
ELDER DEPENDENCY RATIOS (EDR) FOR 2000 TO 2050,
ARRANGED IN ORDER OF MEDIAN AGE IN 2000

Country	Median Age in 2000	EDR in 2000	Percentage Change from 2000 to 2025	EDR in 2025	Percentage Change from 2025 to 2050	EDR in 2050
Italy	39.9	29.0	32.2	42.7	42.9	74.7
Germany	39.8	26.0	34.5	39.6	26.5	53.9
Sweden	39.5	29.5	30.0	42.2	16.4	50.5
Finland	39.4	24.6	44.4	44.3	13.4	51.1
Belgium	39.0	28.2	30.7	40.7	24.3	53.7
Greece	38.9	28.5	28.9	40.0	41.3	68.2
Switzerland	38.9	24.3	43.9	43.4	26.5	59.0
Denmark	38.4	24.2	35.4	37.5	16.9	45.2
Austria	38.2	24.9	33.3	37.3	34.4	56.9
Hungary	38.0	23.5	34.8	36.1	39.4	59.5
Spain	37.7	27.3	30.1	39.0	50.1	78.2
France	37.6	27.3	31.1	39.6	23.1	51.5
Netherlands	37.6	21.9	41.6	37.5	23.5	49.0
United Kingdom	37.6	26.6	27.6	36.7	26.4	49.8
Luxembourg	37.5	22.8	24.5	30.1	29.9	43.0
Norway	37.0	25.8	28.6	36.1	18.6	44.4
Canada	36.8	20.7	42.0	35.6	21.7	45.5
Russia	36.8	20.6	33.6	31.0	35.5	48.1
Portugal	36.7	25.3	28.5	35.4	41.0	60.0
Lithuania	35.7	22.3	25.3	29.8	35.4	46.2
United States	35.7	21.4	36.3	33.6	11.8	38.1
Poland	35.3	20.5	41.6	35.1	19.6	43.7
Australia	35.1	20.7	38.6	33.8	25.0	45.1
Romania	34.5	21.8	27.7	30.2	45.8	55.7
New Zealand	32.5	19.4	29.9	27.7	36.5	43.7
Ireland	32.3	19.4	33.2	29.1	37.8	46.8

SOURCE: United States Census Bureau's (2001) international database.
NOTE: Elder dependency ratio = the ratio of the number of persons sixty-five and older to every 100 persons ages twenty to sixty-four.

each birth cohort entering their reproductive age range consists of similar or smaller numbers of women. The women in each cohort would have to increase their fertility to levels significantly higher than replacement-level fertility to increase the size of later birth cohorts and reverse the population aging process. This is unlikely to happen since the social institutions and attitudes sustaining low fertility are likely to remain in place.

The age of a population is measured using the median age[5] of the population (see Table 8). As a whole, the economically developed countries constitute the oldest region of the world. In 2000, the median ages range from 39.9 in Italy to 32.3 in Ireland. Within this region, the Scandinavian and western European countries are among the oldest populations, due to their prolonged fertility decline and greater life expectancy. They are followed by southern and eastern Europe, where more recent sharp declines have increased the pace of aging. The youngest are the English-speaking countries where fertility rates are generally higher and the post–World War II baby boom made the population age structure younger. While the median age is instructive as an indication of the population age structure, the elder dependency ratio better measures the problem at hand; that is, how will the labor force support the growing elderly population in the future and continue to reproduce itself?

The major problem associated with population aging is accommodating the economic costs associated with a larger older population. These costs include paying public pensions through the prolonged period that the retired population spends outside of the labor force,[6] the ability of families to care for aging parents in personal and financial terms, and the heavy demands that older people place on health care systems (National Research Council 2001). These costs are more easily borne when the national economy is productive and growing—and the size and quality of the labor force are two keys to keeping the economy productive. The elder dependency ratio—that is, the ratio of the number of persons sixty-five and older to every 100 persons ages twenty to sixty-four—approximates, though imperfectly, the burden of the elderly population on the working-age population. Table 8 displays estimates of these ratios in 2000, 2025, and 2050. These estimates incorporate the assumptions that fertility will stabilize at replacement-level fertility, mortality will continue to decline though at a slower pace, and migration will also slow. These assumptions are the statistical best guess of what will happen in the future. Although unforeseen or planned changes will certainly alter the rate of population aging and the elder dependency ratios to a greater or lesser extent, the long-term trend toward an older population age structure is irreversible.

Regional differences in the rate of population aging mostly reflect the regions recent fertility histories. The southern European countries are expected to age rapidly in the next half century (see Table 8). In 2025, dependency ratios will range from 35 elders per 100 working-age persons in Portugal to 43:100 in Italy. In the following twenty-five years, the population will age rapidly, increasing the ratio to 60:100 in Portugal and 78:100 in Spain, thus achieving some of the highest elder dependency ratios. Given the somewhat lower employment rates of young men and especially young women in these populations, this older population will place a heavy burden on the working-age population. The Scandinavian and western European countries also have relatively older populations and will experience rapid population aging in the next twenty-five years to achieve elder dependency ratios ranging from 30:100 in Luxembourg to 44:100 in Finland in 2025. The pace of aging will slow in the following twenty-five years, ranging from a low of 43:100 in Luxembourg to 59:100 in Switzerland. The eastern European countries were relatively young in 2000, but their elder dependency ratios are increasing quite rapidly since fertility there has dropped precipitously in the past decades. By 2050, their elder dependency ratios will range from a low of 44:100 in Poland to a high of 60:100 in Hungary. The youngest of all these countries are the English-speaking countries, which, due to the retirement of the post–World War II baby boom cohort, will experience rapidly increasing elder dependency ratios in the next twenty-five years, though reaching lower levels than European countries. In the following twenty-five years, the pace of aging will slow so these countries will have relatively low elder dependency ratios ranging from a low of 38:100 in the United States to a high of 50:100 in the United Kingdom. The extent to which these growing elder populations can be supported depends heavily on the rates of economic participation of the working-age population and the productivity of the labor force.

Since population aging is inevitable, it may be more reasonable to ask not how to slow population aging but how old nations can sustain their new population regime. National governments and the European Community have considered adopting policies aimed at slowing population aging, including encouraging immigration of young migrants and implementing policies to encourage women to have more children. Encouraging immigration is a good short-term fix, but it is unlikely to affect population aging in the long run since migrants often become permanent residents, thus contributing to the age of the population, and they adjust their fertility levels to the norms of the nation in which they reside (Le Bras 1991). Policies encouraging women to have additional children may slow aging by adding newborns to the population. Generally these policies consist of some combination of cash benefits to parents, parental leave policies, job protection, and subsidized or state-supported child care. Family support programs have had modest impacts on total fertility rates although rates still remain below replacement level (Gauthier 1996; Blanchet and Ekert-Jaffé 1994). However, they have been successful in raising fertility rates in Sweden, especially when they were complemented by economic growth (Hoem 1993; Hoem and Hoem 1997). While these rejuvenating policies have had modest success, there is still room for policy changes that support an old population age structure.

Most discussions of policy reform have focused on reducing the economic burden of the elder population through modifications to public pension and health care plans. These policies may be more politically palatable in a time of government downsizing and slow economic growth in some countries (Walker 1993; Bengstsson and Fridlizius 1994). However, programs that effectively redistribute public monies to the elder population with the lowest incomes could be maintained if the official retirement age were raised and the incentives to retire early were removed (National Research Council 2001). Raising the retirement age would be a justifiable adjustment to the public pension system given the gains in life expectancy experienced since these plans were established. These reforms, though unpopular among the working-age population nearing retirement, would increase the size of the labor force without significantly altering public pension systems. However, these policies would only indirectly address the issues raised by changes in the early life course during the past century and population aging.

The review of the causes of delays in the timing of the transition to adulthood carried out in the previous section of this article identifies a new set of life course activities that could be targeted as a priority area for sustaining the health and well-being of the whole population in the new "old" demographic regime. To effectively support this older age structure, the labor force must be more productive to compensate for its smaller relative size. The focus of educational policy on increasing human capital has paid off in terms of keeping the labor force of industrialized countries highly productive. However, making a smooth transition from school to work is also critical for maintaining a highly productive labor force. Heinz (2000) argued that to stabilize the life course of young adults who are pursuing occupations that require less education and demand fewer skills, there needs to be a greater articulation between industries and services and the education system. This coordination of education and industry would stabilize the early occupational trajectories of these adults and increase productivity. More generally, the shift from Fordist

to flexible employment relationships (briefly defined, the movement from full-time, lifetime employment to more part-time work without benefits and more contractual employment) has contributed to worker insecurity in general (Harvey 1989). This shakier path to economic independence is one of the most important factors contributing to delays in family formation and greater economic instability after a family is formed.

In addition to difficulty in achieving economic independence, higher rates of female employment also contribute to later and less childbearing. Women's early involvement in education and the labor force causes them to delay entry into family roles. After they begin childbearing, working women may have fewer children since the direct and opportunity costs of children are higher, especially for women who bear the majority of child rearing and domestic labor (Gerson 1985; Pinnelli 1995). Single-female-headed households are at an even greater disadvantage with only one income and one parent to carry the economic and social costs of child rearing. These obstacles to gender equality, both in the labor market and at home, contribute to lower fertility levels (Bernhardt 1988; Pinnelli 1995). Again, we can look to Sweden as an example of how gender-egalitarian family policies may effectively raise fertility rates and support young families through an economically unstable point in the life course (Hoem and Hoem 1997).

While the aforementioned trends exert economic force on family formation, changes in ideology are also quite salient though less easily measured. Lesthaeghe (1995) argued that the value placed on gender equality, changes in the commitment to and the meaning of marriage, growing individualism, and the strengthening of market orientation also discourage family formation. Today we live in a society in which childbearing is more optional and perhaps can be characterized increasingly as an expression of one's individuality and decreasingly as a normative stage in the life course (Hall 1993). These social forces are more difficult to reverse and perhaps make the case for why policy should focus on sustaining an older, more educated population rather than trying to slow or reverse population aging.

CONCLUSION

The relationship between changes in the early adult life course and population aging are clear. More time spent in school and early, often unstable or apprenticeship-like labor force experiences cause young adults to delay entering into marriage and childbearing. Employers today demand more human capital and more flexibility from their employees, especially those just entering the labor market and with the least employment experience. This may be seen as the increasing individualization of the life course, something that many of us value. But it can also be seen as greater economic instability, which either causes young people to delay family formation or causes them economic distress when they do form families. In either case, by delaying or forgoing childbearing, young adults contribute to the aging of the population.

In some countries, population aging is one of the most certain threats to the national economy given the burden the growing elderly population will place on the public pension system and the declining relative size of the labor force. There are multiple policy interventions that can address this situation in the short term by reducing public transfers to the retired or raising the retirement age. However, a shift in focus from the elder population to youth provides us with a long-term and forward-thinking solution to the problem of maintaining an older population. By investing in youth through education and facilitating the school-to-work transition and supporting their family formation goals by helping men and women to combine work and family, governments can foster an increasingly productive labor force, and they can ensure that the population will be reproduced at a more stable rate. Indeed, the challenge for governments is to adjust the intergenerational social contract to our new, older age structure so that people in all stages of life support each other rather than compete with each other.

Notes

1. On average, men marry at older ages then women.

2. Male and female students are not separated because their enrollment rates are nearly identical.

3. These data are available separately for men and women, but the differences by gender

are not great. Note that economic activity is not necessarily full-time activity.

4. Finland is an odd case because so many fifteen- to nineteen-year-olds in school are also unemployed, a circumstance that may be encouraged by a generous welfare state.

5. The median age is the age above which and below which half the population falls.

6. While the normal age of pension eligibility is sixty-five in most industrialized countries, a growing proportion of older workers are retiring earlier (National Research Council 2001). With increased life expectancy, the period of life spent out of the labor force and dependent on public pensions has increased significantly since the retirement age was established in the first half of the twentieth century.

References

Arum, Richard, and Yossi Shavit. 1995. Secondary vocational education and the transition from school to work. *Sociology of Education* 68 (3): 187-204.

Becker, Gary. 1981. *Treatise on the family.* Cambridge, MA: Harvard University Press.

Bengstsson, Tommy, and Gunnar Fridlizius. 1994. Public intergenerational transfers as an old-age pension system: A historical interlude? In *The family, the market, and the state in ageing societies*, edited by John Ermisch and Naohiro Ogawa, 198-215. Oxford, UK: Clarendon.

Bernhardt, Annette, Martina Morris, Mark S. Handcock, and Marc A. Scott. 2001. *Divergent paths: Economic mobility in the new American labor market.* New York: Russell Sage.

Bernhardt, Eva M. 1988. Changing family ties, women's position and low fertility. In *Women's position and demographic change*, edited by Nora Federici, Karen Oppenheim Mason, and Sølvi Sogner, 80-103.

Blanchet, Didier, and Olivia Ekert-Jaffé. 1994. The demographic impact of family benefits: Evidence from a micromodel and from macro-data. In *The family, the market and the state in Ageing societies*, edited by John Ermisch and Naohiro Ogawa, 79-103. Oxford, UK: Clarendon.

Chafetz, Janet Saltzman, and Jacqueline Hagan. 1996. The gender division of labor and family change in industrial societies: A theoretical accounting. *Journal of Comparative Family Studies* 27 (2): 187-219.

Cherlin, Andrew. 1992. *Marriage, divorce, remarriage*, Rev. ed. Cambridge, MA: Harvard University Press.

Coale, Ansley. 1964. How a population ages or grows younger. In *Population: The vital revolution*, edited by Ronald Freedman, 47-58. New York: Doubleday.

Coale, Ansley J., and Susan Cott Watkins, eds. 1986. *The decline of fertility in Europe.* Princeton, NJ: Princeton University Press.

Davis, Kingsley, Mikhail S. Bernstam, and Rita Ricardo-Campbell. 1986. Below-replacement fertility in industrial societies: Causes, consequences, policies. *Population and Development Review* 12 (Suppl.): 1-359.

Easterlin, Richard A. 1987. *Birth and fortune.* 2d ed. Chicago: University of Chicago Press.

Fussell, Elizabeth. 2002. Youth in aging societies. In *The future of adolescent experience: Societal trends and the transition to adulthood*, edited by Jeylan Mortimer and Reed Larson. New York: Cambridge University Press.

Gaude, J. 1997. L'Insertion des jeunes et les politiques d'emploi formation. In *Employment and training papers.* No. 1. Geneva, Switzerland: International Labor Organization.

Gauthier, Anne H. 1996. *The state and the family: A comparative analysis of family policies in industrialized countries.* Oxford, UK: Clarendon.

Gerson, Kathleen. 1985. *Hard choices: How women decide about work, career, and motherhood*. Berkeley: University of California Press.

Hajnal, John. 1953. Age at marriage and proportions marrying. *Population Studies* 7:111-36.

———. 1965. European marriage patterns in perspective. In *Population in history: Essays in historical demography*, edited by D. V. Glass and D.E.C. Eversley, 101-43. London: Edward Arnold.

———. 1982. Two kinds of preindustrial household formation systems. *Population and Development Review* 8 (3): 449-94.

Hall, R. 1993. Reproductive individualism: Exploring the relationship between religion, cohabitation and divorce. Discussion Paper No. 93-9. London, Ontario, Canada: Population Studies Centre, University of Western Ontario.

Harvey, David. 1989. *The condition of postmodernity: An enquiry into the origins of cultural change*. Cambridge, MA: Blackwell.

Heinz, Walter R. 2000. Youth transitions and employment in Germany. *International Social Science Journal* 164:161ff.

Hoem, Britta, and Jan M. Hoem. 1997. Fertility trends in Sweden up to 1996. Paper presented at the Expert Group Meeting on Below-Replacement Fertility, UN Population Division, New York, 4-6 November.

Hoem, Jan M. 1993. Public policy as a fuel of fertility: Effects of policy reform on the pace of childbearing in Sweden in the 1980s. *Acta Sociologica* 36 (1): 19-32.

Le Bras, Hervé. 1991. Demographic impact of post-war migration in selected OECD countries. In *Migration: The demographic aspects*, 15-27. Paris: Organization for Economic Cooperation and Development.

Lesthaeghe, Ron. 1995. The second demographic transition in Western coun-

tries: An interpretation. In *Gender and family change in industrialized countries*, edited by Karen Oppenheim Mason and An-Magritt Jensen, 17-62. Oxford, UK: Clarendon.

Levy, Frank. 1998. *The new dollars and dreams: American incomes and economic change*. New York: Russell Sage.

Lichter, Daniel T., G. K. McLaughlin, and D. J. Landry. 1992. Race and the retreat from marriage: A shortage of marriageable men? *American Sociological Review* 57:781-99.

Liefbroer, Aart C., and Martine Corijn. 1999. Who, what, where, and when? Specifying the impact of educational attainment and labour force participation on family formation. *European Journal of Population* 14:45-75.

Modell, John, Frank F. Furstenberg Jr., and Theodore Hershberg. 1976. Social change and transitions to adulthood in historical perspective. *Journal of Family History* 1 (1): 7-32.

Monnier, Alain, and Jitka Rychtarikova. 1992. The division of Europe into east and west. *Population: An English Selection* 4:129-60.

Morris, Martina, and Bruce Western. 1999. Inequality in earnings at the close of the twentieth century. *Annual Review of Sociology* 25:623-57.

National Research Council. 2001. *Preparing for an aging world: The case for cross-national research*. Washington, DC: National Academy Press.

O'Higgins, Niall. 1997. The challenge of youth unemployment. In *Employment and training papers*. No. 7. Geneva, Switzerland: Employment and Training Department, International Labor Office.

Oppenheimer, Valerie. 1988. A theory of marriage timing: Assortative mating under varying degrees of uncertainty. *American Journal of Sociology* 94:563-91.

Oppenheimer, Valerie Kincade, Matthijs Kalmijn, and Nelson Lim. 1997. Men's career development and marriage timing during a period of rising inequality. *Demography* 34 (3): 311-30.

Organization for Economic Cooperation Development (OECD). 1995. *Education at a glance: OECD indicators.* Paris: Centre for Educational Research and Innovation, OECD.

———. 1998. *Education at a glance, OECD education indicators.* Retrieved from www.oecd.org/els/edu/EAG98. htm

Pinnelli, Antonella. 1995. Women's condition, low fertility, and emerging union patterns in Europe. In *Gender and family change in industrialized countries*, edited by Karen Oppenheim Mason and An-Magritt Jensen, 82-104. Oxford, UK: Clarendon.

Preston, Samuel. 1984. Children and the elderly: Divergent paths for America's dependents. *Demography* 21:435-57.

Rindfuss, Ronald R. 1991. The young adult years: Diversity, structural change, and fertility. *Demography* 28 (4): 493-512.

Sardon, Jean-Paul. 1993. Women's first marriage rates in Europe: Elements for a typology. *Population: An English Selection* 5:119-52.

Smock, Pamela J., and Wendy D. Manning. 1997. Cohabiting partners' economic circumstances and marriage. *Demography* 34:331-41.

United States Census Bureau. 2001. International database. Available from www.census.gov

Walker, Alan. 1993. Intergenerational relations and welfare restructuring: The social construction of an intergenerational problem. In *The changing contract across generations*, edited by Vern L. Bengtson and W. Andrew Achenbaum, 141-65. New York: Aldine de Gruyter.

Western, Bruce, and K. Healy. 1999. Explaining the OECD wage slowdown: Recession or labor decline? *European Sociological Review* 15:233-49.

Wyn, Johanna, and Peter Dwyer. 2000. New patterns of youth transition in education. *International Social Science Journal* 164:147ff.

ANNALS, *AAPSS*, **580**, March 2002

Regional Differences in the Transition to Adulthood

By MARIA IACOVOU

ABSTRACT: This article examines the living arrangements of people between ages fifteen and thirty-five in Europe and the United States. Three regional patterns emerge in Europe. In southern Europe, young people remain for extended periods in the parental home and tend to make direct transitions from living at home to (formal) marriage and parenthood. In northern Europe, youngsters leave home earlier and more commonly live alone or in cohabiting unions. The Scandinavian countries form an extreme example of northern behavior, with particularly early home leaving and high levels of nonmarital cohabitation. In the United States, there are large differences between young blacks, whites, and Hispanics. Formal marriage is as common among whites as it is in southern Europe; the extended family is common for blacks and Hispanics, and lone motherhood among young black American women far outstrips the highest rates in Europe.

Maria Iacovou is a researcher at the Institute of Social and Economic Research at Essex University. Her research interests include the transition to adulthood; the educational attainments of children and young people; and the relationship between the family, the education system, and the labor market.

NOTE: This article is part of a project funded by the European Union under the Targeted Socio-Economic Research program. The European Community Household Panel data on which the article is based were provided by Eurostat. I thank all those who gave useful feedback at seminars at Essex University, at the European Science Foundation's European Families conference in Castelveccio de Pascoli, and at the Centre for Economic Policy Research in London. Thanks also to Richard Berthoud, John Ermisch, and the editors of this issue for helpful comments. All errors and deficiencies remaining in the article are my own.

THE purpose of this article is to describe young people's living arrangements across Europe and the United States. In this context, "living arrangements" means the people with whom one shares a household: young people may live alone or with parents, partners, children, other relatives, and friends.

Why are living arrangements important? First, they are linked crucially to economic well-being. Poverty is more common among certain household types than others: families with children (in particular lone-parent families) are more likely to be poor than others. Income pooling within a household may provide a cushion for young people against deprivation and social exclusion (Iacovou and Berthoud 2001).

Second, living arrangements are of interest to anyone studying transitions to adulthood. The transition to adulthood may be conceptualized as incorporating transitions from dependence to independence in a number of different areas (Cavalli and Galland 1995), with the two major transitions being residential (moving from the parental home to having one's own home and family) and economic (moving from financial dependence on one's parents to the independence of living on one's own earnings or on the earnings of a partner). The changing composition of young people's households as they move toward adulthood provides much useful information about the transition from the family of origin to having one's own family.

Several authors have noted the increasing tendency of young people in many countries to defer marriage and childbearing (Cordon 1997; Commission of the European Communities 1991); the tendency for young people to live alone, with friends, or in informal cohabiting unions as a prelude or an alternative to marriage (Commission of the European Communities 1982, 1988); and the increasing tendency of the home-leaving process to be protracted, reversed, and possibly subject to several trial runs (Jones 1987; Davanzo and Goldscheider 1990). However, these characteristics are far from uniform across the countries considered. As will be seen, young people's living arrangements vary to an extraordinary extent between countries, and adding to the understanding of this diversity is a primary aim of this article.

The focus of this article is unashamedly descriptive. A large number of articles have been written examining the determinants of young people's living arrangements in an analytical framework, including Berrington and Diamond (2000), Buck and Scott (1993), Nilsson and Strandh (1999), Ermisch (1996), Ermisch and Di Salvo (1997), Holdsworth (2000), Aquilino (1991), White (1994), Avery, Goldsheider, and Speare (1992), and very many more. However, almost all these articles deal with only a single country or exceptionally two or three countries. An understanding of how young people's lives vary between countries is crucial to interpreting these single-country findings in a wider context. Various aspects of young people's family lives (e.g., statistics on fertility and household size) may be obtained from official statistics.

Kiernan (1986) described the proportions living with parents, living with partners, and living alone in six countries. Vogel (1997), IARD (2001), and Iacovou and Berthoud (2001) described several aspects of young people's lives in Europe, including living arrangements. However, this is the first time that a comprehensive description of living arrangements across Europe and the United States has been presented.

Before proceeding with the rest of the article, one or two points of explanation should be made. The first is that the article deals with living arrangements up until the age of thirty-five. Although it is hard to imagine a definition of "youth" that extends halfway into the fourth decade of life, home leaving, partnership, and parenthood have been delayed to such an extent in some countries that to restrict the focus to a younger age group would miss a great deal of interesting information.

Second, it is necessary to explain the groupings of countries used in the article. Within Europe, convincing evidence emerges to suggest the existence of three broad models of household formation: a southern model characterized by late home leaving and more or less direct transitions from the family of origin to marriage and parenthood; a northern model of early home leaving and multiple transitions en route to the state of marriage and parenthood, which is still the destination of the majority of individuals; and a Nordic model that may be thought of as an extreme version of the northern model. Many of the results are presented in a way that highlights these

groups of countries, and to avoid offending purists, it is worth noting that these terms are not used in a strict geographical sense. The Nordic group of countries consists of Finland, Denmark, and the (behaviorally similar though not geographically Nordic) Netherlands. The northern European group consists of the United Kingdom, France, Belgium, Germany, and Austria. The southern group consists of Italy, Spain, Portugal, and Greece, with the (geographically not quite accurate) addition of Ireland.

An alternative way of viewing this schema is in terms of religion:[1] the southern countries are predominantly Catholic or, in the case of Greece, Orthodox; the northern countries are partly Catholic; and the Nordic countries are non-Catholic. Again, this categorization does not describe the schema quite accurately; however, it will be seen that the countries concerned do fall naturally into these groupings, and they clearly have some validity.

Within the United States, it is clear that major differences in living arrangements are to be seen between different ethnic groups, and therefore information is tabulated separately for white, black, and Hispanic groups. Although the Panel Study of Income Dynamics (PSID) defines several other ethnic groups, none of these are present in sufficient numbers to allow detailed analysis of living arrangements, and rather than being amalgamated or tagged onto another group, the less numerous ethnic groups have been excluded from the analysis.

FIGURE 1
AGE GAP BETWEEN MEN AND WOMEN IN PARTNERSHIPS

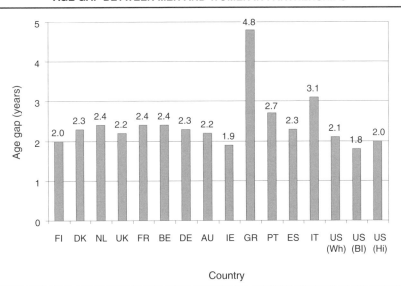

NOTE: FI = Finland; DK = Denmark; NL = Netherlands; UK = United Kingdom; FR = France; BE = Belgium; DE = Germany; AU = Austria; IE = Ireland; GR = Greece; PT = Portugal; ES = Spain; IT = Italy; US (Wh) = United States (White); US (Bl) = United States (Black); US (Hi) = United States (Hispanic).

In the analysis that follows, results are often presented separately for women and men; however, where space does not permit, some results are presented only for women. In fact, living arrangements for women and men are very similar, with one important difference: women tend to make transitions out of the parental home and into partnerships and parenthood at an earlier age than men. This is associated with the fact that men tend to be older than their female partners. This age gap does not vary by cohort, and it is approximately the same for married and cohabiting couples. However, it does vary between countries. Figure 1 shows that in most countries the average age gap is something more than two years. In Italy it is three years, and the age gap is largest of all in Greece, where it approaches five years. The smallest age gaps are found in Ireland, Finland, and among Hispanics in the United States, where men are on average less than two years older than their female partners; the very smallest gap is 1.7 years, for blacks in the United States.

The article is structured as follows. Section 1 presents the data used. Section 2 discusses the major transitions in living arrangements— leaving the parental home, entering partnerships, and having children— and presents some basic figures on these. Section 3 analyzes living arrangements in more detail, presenting data on the proportions of young people living at home, living in extended families, and living in partnerships; the proportion who have children; and those who live alone and with friends. Section 4 summarizes the findings of the previous sections graphically. Section 5 concludes by discussing possible reasons for intercountry variations and suggesting directions for further research.

1. DATA: THE EUROPEAN COMMUNITY HOUSEHOLD PANEL (ECHP) AND THE PSID

Data for thirteen European countries come from the ECHP, a set of comparable large-scale longitudinal studies set up and funded by the European Union.[2] The ECHP contains data on individual characteristics, incomes and expenditures, education, employment and unemployment, and various measures of life satisfaction. This data set has the advantage of being a household survey (and thus collecting information on all members of respondents' households, which is particularly useful in the analysis of living arrangements). Because the same questions are asked in each country, results are directly comparable across countries. In addition, the ECHP is relatively large compared to some other data sets, containing information on more than 37,000 individuals between fifteen and thirty-five.[3]

The first wave of the ECHP was collected in 1994. Although two later waves of data are available, the first wave has been used for analysis, since in several countries young people were not consistently followed when they left the parental home. Thus, although the 1994 data are a little older, they are more reliably a representative sample. Two countries were late joiners to the project, and data for the first available year have been used for these countries: 1995 for Austria and 1996 for Finland. Although Luxembourg is a participant in the ECHP, sample sizes are too small for meaningful analysis.

Data for the United States come from the PSID, which like the ECHP is a large-scale, longitudinal, household-level data set. The PSID is run by the University of Michigan and is of long standing, with the first wave of data collected in 1968. PSID data for 1993 are used here—thus the U.S. data are one year older than the European data, but this has only a minimal impact on the comparability of results. Table 1 gives sample sizes for all the countries in the sample, for the group of young people ages fifteen to thirty-five.

2. THREE MAJOR TRANSITIONS

In terms of living arrangements, the most important components of the transition to adulthood are the transition out of the parental home, the transition from single status to living with a partner, and the transition from childlessness to parenthood. These transitions do not constitute a perfect definition of the transition to adulthood: some people never make one or more of the transitions, some people make a transition

TABLE 1

EUROPEAN COMMUNITY HOUSEHOLD PANEL AND PANEL STUDY OF INCOME DYNAMICS SAMPLE SIZES

Country	Sample Size (Ages 15-35)
Finland	3,200
Denmark	2,281
Netherlands	4,142
United Kingdom	4,063
France	5,732
Belgium	2,799
Germany	3,654
Austria	2,959
Ireland	4,893
Greece	4,956
Portugal	4,267
Spain	7,667
Italy	7,477
United States	9,784
White	4,154
Black	2,949
Hispanic	2,681

twenty for women in Finland and Denmark to older than twenty-seven for women in Italy and almost thirty for men in Italy. Home leaving occurs a good deal earlier in northern European countries than in southern European countries and earliest of all in Nordic countries. It also occurs relatively early in the United States, particularly among white Americans, where the median age for leaving home is twenty-one for women and twenty-two for men. In every country, women leave home earlier than men do. This is particularly pronounced in Greece, where the median age at which women leave home is more than five years earlier than the median age for men and where it is associated with a particularly large age gap between men and women in partnerships.

Figure 2(b) shows the age by which 50 percent of young people in each country are living with a partner. Partnerships are entered earliest in Finland and Denmark, where half of young people are partnered shortly after ages twenty-two (women) and twenty-five (men). The latest of all to enter partnerships are the Italians: the median Italian woman does not enter a partnership until she is older than twenty-seven, and the median Italian man does not enter a partnership until after the age of thirty. It will be observed that whereas northern Europeans leave home very much earlier than southern Europeans, they enter partnerships only slightly earlier. The transitional arrangements that are common in northern Europe between leaving home and before entering a partnership will be discussed later.

only to reverse it later (e.g., by moving back to the parents' home or by splitting up with a partner), and some people make and reverse transitions repeatedly. Because this analysis is cross-sectional, it does not deal with issues such as reversed or repeated transitions; however, a snapshot of how living arrangements vary with age at any one time is extremely informative, as long as one remembers that it gives only a broad indication of the age at which transitions are made for the first time.

Figure 2 illustrates that there are significant intercountry differences in the ages at which people make these three important transitions. Figure 2(a) shows the age by which 50 percent of young people in each country are living outside the parental home. This age ranges from

FIGURE 2
AGE BY WHICH PEOPLE MAKE TRANSITIONS

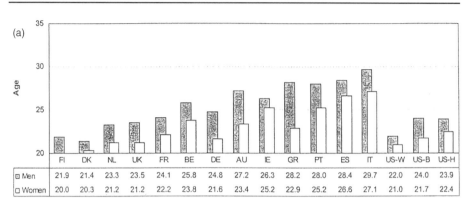

(a)

	FI	DK	NL	UK	FR	BE	DE	AU	IE	GR	PT	ES	IT	US-W	US-B	US-H
Men	21.9	21.4	23.3	23.5	24.1	25.8	24.8	27.2	26.3	28.2	28.0	28.4	29.7	22.0	24.0	23.9
Women	20.0	20.3	21.2	21.2	22.2	23.8	21.6	23.4	25.2	22.9	25.2	26.6	27.1	21.0	21.7	22.4

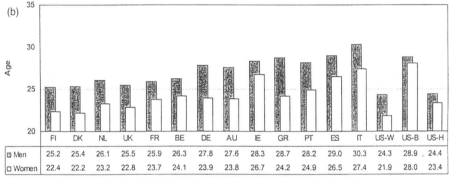

(b)

	FI	DK	NL	UK	FR	BE	DE	AU	IE	GR	PT	ES	IT	US-W	US-B	US-H
Men	25.2	25.4	26.1	25.5	25.9	26.3	27.8	27.6	28.3	28.7	28.2	29.0	30.3	24.3	28.9	24.4
Women	22.4	22.2	23.2	22.8	23.7	24.1	23.9	23.8	26.7	24.2	24.9	26.5	27.4	21.9	28.0	23.4

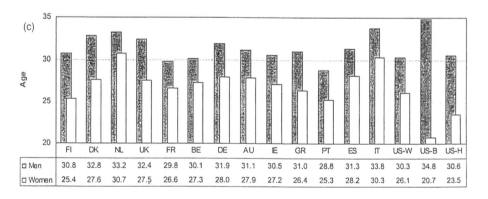

(c)

	FI	DK	NL	UK	FR	BE	DE	AU	IE	GR	PT	ES	IT	US-W	US-B	US-H
Men	30.8	32.8	33.2	32.4	29.8	30.1	31.9	31.1	30.5	31.0	28.8	31.3	33.8	30.3	34.8	30.6
Women	25.4	27.6	30.7	27.5	26.6	27.3	28.0	27.9	27.2	26.4	25.3	28.2	30.3	26.1	20.7	23.5

NOTE: (a) = age by which 50% of people have left home; (b) = age by which 50% of people are living with a partner; (c) = age by which 50% of people are living with children. FI = Finland; DK = Denmark; NL = Netherlands; UK = United Kingdom; FR = France; BE = Belgium; DE = Germany; AU = Austria; IE = Ireland; GR = Greece; PT = Portugal; ES = Spain; IT = Italy; US (Wh) = United States (White); US (Bl) = United States (Black); US (Hi) = United States (Hispanic).

There is a large difference between groups in the United States in the ages at which partnerships are entered. White Americans find themselves in partnerships even earlier than the Finns and the Danes, and Hispanic Americans are also in partnerships much earlier than most Europeans. However, black Americans are relatively unlikely to be in partnerships at an early age: not until ages twenty-eight (women) and twenty-nine (men) are half of all black Americans in a partnership.

Figure 2c shows the age by which half of young people in each country are living with children. Living with children is a slightly more complicated concept than the previous two discussed since a person may live with his or her natural children, may live with the children of a spouse or partner without being a biological parent, or may have had or fathered children without living in the same household as those children. Here, "living with children" is defined as living in the same household as one's own natural children or the children of a partner. For women, this is essentially the same as ever having had a child; for men, particularly where there are high rates of divorce and/or lone parenthood, the two figures may differ substantially. The proportion of men who have children living in a different household will be discussed later.

In the European sample, there is no discernible pattern between groups of countries when it comes to living with children. Of the two countries with the earliest fertility (Finland and Portugal), one is in the Nordic group, and the other is in the southern European group; of the two countries with the latest fertility (Netherlands and Italy), again one in the Nordic group and the other in the southern group. There are substantial intercountry variations: in early-fertility countries, the median woman has a child by the age of 25.4 (Finland) or 25.3 (Portugal), whereas in late-fertility countries, the median woman does not have a child until age 30.3 (Italy) or 30.7 (Netherlands). European countries where the median woman has her first child by 27.5 years of age are Finland, the United Kingdom, France, Belgium, Ireland, Greece, and Portugal; countries where the median woman has her first child later than this are Denmark, the Netherlands, Germany, Austria, Spain, and Italy.

All groups of American women enter motherhood relatively early: median black and Hispanic American women have a first child at 20.7 and 23.5 years of age, respectively, younger than in any European country. The median white American woman has her first child at 26.1 years, which is later than Portuguese or Finnish women, but earlier than all other European women.

The gap between women and men in the age at which 50 percent live with children reflects two things: the age gap between men and women in relationships (so Greece has a large gap), and the prevalence of lone parenthood and/or relationship breakdown (so the gap is also large in Scandinavian countries and for black and Hispanic Americans). It is particularly large for black Americans: half of black American women are living with a child by age 20.7, but only by

FIGURE 3
PROPORTION LIVING AWAY FROM PARENTAL HOME

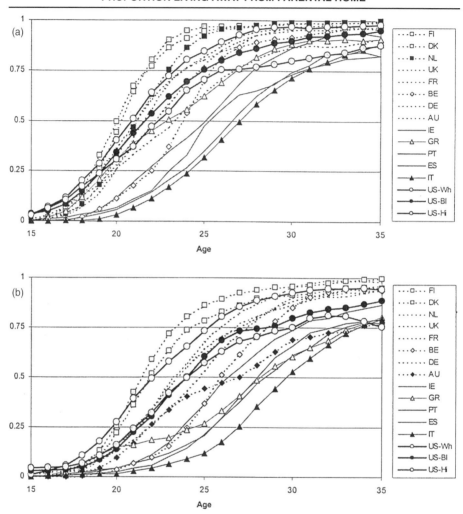

NOTE: (a) = proportion living away from parental home (women); (b) = proportion living away from parental home (men). FI = Finland; DK = Denmark; NL = Netherlands; UK = United Kingdom; FR = France; BE = Belgium; DE = Germany; AU = Austria; IE = Ireland; GR = Greece; PT = Portugal; ES = Spain; IT = Italy; US (Wh) = United States (White); US (Bl) = United States (Black); US (Hi) = United States (Hispanic).

age 34.8—more than fourteen years later—do half of all black American men live with a child.

Of course, the age by which half of young people are in a certain situation is only one indicator of the way in which transitions are made and gives no information about the ages at which transitions are made either side of the median mark. The sections that follow examine all three transitions in a little more detail.

3. LIVING ARRANGEMENTS

Living at home and the extended family

Figure 3 shows the proportions of young women and men who are living away from home between ages fifteen and thirty-five. There is not space to mark every country on the graph; therefore, only selected countries of particular interest have been marked.

The Finns, Danes, and Dutch are the most likely at all ages to be living away from their parents' home: in fact, after the age of twenty-five, hardly any young women in these countries live with their parents. At all ages, Italians are the least likely to have left home. In Belgium, living away from the parental home before the mid-twenties is much rarer than in other northern countries before ages twenty-five (women) and thirty (men), although after this age Belgians behave similarly to other northerners. Austrian men, by contrast, behave similarly to other northern Europeans in their early twenties but are much less likely to have left the parental home than are other northerners by their late twenties. Figure 3 also reveals that the median figures given in the previous section tell only a partial story: although for Greek men, the median age for living away from home is fairly typical of southern European countries, at younger ages Greek men are actually much more likely than other southern Europeans to be living away from home.

Similarly, although the median age for living away from home is lowest among Finns and Danes, the graphs show that Americans, and particularly American women, are the most likely to be living apart from their parents at very early ages (seventeen or younger). White Americans are more likely to be living away from their parents than are black or Hispanic Americans; this is particularly the case for American men.

The variation in the proportion of young people who have left home is less toward the beginning and end of the age range and larger in the middle. Table 2 provides information in numerical form on the proportion of young people living at home for young men and women in their early and late twenties, where the variation is largest.

Most young people who live at home live in a nuclear family: with one or both parents and possibly with siblings. However, in many countries a significant proportion live in extended families. Figure 4 graphs the proportions of women ages fifteen to twenty-four and twenty-five to thirty-four who live in extended families and whether they also live with a partner and/or a child.

Living in an extended family is most common in Austria and among black and Hispanic Americans; it also accounts for about 10 percent of women in the younger age group in the southern European countries. In general, younger women who live in

TABLE 2
PERCENTAGE OF YOUNG PEOPLE LIVING AT HOME

Country	Women's Age		Men's Age	
	20-24	25-29	20-24	25-29
Finland	25.9	3.4	53.0	13.4
Denmark	22.8	2.9	41.0	6.5
Netherlands	37.8	3.5	64.7	19.1
United Kingdom	39.2	8.8	65.4	24.3
France	52.6	11.1	69.9	24.3
Belgium	71.0	14.1	89.3	39.0
Germany	40.7	11.6	74.3	28.2
Austria	59.0	25.3	75.9	47.8
Ireland	73.9	34.1	88.5	45.5
Greece	55.9	24.4	80.5	59.9
Portugal	85.0	39.3	90.7	58.5
Spain	85.9	47.1	94.2	62.5
Italy	89.3	50.3	95.6	73.2
United States				
White	38.7	7.0	51.7	15.7
Black	47.2	15.9	69.4	29.7
Hispanic	54.1	24.5	66.3	34.0

an extended family are predominantly single and childless. However, in Ireland and among black and Hispanic Americans, there are also a sizeable number of lone parents. The proportion of women living with a partner (with or without children) in an extended family is relatively small for this age group, being more than 5 percent only among Hispanic Americans.

In the twenty-five to thirty-four age group, the proportions living in extended families are lower, particularly in northern Europe, where they are negligible. In southern Europe, most of those living in extended families are also living with a partner and children, except in Ireland, where it is more common to be a lone parent. There are also many more lone parents than couple parents among black American women in extended families (7 percent versus 2 percent); among Hispanic Americans, who have the highest proportion of women in extended families, there are more couple parents than lone parents (12 percent versus 6 percent).

*Partnership: Marriage
and cohabitation*

Figure 5 shows how the proportion of men and women living with a partner varies with age and between countries. Comparing Figure 5 with Figure 2, it is generally the case that countries with late median ages at partnering are the same countries where fewer people live with their partners in their teens and early twenties, and countries with early median ages are countries where more people live with partners at this time. The exception is Belgium,

FIGURE 4
THE EXTENDED FAMILY

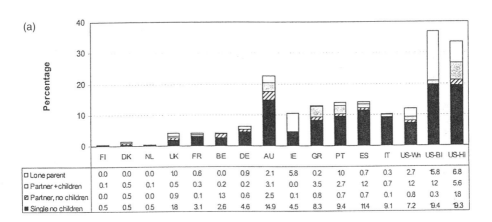

(a)

	FI	DK	NL	UK	FR	BE	DE	AU	IE	GR	PT	ES	IT	US-Wh	US-Bl	US-Hi
☐ Lone parent	0.0	0.0	0.0	1.0	0.6	0.0	0.9	2.1	5.8	0.2	1.0	0.7	0.3	2.7	5.8	6.8
☐ Partner + children	0.1	0.5	0.1	0.5	0.3	0.2	0.2	3.1	0.0	3.5	2.7	1.2	0.7	1.2	1.2	5.6
▨ Partner, no children	0.0	0.5	0.0	0.9	0.1	1.3	0.6	2.5	0.1	0.8	0.7	0.7	0.1	0.8	0.3	1.8
■ Single no children	0.5	0.5	0.5	1.8	3.1	2.6	4.6	14.9	4.5	8.3	9.4	11.4	9.1	7.2	19.4	19.3

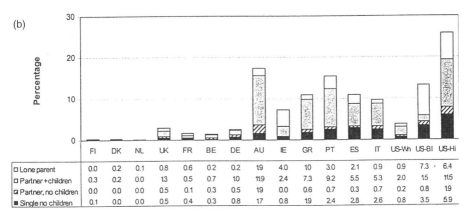

(b)

	FI	DK	NL	UK	FR	BE	DE	AU	IE	GR	PT	ES	IT	US-Wh	US-Bl	US-Hi
☐ Lone parent	0.0	0.2	0.1	0.8	0.6	0.2	0.2	1.9	4.0	1.0	3.0	2.1	0.9	0.9	7.3 ·	6.4
☐ Partner + children	0.3	0.2	0.0	1.3	0.5	0.7	1.0	11.9	2.4	7.3	9.2	5.5	5.3	2.0	1.5	11.5
▨ Partner, no children	0.0	0.0	0.0	0.5	0.1	0.3	0.5	1.9	0.0	0.6	0.7	0.3	0.7	0.2	0.8	1.9
■ Single no children	0.1	0.0	0.0	0.5	0.4	0.3	0.8	1.7	0.8	1.9	2.4	2.8	2.6	0.8	3.5	5.9

NOTE: (a) = the extended family (women ages 15-24); (b) = the extended family (women ages 25-34). FI = Finland; DK = Denmark; NL = Netherlands; UK = United Kingdom; FR = France; BE = Belgium; DE = Germany; AU = Austria; IE = Ireland; GR = Greece; PT = Portugal; ES = Spain; IT = Italy; US (Wh) = United States (White); US (Bl) = United States (Black); US (Hi) = United States (Hispanic).

where it is relatively uncommon to live with a partner before the early twenties but relatively common thereafter.

However, the relatively early median age at partnering among white and Hispanic Americans masks the fact that they are much more likely than Europeans to live with a partner during their teens than Europeans in any country. And black Americans, whose median age at partnering is among the latest, are as likely as any Europeans to live with a partner at an early age. Therefore, relative to Europeans,

FIGURE 5
PROPORTION LIVING WITH A PARTNER

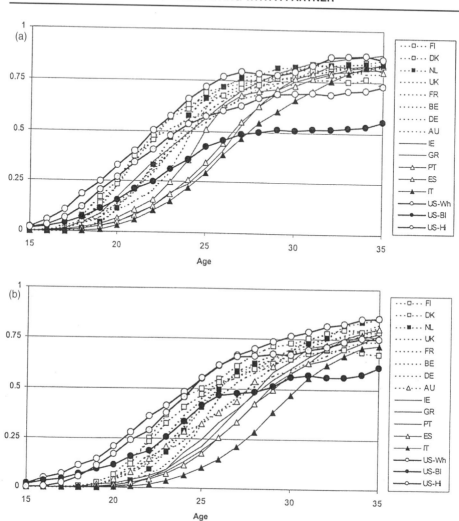

NOTE: (a) = proportion living with a partner (women); (b) = proportion living with a partner (men).
FI = Finland; DK = Denmark; NL = Netherlands; UK = United Kingdom; FR = France; BE = Belgium; DE
= Germany; AU = Austria; IE = Ireland; GR = Greece; PT = Portugal; ES = Spain; IT = Italy; US (Wh) =
United States (White); US (Bl) = United States (Black); US (Hi) = United States (Hispanic).

Americans live with partners a good deal earlier than the median figure would suggest.

It is interesting to note, particularly for women, that in the United States and in those European

FIGURE 6
PROPORTION COHABITING AND MARRIED

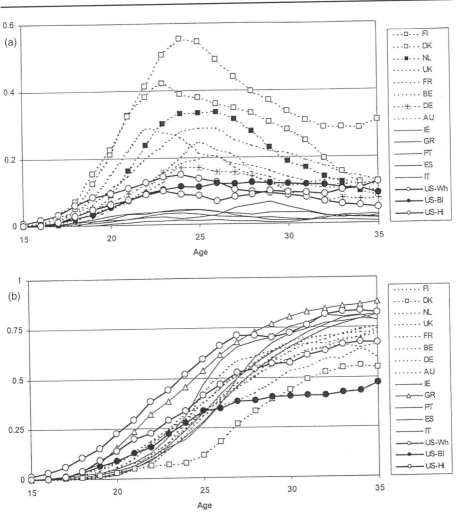

NOTE: (a) = proportion cohabiting (women); (b) = proportion married (women). FI = Finland; DK = Denmark; NL = Netherlands; UK = United Kingdom; FR = France; BE = Belgium; DE = Germany; AU = Austria; IE = Ireland; GR = Greece; PT = Portugal; ES = Spain; IT = Italy; US (Wh) = United States (White); US (BI) = United States (Black); US (Hi) = United States (Hispanic).

countries where partnering occurs very early, the curves flatten off distinctly after the mid-twenties. This does not indicate that no new partnerships occur in these countries after the mid-twenties but rather that the rate of new partnerships is almost matched by the rate of partnership dissolution. In southern European countries, by contrast, the curves remain steep well into the thirties, indicating that new partnerships are being entered in considerable numbers, which well outstrips any partnership dissolution that is occurring at the same time.

One obvious reason partnering occurs earlier in northern than in southern Europe is that nonmarital cohabitation, still rare in southern Europe, has become acceptable and commonplace in northern Europe and is increasingly used as a prelude or an alternative to marriage. Figure 6, which plots the rates of nonmarital cohabitation and marriage for women, shows that the rates of cohabitation in Ireland, Greece, Spain, Portugal, and Italy are tiny compared to rates of cohabitation in northern and Nordic countries—particularly Denmark, where more than half of women in their mid-twenties are in nonmarital cohabitation and where marriage is correspondingly uncommon at this age.

Americans of all groups are more likely than southern Europeans to be cohabiting, but they are much less likely than northern Europeans to be cohabiting. Cohabitation rates for all groups of American women are similar (around 10 percent between ages twenty and thirty-five), though rates are higher for whites at earlier ages and slightly higher for blacks at later ages.

Americans (particularly white Americans) are more likely than Europeans to be formally married at an early age. Of all Europeans, only Greek women are anywhere near as likely as white or Hispanic American

women to be married in their early or mid-twenties. Even black American women, who are a good deal less likely to be married than their white and Hispanic compatriots, are more likely then most Europeans to be married in their teens and early twenties. However, the curve flattens off markedly after the mid-twenties for black American women, indicating that the rate of new marriages is approximately equal to the rate of marital dissolution. Thus, by the age of thirty or so, black American women are less likely than any other women to be married.

Figure 6 combines women with and without children, but these groups of women are separated out in Table 3, revealing some interesting insights. First, there are some countries where cohabitation is common among childless women but extremely uncommon among mothers: this is most strikingly the case for the Netherlands and also for Germany among the older age group.

Marriage is relatively rare among childless women in the twenty to twenty-four age group: only in the United Kingdom, in Austria, and among all groups of American women are more than 10 percent of childless women married. In all countries, marriage is a good deal more common among women with children than among childless women. Marriage is least common among mothers in Denmark and Finland (where only one in four mothers in this age group are married) and among black American women (where only one in five are married). However, in the Scandinavian countries, cohabitation is extremely common, account-

TABLE 3
MARRIAGE AND COHABITATION

	All Women		Women without Children		Women with Children		
	Cohabiting	Married	Cohabiting	Married	Cohabiting	Married	Single
Women ages 20-24							
Finland	35.9	7.1	33.0	3.5	49.7	24.8	25.5
Denmark	42.3	5.1	40.4	2.6	58.6	26.9	14.5
Netherlands	24.8	10.2	25.7	6.8	5.1	83.3	11.6
United Kingdom	25.3	18.9	24.8	11.5	27.3	48.2	24.5
France	19.7	11.4	17.5	6.3	35.6	48.6	15.9
Belgium	11.6	12.7	10.6	7.2	22.2	69.2	8.6
Germany	13.9	19.5	14.2	9.9	12.3	69.6	18.1
Austria	9.8	21.1	9.0	12.9	13.4	58.1	28.5
Ireland	3.6	9.2	1.9	3.7	10.9	31.8	57.2
Greece	2.4	30.3	3.1	8.9	0.0	98.8	1.2
Portugal	3.6	12.4	1.1	5.3	22.0	64.3	13.8
Spain	1.8	10.9	1.6	5.6	4.2	79.9	15.9
Italy	0.9	9.4	0.4	5.2	9.3	85.0	5.8
United States							
White	12.2	36.2	11.2	22.2	15.0	70.4	15.8
Black	9.1	16.2	9.5	11.0	8.7	20.5	72.1
Hispanic	7.8	32.6	6.3	18.0	10.5	53.2	37.8
Women ages 25-29							
Finland	34.0	40.1	47.0	15.2	25.0	57.2	17.8
Denmark	44.2	26.4	48.7	13.2	38.5	43.1	18.4
Netherlands	29.1	46.1	35.7	35.3	5.1	85.3	9.2
United Kingdom	18.8	50.3	23.8	38.4	13.1	63.9	23.0
France	25.9	46.3	28.3	21.6	23.7	68.7	7.6
Belgium	16.9	57.9	22.7	34.0	10.7	83.3	6.0
Germany	15.0	51.6	21.3	28.4	7.0	81.0	12.1
Austria	21.5	44.1	25.6	17.4	16.8	74.4	8.8
Ireland	3.7	47.8	3.3	25.2	4.1	70.7	25.1
Greece	2.3	66.4	4.2	33.9	0.5	95.9	3.6
Portugal	2.7	62.8	0.8	24.6	3.9	87.4	8.7
Spain	4.7	48.9	4.1	23.9	5.6	88.2	6.2
Italy	0.9	45.1	0.9	28.2	0.7	92.9	6.3
United States							
White	10.8	68.4	15.4	50.0	6.6	83.8	11.8
Black	12.1	38.6	11.9	30.2	11.2	43.5	46.2
Hispanic	8.9	57.3	8.3	37.1	8.5	67.2	27.9

ing for half or more of all mothers, whereas among black American women cohabitation among mothers is rather rare, accounting for less than one in ten mothers; thus black American women have a correspondingly high rate of lone motherhood.

Among the twenty to twenty-four age group, the proportion of mothers who do not live with a partner ranges from just 1 percent in Greece to around a quarter of all mothers in Denmark, the United Kingdom, and Austria, to 57 percent in Ireland and

TABLE 4

PERCENTAGE LIVING WITH CHILDREN, BY SEX AND AGE GROUP

Country	Women's Age		Men's Age	
	20-24	25-29	20-24	25-29
Finland	17.14	59.24	4.44	33.59
Denmark	10.30	44.20	4.07	22.64 (24.36)
Netherlands	4.57	21.57	1.01	9.98
United Kingdom	20.18	46.65	8.53 (12.32)	23.36 (27.88)
France	12.05	52.53	2.83	30.14
Belgium	8.85	48.41	2.01	21.94 (24.00)
Germany	16.04	44.04	3.09	21.68
Austria	18.13	46.90	4.81	24.98
Ireland	19.41	49.59	2.73 (4.03)	27.90
Greece	23.83	52.44	2.29	21.54
Portugal	11.97	60.90	4.49	33.03
Spain	7.11	38.83	2.83	18.27
Italy	5.31	26.20	1.02	10.66
United States				
White	29.47	55.17	13.65 (15.63)	34.47 (39.46)
Black	54.03 (56.38)	64.46 (68.98)	9.96 (29.15)	29.89 (54.02)
Hispanic	40.97 (42.69)	67.45 (70.13)	16.22 (25.23)	41.94 (54.48)

NOTE: "Living with children" means living in a household where one or more of one's natural children or stepchildren also live. Figures in parentheses indicate the percentage of people who have had children; where no figure in parentheses is given, data were either unavailable (Finland, Germany, and Austria) or the proportion of people who had children but did not live with any of them was less than 1 percent.

72 percent among black Americans. However, this is not to say that lone motherhood is a common phenomenon among young women in all these countries, since in most countries only a minority of women in this age group have become mothers.

Having children

Table 4 shows the percentage of people in their twenties who live with children—here, this means living in the same household as one or more of one's own natural children or stepchildren.

As noted in section 2, no systematic regional divide is evident in Europe in the proportions of young people living with children; there are early and late fertility countries in both Nordic and southern groups.

Americans are much more likely to live with children than are Europeans. Among American men, blacks are the least likely to be living with children in both age groups; however, even black American men are more likely than are men in Europe to be living with children. Hispanic American men are the most likely to be living with children, with 16 percent of the twenty to twenty-four age group and 42 percent of the twenty-five to twenty-nine age group living with children.

Among American women, white women are the least likely to be living with children (29 percent in the twenty to twenty-four age group and 55 percent in the twenty-five to twenty-nine age group). However, they are still more likely than women virtually everywhere in Europe to be living with children. Black and Hispanic women are more likely than are white women to be living with children: among the twenty to twenty-four age group, black women are most likely to live with children (54 percent), while in the twenty-five to twenty-nine age group, Hispanic women are the most likely (67 percent).

These figures have looked at the percentage of people living with children rather than those who have had or fathered children. In most countries, and particularly for women, the two figures are very similar, with differences of less than 1 percent between them. However, in countries where there is a high incidence of relationship breakdown and/or lone parenthood, the two figures can be very different, particularly for men. Where more than 1 percent of the sample report having had or fathered children but not living with any of them, this percentage is shown in parentheses. In Europe, the country with the highest proportion of men not living with their children is the United Kingdom (with about 4 percent of men in this situation). In the United States, black men are most likely to have children they do not live with. Nineteen percent of black men aged twenty to twenty-four have children they do not live with, and this figure rises to 24 percent in the twenty-five to twenty-nine age group.

Living alone and with friends

Having dealt with parents, extended families, partners and children, we turn briefly to look at young people who live on their own. The proportions of young people living alone are shown in Figure 7. Living alone is most common in Finland, Denmark, the Netherlands, and Germany and also among black American men. Women in these and other countries are most likely to live alone between the ages of twenty and twenty-four, while men are slightly more likely to live alone in their late twenties and even into their thirties.

Those least likely to live alone are young people in Mediterranean countries (where, with the exception of Greece, the proportions are tiny) plus Ireland and the United Kingdom, and Hispanic Americans. Part of the reason young Britons are so unlikely to live alone may be found in Figure 8, which shows the proportion of young women sharing accommodation with unrelated others. This category includes young people living in another family as a lodger, but (for Europe, where data are available) the most common arrangement is where accommodation is shared with friends.

This living arrangement is relatively uncommon, accounting for less than 2 percent of young people in most countries. However, more than 5 percent of young people share with friends throughout the teens and twenties in the United Kingdom, through the twenties in Ireland, and in the teens and early twenties for Hispanic Americans.

FIGURE 7
PROPORTION OF PEOPLE LIVING ALONE

(a)

	FI	DK	NL	UK	FR	BE	DE	AU	IE	GR	PT	ES	IT	US-W	US-B	US-L
■ 15-19	8.5	0.6	4.1	1.3	5.0	0.0	0.4	1.7	0.4	3.8	0.0	0.3	0.0	1.7	0.8	0.6
□ 20-24	26.8	27.3	22.3	3.6	12.5	4.2	21.2	9.8	2.9	8.0	1.6	0.4	0.8	9.9	5.2	2.2
▨ 25-29	11.9	18.3	16.5	6.0	11.8	9.3	15.8	10.1	3.3	5.4	0.7	1.4	3.6	9.6	8.6	2.3
□ 30-34	10.3	9.1	9.9	6.4	8.3	6.4	10.2	6.0	2.5	3.9	1.6	2.2	3.3	4.1	4.9	1.3

(b)

	FI	DK	NL	UK	FR	BE	DE	AU	IE	GR	PT	ES	IT	US-W	US-B	US-L
■ 15-19	0.6	4.9	2.5	1.4	3.4	0.0	2.9	0.6	0.0	3.7	0.0	0.0	0.4	1.3	0.5	0.3
□ 20-24	24.0	31.1	19.9	6.9	12.5	3.7	13.3	8.4	3.6	11.7	0.0	0.6	1.2	14.0	8.1	5.7
▨ 25-29	22.4	32.1	18.5	9.4	16.5	10.1	24.1	12.7	9.4	7.7	1.9	2.7	5.2	14.8	18.4	6.9
□ 30-34	16.6	27.1	20.5	12.5	15.6	15.8	24.4	9.4	7.1	8.0	1.3	3.3	6.1	10.7	20.3	7.9

NOTE: (a) = proportion of women living alone; (b) = proportion of men living alone. FI = Finland; DK = Denmark; NL = Netherlands; UK = United Kingdom; FR = France; BE = Belgium; DE = Germany; AU = Austria; IE = Ireland; GR = Greece; PT = Portugal; ES = Spain; IT = Italy; US (Wh) = United States (White); US (Bl) = United States (Black); US (Hi) = United States (Hispanic).

FIGURE 8
PROPORTION OF WOMEN LIVING WITH FRIENDS

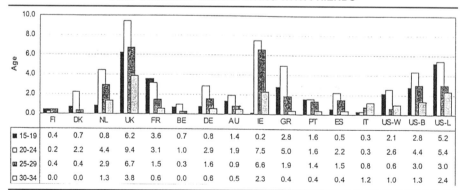

	FI	DK	NL	UK	FR	BE	DE	AU	IE	GR	PT	ES	IT	US-W	US-B	US-L
■ 15-19	0.4	0.7	0.8	6.2	3.6	0.7	0.8	1.4	0.2	2.8	1.6	0.5	0.3	2.1	2.8	5.2
□ 20-24	0.2	2.2	4.4	9.4	3.1	1.0	2.9	1.9	7.5	5.0	1.6	2.2	0.3	2.6	4.4	5.4
▨ 25-29	0.4	0.4	2.9	6.7	1.5	0.3	1.6	0.9	6.6	1.9	1.4	1.5	0.8	0.6	3.0	3.0
□ 30-34	0.0	0.0	1.3	3.8	0.6	0.0	0.6	0.5	2.3	0.4	0.4	0.4	1.2	1.0	1.3	2.4

NOTE: FI = Finland; DK = Denmark; NL = Netherlands; UK = United Kingdom; FR = France; BE = Belgium; DE = Germany; AU = Austria; IE = Ireland; GR = Greece; PT = Portugal; ES = Spain; IT = Italy; US (Wh) = United States (White); US (Bl) = United States (Black); US (Hi) = United States (Hispanic).

4. THE WHOLE PICTURE

Figure 9 summarizes the discussions in the previous sections graphically, indicating how household structure varies by country and age. Graphs are presented for women; graphs for men are similar, but all curves are shifted over to the right.

To read these graphs, note that age is measured on the horizontal axis and the proportion of people in any situation is measured on the vertical axis. Household situation is denoted by three criteria. Parenthood status is indicated by the thick black line running down the middle of each graph. Those below the line are childless, and those above have children. Thus, as expected, the proportion of childless people shrinks with increasing age in every country.

Marital status is indicated by color: those in marital unions are denoted by dark gray areas, those in cohabiting unions by light gray areas, and single people (i.e., those not living with a partner) by the white areas. Single people living alone are shown by unpatterned white, those living with friends are shown by white with diagonal shading, those living in the parental home are shown by vertical shading, and those living in an extended family by heavy vertical shading.

The large areas of light gray in the graphs for the Nordic group of countries, and to a lesser extent for northern European countries, indicate the prevalence of cohabiting unions in these countries. By contrast, the graphs for the southern countries show almost no light gray. Notice that in every European country where cohabiting is common, the light gray area below the bold line is larger than the light gray area above the bold line, indicating that cohabiting is much more common among childless women than among those with children. The Netherlands is a particularly good example of this.

Large areas of unshaded white are visible in the lower portion of the graphs for the Nordic group and to a lesser extent for the other northern countries, denoting people living alone. Again, there is almost no unshaded white on the graphs for the southern countries and very little in the lower portion of the graphs for the United States, indicating that living alone is uncommon among childless women in the United States, particularly for blacks and Hispanics.

The white areas with vertical shading toward the bottom left of the graphs indicate young single people without children, living with their parents. This is by far the most common living arrangement among seventeen-year-olds, but it is extremely uncommon in the Nordic countries after the early twenties and in the other northern countries and the United States after the mid-twenties. However, the fact that these shaded areas extend well over to the right-hand side of the graphs for the southern European countries indicates that these are countries where young people stay for extended periods in the family home.

The heavily shaded areas right at the bottom of the graphs denote young people living in extended families. These areas are virtually absent from graphs for northern and Nordic

FIGURE 9
LIVING ARRANGEMENTS IN EUROPE AND THE UNITED STATES

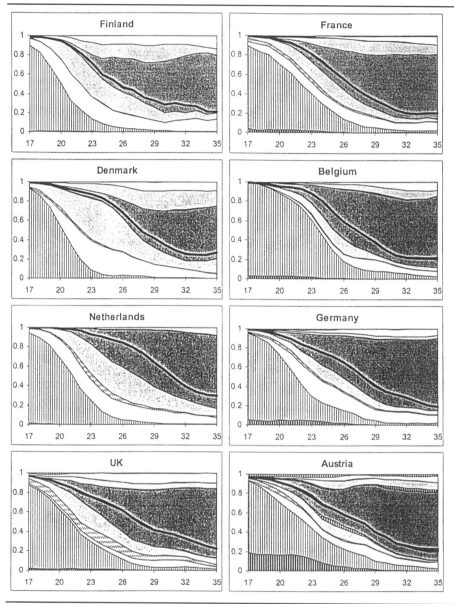

FIGURE 9 Continued

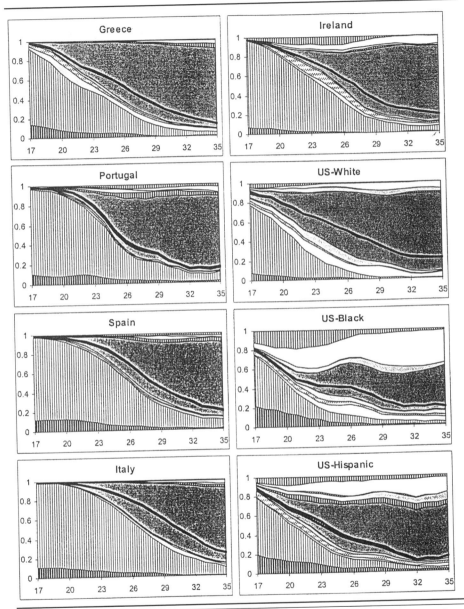

NOTE: White area = single; light gray area = cohabiting; dark gray area = married; light shading = living with parents; diagonal shading = living with friends; heavy shading = extended family; above black line in center = people who have children; below black line in center = people who are childless.

countries except for Austria, but they are of substantial size in all the Mediterranean countries and largest of all among black and Hispanic groups in the United States. Although the extended family is most common among single people at the younger end of the age range, there are also areas of dark shading at the top of the graph indicating single women with children who live in three-generation families (usually consisting of themselves, their parents, and their children). The proportion of lone mothers living in this type of extended family is relatively high in Ireland and among Hispanic Americans but is far higher among black American women. Black American women are also the most likely to be living as single mothers outside the extended family (the white-shaded area at the top of the graph), closely followed by Hispanic American women.

One of the most striking features of these graphs shown all together is that in southern Europe, two states are dominant to the virtual exclusion of others: single, childless, and living with parents dominates at the younger end of the age range, and married with children dominates at the other end. The proportion of young people married without children is small in these countries, suggesting that the transition to marriage is usually contemporaneous with the transition from the parental home, and the transition to parenthood follows soon after. By contrast, outside of southern Europe, a far greater diversity of situations is apparent. In the Nordic countries, in northern Europe, and among white Americans, this diversity is particularly apparent among

childless people: before they have children, northern Europeans may live with parents, live alone, cohabit, or live with a spouse. After having children, there is less diversity—marriage predominates but is by no means universal. For black and Hispanic women in the United States, while there is a good deal of diversity in living arrangements before childbearing, there is a greater deal of diversity afterward, with some mothers married, a few cohabiting (in the case of Hispanic women, with some couples living in extended families), and many unpartnered, living either in or outside the parental home.

Finally, it is worth repeating an observation made earlier: intercountry variation is far greater toward the middle of the age range than at the beginning or end. A narrow vertical slice taken from the left-hand part of any one of the ten graphs, at age seventeen, would be virtually indistinguishable from any other, but slices taken at age twenty-five would be highly dissimilar between countries. By age thirty-five, there would remain some differences between slices from different countries, but with the exception of non-white groups in the United States, they would have become much more alike.

5. CONCLUSIONS AND DIRECTIONS FOR FURTHER RESEARCH

This article has made reference to three groups of countries in Europe: a Nordic cluster, consisting of the Scandinavian countries plus the Netherlands; a northern European cluster, consisting of the United

Kingdom, France, Belgium, Germany, and Austria; and a southern European cluster, consisting of Greece, Portugal, Spain, Italy, and Ireland. None of the U.S. groups fits easily into any of the European clusters. Whites in the United States have rates of formal marriage comparable to southern European countries but early home leaving more similar to the Nordic countries. The popularity of the extended family among black and Hispanic Americans is similar to the southern European group of countries, but again, early home leaving by these groups is more characteristic of the Nordic countries, and their rates of lone motherhood are outside the European ballpark altogether.

These groups correspond to some extent with Esping-Andersen's (1990) schema of welfare states. The Nordic cluster corresponds to Esping-Andersen's "social-democratic" regime, characterized by high levels of state support and an emphasis on the individual rather than the family. The northern European cluster corresponds roughly to Esping-Andersen's "conservative" regime characterized by an emphasis on insurance-based benefits providing support for the family rather than the individual, although Esping-Andersen included Italy in this group whereas Italy clearly falls into a different group as far as living arrangements are concerned. However, the parallels end here. First, Esping-Andersen did not define a category into which southern European welfare states might be placed. Second, Esping-Andersen's "liberal" regime (characterized by modest welfare provisions with an emphasis on means testing) included the United States, with the United Kingdom as a sort of associate member. However, within the United States, living arrangements vary so much between groups that it is impossible to assign all groups to a single welfare state category. It may be that this diversity within the United States is a feature of the social polarization brought about by the liberal welfare regime, but it is difficult enough to find many common features between the different groups of Americans without mapping them all onto a single welfare state model.

Another reason too much emphasis should not be placed on groupings of countries is that these groupings may deflect attention from other interesting differences between countries. For example, although on most criteria the Netherlands belongs in a group with Scandinavian countries, it is set apart by the virtual absence of cohabiting unions among parents. Although Austria may belong with other central European countries, the popularity of the extended family in this country is more characteristic of the southern European group. There is also evidence for an Anglo-Saxon dimension in Europe, with young people in the United Kingdom and Ireland much more likely than those elsewhere in Europe to share with other unrelated adults and also more likely than other Europeans to be single mothers.

This article has identified a host of differences in young people's living arrangements between regions in Europe and groups of young men and

FIGURE 10

AGE BY WHICH EUROPEAN MEN LEAVE HOME, BY RELIGION AND COUNTRY

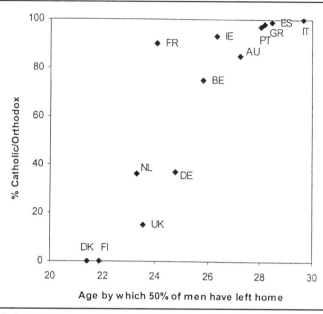

SOURCE: Central Intelligence Agency (1998) for the religion data; ECHP data for the age by which 50% of men have left home.

NOTE: FI = Finland; DK = Denmark; NL = Netherlands; UK = United Kingdom; FR = France; BE = Belgium; DE = Germany; AU = Austria; IE = Ireland; GR = Greece; PT = Portugal; ES = Spain; IT = Italy.

women in the United States. It is well beyond the scope of this descriptive article to test hypotheses as to the causes of these differences, but it is worth pointing to a number of possible factors that may provide avenues for further investigation.

Religion

It has already been noted that the southern group of countries in Europe may be characterized as mainly Catholic, and the northern group as mainly Protestant. In addition, Belgium and France, which are less extreme examples of the northern model, are also countries with large Catholic populations. Figure 10 shows that there is a strong relationship between the proportion of Catholics living in a country and at least one aspect of living arrangements.

However, the reasons behind this association are far from clear. Does the relationship between Catholicism and family formation arise at an individual level (individuals coming from a Catholic family are more likely to behave in a particular way), at a social level (living in a Catholic country causes people to behave in a particular way), or via a third factor associated with both religion and lifestyle? Because the ECHP does not

FIGURE 11
AGE BY WHICH MEN LEAVE HOME, BY SOCIAL EXPENDITURE IN COUNTRY

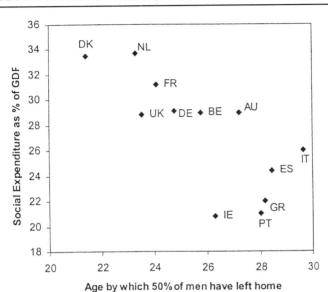

SOURCE: Eurostat (1999) for social expenditure; ECHP data for the age by which 50% of men have left home.

NOTE: FI = Finland; DK = Denmark; NL = Netherlands; UK = United Kingdom; FR = France; BE = Belgium; DE = Germany; AU = Austria; IE = Ireland; GR = Greece; PT = Portugal; ES = Spain; IT = Italy.

contain information on individuals' religious beliefs, it does not allow the researcher to identify the level at which the relationship operates. However, this will certainly be possible using other data sets, and this is a fruitful direction for further research.

The welfare state

A welfare state in northern Europe that allows young people to live independently even when they are jobless or low paid may be a reason so many northern Europeans leave the family home so early. Figure 11 establishes a relationship

between early home leaving and more generous welfare states, using a very general measure of social expenditure. However, it is not clear whether welfare state provision has reacted to behavioral norms or vice versa. In the absence of large-scale welfare experiments, we know little about cause and effect; however, changes in welfare state provision may provide the key to further insights into this relationship.

The housing market

High house prices relative to wages and a scarcity of rented housing or housing suitable for single

FIGURE 12
AGE BY WHICH MEN LEAVE HOME, BY RENTAL AVAILABILITY IN COUNTRY

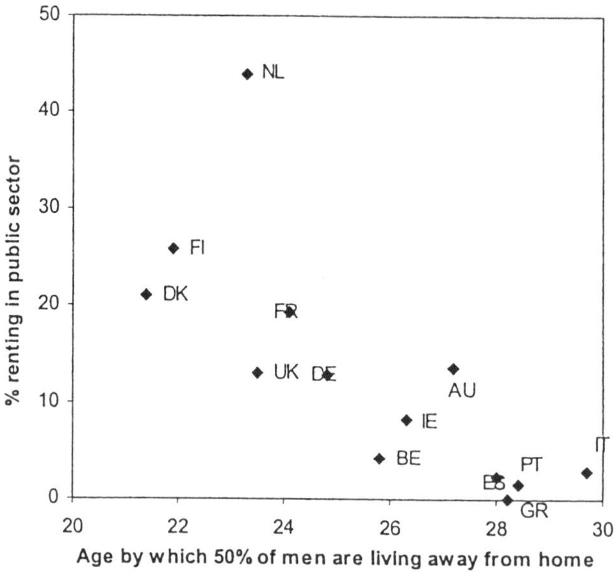

SOURCE: ECHP data for the percentage renting.

NOTE: FI = Finland; DK = Denmark; NL = Netherlands; UK = United Kingdom; FR = France; BE = Belgium; DE = Germany; AU = Austria; IE = Ireland; GR = Greece; PT = Portugal; ES = Spain; IT = Italy; US (Wh) = United States (White); US (Bl) = United States (Black); US (Hi) = United States (Hispanic).

people are often given as reasons southern Europeans delay leaving home and partnering. Figure 12 shows that the stock of public sector housing is related to the age at which young people leave home, and the stock of private rented accommodation is also related to home-leaving behavior (not shown). However, it is unclear whether a good supply of affordable housing suitable for young people causes them to leave home early or whether it is simply a response to demand for such housing. Variations within countries in the cost and supply of housing may allow further insights into the relationship between housing factors and living arrangements.

The labor market

Low wages, high unemployment, and insecure employment have been advanced as reasons for young people in southern Europe remaining for long periods in the family home. Figure 13 shows that (except for Spain) there is a slight relationship between the rates of insecure employment in Europe and the age at leaving home. It is clear that individuals' economic circumstances will affect the choices they make about where and with whom they will live. However, if economic circumstances were the main driving force behind young people's behavior, one would expect to see a far greater degree of congruence between north and south than is

FIGURE 13
AGE BY WHICH MEN LEAVE HOME, BY EMPLOYMENT SECURITY IN COUNTRY

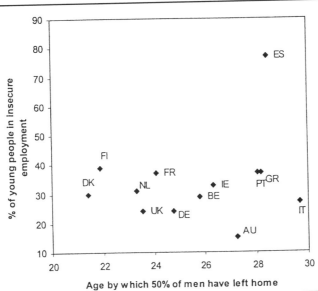

SOURCE: Iacovou and Berthoud (2001) for employment security and ECHP data for the age by which 50% of men have left home.
NOTE: FI = Finland; DK = Denmark; NL = Netherlands; UK = United Kingdom; FR = France; BE = Belgium; DE = Germany; AU = Austria; IE = Ireland; GR = Greece; PT = Portugal; ES = Spain; IT = Italy.

observed in practice. Young people in the south face generally difficult labor market conditions, but many do have secure employment and would be able to live independently if they so desired. Further research into the relationship between what young people could afford if they left home and their actual home-leaving behavior is possible with current ECHP data.

Education systems

Young people's family formation depends in a number of ways on education systems. Staying on longer in education will generally lead to delayed marriage and parenthood, but depending on factors such as cultural norms and the location of universities within the country, it may lead either to accelerated or to delayed home leaving. Mechanisms for funding students in higher education, and the returns to education in different countries, will also affect young people's behavior. This is another potentially fruitful avenue for research into the reasons for cross-national differences in living arrangements.

Culture and custom

A large part of behavior is determined by what is culturally usual and acceptable. Thus, a young Dane and a young Italian facing similar economic circumstances may behave differently according to what is usual in their particular milieu. One might attempt to test the role of culture and custom in two ways. First, one may attempt to match people according to their economic circumstances, education, and so on, and attribute some or all of the residual variation in behavior to cultural factors.

Second, one may look at young people from migrant families, who were brought up and educated in one country and who face the economic conditions pertaining to that country but who were born, or whose parents were born, in another part of Europe. The extent to which people from migrant families differ from people from nonmigrant families might yield further information about the role of culture and custom in family formation.

*Dynamics: One versus
    many transitions*

In southern Europe, the fact that two states (single, childless, and living at home; and married with children) dominate to the virtual exclusion of all others indicates that young people nearly always make the transition directly from the family home to marriage and tend to become parents relatively quickly after getting married. However, in the rest of Europe and in the United States, living arrangements are far more diverse, incorporating a range of transitional arrangements such as living alone and nonmarital cohabitation. These living arrangements may be labeled transitional with some confidence, as by the age of

thirty-five they are much less common than they are in the mid-twenties. However, this study has not yet established the frequency with which transitions are made. For women in the United Kingdom in their late twenties, living alone, living with friends, and childless cohabitation are approximately equally common. But this may be because nearly all women pass through one of these states for a short time on the way to becoming a mother and/or a wife, because a smaller number of women remain in each of these states for a relatively long period, or because a smaller number of women are cycling repeatedly between these states. As the ECHP matures, researchers will be able to answer these important questions of dynamics.

Notes

1. See Figure 10.
2. European Community Household Panel data are supplied by Eurostat, the Statistical Office of the European Communities, Batiment Jean Monnet, rue Alcide de Gasperi, Luxembourg-Kirchberg.
3. Individuals are interviewed only on reaching age sixteen, but some information is available on fifteen-year-olds and their households.

References

Aquilino, William S. 1991. Family structure and home-leaving: A further specification of the relationship. *Journal of Marriage and the Family* 53:999-1010.

Avery, Roger, Frances Goldscheider, and Alden Speare Jr. 1992. Feathered nest/gilded cage: Parental income and leaving home in the transition to adulthood. *Demography* 29 (3): 375-88.

Berrington, Ann, and Ian Diamond. 2000. Marriage or cohabitation: A competing risks analysis of first-partnership formation among the 1958 British Birth Cohort. *Journal of the Royal Statistical Society A* 163 (2): 127-51.

Buck, N., and J. Scott. 1993. She's leaving home: But why? An analysis of young people leaving the parental home. *Journal of Marriage and the Family* 55:863-74.

Cavalli, A., and O. Galland. 1995. *Youth in Europe*. London: Pinter.

Central Intelligence Agency. 1998. *The world factbook*. Washington, DC: Central Intelligence Agency.

Commission of the European Communities. 1982. *The young Europeans*. Brussels, Belgium: Commission of the European Communities.

———. 1988. *Young Europeans in 1987*. Luxembourg: Office for Official Publications for the European Communities.

———. 1991. *Young Europeans in 1990*. Luxembourg: Office for Official Publications for the European Communities.

Cordon, J.A.F. 1997. Youth residential independence and autonomy: A comparative study. *Journal of Family Issues*, 18:576-607.

Davanzo, J., and F. K. Goldscheider. 1990. Coming home again—Returns to the parental home of young-adults. *Population Studies—A Journal of Demography* 44 (2): 241-55.

Ermisch, John. 1996. Analysis of leaving the parental home and returning to it using panel data. Paper 96-1. In *Working papers of the ESRC Research Centre on Micro-Social Change*. Colchester, UK: University of Essex.

Ermisch, John, and Pamela Di Salvo. 1997. The economic determinants of young people's household formation. *Economica* 64:627-44.

Esping-Andersen, Gosta. 1990. *Three worlds of welfare capitalism*. Cambridge, MA: Polity.

Eurostat. 1999. *Statistics in focus: Theme 3—5 / 1999*. Luxembourg, Belgium: Eurostat.

Holdsworth, Clare. 2000. Leaving home in Britain and Spain. *European Sociological Review* 16 (2): 201-22.

Iacovou, Maria, and Richard Berthoud. 2001. *Young people's lives: A map of Europe*. Colchester, UK: Institute of Social and Economic Research, Essex University.

IARD. 2001. *Study on the state of young people and youth policy in Europe*. Milano, Italy: IARD.

Jones, G. 1987. Leaving the parental home: An analysis of early housing careers. *Journal of Social Policy* 16:49-74.

Kiernan, K. 1986. Leaving home—Living arrangements of young-people in 6 West-European countries. *European Journal of Population—Revue Européenne De Démographie* 2 (2): 177-84.

Nilsson, Karina, and Mattias Strandh. 1999. Nest leaving in Sweden: The importance of early educational and labor market careers. *Journal of Marriage and the Family* 61:1068-79.

Vogel, J. 1997. Living conditions and inequality in the European Union 1997. Working paper, Eurostat, Luxembourg, Belgium.

White, Lynn. 1994. Coresidence and leaving home: Young adults and their parents. *Annual Review of Sociology* 20:81-102.

ANNALS, *AAPSS*, **580**, March 2002

Cross-National Variation in Educational Preparation for Adulthood: From Early Adolescence to Young Adulthood

By LAURA LIPPMAN

ABSTRACT: This article presents key indicators of educational and employment success for adolescents and young adults preparing for adulthood in representative OECD countries. Nations are compared on mathematics achievement, educational attainment, literacy, and unemployment, as well as on national expenditures for education circa 1995. Nations with high-performing students on mathematics assessments are found also to have high levels of literacy in their population, and high rates of graduation from secondary school. National rates of tertiary degree attainment, however, appear to be unrelated to national performance on mathematics and literacy assessments in the countries studied. Indicators of educational performance in the countries studied did not track either an indicator of national investment in education or an indicator of success of young adults in the labor market, which may be more related to country economic cycles and labor force characteristics.

Laura Lippman is a senior research associate at Child Trends where she works on a variety of projects related to indicators of child well-being, early childhood education, positive youth development, and international comparisons. Previously, she was a demographer and senior analyst in the Early Childhood, International, and Cross-Cutting Studies Division of the National Center for Education Statistics, U.S. Department of Education. She was instrumental in forming the Federal Interagency Forum on Child and Family Statistics, and as chair of its Reporting Committee, she led the development of the first official federal effort to monitor child well-being, America's Children: Key National Indicators of Well-Being, and developed its website, childstats.gov. She has produced landmark studies, including Urban Schools: The Challenge of Location and Poverty, and Children's Well-being: An International Comparison. She has served as an advisor to various state, national, and international child well-being indicator efforts, including those conducted by the Annie E. Casey Foundation, the European Union, and international expert groups.

NOTE: An earlier version of this article, titled "The Transition to Adulthood: Explaining National Differences," was presented at the Johann Jacobs Foundation Conference, 28-30 October 1999 in Marbach, Germany.

T HIS article presents key indicators of educational and employment status for students making the transition from adolescence to early adulthood in selected Organization for Economic Cooperation and Development (OECD) countries. The data that are presented include international comparisons of student achievement, educational attainment, literacy, and unemployment among young adults. Data on expenditures for education are presented as a measure of national investment in education. This is by no means an exhaustive presentation of available data; rather, it is selective, presenting data on important educational markers from international surveys and collections, offered as representative of key aspects of transitioning from education to the workforce in each country.

To ensure comparability of data across countries, the data are derived from international surveys or from data collection efforts in which data have been harmonized. The time frame to which the data refer is the middle of the 1990s, between 1994 and 1996. Time trends are not presented, since the surveys are only available for one point in time. Although some trends in administrative data are available, it was deemed more important to present data for a time period corresponding to that of the assessment and survey data in order to observe patterns across the milestones presented.

The countries chosen for comparison are OECD members that are representative of the regions of Europe (northern, central, southern, and eastern), English-speaking countries, and Asia. The coverage of countries will vary by source, as the same countries did not participate in each of the surveys and data collections. However, every effort was made to include seven countries that are of particular interest, and they are the focus of the discussion in the text and appear in the figures when data are available: the United States, the United Kingdom, France, Germany, the Netherlands, Sweden, and Italy.

STUDENT ACHIEVEMENT
IN MATHEMATICS

Assessments of student achievement measure individual academic performance as well as the performance of education systems. Mathematics is the subject most often chosen in international comparative studies of achievement for several reasons. Mathematics could be considered the most likely subject to be similar across countries since the content of school mathematics curricula is more similar than other subjects and much of it needs to be taught in sequence. Mathematics achievement is a high priority for nations. A workforce that is highly skilled in mathematics is valued and often cited as a policy goal by nations, as the global economy increasingly demands technical skills that require mathematics proficiency at their base. Since mathematics is the gateway to careers in science and technology, assessments of achievement in mathematics indicate student preparedness for these careers. Finally, advanced coursework in mathematics in middle school is often considered a gateway to entrance to higher education in general.

The Third International Mathematics and Science Study (TIMSS) is the source of the data. It is the largest, most ambitious, and most technically advanced international assessment of students in mathematics and science achievement conducted to date. It was conducted by the International Association for the Evaluation of Educational Achievement (IEA) in 1995 in forty-five countries in middle school and twenty-four countries in the final year of secondary school. Results have been reported for forty-one and twenty-one countries, respectively (IEA 1996, 1998). There is also a primary school sample, but these results were considered outside the scope of this article.

Middle school

TIMSS sampled middle school students in the two grades with the largest proportion of thirteen-year-olds—seventh and eighth grade—in most countries. Results for eighth grade mathematics are presented in this article. Proficiency in six content areas were included in the mathematics assessment, including fractions and number sense; measurement; proportionality; data representation, analysis, and probability; geometry; and algebra. An international committee that considered the varied curricula across the participating countries developed assessment items. A discussion of performance in each content area is beyond the scope of this article; only summary measures of national differences in performance in overall

mathematics achievement are presented.

Table 1 presents means and percentile distributions of the mathematics assessment for eighth graders in nineteen representative countries. To give meaning to the scores, the average score of all countries participating in TIMSS was 513, and on average, students advance thirty-three points from seventh to eighth grade. The range in mean scores of the selected countries is from the 480s in the southern European countries of Spain and Greece to 605 in Japan. This range in mean scores across counties is greater than three times the average gain in achievement from seventh to eighth grade. Among the countries of interest, presented in Figure 1, the means range from 541 in the Netherlands to 500 in the United States (Italy did not report scores in time to be included in the TIMSS reports).

The distribution of scores within countries is larger than that across countries. Standard deviations among the countries in Table 1 range from 73 in Spain to 102 in Japan, or more than two to three times the average gain in achievement from seventh to eighth grade. All countries tested demonstrated a similarly large dispersion, and among the countries of interest, it ranges from 76 in France to 93 in England (see Figure 1 and Table 1). The interquartile range—the range from the seventy-fifth percentile score and the twenty-fifth percentile score—is another useful measure of dispersion in the performance of the middle half of all students. It ranges among the countries of interest from 107 in

TABLE 1

DISTRIBUTION OF MATHEMATICS ACHIEVEMENT SCORES, EIGHTH GRADE, 1995

Country	M	SE	Fifth Percentile Score	SE	Twenty-Fifth Percentile Score	SE	Seventy-Fifth Percentile Score	SE	Ninety-Fifth Percentile Score	SE	SD
Anglo											
Australia[a]	530	4.0	372	4.1	460	1.5	600	7.2	690	5.4	98
Canada	527	2.4	389	3.3	468	2.0	587	2.4	670	3.7	86
Ireland	527	5.1	381	6.5	462	4.9	594	9.6	681	3.3	93
United Kingdom (England)[b]	506	2.6	361	8.8	443	4.8	570	2.7	665	4.1	93
United Kingdom (Scotland)[a]	498	5.5	364	2.1	436	3.2	559	7.1	649	15.3	87
United States[b]	500	4.6	356	3.3	435	3.4	563	8.2	653	3.7	91
Northern Europe											
Denmark[a]	502	2.8	369	9.8	443	2.9	561	2.2	641	5.9	84
Sweden	519	3.0	384	2.9	460	6.0	579	3.4	661	4.7	85
Western Europe											
Belgium (Flemish)[b]	565	5.7	416	7.7	502	8.7	631	5.7	710	3.5	92
Belgium (French)[a]	526	3.4	385	13.8	467	1.1	587	3.7	658	6.2	86
France	538	2.9	415	5.2	484	1.4	591	2.5	666	3.4	76
Germany[a]	509	4.5	368	8.2	448	9.4	572	7.5	661	10.9	90
Netherlands[b]	541	6.7	397	10.6	477	9.1	604	7.4	688	6.9	89
Switzerland[b]	545	2.8	401	6.3	485	2.1	607	2.9	685	2.8	88
Southern Europe											
Greece[a]	484	3.1	347	2.8	422	1.9	546	3.6	633	6.6	88
Spain	487	2.0	376	2.0	436	2.5	536	3.5	616	3.9	73
Eastern Europe											
Hungary	537	3.2	391	2.3	471	2.1	602	2.7	693	9.2	93
Russia	535	5.3	388	4.5	471	5.6	600	8.2	687	2.9	92
Asia											
Japan	605	1.9	435	2.1	536	6.8	676	1.4	771	4.8	102

SOURCE: International Association for the Evaluation of Educational Achievement (1996).

NOTE: Because results are rounded to the nearest whole number, some totals may appear inconsistent.

a. Countries did not meet Third International Mathematics and Science Study (TIMSS) sampling requirements.

b. Countries met TIMSS sampling requirements only partially.

FIGURE 1
THIRD INTERNATIONAL MATHEMATICS AND SCIENCE STUDY
EIGHTH GRADE AVERAGE MATHEMATICS ACHIEVEMENT SCORES, 1995

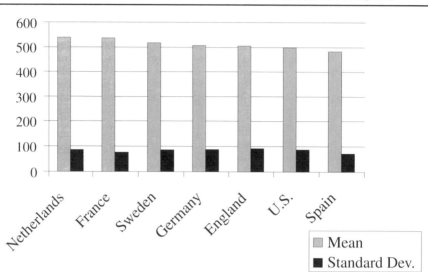

France to 128 in the United States (as may be seen in Figure 2 and Table 1), or three to four times the average gain from seventh to eighth grade.

The Netherlands and France have the highest mean scores among the countries of interest (and they are not significantly different from each other at 541 and 538), but their distributions of performance are different, with a larger dispersion of scores in the Netherlands, where the interquartile range is 127 compared to 107 in France (see Figure 2). Low scorers in the Netherlands at the fifth percentile score 397 compared to 415 at the fifth percentile in France, and high scorers in the Netherlands at the ninety-fifth percentile score 688 compared to 666 in France. France demonstrates that a wide range in performance is not a prerequisite for high overall levels of achievement. Interestingly, students at only the twenty-fifth percentile in France have a score that is about the same as the mean for the United States.

Sweden's mean score is 519, which is not significantly different from that of the Netherlands (because of the large standard error in the Netherlands), but it is below that of France. Germany's mean score is not significantly different from Sweden's at 509, and also not significantly different from England's and the United States' at 506 and 500, respectively. Germany, England, and the United States also have large dispersions of scores, with their interquartile ranges among the highest at 124, 127, and 128, respectively. Differences in the mean scores between one country and the next lowest scoring country are, in

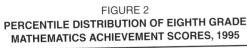

FIGURE 2
PERCENTILE DISTRIBUTION OF EIGHTH GRADE
MATHEMATICS ACHIEVEMENT SCORES, 1995

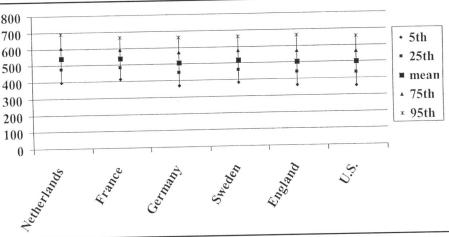

general, small or insignificant among the countries of interest.

Gender differences in eighth grade mathematics achievement across countries are presented in Table 2. They are small or virtually nonexistent. Among the countries presented in Table 2, only Denmark, the southern European countries, and Japan have gender differences that are statistically significant, and in all cases, boys score higher than do girls. In the six countries of interest for which data are available, gender differences range from two points in Sweden to eight points in France, but these differences are not statistically significant.

Differences in performance in TIMSS among countries at the eighth grade have been attributed to differences in curriculum and instructional practices, which influence students' opportunity to learn content areas in mathematics (National Center for Education Statistics 2000; Schmidt et al. 1997). Some of these differences as well as other school system characteristics of each country participating in TIMSS are detailed in *National Contexts for Mathematics and Science Education: An Encyclopedia of the Education Systems Participating in TIMSS* (Robitaille 1997). In all participating countries, student-level factors that were strongly related to higher achievement included higher parent education, more educational resources and books in the home, and less time watching television (IEA 1996).

End of secondary school

Twenty-four countries participated (and twenty-one reported data) in the TIMSS assessment of mathematics and science achievement in the final year of secondary school—intended as an assessment of the yield of education systems. The

TABLE 2

**GENDER DIFFERENCES IN MATHEMATICS ACHIEVEMENT,
EIGHTH GRADE (IN MOST COUNTRIES), 1995**

Country	M	SE	Boys M	Boys SE	Girls M	Girls SE	Difference	SE
Anglo								
Australia[a]	530	4.0	527	5.1	532	4.6	5	6.9
Canada	527	2.4	526	3.2	530	2.7	4	4.2
Ireland	527	5.1	535	7.2	520	6.0	14	9.3
United Kingdom (England)	506	2.6	508	5.1	504	3.5	4	6.2
United States	500	4.6	502	5.2	497	4.5	5	6.9
Northern Europe								
Denmark[c]	502	2.8	511	3.2	494	3.4	17	4.7
Norway	503	2.2	505	2.8	501	2.7	4	3.9
Sweden	519	3.0	520	3.6	518	3.1	2	4.7
Western Europe								
Belgium (Flemish)	565	5.7	563	8.8	567	7.4	4	11.5
Belgium (French)[a]	526	3.4	530	4.7	524	3.7	6	6.0
France	538	2.9	542	3.1	536	3.8	6	4.9
Germany[b]	509	4.5	512	5.1	509	5.0	3	7.1
Netherlands[a]	541	6.7	545	7.8	536	6.4	8	10.1
Switzerland	545	2.8	548	3.5	543	3.1	5	4.7
Southern Europe								
Greece[c]	484	3.1	490	3.7	478	3.1	12	4.8
Portugal	454	2.5	460	2.8	449	2.7	11	3.9
Spain	487	2.0	492	2.5	483	2.6	10	3.6
Eastern Europe								
Hungary	537	3.2	537	3.6	537	3.6	0	5.1
Russia	535	5.3	535	6.3	536	5.0	1	8.0
Asia								
Japan	605	1.9	609	2.6	600	2.1	9	3.3

SOURCE: International Association for the Evaluation of Educational Achievement (1996).
NOTE: Because results are rounded to the nearest whole number, some totals may appear inconsistent.
a. Countries not satisfying guidelines for sample participation rates.
b. Countries not meeting age/grade specifications (high percentage of older students).
c. Countries with unapproved sampling procedures at classroom level.

end of upper secondary education is defined differently across countries, and students vary by average age, enrollment rates in any educational program, and type and length of programs or tracks in which they are enrolled (academic, technical, or apprenticeship). The appendix describes the structure of the upper secondary systems in the six countries of interest that participated in this assessment.

Since the end of upper secondary education varies across countries, it is important to be conscious of differences in the coverage of students who are being assessed, so that comparisons between selected highly academic students in one country and the general population in another can be avoided. An index was created to represent the percentage of the school-leaving population of a country covered by the TIMSS sample: the TIMSS Coverage Index (TCI). Countries with high TCIs have high proportions of the age cohort still in school, and they are represented in the TIMSS sample. Low TCIs indicate that smaller proportions of the cohort were still in school and/or students in certain programs may have been excluded from their sample. Among the six countries of interest, the TCI was 84 percent in France, 78 percent in the Netherlands, 75 percent in Germany, 71 percent in Sweden, 63 percent in the United States, and 52 percent in Italy. (The United Kingdom did not participate at this school level.) Countries with higher TCIs tended to have higher performance on the assessment (IEA 1998).

Results for the mathematics literacy test are presented here. This test measures general mathematics knowledge of all final-year students who are at the point of leaving school and entering the workforce or postsecondary education. It can indicate how well the overall population of school leavers is prepared to apply general mathematics knowledge to their future tasks in the workplace or in further education. The mathematics curriculum varies across countries, and the sample includes students who have specialized in mathematics, as well as those who may have not had mathematics courses in several years. TIMSS also assessed general science literacy, as well as advanced mathematics and

physics at this level, but these were considered outside the scope of this article.

Table 3 presents mean and percentile scores for selected countries representing each region, and Figure 3 displays the means and standard deviations for the countries of interest. The average score of all countries that participated was 500. The mean scores range from 461 in the United States to 560 in the Netherlands, which is a wider range in scores than among eighth graders. But standard deviations are again large, ranging from 79 in France to 99 in Sweden, indicating again that within-country differences are larger than between-country differences in mean scores. The interquartile range between the seventy-fifth and the twenty-fifth percentiles of performance ranged among the countries of interest from 110 in France to 126 in the United States. Once again, the lowest twenty-fifth percentile in France scores similarly to the mean score for the United States (see Figure 4).

The Netherlands is again the highest scorer among the countries of interest in mathematics at the end of secondary school with a score of 560, although Sweden's score was not significantly lower at 552. France was next highest at 523, and then Germany and Italy, at 495 and 476, respectively; these scores were not significantly different from each other. The United States scored 461, which was significantly lower than all of the other countries of interest except Italy. The Netherlands, Sweden, and France all scored significantly higher than the international mean.

FIGURE 3
THIRD INTERNATIONAL MATHEMATICS AND SCIENCE STUDY GENERAL
MATHEMATICS LITERACY SCORES, END OF SECONDARY SCHOOL, 1995

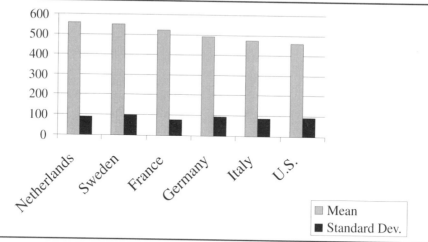

FIGURE 4
PERCENTILE DISTRIBUTION OF END OF SECONDARY SCHOOL
GENERAL MATH LITERACY SCORES, 1995

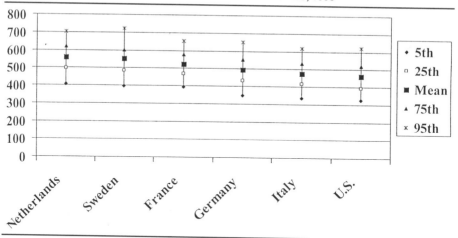

Gender differences are larger at the end of secondary education than at eighth grade. For all of the countries of interest except the United States, young men score significantly higher than young women do in mathematics literacy (see Table 4). Gender differences are largest in the Netherlands at 53 points, a bit less in Sweden and France at 42 and 38 points, respectively, and more moderate in Germany and Italy at 29 and 26 points, respectively.

Overall, countries that ranked high in eighth grade mathematics achievement did not necessarily do

TABLE 3

DISTRIBUTION OF MATHEMATICS LITERACY SCORES, FINAL YEAR OF SECONDARY SCHOOL, 1995

Country	M	SE	Fifth Percentile		Twenty-Fifth Percentile		Seventy-Fifth Percentile		Ninety-Fifth Percentile		SD	SE
			Score	SE	Score	SE	Score	SE	Score	SE		
Anglo												
Australia[a]	522	9.3	357	17.5	459	9.4	585	9.5	684	10.4	97	4.9
Canada[a]	519	2.8	375	5.8	461	7.9	579	3.8	674	5.3	90	1.7
United States[a]	461	3.2	325	4.4	395	3.8	521	6.7	621	7.4	91	1.9
Northern Europe												
Denmark[b]	547	3.3	406	8.2	487	5.6	609	4.7	689	9.2	87	2.8
Norway	528	4.1	384	7.7	461	6.1	592	4.5	691	6.8	94	1.9
Sweden	552	4.3	396	6.4	483	5.1	601	5.5	722	6.8	99	2.3
Western Europe												
France[a]	523	5.1	392	8.6	468	6.3	578	6.9	655	9.9	79	2.8
Germany[c]	495	5.9	347	10.5	432	11.3	554	8.9	652	8.0	94	3.2
Netherlands[b]	560	4.7	407	5.7	498	7.1	622	5.2	704	16.0	90	3.5
Switzerland	540	5.8	395	7.4	478	7.9	601	5.5	684	5.3	88	2.5
Southern Europe												
Italy[a]	476	5.5	336	15.3	417	7.5	534	4.6	619	11.7	87	3.9
Eastern Europe												
Hungary	483	3.2	343	3.8	417	3.1	545	3.5	644	6.6	92	2.2
Russia	471	6.2	342	6.4	410	4.8	528	7.8	622	16.6	85	3.2

SOURCE: International Association for the Evaluation of Educational Achievement (1998).

a. Countries not satisfying guidelines for sample participation rates.

b. Countries with unapproved sampling procedures and low participation rates.

c. Countries with unapproved student sampling.

TABLE 4
GENDER DIFFERENCES IN MATHEMATICS LITERACY, FINAL YEAR OF SECONDARY SCHOOL, 1995

Country	M	SE	Boys M	Boys SE	Girls M	Girls SE	Difference	SE
Anglo								
Australia[a]	522	9.3	540	10.3	510	9.3	30	13.9
Canada[a]	519	2.8	537	3.8	504	3.5	34	5.2
United States[a]	461	3.2	466	4.1	456	3.6	11	5.5
Northern Europe								
Denmark[b]	547	3.3	575	4.0	523	4.0	52	5.7
Norway	528	4.1	555	5.3	501	4.8	54	7.1
Sweden	552	4.3	572	5.9	531	3.9	42	7.0
Western Europe								
France[a]	523	5.1	544	4.6	506	5.3	38	7.7
Germany[c]	495	5.9	509	8.7	480	8.8	29	12.4
Netherlands[b]	560	4.7	585	5.6	533	5.9	53	8.2
Switzerland	540	5.8	555	6.4	522	7.4	33	9.8
Southern Europe								
Italy[a]	476	5.5	490	7.4	464	6.0	26	9.5
Eastern Europe								
Hungary	483	3.2	485	4.9	481	4.8	5	6.9
Russia	471	6.2	488	6.5	460	6.6	27	9.2

SOURCE: International Association for the Evaluation of Educational Achievement (1998).
a. Countries not satisfying guidelines for sample participation rates.
b. Countries with unapproved sampling procedures and low participation rates.
c. Countries with unapproved student sampling.

so at the end of secondary school. Yet among the countries of interest, both the Netherlands and France scored above the international average at both levels. Higher scores were generally found among students who were still taking math classes in their final year of secondary school and among students who were enrolled in academic versus vocational programs. As in eighth grade, high levels of parent education were strongly related to better student performance across the countries tested (IEA 1998). However, these relationships do not necessarily translate into explanations for differences in country performance. For example, although end-of-secondary students in both France and the Netherlands were high performers, 85 percent of students in France were still taking mathematics in their final year of school, but less than a third were in the Netherlands.

EDUCATIONAL ATTAINMENT

Completion of secondary education is a minimum qualification for a job or further education in most OECD countries. Increasingly, a postsecondary degree is necessary for a job with a decent wage and increased access to employment

(OECD 1998). Although there are major differences in the structure of secondary and tertiary education across countries (see the appendix), tremendous strides have been made in compiling and presenting comparable data on educational attainment through the development of the International Standard Classification of Education and the OECD Indicators of Education Systems project.

Upper secondary

There has been a marked increase in the proportion of the population who has completed upper secondary education over the past generation. While an average of 42 percent of fifty-five- to sixty-four-year-olds in OECD countries had completed an upper secondary degree as of 1996, 72 percent of those aged twenty-five to thirty-four had done so (OECD 1998). Upper secondary programs have become more diverse, including general, vocational, and technical programs, with more flexible entrance pathways. Students who are older than the typical age of graduation are enrolling in greater numbers. In many European countries, the majority of students are enrolled in vocational or apprenticeship programs, and it is possible to complete more than one upper secondary program. To make valid international comparisons, then, the data presented here are restricted to graduates of the first upper secondary education programs in which students enrolled. The number of first-time upper secondary graduates is divided by the population at the typical age of graduation, as defined by each country.

Table 5 presents upper secondary graduation ratios per population at the typical age of graduation for selected countries by region, and Figure 5 for the six countries of interest for which data were available. In all of the selected countries, and all OECD countries for that matter, graduation ratios are at least 72 percent (United States), ranging up to 100 percent in Belgium and Norway. Among the countries of interest, the range is much smaller. Germany and France have the highest rates (86 and 85 percent, respectively), followed by the Netherlands and Sweden at 81 percent, then by Italy (79 percent) and the United States (72 percent). For all of the countries of interest except the United States, the majority of graduates have completed vocational or apprenticeship programs rather than general programs (OECD 1998).

Gender gaps in upper secondary graduation ratios, where they exist, tend to favor women (reversing historical trends in some countries) and tend to be larger in countries with lower graduation ratios overall. While there is no gender gap in Germany and France, a higher proportion of women than men graduate from upper secondary programs in Sweden, Italy, and the United States. These gaps are due to the higher rates of women graduating from general rather than vocational programs in those countries, as men continue to dominate in vocational programs.

TABLE 5

**RATIO OF UPPER SECONDARY GRADUATES TO POPULATION
AT TYPICAL AGE OF GRADUATION (TIMES 100),
BY TYPE OF PROGRAM (FIRST EDUCATION PROGRAMS), 1996**

Country	Total			General			Vocational and Apprenticeship		
	Men and Women	Men	Women	Men and Women	Men	Women	Men and Women	Men	Women
Anglo									
Canada	73	70	77	x	x	x	x	x	x
Ireland	79	75	83	77	72	82	2	2	2
United States	72	69	76	x	x	x	x	x	x
Northern Europe									
Denmark	81	76	87	46	38	55	35	38	32
Finland	98	93	104	48	40	57	50	53	47
Norway	117	133	101	49	43	56	68	90	45
Sweden	81	80	82	27	21	34	54	59	48
Western Europe									
Belgium (Flemish)	117	104	130	34	30	39	82	74	90
France	85	85	86	34	29	40	51	56	46
Germany	86	86	86	25	22	29	61	64	58
Netherlands	81	NA	NA	33	NA	NA	48	NA	NA
Switzerland	81	86	76	20	18	23	61	68	53
Southern Europe									
Greece	80	75	86	54	46	63	26	29	23
Italy	79	76	82	19	16	22	59	59	59
Portugal	91	115	66	79	99	58	17	22	12
Spain	73	65	81	44	NA	NA	27	25	29
Eastern Europe									
Hungary	86	NA	NA	25	18	33	59	NA	NA
Poland	94	NA	NA	25	NA	NA	69	NA	NA
Russia	88	82	94	49	47	52	38	35	40
Asia									
Japan	99	96	102	73	69	76	26	27	26

SOURCE: Organization for Economic Cooperation and Development (1998).
NOTE: x = data included in another category/column of the table; NA = data not available.

Tertiary education

The OECD has estimated that adults with a tertiary degree spend half as much time in unemployment and add a decade to their time employed compared to those without an upper secondary degree (OECD 1998). Participation in tertiary education has increased in both university and nonuniversity programs across all OECD countries, and since 1990, enrollment has grown by more than 20 percent in many countries. This growth was largely due to higher enrollment rates rather than a larger cohort of students. On average, one out of three youth today in OECD countries will enter a university program

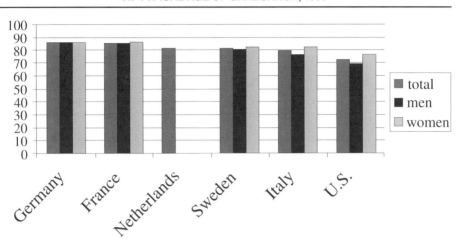

FIGURE 5
**RATIO OF UPPER SECONDARY GRADUATES TO POPULATION
AT TYPICAL AGE OF GRADUATION, 1996**

during the course of their lives, and one out of five will enter a nonuniversity program.

Tertiary programs vary greatly across and sometimes within countries. The types of programs in a country influence the age at entry, the length of time that students stay in tertiary education, and their likelihood of completing the program. International comparisons of graduation rates from tertiary education need to be considered with caution because of major differences in program types and length as well as the typical age of students. However, it is a worthwhile exercise to compare countries according to their ability to provide this level of education to their students, which is so valuable in their transition to the adult workforce.

The OECD identifies five categories of tertiary programs: (1) nonuniversity programs; (2) short first university programs that are usually four years or less, such as a U.S. bachelor's degree program; (3) long first university programs that last longer than four years, such as the German *Diplom* or the Italian *Laurea*; (4) second university programs such as a U.S. master's program; and (5) an advanced research degree such as a Ph.D. Some programs may not precisely fit into these categories, and countries may differ in their assignments of programs to a category.

Table 6 presents rates of graduation from the five types of tertiary programs per population at the typical age of graduation, for selected countries by region for 1996. Most countries have either a short or long first university program, and some have both, so it is possible to compare graduation rates from first university programs whether they are short or long and when both exist in the same country by combining the graduation rates from the two. Figure 6 displays this comparison of graduation ratios from first university programs, which can be seen as a basic university-level credential, among the countries of interest. Countries with short first university degree programs, such as the United States and the United Kingdom, have higher rates of graduation (35 and 34 percent, respectively) than do countries with long first degree programs, such as the Netherlands (20 percent), Germany (16 percent), France (14 percent), and Italy (12 percent). Sweden has both types of programs and, when they are combined, graduates students from first university programs at a rate of 19 percent. It stands to reason that shorter programs would have higher graduation ratios since they require less investment of time and money. Students attending long university programs tend to be older at graduation, and the credential is more similar to a second university degree such as a master's, with its greater specialization and selectivity.

Women are more likely than are men to graduate from first university programs, whether they are long or short (see Table 6 and Figure 6). Germany is an exception to this among the countries of interest, where 18 percent of men versus 14 percent of women have completed the German *Diplom*. Graduation ratios from second university programs are similar among men and women in all countries, but men are more likely than are women to obtain a Ph.D. or equivalent.

LITERACY

While comparisons of achievement and educational attainment reveal country differences in the academic knowledge and credentials obtained by youth as they make their transition to adulthood, assessments of literacy more directly measure the actual skills and competencies possessed by youth at the time of entry into adulthood. Literacy is a measure of everyday functioning rather than academic achievement. It is defined (in the International Adult Literacy Survey [IALS]) as the ability to understand and employ printed information in daily activities at home, at work, and in the community and to use it to achieve one's goals and to develop one's knowledge and potential (OECD and Statistics Canada 1995). Cross-national comparisons of literacy among young adults can speak to the yield of education systems in producing educated and literate populations as well as to the preparedness of young adults for work.

Prior to the 1990s, literacy was often defined as a single skill—the basic ability to read—that was either possessed or not possessed. It was usually measured by proxy measures, such as the percentage of the population who had completed four to six of years of school (during which it was assumed that basic reading skills would be mastered), or by attaining a certain grade-level score on school-based reading tests. By these measures, all highly developed countries had populations with literacy rates that approached 100 percent. During the 1990s, pioneering studies

TABLE 6

RATIO OF TERTIARY GRADUATES TO THE POPULATION AT THE TYPICAL AGE OF GRADUATION (TIMES 100), BY THE TYPE OF PROGRAM AND GENDER, 1996

	Nonuniversity Tertiary Program			Short First University Degree Program (e.g., U.S. bachelor's)			Long First University Degree Program (e.g., German Diplom)			Second University Degree Program (e.g., U.S. master's)			Ph.D. or equivalent		
	Men and Women	Men	Women	Men and Women	Men	Women	Men and Women	Men	Women	Men and Women	Men	Women	Men and Women	Men	Women
Anglo															
Australia	NA	NA	NA	36	29	43	x	x	x	12.2	11.2	13.1	0.8	1.0	0.6
Canada	57	58	56	32	26	37	x	x	x	5.1	5.0	5.2	0.8	1.1	0.5
Ireland	16	17	15	14	12	16	11	12	10	4.5	4.6	4.4	0.6	0.8	0.5
United Kingdom	12	10	13	34	33	36	x	x	x	12.3	12.0	12.7	1.1	1.4	0.7
United States	22	18	27	35	31	39	x	x	x	12.5	11.7	13.4	1.2	1.4	0.9
Northern Europe															
Denmark	8	10	6	20	15	26	8	8	7	4.4	4.4	4.3	0.6	0.9	0.4
Finland	19	13	26	11	11	10	13	12	15	x	x	x	1.9	2.0	1.8
Norway	50	42	58	22	15	29	6	5	6	9.3	10.1	8.4	0.9	1.1	0.6
Sweden	4	4	4	11	7	16	8	9	7	3.0	2.5	3.6	1.9	2.6	1.2
Western Europe															
Belgium (Flemish)	28	24	30	—	—	—	16	17	15	4.9	4.5	5.3	0.7	0.9	0.4
France (1994)	25	22	23	x	x	x	14	13	15	—	—	—	5.3	5.6	5.1
Germany	11	9	13	—	—	—	16	18	14	—	—	—	1.6	2.2	1.0
Netherlands	—	—	—	x	x	x	20	18	21	10.0	10.4	9.5	1.9	2.3	1.5
Switzerland	26	36	17	—	—	—	9	12	7	—	—	—	2.9	3.9	1.9
Southern Europe															
Greece	5	5	6	x	x	x	13	11	15	0.3	0.3	0.3	0.4	0.5	0.2
Italy	3	2	4	1	1	1	12	11	13	1.2	1.3	1.1	0.1	0.2	0.1
Portugal	6	4	9	2	1	2	14	10	18	1.5	1.4	1.6	n	n	n
Spain	2	3	2	11	9	14	15	13	17	x	x	x	0.9	1.1	0.8
Eastern Europe															
Hungary	—	—	—	x	x	x	22	18	26	2.5	2.8	2.2	0.1	0.2	0.1
Poland	10	NA	NA	NA	NA	NA	NA	NA	NA	NA	NA	NA	NA	NA	NA
Asia															
Japan	30	18	43	23	31	15	x	x	x	1.9	3.1	0.7	0.4	0.7	0.1

SOURCE: Organization for Economic Cooperation and Development (1998).

NOTE: NA = data not available; — = not applicable because category does not apply; x = data included in another category/column of the table.

85

FIGURE 6
**RATIO OF SHORT AND LONG FIRST UNIVERSITY PROGRAM GRADUATES
TO POPULATION AT THE TYPICAL AGE OF GRADUATION, 1996**

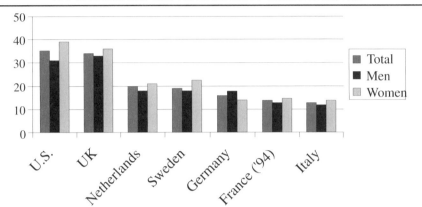

in the United States and Canada developed scales for assessing literacy using tasks with varying levels of difficulty to differentiate skill levels within populations. The IALS, first conducted in 1994, adopted this approach and defined three domains of literacy:

- Prose literacy—the knowledge and skills needed to understand and use information from texts including editorials, news stories, poems, and fiction;
- Document literacy—the knowledge and skills required to locate and use information contained in various formats, including job applications, payroll forms, transportation schedules, maps, tables and graphics; and
- Quantitative literacy—the knowledge and skills required to apply arithmetic operations, either alone or sequentially, to numbers embedded in printed materials, such as balancing a check book, figuring out a tip, completing an order form, or determining the amount of interest on a loan from an advertisement.

This article will present data on document literacy, which can be considered the most basic domain needed to function in society. Levels of performance are similar across the three domains within each of the participating countries, so document literacy can be seen as exemplary of literacy skills overall (OECD and Statistics Canada 1995). Four types of tasks were included in the document literacy test: locating, cycling, integrating, and generating information. The scale of items is divided into five levels of difficulty that correspond to the following ranges on a 500-point scale:

- Level 1: 0 to 225
- Level 2: 226 to 275
- Level 3: 276 to 325
- Level 4: 326 to 375
- Level 5: 376 to 500

Level 3 is the level considered the necessary minimum to cope with the demands of everyday life and work in modern society. It denotes the ability to match and integrate several sources of information and to use several parts of a document to provide multiple answers (OECD and Statistics Canada 1995). It is used here as a cut point with which to compare countries.

The first point to be made is that while literacy skill levels are positively related to educational attainment in all countries (see Table 7), the same level of educational attainment does not produce the same level of literacy across countries. Young adults who have recently graduated from an upper secondary program across countries, for example, are not equally likely to demonstrate similar levels of literacy. Table 8 presents the proportion of sixteen- to twenty-nine-year-olds with upper secondary and tertiary degrees who perform at levels 1 and 2 on the document scale or below the level 3 minimum for selected participating countries: Canada, the United States, Sweden, Germany, the Netherlands, Switzerland (French), Switzerland (German), and Poland. Figure 7 displays the data for the upper secondary graduates only for the countries of interest that participated in the study: the United States, Germany, Sweden, and the Netherlands.

In the United States, 48 percent of young adults with a high school degree perform below level 3 on the document scale. Canada and Switzerland have more than 30 percent of young adults at these levels. The percentage of upper secondary graduates with low levels of literacy is 22 percent in Germany, 19 percent in Sweden, and 13 percent in the Netherlands. These latter three countries have been able to foster high degrees of literacy even among less educated adults who have received no formal qualification beyond lower secondary (OECD 1996b).

Sweden, the Netherlands, and Germany have higher levels of literacy overall, not just among those who have completed upper secondary and tertiary programs. Table 9 presents the proportion of two selected age cohorts (sixteen to twenty-five and forty-six to fifty-five) who are at document literacy level 3 or higher, and Figure 8 presents the data for the countries of interest. In Sweden and the Netherlands, more than three-quarters of young adults ages sixteen to twenty-five are at level 3 or above, and in Germany, two-thirds are at that level or above. In the United Kingdom and the United States, 56 and 45 percent, respectively, perform at level 3 or above.

The level of literacy attained by the young adult (ages sixteen to twenty-five) cohort is higher than that attained by the older cohort (ages forty-six to fifty-five) in all countries except the United States, largely reflecting higher levels of educational attainment among the younger cohort in all countries. The most dramatic increase was in the Netherlands, where one-half of the older cohort perform at level 3 or higher but three-quarters of the younger cohort perform at those levels. Sweden has the highest level of literacy among both cohorts, indicating long-standing factors that encourage high levels of literacy.

The literacy skills of young adults, then, reflect factors that go beyond levels of educational attainment.

TABLE 7

**PROPORTION OF POPULATION AT EACH LEVEL OF EDUCATIONAL ATTAINMENT
WHO ARE AT EACH LITERACY LEVEL, DOCUMENT SCALE, 1994-1995**

Country	Educational Level	Level 1	Level 2	Level 3	Level 4/5
Anglo					
Canada	Less than ISCED 02	73.6	15.4	9.7	1.3
	ISCED 02	23.2	40.2	26.3	10.3
	ISCED 03	10.5	28.4	36.9	24.1
	ISCED 05	4.2	17.6	39.1	39.1
	ISCED 06/07	3.3	10.1	38.5	48.1
United States	Less than ISCED 02	74.0	18.8	6.3	1.0
	ISCED 02	45.2	27.9	21.1	5.9
	ISCED 03	21.2	33.7	32.5	12.6
	ISCED 05	11.7	25.0	39.4	24.0
	ISCED 06/07	6.7	13.3	38.9	41.1
Northern Europe					
Sweden	Less than ISCED 02	22.5	38.1	33.2	6.2
	ISCED 02	6.8	16.9	45.5	30.8
	ISCED 03	3.9	19.1	42.1	34.9
	ISCED 05	1.1	11.1	37.8	50.1
	ISCED 06/07	0.7	8.1	29.8	61.4
Western Europe					
Germany	Less than ISCED 02	55.5	30.2	14.3	0.0
	ISCED 02	10.5	38.3	39.2	12.0
	ISCED 03	4.7	26.7	43.5	25.1
	ISCED 05	4.7	20.2	48.3	26.8
	ISCED 06/07	1.1	17.9	34.8	46.2
Netherlands	Less than ISCED 02	36.0	38.7	19.2	6.2
	ISCED 02	11.2	36.9	43.1	8.8
	ISCED 03	2.9	18.2	52.4	26.5
	ISCED 05	NA	NA	NA	NA
	ISCED 06/07	1.3	13.8	50.0	34.9
Switzerland (French)	Less than ISCED 02	41.9	39.7	16.4	2.0
	ISCED 02	31.1	46.9	19.9	2.1
	ISCED 03	9.0	31.1	45.1	14.8
	ISCED 05	2.0	19.5	47.9	30.6
	ISCED 06/07	4.9	7.1	47.9	40.1
Switzerland (German)	Less than ISCED 02	72.6	16.7	10.6	0.0
	ISCED 02	31.6	40.2	17.9	10.3
	ISCED 03	9.7	30.9	42.9	16.5
	ISCED 05	5.1	24.9	49.1	20.9
	ISCED 06/07	6.8	15.7	39.1	38.4
Eastern Europe					
Poland	Less than ISCED 02	74.6	18.8	5.2	1.4
	ISCED 02	46.9	33.9	15.2	4.0
	ISCED 03	27.8	38.3	27.2	6.8
	ISCED 05	16.4	35.5	36.1	12.1
	ISCED 06/07	15.6	29.6	32.8	22.0

SOURCE: International Adult Literacy Survey (1994-1995), Organization for Economic Cooperation and Development and Statistics Canada (1995).

NOTE: ISCED = International Standard Classification of Education; ISCED 02 = some secondary
education, but not completed; ISCED 03 = secondary education completed; ISCED 05 = tertiary,
nonuniversity education; ISCED 06/07 = tertiary, university education.

TABLE 8
**LITERACY LEVEL BY EDUCATIONAL ATTAINMENT FOR
16- TO 29-YEAR-OLDS, DOCUMENT SCALE, 1994**

Country	ISCED Levels	Literacy Level 1		Literacy Level 2	
		%	SE	%	SE
Anglo					
Canada	03	9.3	2.3	23.6	2.4
	05/06/07	1.7	1.7	10.8	2.6
United States	03	14.4	NA	33.7	NA
	05/06/07	3.7	NA	16.7	NA
Northern Europe					
Sweden	03	2.5	0.6	16.4	1.5
	05/06/07	0.0	0.0	5.8	2.3
Western Europe					
Germany	03	4.5	2.3	17.4	4.6
	05/06/07	0.0	0.0	11.9	6.8[a]
Netherlands	03	1.0	1.0	12.0	1.5
	05/06/07	0.8	0.9	8.8	2.7
Switzerland (French)	03	4.7	1.5	25.8	3.3
	05/06/07	1.7	1.3	8.1	2.7
Switzerland (German)	03	6.1	1.8	25.4	4.0
	05/06/07	3.7	2.5[a]	18.4	5.6[a]
Eastern Europe					
Poland	03	15.2	2.9	39.4	3.2
	05/06/07	8.5	2.7	25.0	3.0

SOURCE: Organization for Economic Cooperation and Development and Statistics Canada (1995).

NOTE: ISCED = International Standard Classification of Education; ISCED 03 = completed upper secondary education; ISCED 05/06/07 = completed tertiary university or nonuniversity education; NA = data not available.

a. Sample size is insufficient to permit reliable estimate.

Canada and the United States have higher levels of attainment of tertiary education but relatively lower levels of literacy than do the other countries in the study, such as Sweden, the Netherlands, and Germany, which have high levels of literacy even among those with low levels of educational attainment. The content of curriculum at lower levels of education and/or institutional or cultural factors may be related to these different literacy profiles across countries (OECD and Statistics Canada 1995; OECD 1996a).

UNEMPLOYMENT
AMONG YOUNG ADULTS

The transition from school to work is an area of concern for many countries. Despite a perception that the unemployment rate among youth and young adults is problematic, the amount of time spent in unemployment among youth actually declined between 1985 and 1996 (OECD 1998). Part of the reason for this is an increase in the number of years that youth remain in education and a corresponding decline in the amount of time in any employment status.

FIGURE 7
**PERCENTAGE OF UPPER SECONDARY SCHOOL COMPLETERS WITH LOW LEVELS
OF LITERACY, AGES SIXTEEN TO TWENTY-NINE, DOCUMENT SCALE, 1994**

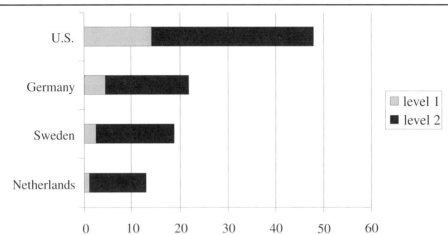

Between 1985 and 1996, there was an average increase of two to three years among OECD countries in the time spent in education of fifteen- to twenty-nine-years olds (OECD 1998). A corresponding trend is an increase in the length of the transition from school to work in some countries (OECD 1996b). In addition, a growing number of students are combining school and work, so the distinction between those worlds is becoming more blurred.

Cross-national comparisons of unemployment rates among young adults in their twenties is one measure of how well youth succeed in making the transition from school to work. Among OECD countries in general and the countries of interest in particular, high proportions of young adults ages twenty to twenty-four are still in school. In 1996, the proportion of twenty- to twenty-four-year-olds still in school ranged

among the countries of interest from 28 percent in the United Kingdom to about 32 percent in Germany, Italy, and the United States to 40 percent in Sweden to 51 percent in France (OECD 1998). The unemployment rates of young adults in their late twenties, then, more accurately reflects the completion of the transition. Therefore, the rates presented here are for twenty-five- to twenty-nine-year-olds, contrasted with the rates for fifteen- to twenty-four-year-olds.

To present a more comparable picture of youth unemployment, given country differences in the size of the labor force as a function of different rates of participation in education, the rates presented here are for youth not in school. They are taken from one source for the European Union (the European Union Labor Force Survey), which should minimize data comparability problems.

TABLE 9
PROPORTION OF PERSONS AGES 16-25 AND 46-55
WHO ARE AT EACH DOCUMENT LITERACY LEVEL, 1994-1995

Country	Age	Level 1		Level 2		Level 3		Level 4/5	
		%	SE	%	SE	%	SE	%	SE
Anglo									
Australia	16-25	9.7	0.7	28.4	1.5	42.6	1.8	19.2	1.4
	46-55	23.6	1.2	27.5	1.4	34.3	1.9	14.5	1.1
Canada	16-25	10.4	1.3	22.3	3.6	36.4	2.1	31.0	4.7
	46-55	23.0	4.7	31.0	3.4	23.6	6.8	22.4	10.7
Ireland	16-25	17.0	1.6	32.9	2.1	36.9	2.3	13.2	1.8
	46-55	36.1	3.6	29.8	2.2	24.8	1.5	9.2	2.2
United Kingdom	16-25	17.8	1.7	26.6	1.8	34.1	2.3	21.5	2.0
	46-55	24.5	2.3	28.2	1.7	31.1	2.9	16.2	1.5
United States[a]	16-25	24.7	2.2	30.9	2.8	28.4	3.0	16.1	x
	46-55	21.4	2.1	28.2	2.8	33.2	2.1	17.3	x
Northern Europe									
Sweden	16-25	3.1	0.8[b]	16.6	1.9	39.6	1.5	40.7	1.6
	46-55	6.8	1.0	19.7	1.8	43.1	2.5	30.3	2.1
Western Europe									
Belgium (Flanders)	16-25	5.8	5.2	17.8	12.5	51.4	18.2	25.0	2.5
	46-55	20.5	3.1	27.8	2.5	41.5	2.9	10.3	1.6
Germany	16-25	5.2	1.4[b]	29.0	3.5	43.0	4.9	22.8	3.7
	46-55	7.4	1.3[b]	35.0	4.3	43.1	3.4	14.5	2.5
Netherlands	16-25	6.1	1.8[b]	16.8	1.9	51.1	3.0	26.0	2.5
	46-55	12.6	1.7	35.7	2.0	38.0	2.4	13.7	1.8
Switzerland (French)	16-25	8.7	2.0[b]	24.9	2.4	40.4	3.9	26.0	3.8
	46-55	18.0	3.3	29.8	3.8	42.4	3.9	9.7	2.0
Switzerland (German)	16-25	7.1	1.9[b]	25.7	4.2	41.0	3.7	26.3	3.2
	46-55	21.0	3.0	33.8	3.3	35.0	2.4	10.2	1.6[b]
Eastern Europe									
Poland	16-25	32.2	2.1	33.1	1.8	26.2	1.8	8.5	0.9
	46-55	55.6	2.4	27.0	2.5	13.3	2.0	4.1	0.8[b]

SOURCE: International Adult Literacy Survey (1994-1995), Organization for Economic Cooperation and Development and Statistics Canada (1997).
    NOTE: x = data included in another category/column of the table.
    a. Because of a sampling anomaly, National Adult Literacy Survey data have been substituted for
the group aged sixteen to twenty-five.
    b. Unreliable estimate.

The Canadian data come from the Canadian Labor Force Survey, and for the United States, data come from the Current Population Survey (OECD 1998).

Unemployment rates for youth ages fifteen to twenty-four and twenty-five to twenty-nine who were not in school for 1996 are presented in Table 10 and in Figure 9 for the countries of interest. Among fifteen- to twenty-four-year-olds, the rate ranges among the countries of interest from about 10 percent in the Netherlands to 33 percent in Italy. The mean of the selected countries in Table 10 is 20.4. Rates of unemployment for twenty-five- to twenty-nine-

FIGURE 8
**PERCENTAGE OF POPULATION SCORING AT LITERACY LEVEL 3 OR
HIGHER, DOCUMENT SCALE, BY SELECTED AGE GROUP, 1994-1995**

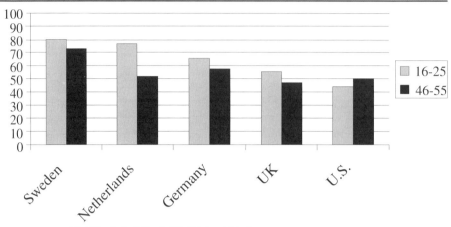

TABLE 10
UNEMPLOYMENT RATES FOR YOUTH NOT IN SCHOOL, BY AGE, 1996

Country	Age Group	
	15-24	25-29
Anglo		
Canada	20.7	10.6
Ireland	20.1	11.7
United Kingdom	19.1	11.2
United States	12.4	5.8
Northern Europe		
Denmark	12.9	7.4
Finland	32.9	13.3
Western Europe		
Austria	7.6	5.4
Belgium	20.7	10.6
France	29.9	15.8
Germany	13.5	8.7
Netherlands	9.9	6.6
Southern Europe		
Greece	29.8	14.7
Italy	33.0	17.7
Spain	38.9	27.6
Country mean	20.4	11.4

SOURCES: European Countries: European Union Labour Force Survey (EUROSTAT); United States: Current Population Survey; Canada: Labour Force Survey; Organization for Economic Cooperation and Development (1998) and the U.S. Bureau of Labor Statistics, unpublished tabulations.

NOTE: United Kingdom data are from 1994; United States data are for sixteen- to twenty-four-year olds not in school and all twenty-five- to twenty-nine-year-olds in labor force and were tabulated by the U.S. Bureau of Labor Statistics.

FIGURE 9
UNEMPLOYMENT OF YOUTH NOT IN SCHOOL, BY AGE GROUP, 1996

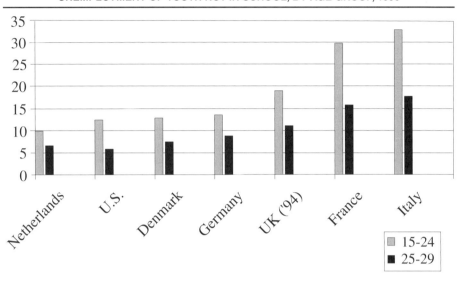

year-olds parallel those for fifteen- to twenty-four-year-olds, but at a much lower level, ranging from about 6 percent in the Netherlands and the United States to 17.7 percent in Italy, with a mean among the selected countries at 11.4. Countries with larger labor force participation rates, such as Germany, the Netherlands, and the United States, generally have lower unemployment rates. Countries with overall high levels of unemployment have high unemployment rates among twenty-five- to twenty-nine-year-olds as well, as rates in this age group tend to reflect the state of the labor market overall (OECD 1998).

Countries with higher proportions of students in apprenticeship programs tend to have lower unemployment rates. This may be because students in these programs are better trained and linked to jobs on leaving school. But a measurement issue may also affect these rates: apprenticeships are generally counted as employment in labor force surveys, which would have the effect of increasing the percentage employed over countries without these programs (OECD 1996a). Germany and Denmark have more than 50 percent of upper secondary students enrolled in apprenticeship programs and have among the lowest unemployment rates among the countries of interest.

Such explanations do not explain the low unemployment in the United States, which may result from a larger labor force relative to other countries, higher levels of work experience while in school, and in the year for which data are presented, a stronger economy. One year of unemployment data is not sufficient for conducting cross-national comparisons, since these rates fluctuate with economic conditions. However, it may be expected that the relative levels of unemployment among the countries and the relationships between the rates of the younger age group to the older age groups in each country would be relatively consistent over time. Another explanation for the lower U.S. rates may be that lower unemployment rates among youth have been found among countries where employment protection legislation is relatively weaker, which is the case in the United States, the Netherlands, and the United Kingdom (OECD 1998a).

The reasons given by survey respondents for their unemployment indicate that finding that first job is difficult, particularly among fifteen- to twenty-four-year-olds in Italy (81 percent) and the Netherlands (58 percent) and to a lesser extent in France (35 percent), Germany (24 percent), and the United States and the United Kingdom (27 percent each). However, other reasons are important also. Dismissal or redundancy is the second most frequent reason given among both those ages fifteen to twenty-four and those ages twenty-five to twenty-nine in Germany, the Netherlands, the United Kingdom, and the United States. In France, about half of both age groups are unemployed because their jobs were temporary (OECD 1998).

PUBLIC EXPENDITURE
ON EDUCATION

The level of public expenditure on education varies greatly across the countries studied and does not appear to be related to student achievement as measured by TIMSS (IEA 1998). It can, however, be viewed as an indicator of a nation's institutional support for education. Education funding varies greatly across countries by level of education—primary, secondary, or tertiary—particularly at the tertiary level. Some of the factors related to this variability at the tertiary level include national differences in the length of study in tertiary education, differences in the propensity of students to attend full-time versus part-time, and differences in the proportion of funds spent on research versus teaching. Because of this lack of comparability at the tertiary level, the focus here will be on expenditures on secondary education. Expenditures for public and private institutions at all levels of education are presented in Tables 11 and 12, however.

Figure 10 displays expenditures per student on public and private secondary institutions in 1995, based on full-time equivalents and converted to U.S. dollars using purchasing power parities, for the countries of interest. Country differences in the cost of educational resources are not accounted for in this conversion. The OECD mean for secondary institutions is $4,606 per student. Among the countries of interest, the United States, Germany, France, Sweden, and Italy spend more than the OECD mean, while the Netherlands and the United Kingdom spend less than the mean. Clearly, the lower level of expenditures is not related to the higher level of performance in the Netherlands. The range in expenditures among the countries of interest

TABLE 11

EXPENDITURE PER STUDENT (U.S. DOLLARS CONVERTED USING PURCHASING POWER PARITIES) ON PUBLIC AND PRIVATE INSTITUTIONS, BY LEVEL OF EDUCATION (BASED ON FULL-TIME EQUIVALENTS), 1995

	Early Childhood	Primary	Secondary	Tertiary All	Nonuniversity	University Level	All Levels of Education Combined
Anglo							
Australia	NA	3,121	4,899	10,590	7,699	11,572	NA
Canada	5,378	x	x	11,471	10,434	12,217	6,717
Ireland	2,108	2,144	3,395	7,249	x	x	3,272
United Kingdom[a]	5,049	3,328	4,246	7,225	x	x	4,222
United States	NA	5,371	6,812	16,262	7,973	19,965	7,905
Northern Europe							
Denmark	4,964	5,713	6,247	8,157	x	x	5,968
Finland	5,901	4,253	4,946	7,315	6,933	7,412	5,323
Norway[b]	NA	NA	NA	9,647	x	x	6,360
Sweden	3,287	5,189	5,643	13,168	x	x	5,993
Western Europe							
Belgium (Flemish)[a]	2,391	3,270	5,770	6,043	x	x	4,694
France	3,242	3,379	6,182	6,569	x	x	5,001
Germany[b]	4,381	3,361	6,254	8,897	6,817	9,001	5,972
Netherlands	3,021	3,191	4,351	9,026	—	9,026	4,397
Switzerland	2,436	5,893	7,601	15,685	8,226	18,365	7,241
Southern Europe							
Greece[a]	x	x	1,950	2,716	1,750	3,169	1,991
Italy[b]	3,316	4,673	5,348	5,013	6,705	4,932	5,157
Portugal[b]	NA	NA	NA	6,073	x	x	NA
Spain	2,516	2,628	3,455	4,944	3,973	4,966	3,374
Eastern Europe							
Hungary[b]	1,365	1,532	1,591	4,792	—	4,792	1,782
Asia							
Japan	2,476	4,065	4,465	8,768	6,409	9,337	4,991
OECD Mean	3,180	3,546	4,606	8,134	6,016	8,781	4,713

SOURCE: Organization for Economic Cooperation and Development (1998).

NOTE: NA = data not available; x = data included in another category/column; — = data not applicable because the category does not apply; OECD = Organization for Economic Cooperation and Development.

a. Public and government-dependent private institutions.

b. Public institutions.

is from $6,812 per student in the United States to $4,246 in the United Kingdom at the secondary level. Extended to all of the selected countries in Table 11, the range extends from $7,601 in Switzerland to $1,591 in Hungary. Staffing costs are the largest component of educational expenditures, so variability across countries can be attributed to differences in teacher salaries, student/teacher ratios, and staffing patterns (OECD 1998).

Another way of looking at expenditures is in relation to per capita GDP, which indicates spending in

TABLE 12

**EXPENDITURE PER STUDENT RELATIVE TO GDP PER CAPITA ON
PUBLIC AND PRIVATE INSTITUTIONS, BY LEVEL OF EDUCATION, 1995**

	Early Childhood	Primary	Secondary	Tertiary All	Tertiary Nonuniversity	Tertiary University Level	All Levels of Education Combined
Anglo							
Australia	NA	16	25	54	39	59	NA
Canada	26	x	52	55	50	58	32
Ireland	12	12	20	42	x	x	19
United Kingdom[a]	28	19	24	40	x	x	24
United States	NA	20	26	61	30	75	30
Northern Europe							
Denmark	23	27	29	38	x	x	28
Finland	33	24	28	41	39	41	30
Norway[b]	NA	NA	NA	42	x	x	28
Sweden	18	28	30	70	x	x	32
Western Europe							
Belgium (Flemish)[a]	11	16	27	29	x	x	23
France	16	17	31	33	x	x	25
Germany[b]	21	16	31[c]	43	33	44	29
Netherlands	15	16	22	45	—	45	22
Switzerland[b]	10	24	30	63	33	74	29
Southern Europe							
Greece[a]	x	17	16	22	14	26	16
Italy[b]	17	24	27	26	34	25	26
Portugal[b]	NA	NA	NA	49	x	x	NA
Spain	18	18	24	35	28	35	24
Eastern Europe							
Hungary[b]	20	22	23	70	—	70	26
Asia							
Japan	11	19	20	40	29	43	23
OECD Mean	18	19	27	46	32	50	26

SOURCE: Organization for Economic Cooperation and Development (1998).

NOTE: NA = data not available; x = data included in another category/column; — = data not applicable because the category does not apply; OECD = Organization for Economic Cooperation and Development.

a. Public and government-dependent private institutions.

b. Public institutions.

c. Author's estimate from OECD (1998) figure.

relationship to a country's relative wealth. Table 12 presents data on expendi-tures relative to GDP per capita on public and private institutions by level of education in 1995. In general, richer countries spend rela-tively more on secondary education than do poorer countries. Among the countries of interest, the general pat-terns observed above persist. Ger-many, France, Italy, and Sweden spend more than the OECD mean, and the United Kingdom and the Netherlands spend less than the

FIGURE 10
**EXPENDITURE PER STUDENT ON PUBLIC
AND PRIVATE SECONDARY INSTITUTIONS, 1995**

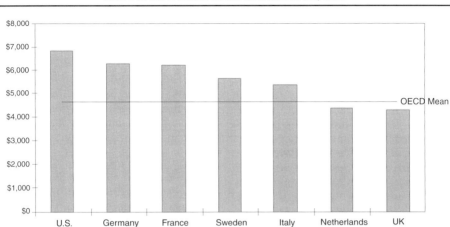

mean. Interestingly, in this measure, the United States does not maintain its high position, spending just less than the mean.

SUMMARY

Some patterns can be observed among the seven countries of interest in their performance across the areas in which data were presented.

- Several countries perform consistently well across the areas of achievement, literacy, and graduation from secondary school. The countries with the highest levels of achievement on TIMSS (the Netherlands and Sweden) also exhibit high levels of literacy in their populations, as well as higher than average graduation rates from secondary school. France is among the top scorers on TIMSS and has among the highest graduation rates from secondary school (France did not participate in the literacy survey).

Germany exhibits high rates of graduation from secondary school and high literacy, and it scored near the middle of the countries of interest in eighth grade and at the end of secondary school on TIMSS.

- High levels of tertiary educational attainment in a population, however, do not necessarily translate into high achievement or high levels of literacy. The United States and the United Kingdom have the highest graduation rates from tertiary education but have relatively lower proportions of the population performing above a minimum level of literacy, among the countries of interest that participated in the literacy survey.

- Youth unemployment rates track performance in the other areas for only a couple of the countries of interest. Youth unemployment is relatively low in the Netherlands and Germany, where performance in mathematics achievement, literacy, and secondary school graduation was high. In the other countries of interest, youth unemployment rates relative to the other countries do not appear to track relative levels of mathematics achievement, literacy, or educational attainment. The overall youth unemployment rate is too crude a measure to capture country differences in the successful employment of youth with credentials in specified fields and may be more reflective of the state of a country's economy and in particular the extent of the service sector, which attracts employment of young adults. Countries with strong service sectors, such as the United States and the Netherlands, tend to have lower unemployment rates among young adults. A strong economy with low unemployment rates can actually be such a strong attraction to students that they choose to enter the job market rather than complete their education. Thus, a country's performance on educational indicators is not strongly related to this indicator of success in the labor market.

- Expenditures on secondary education in the countries of interest appear unrelated to the outcome measures presented. All of the countries spent more than the OECD mean on this level of education except for the Netherlands and the United Kingdom, which spent less than the mean.

While the data presented in this article provide snapshots of country performance at important points in the transition to adulthood, they fall short of illuminating important differences across countries in the patterns of the transition. The levels of country performance are suggestive of supports for, or obstacles to, a successful transition, but they are not explicit in the data. Panel surveys would probably be more useful for identifying these patterns and related supports or obstacles, although they are not typically able to provide the assessments of skills in populations that the TIMSS and the IALS can and are not comparable across countries.

The cross-sectional data presented here do, however, enable us to place each country on a spectrum of performance on each measure and permit us to identify strengths and weaknesses of each country relative to others at important milestones in the transition to adulthood. The data also give a sense of the distribution of performance on each measure among the youth within each country, suggesting the distribution of achievement and opportunity. It is important to note that the seven countries of interest are much more similar to each other on many of these measures than they are to many of the other countries presented in the tables. Although the latter were not the focus of this article, they are more representative of the full range of performance.

APPENDIX
DESCRIPTION OF SCHOOL SYSTEMS IN SEVEN COUNTRIES

This section summarizes information found in *National Contexts for Mathematics and Science Education: An Encyclopedia of the Education Systems Participating in TIMSS*, edited by David F. Robitaille.

England (the entire United Kingdom did not participate in TIMSS)

England has a centralized education system in which the secretary of state for education and employment is responsible for providing education services and national policy and planning. Policies are implemented by local education authorities and schools' governing bodies. The local school now carries out most school administration and management functions.

Education is compulsory between ages five and sixteen. Preprimary education is voluntary. Primary education is attended by children ages five to eleven. Secondary education is for students ages eleven to eighteen. Postcompulsory education is provided in institutions of further education. The first five years of secondary education are compulsory; thereafter, school is voluntary. Further and higher education is provided by colleges or vocational schools.

State schools are attended by 93 percent of the school-age population and are funded by the central government. There are private schools maintained by public funds at all levels of education, often known as independent schools.

France

France has a centralized school system run by the Ministry of Education. There are twenty-eight regions, known as *Académies*. France has a strong preprimary tradition; most preprimary schools are public and were attended by 85 percent of two- to five-year-olds in 1995. Compulsory education begins at age six and lasts until age sixteen. Private schools comprise 86 percent of primary schools and 20 percent of secondary schools.

There are three types of secondary schools:

1. *Colléges*, or lower secondary schools for grades 6 to 9;
2. *Lycées*, or upper secondary schools for grades 10 to 12; and
3. *Lycées professionnels*, or vocational upper secondary schools, which may end at grades 11 to 13.

Although vocational education is available after grade 7, most students in grade 8 and 9 attend general studies. In grade 10, a clear distinction is made between general or technical education and vocational education. Sixty-eight percent of grade 10 students were enrolled in general or technical education in 1994-1995. In grade 11, students choose between three tracks leading to the *baccalauréat général* or four tracks leading to the *baccalauréat technologique*. Both lead to university.

The grade 10 vocational students attend a program leading to the *Brevet d'études professionnelles* at the end of grade 11 or to the *Certificat d'aptitude professionnelle*. Most students do the former and can continue their education in a technological track or in vocational upper secondary for two years to achieve the *baccalauréat professionnel*, which leads to university. Youth ages sixteen to twenty-five in vocational track can be apprentices. Fewer than one-third enter the apprenticeship program from the ninth grade.

Germany

Germany has a regional educational governance system, with each of the sixteen *Laender* having jurisdiction over educational policy in their area. Compulsory schooling extends from age six through age eighteen. Nine or ten of those years must be spent in full-time schooling and the rest in full-time schooling or part-time vocational schools in conjunction with a trade or apprenticeship program. Only about 6 percent of students attend private schools.

Kindergarten is voluntary, and primary schools comprise grades 1 to 4 for students ages six to ten. Secondary level one is for students ages ten to sixteen, and students are differentiated into one of the following systems (about a third of students in each):

1. *Hauptschule*, which provides a basis for vocational training;
2. *Realschule*, which provides the basis for careers between the purely theoretical and purely practical; and
3. *Gymnasium*, which prepares students for higher education.

Secondary level two is for students ages sixteen to nineteen and prepares them for university. Full-time and part-time vocational education is available at this level, in a dual system involving cooperative apprenticeships at two learning sites, the school and the workplace. In 1993, about 31 percent of students were in *gymnasium* and comprehensive schools, grades 11 to 13; 16 percent were in full-time vocational education; and 53 percent were in part-time vocational education.

Italy

Italy has a centralized school system in which the Ministry of Education defines official intended curricula. There are four levels of the education system: preprimary, primary, secondary, and university. Secondary schools are divided into two levels: level 1 includes middle or junior high schools, and level 2 includes senior high schools. Compulsory education begins at age six and continues through age fourteen, at the end of junior secondary school. In 1993-1994, about 8 percent of primary, 4 percent of junior secondary, and 9 percent of senior secondary students attended nonstate schools.

Junior secondary school lasts three years and is attended normally during ages eleven to fourteen. There is a junior secondary school leaving examination, after which students may attend senior secondary school for an additional three, four, or five years.

Senior secondary school is not free; students pay fees to the state and the school. There are four types of schools at this level:

1. Classical schools, which prepare students in different specialty areas for university or teaching careers, including *Liceo Classico* for the humanities, *Liceo Scientifico* for mathematics and science, *Liceo Linguistico* for the languages, *Istituto magistrale* for primary teacher education, and *Scuola magistrale* for preprimary teacher education;
2. Art schools, which train students in the visual arts for university or fine arts academies;
3. Technical schools, which prepare students for professional, technical, or administrative jobs in agriculture, industry, or business, and can lead to university; and
4. Vocational schools, which train students to become technicians and may lead to university.

The Netherlands

There are a wide variety of schools in the Netherlands resulting from the constitutional principle of freedom of education. Public schools constituted only 27 percent of schools in 1993, and private schools constituted 73 percent. The Dutch system combines a decentralized administration and school management with centralized education policy. The school system is divided into primary, secondary (lower and upper), and tertiary. Primary education starts at age four and covers eight grades. Compulsory education is from ages five to sixteen, but

95 percent of children begin school at age four.

Secondary students are tracked into one of the following four tracks based on ability (percentages refer to 1993):

1. Preuniversity education, a six-year program leading to university or colleges of higher professional education (26 percent);
2. Senior general education (HAVO), a five-year program preparing students for higher professional education (22 percent);
3. Junior general secondary education, a four-year program after which students may go on to the final year of HAVO, take a short or long senior secondary vocational education course, join an apprenticeship course, or enter the labor market (28 percent);
4. Junior secondary vocational education, a four-year course of prevocational education specializing in technical, home economics, commercial, trade, and agricultural studies, which can lead to senior secondary vocational education courses, an apprenticeship course, or the labor market (24 percent).

Sweden

Sweden's education system has national goals and curricula, but schools are free to implement these based on local concerns. Compulsory education is from age seven to age sixteen, and since 1995 the concept of levels has disappeared. Preschool includes all daycare activities for children ages one to six and is organized by schools. There are goals and objectives for the end of grades 5 and 9.

In the early 1990s, upper secondary school was divided into sixteen national programs, all lasting three years. Students may follow a specially designed or individual program. Students may attend university from all programs; however, two programs, natural science and social science, are geared for students planning to attend university.

The United States

The United States has a decentralized system of education wherein education is primarily the responsibility of states and local school districts which are responsible for the daily operation of schools. The federal government is involved in setting federal education policy governing the receipt of federal funds, which account for less than 9 percent of all educational expenditures. In fall of 1995, 86 percent of students at all levels were enrolled in public schools.

Public school generally begins with kindergarten at age five. The final year of compulsory schooling is generally considered to be grade 12, which finishes at age eighteen, but states vary in the final age of mandatory attendance, from age sixteen to age eighteen. Grades 1 through 12 are generally divided into three levels, but they have varying grade ranges. Commonly, though, elementary schools contain kindergarten through grade 5 or 6, junior secondary or middle schools are grades 7 to 9 or 6 to 8, and senior secondary schools are grades 9 to 12 or 10 to 12.

Grouping by ability occurs in many schools. Students may choose from a variety of courses in secondary school based on their interests or ability. Students who choose a larger proportion of courses that prepare them for university are said to be in a college preparatory or academic track. Those who choose a higher proportion of vocational classes are said to be in a vocational track. Those who do not concentrate in either vocational or academic courses are in a "general" school program.

References

International Association for the Evaluation of Educational Achievement (IEA). 1996. *Mathematics achievement in the middle school years.* Chestnut Hill, MA: Boston College.

————. 1998. *Mathematics and science achievement in the final year of secondary school.* Chestnut Hill, MA: Boston College.

National Center for Education Statistics. 2000. *Mathematics and science in the 8th grade: Findings from the third international mathematics and science study.* Washington, DC: National Center for Education Statistics.

Organization for Economic Cooperation and Development (OECD). 1996a. *Education at a glance: Analysis.* Paris: OECD.

————. 1996b. *Education at a glance: OECD indicators.* Paris: OECD.

————. 1998. *Education at a glance: OECD indicators, 1998.* Paris: OECD.

Organization for Economic Cooperation and Development and Human Resources Development Canada. 1997. *Literacy skills for the knowledge society.* Paris: OECD.

Organization for Economic Cooperation and Development and Statistics Canada. 1995. *Literacy, economy and society.* Paris: OECD.

Robitaille, David F., ed. 1997. *National contexts for mathematics and science education: An encyclopedia of the education systems participating in TIMSS.* Vancouver, Canada: Pacific Education Press.

Schmidt, W., C. McKnight, G. Valverde, R. Houang, and D. Wiley. 1997. *Many visions, many aims: A cross-national investigation of curricular intentions in school mathematics.* Norwell, MA: Kluwer.

ANNALS, *AAPSS*, **580**, March 2002

Cross-National Differences in Employment and Economic Sufficiency

By TIMOTHY M. SMEEDING and KATHERIN ROSS PHILLIPS

ABSTRACT: Economic independence is an important indicator of the transition to adulthood. This article portrays the level of economic independence among young adults, ages eighteen to thirty-two, in seven industrialized countries. The cross-national variations the authors uncover help one understand how work, family, and comparative income packages affect economic self-sufficiency. In all countries, young women are less able than are young men to become economically independent through market work alone. The ability to support a family is affected more by government transfers than the ability to support oneself. The authors also find that family support through additional income, the provision of housing, and caring labor as well as decisions to have roommates are clearly important to the economic well-being of young adults. In closing, the authors suggest several avenues for future research.

Timothy M. Smeeding is the Maxwell Professor of Public Policy, professor of economics and public administration, and director of Maxwell's Center for Policy Research at Syracuse University. He is also the director of the Luxembourg Income Study, which he cofounded in 1983. During 1994-1995, he was a fellow at the Center for Advanced Study in the Behavioral Sciences at Stanford University. Professor Smeeding's research is focused on economic inequality, poverty, and public policy toward vulnerable groups such as children, the aged, and the disabled.

Katherin Ross Phillips is a research associate in The Urban Institute's Income and Benefits Policy Center. Her research focuses on low-income workers with children.

NOTE: The authors would like to thank Kati Foley, Esther Gray, and Mary Santy for their help in preparing the manuscript and Tom Cook, Anne Gauthier, and especially Frank Furstenberg for comments on an earlier draft. Support for the article was provided by the Ford Foundation and the MacArthur Network on Families and Children. The authors assume responsibility for all errors of commission and omission. Please address all correspondence to Timothy M. Smeeding at tmsmeed@maxwell.syr.edu.

E CONOMIC independence is an important indicator of the transition to adulthood. This article portrays the level of economic independence among young adults, ages eighteen to thirty-two, in seven industrialized countries. The snapshots are taken from household surveys conducted early in the 1990s. As such, the article is designed to paint a comparative picture of when, and if, young adults achieve economic independence. We examine men and women separately to compare outcomes by sex as well. Since our data are cross-sectional, we can observe variations at only a single point in time. We cannot ascertain trends over time among young adults or observe the way that individuals transition from youth to middle age over time. However, the cross-national variations we uncover help us to understand how work, family, and comparative income packages affect economic self-sufficiency.

The breadth of our database, the Luxembourg Income Study (LIS), presents an opportunity to examine young persons in a range of countries in the 1990s. To generalize our findings to other nations, our countries were selected on the basis of previous research on similar topics (e.g., Smeeding 1997; Smeeding and Ross 1999; Jäntti and Danziger 2000) and to coincide with the focus of this issue. Besides the United States (1994 data year), we selected one other Anglo-Saxon nation (the United Kingdom 1995), one Scandinavian country (Sweden 1995), three large central and northern European nations (the Netherlands 1991, France 1989, and Germany 1994),

and one southern European nation (Italy 1995).[1] These seven nations paint sometimes similar, but more often widely divergent, experiences among young adults in attaining economic self-sufficiency.

We begin by presenting a brief overview of some of the different welfare state system theories that set the context for employment in the nations that we examine. The theoretical background will help us explain some of the different patterns of the transition to economic independence that we report in this article. A brief description of our data set follows. We then introduce each of our measures of economic participation and describe the results for each measure in a cross-national context. Next we draw brief country-specific summary portraits in an attempt to draw some regional conclusions about patterns of economic independence among young adults in each nation. The final section of the article assesses what we have learned and what topics and questions deserve future research.

YOUTH AND THE WELFARE
STATE: UNDERSTANDING
ECONOMIC INDEPENDENCE

All youth face the challenge of a transformation from economic dependence to economic independence. Schooling choices, no doubt, have an important effect on the pattern and timing of this transition.[2] But regardless of school choice, every transition involves some mix of three important sources of support: market work, welfare state support and support for human capital building investments such as schooling and job training, and familial support in cash and in-kind (living arrangements).

The focus of traditional comparative welfare state frameworks is on state and market interactions. Esping-Andersen (1990) clustered systems of social provision along three dimensions: the relationship between the state and the market in the provision of social welfare, the effects of the welfare state on social stratification, and the character of social rights. From his analysis of these three dimensions, he developed three welfare state regimes. Social-democratic states (the Nordic countries) emphasize universal access to benefits and full employment, have a strong state role in welfare provision, and integrate economic and social policy. In conservative-corporatist countries (such as Germany, France, Italy, and the Netherlands), social insurance dominates, and financial contributions determine benefit receipt. The state provides social services only in the case of family "failures." Countries in this cluster tend to preserve class and status stratification. Finally, liberal welfare states (the United States, Canada, and Australia) are characterized by a strong emphasis on free markets, with state intervention primarily in the case of market "failures." Benefit eligibility is primarily based on economic need.

There have been many critiques of Esping-Andersen's (1990) work and the research it engendered. While employing gender-neutral terms, many analysts argue that he has implicitly assumed a male standard and that female experiences differ across and within these states (O'Connor 1993; Orloff 1993, 1996; Sainsbury 1994). Focusing on interactions between the welfare state and the market, many analysts like Esping-Andersen have also overlooked a major provider of social welfare—the family (Lewis 1993). These elements also deserve our attention.

Unpaid caring work constrains the choices of women within the welfare state (Hobson 1994). The limitations posed by the demands of home production, along with the implications of these limitations for economic and political participation, are not accounted for in traditional analytic frameworks. Moreover, in her review of comparative welfare state research, Orloff (1996) offered a new dimension on which to compare welfare states: how benefits shape women's capacity to form and maintain autonomous households. This dimension should capture the ability of women to support their children in the absence of a male breadwinner. Fraser (1994) proposed two alternative social policy models: the universal breadwinner model and the caregiver parity model. The universal breadwinner model would remove gender-specific barriers to formal employment. The caregiver parity model would remunerate women for their caregiving responsibilities. These two elements, gender and family, need also be added to the Esping-Andersen state-market nexus.

In summary, the welfare state literature suggests that our assessment of the transition to economic independence for youth focus on these critical elements: employment sufficiency, welfare state assistance, and family support. They also suggest that women in these societies may make these transitions in a different way than do men. Each of these factors is investigated below.

DATA AND MEASURES

The database used to carry out this analysis is the LIS database, which now contains information on child poverty for twenty-six nations in 101 databases covering the period 1967 to 1998 (see the LIS homepage at http://lisweb.ceps.lu). The LIS consists of a set of existing household income micro–data sets that have been harmonized (categories of income and demography are made consistent), producing output files that are more comparable than are the raw files. While the LIS process certainly raises the ratio of signal to noise in cross-national comparisons of income, poverty, and economic well-being, some of the noise remains. Hence, footnotes on noncomparabilities that have been reduced but not eliminated still are worthy of note. Recent papers and publications on poverty, inequality, and social protection using LIS include Gottschalk and Smeeding (1997, 2000), Jäntti and Danziger (2000), Smeeding (1997), and Kenworthy (1998).

There are a number of ways to measure economic independence. For this article, we choose nine somewhat related measures, described below, that illuminate the welfare state theories mentioned above. These indicators fall into three broad categories: (1) economic indepen-

dence through market work; (2) economic independence through market work and government transfers; and (3) relative economic status that combines the effects of market, state, and family. For each measure, we estimate the level of economic independence at a point of time averaged over eleven overlapping, five-year age ranges (eighteen to twenty-two, nineteen to twenty-three, twenty to twenty-four, twenty-one to twenty-five, twenty-two to twenty-six, twenty-three to twenty-seven, twenty-four to twenty-eight, twenty-five to twenty-nine, twenty-six to thirty, twenty-seven to thirty-one, and twenty-eight to thirty-two). This technique permits us to assess differences in patterns across ages at a given point in time. Results are presented separately for men and women. We display our results graphically in Figures 1 through 9.[3] The appendix includes detailed information about how we measure income and poverty for our analyses.

DESCRIPTIVE RESULTS

We begin by examining the role of market work alone then progress to include state and family effects. While this analysis attempts to separate the various forces of employment, welfare state, and family, we cannot ignore the interactions among the three. The final set of analyses combines these effects into measures of household-based inequality. Until that time, we do not explicitly account for the living arrangements and marital status of young adults. In the early analyses, we are interested in the effects of the market and state policy on the potential economic independence of young adults in the absence of their decisions about family formation.[4]

Economic independence through market work

Full-time work. The first measure we use to identify young adults who are achieving economic independence is the percentage who are working full-year, full-time. We define full-year as having a job for fifty weeks during the past year; full-time is equivalent to working thirty-five hours per week. Due to data limitations, we can examine full-year, full-time work among only four of our seven nations (Germany, Italy, the United Kingdom, and the United States).

The top half of Figure 1 shows the percentage of young men who are working full-year, full-time in the four countries. In all of these nations, men in our older age ranges are more attached to the labor force than the younger men. Hence, there is more within-country variation than across-country variation. For each country, the rate of increase is fairly steady, but that rate varies by country. Among young men, Germans have the lowest levels of full-year, full-time work in early adulthood. By the time they are approaching their thirties, however, German men have the highest level of full-year, full-time work. In contrast, young men in the United Kingdom have the highest levels of full-year, full-time work during their late teens and early twenties and lowest levels as they approach their thirties. By the end of

our age range, the level of full-year, full-time work among young men converges to around 67 to 69 percent, with the United Kingdom as an outlier at 61 percent. During the earlier years when many young men are transitioning from education into the workforce, there is a wider range of labor market attachment among our countries. But by the end of the age range, we expect that national macroeconomic factors such as unemployment are the main factor behind the small differences that remain.

In contrast, the bottom half of Figure 1 portrays the patterns of full-year, full-time work among young women. Unlike the case with men, two separate patterns emerge from our four nations. Young women from both Italy and the United States generally increase their levels of full-year, full-time work through young adulthood. Young women from the United Kingdom and Germany, however, increase and then decrease their levels of full-year, full-time work. In both of these countries, the maximum level of nearly 41 percent is reached during the twenty-four to twenty-eight range. German women have the steepest increase and the sharpest decline in labor force attachment. Of course, marriage and child rearing explain some but not all of these differences. For instance, in Italy, the United Kingdom, and the United States, women are less likely to work full-year, full-time than are men within each age range. In contrast, young German women are more likely to work full-year, full-time than their male counterparts between the ages of nineteen and twenty-six. By the time they

FIGURE 1
YOUNG ADULTS WORKING FULL-YEAR, FULL-TIME

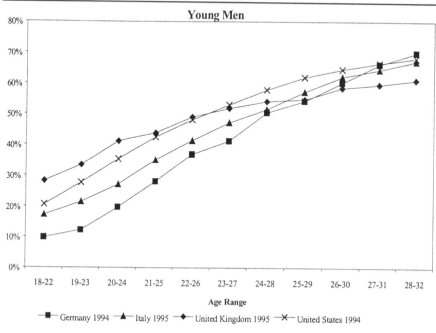

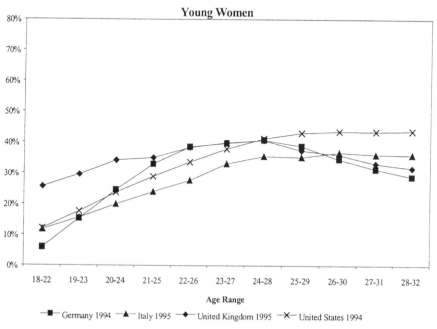

SOURCE: Authors' calculations based on Luxembourg Income Study.

approach their thirties, however, only 29 percent of German women work full-year, full-time compared to 70 percent of German men.

Earnings adequacy. Working full-year, full-time does not necessarily lead to economic independence through the market. Rather, that independence is determined by the wage earned while working and the number of hours worked. One important question to ask is whether young adults, male and female, could afford to live alone based only on their current earnings. This measure is constructed by comparing the earnings of the person in question to the poverty line for a single-person household. We use a relative concept of poverty, the percentage of persons living with incomes below half of median income. In the appendix, we describe our choice of this relative line in more detail (as well as other technical decisions we had to make throughout this article). The effects of taxes and/or transfers are not considered in this measure of economic independence. The comparison does not allow for behavioral change, for example, increased earnings, in response to a demographic transition. For example, a young adult living with her parents may work in a part-time job. If she decides she would like to live on her own, she may increase her hours or work in a higher-wage job. Since our data are cross-sectional, we do not observe any demographic transitions and may understate the percentage of the young adult population who could support themselves if they so chose.[5] Our measure does, however, give us an idea of how many young adults could support themselves, at a point in time, if they had to do so.

Figure 2 shows the percentage of young men (top half of figure) and the percentage of young women (bottom half), by age range, who earn enough to keep themselves out of poverty in our seven countries. Only men and women with earnings (workers) are included in this figure. Both the levels and slopes are of interest here. For all men, earnings increase at a diminishing rate. Comparing the levels in Figures 1 and 2, with the exception of Italy, more young men earn enough to isolate them from poverty (see Figure 2) than actually work full-year, full-time (see Figure 1). This finding implies that wages are high enough in these countries for many men to be able to work either part-time or part-year and still earn enough to support themselves at a non–poverty level.

Unlike the pattern of full-year, full-time work (shown in Figure 1), the countries diverge, rather than converge, over the age range studied. The two outliers among men are Italy and the Netherlands. In Italy, most young men who work full-year, full-time do not earn enough to keep themselves out of poverty. Dutchmen start low but due to their steep profile end up with the highest levels of self-sufficiency through earnings at ages twenty-two to twenty-six and beyond. In both Italy and the United Kingdom, earning sufficiency is much flatter than in other countries, especially in the older age ranges. However, the level of wages in the United Kingdom is higher than that in Italy. Among the very youngest

FIGURE 2
**PERCENTAGE OF YOUNG ADULTS ABLE TO
SUPPORT THEMSELVES WITH THEIR EARNINGS ALONE**

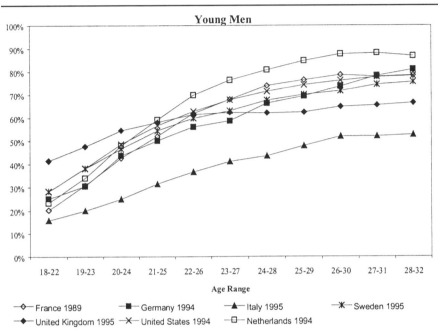

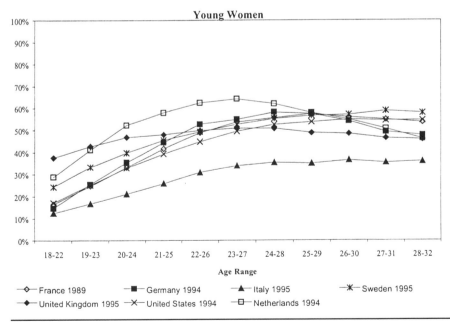

SOURCE: Authors' calculations based on Luxembourg Income Study.

men, the United Kingdom offers the greatest initial promise of wage sufficiency, but by the time men reach their late twenties earnings adequacy falls below all nations but Italy. The fact that young Italian men do so poorly likely reflects the fact that labor market opportunities are fewer and less well paid and that the institutions of the Italian labor market are likely to favor older men.

As indicated by the bottom half of Figure 2, Dutch women show the most variation with a steep increase up to age range twenty-three to twenty-seven (similar to men) then a sharp decrease throughout the rest of the age ranges; Germany follows the same pattern but peaks at a later age range (twenty-four to twenty-eight). Similar to men, the sufficiency pattern for British women is relatively flat, starting highest and ending second lowest, with little variation throughout the age ranges. Like their male counterparts, Italian young women are less likely than are young women from our other countries to earn enough to be economically self-sufficient. The other nations look fairly similar, with young women experiencing only small changes in earnings self-sufficiency.

Overall, the patterns of earnings sufficiency for both men and women up to the mid-twenties are similar. At lower age ranges, women and men who work display similar levels of economic independence. At older age ranges, however, men achieve much higher levels of economic independence, as illustrated in Figure 2. Clearly, men do better than women from market work alone as they move through these age ranges.

Family earnings adequacy. Another important marker of the transition to adulthood is the formation of independent families. Our next indicator of the economic transition to adulthood is the proportion of young adults who are able to support a family of three with their earnings (see also Duncan, Boisjoly, and Smeeding 1996). This measure is similar to the previous measure; it compares the earnings of young adults to the poverty line for a three-person household. We choose three persons because the implicit choice being made by both men and women here is the capacity to start a family with one earner (either male or female) supporting a spouse (partner in the case of cohabitation) and a young child. We assume that the poverty level of half of median income is the lowest level at which a couple would decide to begin a family based on earnings alone. State and family support could, of course, enhance this minimum level of support.[6]

Figure 3 displays the same general patterns found in Figure 2, but at a lower absolute level and with greater across- and within-country variation. For instance, the slopes of the lines for the Netherlands and Italy look essentially the same as in Figure 2, but the levels differ greatly. The United Kingdom is again the flattest, but with a greater slope than in Figure 2, indicating that for some men, wage progression with age is greater than for others. French, Swedish, German, and American

FIGURE 3
**PERCENTAGE OF YOUNG ADULTS ABLE TO
SUPPORT A FAMILY OF THREE WITH THEIR EARNINGS**

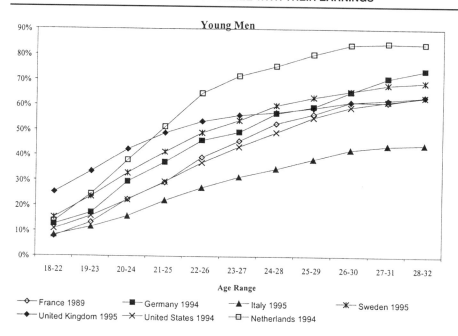

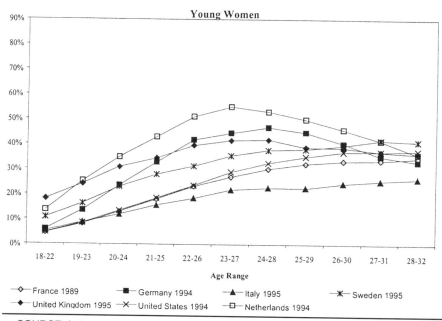

SOURCE: Authors' calculations based on Luxembourg Income Study.

men appear to have similar levels and patterns of market self-sufficiency through young adulthood. Dutch men again show the most rapid pattern of earnings sufficiency growth by this standard.

Among women, levels of family earnings adequacy show less across-country variation, particularly at the youngest ages. Swedish, American, and French women exhibit steady, although small, gains despite women's movement into prime child rearing years. Paralleling their own economic independence, young women from the Netherlands and Germany experience sharp decreases in their ability to support a family through market earnings alone once they reach the middle age ranges. Comparing women to men, the penalties associated with child rearing begin to tell in women. More women have decreasing earnings in prime childbearing years in the United Kingdom, Germany, and the Netherlands. Overall, women are less likely to be able to support a family than men through earnings alone.

Earnings inequality. We also measure the degree of earnings inequality for young adults by comparing—among earners only—the ninetieth percentile of earnings to the tenth percentile of earnings, within our age ranges. This ratio summarizes the breadth of the earnings distribution. Ratios close to 1.0 suggest that the majority of the population have similar earnings, with high earners having similar salaries to low earners; a ratio of 6.0 indicates that a person in the top decile of the earnings distri-

bution has a salary at least six times as large as a person in the bottom decile of the earnings distribution.

Among male workers, we find three sets of patterns. Earnings inequality among Dutch men goes from highest to lowest, demonstrating a strong movement toward earnings parity by the age range of twenty-four to twenty-eight. German and American men experience declining inequality. In the United Kingdom, Italy, and France, earnings inequality stays rather low throughout. By the time young men are age thirty, earnings inequality in five of the six nations is tightly clustered in the 2.0 to 4.5 range for men, except for the United States at 6.1. This suggests that work patterns among men begin with high variance (due to schooling, wage inequality, and other factors) before settling down to more narrow ranges of mostly full-time work with earnings differences related mainly to differences in wage inequality (see Gottschalk and Smeeding 1997, Table 1).

As one might expect, there is both less stability and less predictability of earnings inequality among women. Dutch women have patterns similar to Dutch men until ages twenty-three to twenty-seven, when they flatten and then climb with rising earnings inequality at older ages. German and American women's earnings inequality follows the same general downward pattern as that of men, but with a slight rise in inequality at the end of the period. Earnings inequality for British, French, and Italian women is lower than that for women in other countries, no doubt the result of child rearing and family leave and work patterns at these ages (Gornick, Meyers, and Ross 1998). Although the patterns of inequality experienced by women from these countries are relatively flat throughout the age ranges, the levels of inequality begin to rise in the older age ranges. American women have the widest level of wage inequality at all ages beyond twenty-one to twenty-five. Unlike with men, the earnings inequality for women in other countries does not converge to a similar pattern at older ages. Only French and Italian women have earnings inequality levels similar to their male counterparts, but only in France are the levels of earnings inequality similar.

*Economic independence through
   market work and social transfers*

Markets alone do not provide economic independence for all young adults. Welfare states can act to minimize earnings disparity and increase levels of economic self-sufficiency both within and across age cohorts by transferring income. Our second set of independence measures looks at the combined effect of taxes and public transfers on the ability of young adults to support themselves and to form an economically independent family. Again, we examine whether individuals could support either themselves or a family of three with the combination of their net earnings (less income and payroll taxes) plus a prorated share of the household's total level of public transfers.[7] The role of the family in preventing poverty and low income is not captured in this analysis because

we observe a mix of young adults living alone (or with partners and with children) and those still living in the parental household. Hence, our poverty rate analyses come in the next section of the article where we examine household level incomes. Here we continue to focus on an individual young adult's capacity for self-reliant living.

Since we examine the effects of government programs, in conjunction with earnings, on the ability to support oneself through transfers, the natural comparisons are between Figures 4 and 2 where one can compare ability to support oneself and between Figures 5 and 3 where the bar is raised to the level of supporting a family of three. Comparing Figures 2 and 4, it is clear that the effect of government policy is generally to increase one's ability to live alone at a nonpoverty level in all countries and for both sexes. The net differences of government activity are largest in the youngest and middle age ranges and flatten out at the older ages.

As one might expect, there are substantial cross-national differences in net government support for young adults, and these differences vary throughout the age ranges. Although their ability to support themselves is lower than the ability of young men in other countries, Italian men benefit the most from social transfers. Comparing the top portions of Figures 2 and 4 shows that government tax and transfer policy doubles the percentage of Italian men who are able to support themselves in the early age ranges and continues to increase the percentage

FIGURE 4
**PERCENTAGE OF YOUNG ADULTS ABLE TO SUPPORT
THEMSELVES WITH THEIR NET EARNINGS AND SOCIAL TRANSFERS**

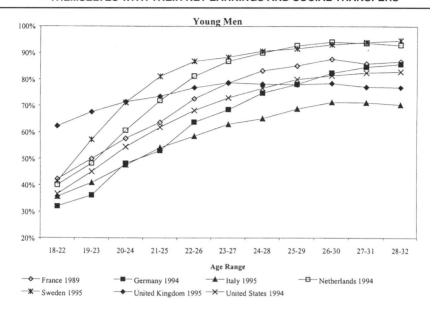

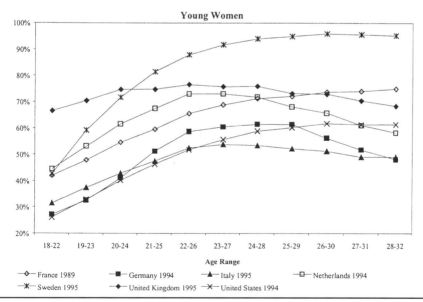

SOURCE: Authors' calculations based on Luxembourg Income Study.

at older ages as well. At the younger age ranges, French taxes and transfers, like Italian government policy, double the percentage of young men who are able to support themselves. At older ages, however, government support is not as effective for French men. The German and U.S. governments provide the least financial support to young men in the younger age ranges; the Netherland and the U.S. governments provide the least to men in the older age ranges. The high relative rankings of men in these countries are driven by the earnings of the men, not the net social support that they receive.

The net effect of taxes and transfers has a larger positive effect on women's economic position than on men's (compare bottom of Figures 4 and 2). Nonetheless, with the exception of Dutch women in the first three age ranges, women are less able than their male counterparts to be able to support themselves through a combination of market work and net government support. This is the same pattern shown in Figure 2. Taxes and transfers increase cross-national variation in young women's ability to support themselves. Swedish support is particularly noteworthy. It enables more than 90 percent of young women in the middle and older age ranges to support themselves economically. Only between 50 and 60 percent of these women could support themselves through their earnings alone.

For the most part, government taxes and transfers do little to change the shape of the curves (compare Figures 2 and 4) or the relative position of young men compared to young women. In other words, governments in the countries we analyze do not transfer income between these age ranges or sexes in a way that influences relative within- country/across-age-range/across-sex economic independence. Instead, social support serves to increase the economic position of young men and women across all the young adult age ranges, while preserving the general age- and sex-related portrait of economic self-sufficiency provided through market work.

Moving to the higher level of economic sufficiency—ability to support a family of three with net earnings and social transfers—we find a much tighter pattern for men but a wider variance for women once government benefits are added to earnings (compare Figures 3 and 5). Government policy, while compressing the across-country range for men, does not always provide net support. In the Netherlands (ages twenty to thirty), Sweden (ages eighteen to twenty-five), and Germany (ages twenty to thirty-two), young men are net taxpayers—government taxes and transfers actually reduce the likelihood that these young men can support a family of three. In contrast, the ability of French and Italian men to support a family of three is substantially increased through the net effect of taxes and transfers—these men are net transfer recipients. The combined effects are to move the higher-level Dutch men and the lower-level Italian men's earnings patterns (see Figure 2) much closer to the others (see Figure 5) especially at the upper end of the age range. Differences between earnings alone and earnings plus net benefits (or minus net taxes) are least in the United States and the United Kingdom.

FIGURE 5
**PERCENTAGE OF YOUNG ADULTS ABLE TO SUPPORT A FAMILY
OF THREE WITH THEIR NET EARNINGS AND SOCIAL TRANSFERS**

Young Men

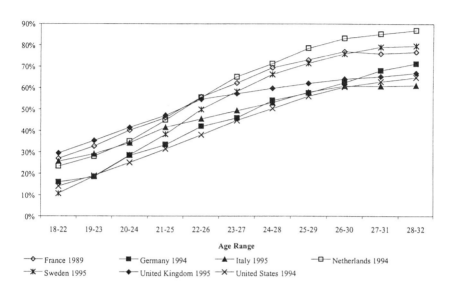

Young Women

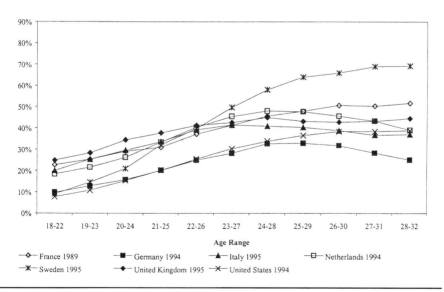

SOURCE: Authors' calculations based on Luxembourg Income Study.

Among women (compare bottom of Figures 3 and 5) the pattern is very different. As expected, women's ability to support a family of three is lower than men's at every age level. With the exception of Sweden, the range across nations is closer at ages eighteen to twenty-nine, but further apart at ages twenty-six to thirty-two. The French, Italian, and Swedish governments exhibit support of women after the twenty-two to twenty-six age range. In each of these countries, the net effect of government taxes and transfers increases the percentage of women in the older age ranges who could support a family of three through earnings alone by more than 16 percentage points. There are some differences in these three countries at the younger age ranges. In Sweden, women in the first three age ranges are net taxpayers, whereas younger women in France and Italy benefit more from government transfers than do women in the older age ranges.

Young women in Germany are net taxpayers in the age ranges bounded by nineteen and thirty-two. In other words, the likelihood that German women in these age ranges can support a family of three is lower when government taxes and transfers are included in their income than when the probability is calculated on their earnings alone. Dutch women are net taxpayers in the age ranges bounded by nineteen and thirty. For the most part, British women receive a small, positive benefit from government taxes and transfers. As with young men, the U.S. welfare state has little impact on a woman's ability to support a family of three (compare Figure 3 to Figure 5).

Across all of our countries, women are less able to support a family than are men. As they reach child rearing age, women's earnings are reduced, and they must rely to a greater extent on both public and private transfers. In some nations, the net effect of government is to exacerbate these differences.

The next section looks at the net effect of the combination of public and private transfers, market income and taxes, and demographic decisions. That is, it examines economic status of young adults accounting for their living arrangements (interfamily transfers) measured at the household level. Thus, it captures the effects of actual differences in living arrangements, not just one's ability to support oneself or to support a family of three.

Relative economic status

Economic independence, as operationalized above, tells us only one aspect of the relative economic well-being of young adults. Since our cutoff for economic independence is a relative poverty line, many of our "independent" young adults may still be economically insecure, living just above the poverty line. Moreover, some of our young adults who do not have the economic capacity for independent living may still appear to be well-off due to interfamily (or interhousehold) transfers and choices about living arrangements. In this last section of results, we examine the actual level of living of younger adults, including family support as well as earnings and government.

We use three measures to describe the economic status of young adults. An individual is deemed to have middle or high income if his or her household has after-tax-and-transfer income equal to 70 percent or more of the median household's after-tax-and-transfer income for his or her country in the year of observation. As explained in the appendix, we adjust household income for family size to compare incomes across households of varying sizes. We measure income inequality among young adults by comparing the level of adjusted household after-tax-and-transfer income at the ninetieth percentile of the income distribution within age range to the level of household after-tax-and-transfer income at the tenth percentile within the same age range. Finally, we examine the poverty rates of young adults. These poverty rates account for all of the disposable income within the household in which the young adult resides.

Middle or high income. The fraction of both men and women who achieve middle or high income (70 percent of median) are judged to be economically secure. Some combination of their own earnings, public programs (net tax-transfer effects), and the income of others with whom they live (parents, spouses, siblings, or friends) is enough to put them 40 percent above the half median income poverty level.[8] Figure 6 suggests a wide range of values across our six nations. Here the nations are found in a different ranking than in earlier charts, suggesting that the impor-

tance of demographic situations and family support in achieving a high-income status varies by country. For instance, young Italian men and women were at the bottom end of most of the earlier economic adequacy tallies, having relatively low chances of achieving minimal independent living status (for a single person or a family of three) whether government benefits were included or not (see Figures 2, 3, 4, and 5). However, Italian men are much better-off, in a relative sense, once living arrangements are taken into account. Most Italian youth live with their parents well into their twenties and up to age thirty in many cases. French youth are also relatively late home leavers and do well, as do Dutch men in particular. As we move from younger to older ages, German men become increasingly well-off; British men have a fairly flat, but also relatively high, proportion of economically secure younger men. It is American young men who are doing least well at every age. Despite the fact that there is an upward slope to the line, only 70 percent of young American men have middle or high income at age thirty, with the remainder closer to 65 percent at younger ages. This fact fits well with what we know about economic inequality in the United States.

With the exception of France, women do worse than men (see Figure 6, bottom panel), particularly as they move into the child rearing years (although the differences are smallest in the United States and the Netherlands). Throughout the age spectrum, a higher proportion of French and Dutch women achieve

FIGURE 6
PERCENTAGE OF YOUNG ADULTS WHO HAVE MIDDLE OR HIGH INCOME

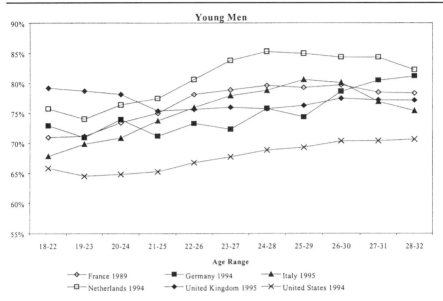

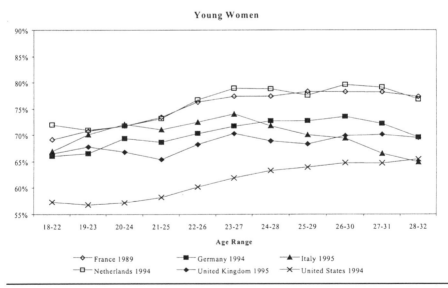

SOURCE: Authors' calculations based on Luxembourg Income Study.
NOTE: Middle- or high-income young adults living in household units with at least 70 percent of adjusted median disposable household income.

middle or higher income status than women in other countries. Women in the United States are the least likely to have middle or higher income until the oldest age range when Italian women take over the bottom rank.

Income inequality. Overall income inequality, as measured by the decile ratio, is generally lower for adjusted household income (see Figure 7) than for earnings inequality alone (see Figure 8). There are two obvious male clusters: the high-inequality countries (the United States, the United Kingdom, Italy) and the low-inequality cluster (Germany, the Netherlands, and France). These groupings are consistent with what we know about national income inequality rankings from other studies (e.g., Gottschalk and Smeeding 1997), and they remain steady across the age ranges.

There is greater overall income inequality among young women (see Figure 7, bottom panel) and less consistent grouping across the countries. Although the United States, the United Kingdom, and Italy become a cluster toward the older age ranges, during the young age ranges, the United States stands alone as a high income-inequality country. The very high U.S. levels, especially at younger ages, reflect relatively high numbers of single-parent families who are much worse-off, on average, than are their similar age counterparts who live in different family circumstances. Young British and Italian women's inequality rises as women age. This explanation may be due to divorce and single parenthood in the United Kingdom. The Italian results are more puzzling because familial living arrangements are different than in the other nations. Younger women in the remaining

three nations experience declining levels of inequality at older ages, especially French and Dutch women.

Poverty. Our final figure captures poverty status among young adults by asking how many men and women live in households with family-size-adjusted incomes below one-half the national adjusted median. This is the most common international measure of poverty (e.g., see Jäntti and Danziger 2000; Smeeding, Rainwater, and Burtless 2002; Smeeding 1997). Among men, young adults from the United States are the poorest. Although poverty rates for American men decrease with age, the rates remain in the 15 to 20 percent range. Poverty rates for British young men remain fairly constant, hovering about 12.5 percent as compared to 17.5 percent in the United States. Italian men tend to be close to British levels up to ages twenty-seven to thirty-one, when they approach U.S. men's levels. These results are as expected, given what we know about overall national poverty rates (e.g., see Jäntti and Danziger 2000). Young Frenchmen have the lowest (or next to lowest) poverty rates at each age level, everywhere below 10 percent. Dutch men show the greatest improvement with age, while German men follow a curious bumped pattern, with poverty rates rising as they leave the household (or schooling) for independent living and then falling with steady employment and relatively higher wages.

Among younger women, a much more varied pattern emerges across nations (see Figure 9, bottom panel), but with somewhat less within-country

FIGURE 7
INCOME INEQUALITY AMONG YOUNG ADULTS

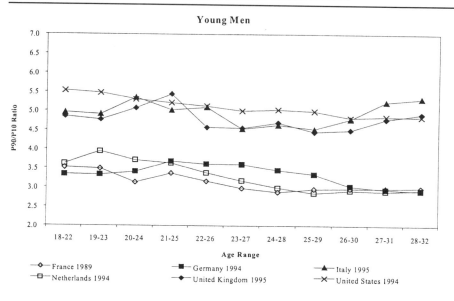

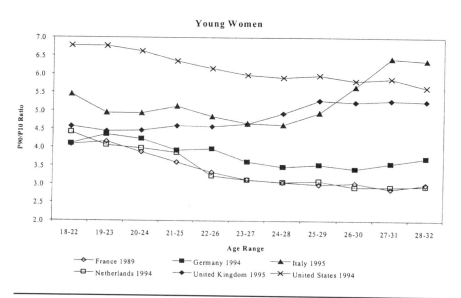

SOURCE: Authors' calculations based on Luxembourg Income Study.
  NOTE: Income inequality if measured by the decile ratio (ninetieth to tenth percentile of adjusted income ratio).

FIGURE 8
EARNINGS INEQUALITY AMONG YOUNG ADULTS

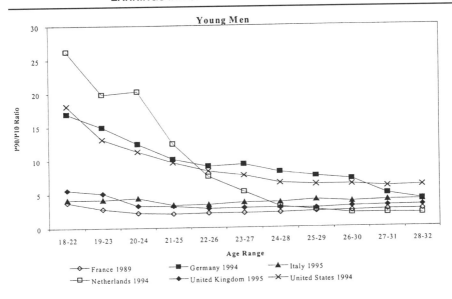

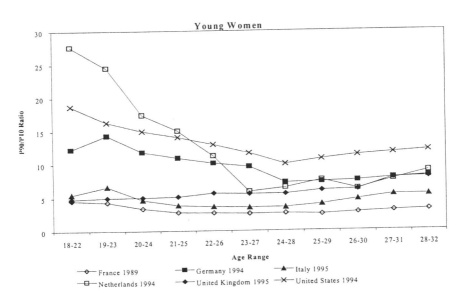

SOURCE: Authors' calculations based on Luxembourg Income Study.

NOTE: Earnings inequality is measured by the decile ratio for the ninetieth to tenth percentile ratio of individual male and individual female earnings.

variation. Young women from the United States are poorest, followed by women from the United Kingdom and Italy. Poverty rates are everywhere above those for men and reflect single parenthood in the United Kingdom and the United States. Dutch and French women do better as they age, with a particularly large drop in poverty from ages twenty to twenty-four to ages twenty-two to twenty-six in the Netherlands. By the time they reach the upper age ranges, French and Dutch women (as well as French and Dutch men) have poverty rates at or below 7 percent. Germany remains pretty much in the middle of the pack, not exhibiting the bumped shape noted for men above.

COUNTRY-SPECIFIC DISCUSSION

Thus far we have assessed information on an across-country basis. The other articles in this issue do a more thorough job illuminating national stories. And here we do find some interesting national pictures among the comparative charts. In general, French, Dutch, and, to the extent measurable, Swedish youth seem to encounter the least inequality, the least poverty, and the most stable economic patterns of the nations shown, both for men and women. We believe that their strong welfare states provide at least adequate minimal levels of support for both sexes as they transition from youth to adulthood. German and British youth have more varying levels of support—finding themselves

within the range of the other nations in almost every age group and within almost all comparative dimensions. Age (from twenty to thirty years) seems to have little to do with changing poverty, inequality, or earnings ability for British youth, with women almost always doing more poorly than men. German youth show a more varied pattern, but still with women doing least well. U.S. youth exhibit the most poverty and the most inequality at younger ages, but without the advantage of having the highest chance to have middle or high income. Clearly, many American youth experience a relatively insecure transition to adulthood as far as these data can tell us. Italian men and women show the greatest differences in our measures of the transition to economic independence in young adulthood. In our measures of economic self-sufficiency that focus on market work or the combination of market work and government transfers, young Italians tend to rank at or near the bottom of our countries. In our measures that implicitly account for living arrangement choices, however, Italians fare much better, in a relative sense. No doubt, differences in patterns of living arrangements and other factors reflecting the wide range of differences between northern and southern Italy are at play here (see Rainwater, Smeeding, and Coder 2001). The other articles in this issue will also help the reader to flesh out these differences on a country-specific basis.

FIGURE 9
PERCENTAGE OF YOUNG ADULTS WHO ARE POOR AFTER TAXES AND TRANSFERS

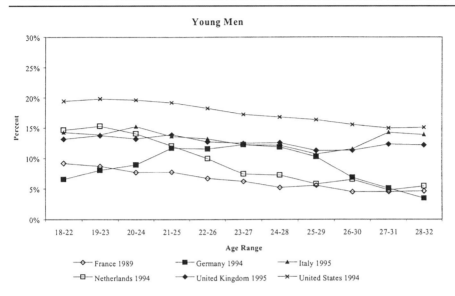

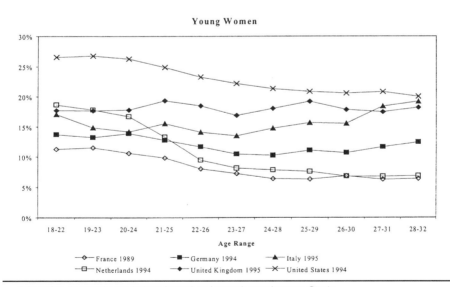

SOURCE: Authors' calculations based on Luxembourg Income Study.
NOTE: Poverty status is measured by the fraction of young adults living in households with incomes less than half of the median.

CONCLUSIONS

The analyses in this article suggest that it is not easy to quantify how and when young adults achieve economic independence. Drawing on the work of welfare state theorists, we examined the transition to economic self-sufficiency through three avenues: (1) market work alone; (2) the combination of market work and net government transfers; and (3) the combination of market work, net government transfers, and family resources. Each of these avenues suggests a different interpretation of cross-national differences in economic self-sufficiency.

Across many of our measures of economic independence through market work alone, there is more within-country variation, by both sex and age, than across-country variation. The pattern of results suggests that young men continue to transition toward economic independence through market work throughout our age ranges (eighteen to thirty-two). Young women begin on the same trajectory toward economic independence as do young men. However, the trajectory either flattens out or begins to descend as women reach prime child rearing age. In all countries, young women are less able than young men to become economically independent through market work alone.

The overall effect of government policy is to increase a young adult's ability to live alone at a nonpoverty level in all countries and for both sexes. Government policy tends to increase cross-national variation among women, particularly in the older age ranges. The ability to support a family is affected more by government transfers than the ability to support oneself. In Germany and the Netherlands, the net effect of government tax and transfer policy, when added to market work alone, reduces the ability of young adults to support a family. In some countries, social support reduces the age and sex differences in economic independence. However, across all countries, the age and sex patterns of the transition to economic independence determined through market work alone dominate.

The relative position of countries changes when we include choices about living arrangements in our outcome measures. Family support through additional income, the provision of housing and caring labor, and decisions to have roommates are clearly important to the economic well-being of young adults. The importance of demographic situations and family support for economic outcomes varies by country. Whether and how living arrangement choices among young adults vary by nation is an important area for future research.

Interestingly, none of our analyses strongly supports the typology of welfare states suggested by Esping-Andersen (1990). The large outcome differences for men and women, consistent across most of our measures, and the different pattern of results for our measures suggest that the feminist critique of traditional welfare state theories is warranted. Including family resources in measures of economic well-being changes the relative rankings of countries because different structures of family support emerge in different ways across the outcomes and nations observed here.

The data that we present in this article illustrate interesting comparative patterns, not only across the various nations, but also between men and women within each nation. The economic heterogeneity between the sexes is no doubt a by-product of national differences in living arrangements, childbearing, and economic differences. School attendance may also be a factor here. The roles of both family (particularly in terms of supported living arrangements) and state (in terms of support for living alone) are difficult to disentangle. Both provide support to young adults, and both vary significantly across nations. While these differences play out in interesting ways, they provide only hints at the economic and social forces that affect young men and young women in these rich nations.

Future research on these topics might begin with our cross-sectional analyses and then move to a dynamic comparison of these transitions using household panel microdata. Currently these data exist for several nations, especially for the United States, Germany, the United Kingdom, and Canada. Following young adults as they transition from basic education to full-time work and economic independence, including differences by gender, higher education, choices, fertility, and place of residence, should rank high on the list of future research priorities for cross-national panel data set users.

APPENDIX
CONCEPTS, MEASURES, AND DATA DETAILS

The snapshot we take is based on a number of choices. Luckily, the database we employ, LIS, permits these choices. In this appendix, we describe our concepts and choices for poverty measurement and measuring economic status. These are important for understanding the results in the main body of the article.

*Concepts and measures:
    Equivalence scales, poverty,
    and income measures*

The measurement of economic poverty in all nations, rich or poor, involves the calculation of economic well-being (or resources) relative to needs. Economic well-being refers to the material resources available to households. The concern with these resources is not with material consumption itself; rather, the capabilities they give household members to participate in these activities produces a particular level of well-being (Rainwater 1990; Coleman and Rainwater 1978). Measurement of these capabilities differs according to the context in which one chooses to measure them, particularly within rich nations as compared to within poor nations and perhaps also particularly among younger persons who have not yet totally separated from their parents.

All advanced or rich societies are highly stratified socially. Some individuals have more resources than do others. The opportunities for social participation are vitally affected by the resources that the family possesses, particularly in nations like the United States, where there is heavy reliance on the market to purchase such social goods as health care, education, and child care services (Rainwater 1974). Money income is the central resource in these societies. But there are still other important kinds of resources such as social capital (Coleman 1988), noncash benefits, education, and access to basic health care, all of which add to human capabilities, but those are not measured by LIS money income and thus are a shortcoming of this article. There are also many forces in rich societies that reduce well-being by limiting capabilities to participate fully in society: for instance, violent, geographically isolated, and socially isolated neighborhoods; poor-quality public education; and earnings and job instability increase economic insecurity in many rich countries. LIS also excludes these factors.

In rich societies, we argue that income—or the ability to consume—is the key measure of economic resources and the ability to avoid poverty. While income—consumption plus change in net worth—brings with it more complicated issues of period of measurement and life cycle considerations, it is a much more appropriate and, we would argue, more easily measured index of well-being for rich nations than is consumption (see Johnson and Smeeding 1998 on this topic). And so in rich nations, one measures poverty based on annual disposable money income. Comparable information exists on money income by source, taxes paid, and certain kinds of transfers that have a cash-like character, such as housing allowances, fuel assistance, and food stamps, for the seven nations which we will investigate here.

While we are able to take into account income stipends for student support and similar cash benefits that help support the incomes of students, we collect information only on regular private transfers received by persons. Hence, a student (or other young adult) who is being supported by a parent or other relative not living with them should report these regular private transfers as income. But our income concepts do not record one-time gifts received by persons as income.

Unfortunately, we cannot take into account the major in-kind benefits that are available in most countries—for example, health care, education (subsidized tuition), housing subsidies other than those in cash, and the like. To the extent that the level and distribution of these resources is different in different countries, our analysis of money income must be treated with some caution. While their inclusion would be attractive to those interested in capabilities and their effects on longer-term poverty (e.g., Bradbury, Micklewright, and Jenkins 1999), we do not have such data on hand. Earlier LIS-based studies indicated that while overall inequality and poverty comparisons were not much affected by these additions, we did find that the relative economic well-being of single persons and couples without children fell while those of the elderly and families with children rose due to these subsidies (Smeeding et al. 1993).

Equivalence scales. Households differ not only in terms of resources but also in terms of their needs. We take differing needs, due to differences in household size (and sometimes other factors such as urban-rural differences) into account by adjusting income for family size using an equivalence scale. The adjustment for household size is designed to account for the different requirements families of different sizes and different circumstances have for participating in society at a given level. Different equivalence scales will yield different distributions of well-being. Several studies in Europe, the United States, and Australia point to an equivalence scale that implies fairly large economies of scale in the conversion of money incomes to social participation among families with children and other larger family types (Buhmann et al. 1988; Bradbury 1989; Rainwater 1990) and also among the aged (Burkhauser,

Smeeding, and Merz 1996). Because choice of equivalence scale may favor small versus large families, depending on which level is selected, we aim to find a middle-ground value that is appropriate for measuring vulnerability for both large families (e.g., those young persons living with two or more relatives) and smaller units (e.g., single younger adults living alone).

Buhmann et al. (1988) have proposed that disposable income be adjusted for family size in the following way:

$$\text{Adjusted income} = \text{Disposable Income/Size}^E \quad (1)$$

The equivalence elasticity, or equivalence factor E, varies between 0 and 1; the larger is E, the smaller are the economies of scale assumed by the equivalence scale. The various studies reviewed in the survey from Buhmann et al. (1988) and later Atkinson, Rainwater, and Smeeding (1995) make use of equivalence scales for analyses of per capita income ranging from E = 0 (or no adjustment for size) to E = 1 (which ignores all economies of scale). Between these extremes, the range of possible values is evenly covered. The reader should keep in mind that all money income estimates in the article are based on adjusted or equivalent income calculated according to the above formula.

The obvious question is which measure of E to use for this study. Following Atkinson, Rainwater, and Smeeding (1995, especially chaps. 2, 3, and 7), we have selected an E value of 0.5, similar to that used by the Organization for Economic Cooperation and Development (OECD) (Förster 1993) and Eurostat (Hagenaars, DeVos, and Zaidi 1994). For the most part, national rankings by overall poverty rates are not sensitive to the measure of E selected (Burkhauser, Smeeding, and Merz 1996; Smeeding 1997).

Having defined equivalent income in this way, we determine the equivalent income of all households and all individuals in each country. We then examine the distribution of equivalent incomes of persons of any age in households in relation to the selected poverty line or level of economic well-being (economic status). That is, we tabulate the percentage of persons of a given age who have given characteristics, where these person's calculations are weighted by the number of persons of each type (all persons including children, adults, and elderly) residing in each household type.

Poverty and economic status measurement. Needs can be measured in two ways: an absolute definition and a relative definition. Relative poverty involves deciding on the income concept for relativity (median or mean) and on the fraction of adjusted income that signifies poverty. Absolute poverty measurement means locating the absolute poverty line and then converting that poverty line into national currency.

We rely here on a relative concept of poverty, the percentage of persons living with incomes below one-half of median income. This income is in line with a well-established theoretical perspective on poverty (Sen 1992; Townsend 1979). Such a measure is now commonly calculated by the European Commission (Hagenaars, DeVos, and Zaidi 1994; Ramprakash 1995), by the OECD (Förster 1993), and by other international groups. Only the British use and one other major international study (Cantillon, Marx, and van den Bosch 1996) used a fraction of mean income as a standard, though Cantillion, Marx, and van den Bosch (1996) used both mean and median income-based poverty rates in their study.

In fact, most studies use the average or median household as the point of reference, as do we. Using the average or mean income means measuring social distance from something other than the average household. Moreover, the decision to use one measure versus the other can lead to quite different results in poverty trends when inequality is changing. In the United States from 1973 to 1994, the mean income grew 15 percent more than the median income, thus assuring that poverty measured relative to the mean grew much more than poverty relative to the median (Burtless 1996).

Absolute poverty is more difficult to measure in rich nations because of our limited tools for converting one currency to another in purchasing power parity terms (Summers and Heston 1991; Smeeding, Rainwater, and Burtless 2002). However, some have used both absolute and relative poverty definitions with LIS and have found roughly similar patterns to those found here (see Kenworthy 1998; Jäntti and Danziger 2000; Smeeding, Rainwater, and Burtless 2002).

Our measure of poverty is the headcount, that is, percentage of households or persons with incomes less than one-half of the median income. We use only the headcount in this article, although measures of poverty gap or more sophisticated measures of poverty, such as the Foster-Greer-Thorbecke (FGH) (1984) and Sen (1976) indexes, could be deployed. Were the purpose of this article poverty measurement, we would stress more measures of both absolute and relative poverty. However, poverty measurement is not the major purpose of this article. And in practice, each of the other measures of poverty suggested above may have severe computational problems. For instance, the poverty gap, FGH, and Sen indexes are all very sensitive to the accuracy of the income measure at the bottom of the income distribution. Differences in survey reporting, survey editing, and bounding of incomes by survey agencies may each drastically affect these measures of poverty, as they in effect artificially present different lower-bound income figures across nations.

Defining resources: Disposable income, earnings inequality, and live alone

Cross-national comparisons of poverty have focused primarily on the distribution of disposable money income after direct taxes (income and employee payroll) and after transfer payments. While this definition of post–tax and transfer disposable income is broad, it falls considerably short of the Haig-Simons comprehensive income definition, typically by excluding much of capital gains, imputed rents, home production, and in-kind income (including employment-related benefits).

Ability to earn income at nonpoverty levels is also an important marker of economic independence. In this article, we examine earnings of young men and young women to determine their capacity for independent living. We do this by comparing their individual earnings (and their earnings plus their share of household government benefits) to the poverty level for one adult and three adults.

We also measure income inequality for individual youth earnings and for overall adjusted incomes employing one summary measure of inequality, the decile ratio: the ratio of the earnings (or adjusted income) at the ninetieth percentile to that at the tenth percentile. Decile ratios are both an intuitive measure of social distance and a measure of inequality that is less dependent on the differential quality of data at both the top and the bottom of the LIS income data sets.

Notes

1. We examine only West German youth here, excluding East Germany, which was the German Democratic Republic from 1948 to 1989. Future waves of Luxembourg Income Study (LIS) data will include this population as well.

2. Unfortunately, the LIS data sets do not contain information about school attendance. Since schooling status no doubt affects economic behavior and living arrangements, this is a shortcoming of the LIS data and hence of this article.

3. One important note below is that the structure of households in Sweden differs from that in other nations studied here. Hence, Sweden is not included in some of our analyses. For additional detail, see the appendix on concepts, measures, and data details.

4. Of course, this is a somewhat arbitrary distinction since decisions about work effort and family formation are strongly tied.

5. On the other hand, an inability to find a job with higher earnings could dictate the living arrangements of the young adults in our countries. The young woman may want to move out of her parents' home, but she is unable to find employment that would allow her to afford such a move.

6. See the appendix for a detailed description of our choice of equivalence scale.

7. LIS data sets include only social transfer information at the household, not the individual, level. Since many social transfers are made to a household, LIS staff members do not attempt to allocate social transfers to individuals within the household because of the difficulty of doing so for transfers other than social retirement benefits for older men and women.

8. The obverse, or one minus the fraction shown in Figure 6, are those who are both poor and economically insecure. Note that Sweden is excluded from these figures because of the difficulty of identifying living arrangements of youth ages eighteen and older. See the appendix for more details.

References

Atkinson, A. B., L. Rainwater, and T. Smeeding. 1995. *Income distribution in OECD countries: The evidence from LIS*. Paris: OECD.

Bradbury, B. 1989. Family size equivalence and survey evaluations of income and well-being. *Journal of Social Policy* 11:383-408.

Bradbury, B., K. Micklewright, and S. P. Jenkins. 1999. *Children in and out of poverty*. Florence, Italy: UNICEF.

Buhmann, B., L. Rainwater, G. Schmaus, and T. Smeeding. 1988. Equivalence scales, well-being, inequality and poverty. *Review of Income and Wealth* 34 (2): 115-42.

Burkhauser, R., T. Smeeding, and J. Merz. 1996. Relative inequality and poverty in Germany and the United States using alternative equivalence scales. *Review of Income and Wealth* 42 (4): 381-400.

Burtless, G. 1996. Trends in the level and distribution of U.S. standards: 1973-1993. *Eastern Economic Journal* 22 (3): 271-90.

Burtless, G., L. Rainwater, and T. M. Smeeding. 2000. United States poverty in a cross-national context. Center for Policy Research, Maxwell School, Syracuse University, NY. Mimeographed.

Cantillion, B., U. Marx, and K. van den Bosch. 1996. Poverty in advanced economies: Trends and issues. Paper presented to the twenty-fourth general conference of the International Association for Research on Income and Wealth, Lillehammer, Norway, August.

Coleman, James S. 1988. Social capital in the creation of human capital. *American Journal of Sociology* 94:S95-S120.

Coleman, J., and L. Rainwater. 1978. *Social standing in America*. New York: Basic Books.

Duncan, Greg J., Johanne Boisjoly, and Timothy M. Smeeding. 1996. Economic mobility of young workers in the 1970s and 1980s. *Demography* 33:497-509.

Esping-Andersen, Gosta. 1990. *The three worlds of welfare capitalism*. Princeton, NJ: Princeton University Press.

Förster, M. 1993. Comparing poverty in 13 OECD countries: Traditional and synthetic approaches. Studies in Social Policy paper no. 10. Paris: OECD.

Foster, J., K. Greer, and E. Thorbecke. 1984. A class of decomposable poverty measures. *Econometrica* 52:761-66.

Fraser, Nancy. 1994. After the family wage: Gender equity and the welfare state. *Political Theory* 22:591-618.

Gornick, Janet C., Marcia K. Meyers, and Katherin E. Ross. 1998. Public policies and the employment of mothers: A cross-national study. *Social Science Quarterly* 79 (1): 35-54.

Gottschalk, P., and T. Smeeding. 1997. Cross-National comparisons of earnings and income inequality. *Journal of Economic Literature* 35:633-86.

———. 2000. Empirical evidence on income inequality in industrialized countries. In *Handbook of income distribution: Handbooks in economics series*, edited by A. B. Atkinson and F. Bourgignon, 263-308. New York: Elsevier–North Holland.

Hagenaars, A., K. DeVos, and A. Zaidi. 1994. Patterns of poverty in Europe. Paper presented to the twenty-third general conference of the International Association for Research on Income and Wealth, St. Andrews, Canada, August.

Hobson, Barbara. 1994. Solo mothers, social policy regimes, and the logics of gender. In *Gendering welfare states*, edited by D. Sainsbury, 170-87. London: Sage.

Jäntti, J., and S. Danziger. 2000. Income poverty in advanced countries. In *Handbook on income distribution*, edited by A. B. Atkinson and F. Bour-

gignon, 309-78. New York: Elsevier–North Holland.

Johnson, D., and T. Smeeding. 1998. Measuring the trend in inequality among individuals and families: Consumption or income? Center for Policy Research, Maxwell School, Syracuse University, NY. Mimeographed.

Kenworthy, L. 1998. Do social welfare policies reduce poverty? A cross-national assessment. Working Paper No. 191, Luxembourg Income Study, Differdange, Luxembourg, and Syracuse University, Syracuse, NY.

Lewis, Jane. 1993. Introduction: Women, work, family and social policies in Europe. In *Women and social policies in Europe: Work, family, and the state*, edited by J. Lewis, 1-24. Aldershot, UK: Edward Elgar.

O'Connor, Julia S. 1993. Gender, class and citizenship in the comparative analysis of welfare state regimes: Theoretical and methodological issues. *British Journal of Sociology* 44:501-18.

Orloff, Ann Shola. 1993. Gender and the social rights of citizenship: The comparative analysis of gender relations and welfare states. *American Sociological Review* 58:303-28.

———. 1996. Gender and the welfare state. Discussion paper no. 1082-96, Institute for Research on Poverty, University of Wisconsin–Madison, March.

Rainwater, L. 1974. *What money buys*. New York: Basic Books.

———. 1990. Poverty and equivalence as social constructions. Working paper no. 91, Luxembourg Income Study and Syracuse University, Syracuse, NY.

Rainwater, Lee, Timothy M. Smeeding, and John Coder. 2001. Child poverty across states, nations and continents. In *Child well-being, child poverty and child policy in modern nations: What do we know?* edited by K. Vleminckx and Timothy M. Smeeding, 33-74. Bristol, UK: Policy Press.

Ramprakash, D. 1995. Poverty in Europe. *European Journal of Social Policy* 15 (1): 161-68.

Sainsbury, Diane. 1994. *Gendering welfare states*. London: Sage.

Sen, A. 1976. Poverty: An ordinal approach to measurement. *Econometrica* 46:437-46.

———. 1992. *Inequality reexamined*. Cambridge, MA: Harvard University Press.

Smeeding, T. 1997. Poverty in developed countries: The evidence from LIS. In *Poverty and human development*, 195-240. New York: United Nations.

Smeeding, T., L. Rainwater, and G. Burtless. 2002. United States poverty in a cross-national context. In *Understanding poverty*, edited by Sheldon H. Danziger and Robert H. Haveman, 162-89. New York: Russell Sage.

Smeeding, T., and K. Ross. 1999. Social protection for the poor in the developed world: The evidence from LIS. Working paper no. 204, Luxembourg Income Study and Syracuse University, Syracuse, NY.

Smeeding, T., P. Saunders, J. Coder, S. Jenkins, J. Fontall, A. Hagenaars, R. Hauser, and M. Wolfson. 1993. Poverty, inequality, and family living standards impacts across seven nations: The effect of noncash subsidies for health, education, and housing. *Review of Income and Wealth* 39 (3): 299-356.

Summers, R., and A. Heston. 1991. The Penn World Table (Mark 5): An expanded set of international comparisons. *Quarterly Journal of Economics* 105:327-68.

Townsend, P. 1979. *Poverty in the United Kingdom*. London: Harmendsworth Penguin Books.

ANNALS, *AAPSS*, **580**, March 2002

Trends in Youth Sexual Initiation and Fertility in Developed Countries: 1960-1995

By JULIEN O. TEITLER

ABSTRACT: The widespread interest in recent changes in fertility, union formation, and union dissolution has largely focused on adult behaviors. Much less attention has been paid to changes in related youth behaviors that foreshadow and may shape adult behaviors. This article identifies some of the changes that have occurred in the timing of sexual initiation and fertility across Western industrialized countries since 1960. Documenting the similarities and differences in these patterns helps us to understand better how youth transition experiences differ across place. This article finds that patterns of youth sexual behavior are converging across developed countries. That is, within- and between-country variation in the timing of sexual initiation has decreased. There also has been a reduction and convergence in levels of teenage fertility, but the decline in fertility was more pronounced among non-English-speaking countries than among English-speaking countries, which has resulted in an increasing gap.

Julien O. Teitler is an assistant professor at Columbia University's School of Social Work. He also directs the Social Indicators Survey Center. His areas of research include nonmarital fertility, social inequality, and research methods. Teitler's recent papers and publications are on neighborhood and school effects on youth sexual behavior, effects of marital disruption and cohabitation on children, and effects of welfare policies on new families.

NOTE: Support for this article was provided by the Lowenstein Foundation, the National Institute of Health (grant no. HD08221), and the Office of Population Research (grant no. 5P30HD/AG32030). I am grateful to all the members of the Transition to Adulthood project for the useful suggestions. Please direct correspondence to Julien O. Teitler, School of Social Work, Columbia University, 622 West 114th Street, New York, NY 10025; e-mail: teitler@columbia.edu.

T REMENDOUS changes in family formation have occurred throughout developed countries since 1960. Among the most dramatic of these changes are an increase in divorce, cohabitation, and extramarital births and a decline in overall fertility levels. The latter phenomenon has been so dramatic that it is commonly referred to as the second demographic transition. These changes have been widely documented and are believed to be related to changes in values, gender roles, and economic factors (Ermisch 1996; Kiernan 1996) in addition to the greater availability of modern contraceptive methods.

The dramatic increase in the diversity of family structures and the equally dramatic reduction in family size have captured the attention of researchers and policy makers alike. Both groups are grappling with the implications of these trends for child and family support programs, work environments, and social security. The widespread interest in recent changes in fertility, union formation, and union dissolution has largely focused on adult behaviors. Much less attention has been paid to changes in related youth behaviors that foreshadow and may shape adult behaviors. This article identifies some of the changes that have occurred in the timing of sexual initiation and fertility across Western industrialized countries since 1960. Documenting the similarities and differences in these patterns helps us to understand better how youth transition experiences differ across place. How much variation exists in adolescent transition experiences of youth,

across Western industrialized countries? Are differences in how adolescents approach sexual relationships related to differences in public discourses about sex and contraception? To what extent are programs and policies that attempt to alter patterns of youth sexual and contraceptive behavior responsible for recent changes in youth fertility? These are some of the questions to which a comparative study of fertility can provide insights, if not definite answers.

The first section of this article focuses on trends in the timing of sexual initiation, the second section examines trends in fertility, and the third section explores possible explanations for between-country differences in fertility by looking at contraceptive use and abortion.

TRENDS IN THE TIMING
OF SEXUAL INITIATION

Much of what we know about youth sexual behavior has come from surveys of adults asking retrospective questions about early sexual experiences. The first of these large-scale studies was conducted by Alfred Kinsey in the late 1940s. A few decades later, more representative studies of sexual behaviors were conducted in the United States and in several European countries.[1] Some of these national studies provided detailed accounts of the contexts within which early romantic and sexual relationships occurred and descriptions of the nature of those relationships; however, in the absence of international cooperation between investigators, questions

FIGURE 1
MEDIAN AGE AT FIRST SEX (MALES), BY BIRTH COHORT

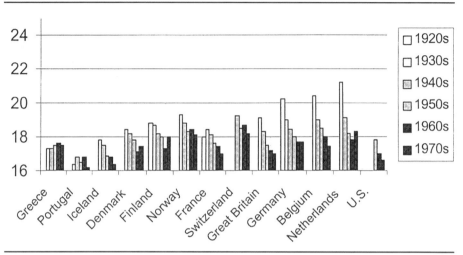

SOURCES: Bozon and Kontula (1998) and Alan Guttmacher Institute (1994).

were not standardized, so comparative studies of sexual behavior were not achievable.

The problem of data comparability has only very recently been resolved, at least to a sufficient extent to make a comparative study manageable. During the past ten years, many European governments and health organizations commissioned or sponsored studies of sexual behavior to better target AIDS prevention efforts. Since these studies focused on sexually transmitted diseases (STDs), they paid special attention to youth who are at particularly high risk of becoming infected. They also sought much more detail about the types of relationship within which sex was occurring, and many were very explicit about how they defined sexual relations. Together, these factors made it much more feasible to

construct comparable measures across countries. Still, comparability is far from perfect.

In 1998, an inter-European collaboration published comparable data from twelve countries that had recently conducted surveys of sexual behavior (Hubert, Bajos, and Sandfort 1998). Most of the data on sexual behavior that are presented in this article are drawn from those studies and, for the United States, from figures published by the Alan Guttmacher Institute ([AGI] 1994).

One of the most notable changes in sexual behavior in Europe since the 1950s has been the reduction in the age of sexual initiation. Figure 1 (males) and Figure 2 (females) illustrate the trends in the median age of sexual initiation for thirteen countries. The decline in the age of sexual onset was particularly important for

FIGURE 2
MEDIAN AGE AT FIRST SEX (FEMALES), BY BIRTH COHORT

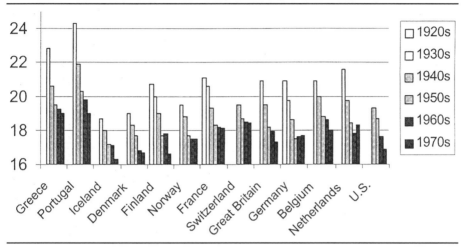

SOURCES: Bozon and Kontula (1998) and Alan Guttmacher Institute (1994).

women. On average, their median age at first sex dropped by about three years. The median age at first sex for men also declined during this period, but not as much, in part because it remained stable in countries where the age at initiation was already very low (i.e., below eighteen years of age).

The decline in the timing of sexual initiation was greatest in countries that started the period with the oldest median ages. This led to a between-country convergence in the timing of sexual initiation. In the 1950s (the 1930s cohort in Figure 1), almost 5 years separated Portuguese men from Dutch men. This gap decreased to 1.2 years by the 1990s (the 1970s cohort). Similarly for women, the median age of sexual initiation was 5.5 years higher in Portugal than in Iceland for the earliest

cohorts, and by the most recent cohorts, the age difference between these countries had declined to fewer than 3 years. Among men, the median age of sexual initiation is now between seventeen and eighteen in most of the countries, except the Mediterranean countries, where it is closer to sixteen. Among women, too, the median age is primarily in the seventeen- to eighteen-year-old range, except in the Mediterranean countries, where it is nineteen.

During this period, there was also a between-gender convergence in the timing of sexual initiation. In the cohort born during the 1930s, Portuguese women initiated intercourse 8 years later than Portuguese men. By the 1970s cohort, the gender gap in age at initiation was 2.8 years. Greece experienced as dramatic a reduction in gender differences. For other countries, the convergence was not as large because the gender differences in the timing of sexual initiation were not as large to begin with. In fact, in a few European countries (Norway, the Netherlands, and Germany), the gender difference in age at initiation was virtually nonexistent even for the earliest cohorts shown in the graphs. By the most recent cohort, the gender difference in the median age of sexual initiation was less than 1 year in ten of the thirteen countries. Exceptions are Greece and Portugal, where gender difference remains substantial, and Finland, where women's age at sexual initiation has recently dropped substantially below that of men. Although the figure for France shows a gender gap of more than 1 year, a more recent study shows that the age difference between men and women has all but disappeared in the 1990s (Lagrange and Lhomond 1997).

In addition to the between-country and between-gender convergence in the timing of sexual initiation, the age of sexual onset has become less variable within almost all European countries. That is, youth transitions are becoming more uniform, and first sexual experiences are occurring within an increasingly narrow age range. Bozon and Kontula (1998) have documented the within-cohort convergence in the timing of sexual initiation by showing that interquartile ranges in the age of sexual initiation are much smaller for the recent cohort than for older ones. In almost all the European countries for which they have data, the interquartile ranges decreased by one-third to one-half.

For example, 3.8 years separated the first and third quartiles of French men born during the 1920s, but for the cohort born in the early 1970s, the interquartile range was 2.4. The interquartile range among women in France, over the same period, declined from 5.7 years to 3.1 years. The narrowing of the transition window was greatest in Finland and West Germany where it was halved over the past forty years. Greece and Portugal saw the smallest reductions in interquartile ranges during this period.

As the ranges in transition experiences have narrowed, the timing differences between social classes have also diminished among many European countries. Educational level, once strongly associated with the timing of first intercourse, is becoming less determinant. In France, for example, only seven to eight months now separate the timing of initiation of the most educated and the least educated (Lagrange and Lhomond 1997). European countries where educational differences in the timing of sexual initiation remain important are Finland, Greece, Great Britain, and the Netherlands, among men, and Belgium, Germany, and Norway, among women (Bozon and Kontula 1998; Wellings et al. 1994).

As the number of years separating early initiators from later initiators has declined, the transitions from nonsexual to sexual dating relationships has lengthened. For adolescents in Europe, a prolonged flirting period ("going out" without having sex) became common only during the 1960s (about ten years later than in the United States). Since then, the median age when youth start kissing, which is a marker for the onset of this phase, has been declining. In France and in Finland, for example, the median age at first kiss is now fourteen (Lagrange 1998; Kontula and Haavio-Mannila 1996), about four years before the median age at first intercourse.

While nonsexual romantic relationships are now part of the romantic transition experience of most youth, it does not follow that first sexual relations increasingly occur within steady, long-term relationships. To the contrary, first sexual relationships decreasingly occur within the context of a steady relationship in all European countries, and the length between first sexual relationships and first cohabiting unions has increased (Sandfort et al. 1998).

The convergence in between-country, between-gender, and within-cohort differences in the timing of sexual initiation and the similarities in transition patterns (from nonsexual romantic relationships to sexual relationships and cohabiting relationships) has greatly diminished national, cultural, and class influences in the manner in which youth experience this particular transition. The transition script in Western industrialized countries appears to be increasingly uniform and universal and adhered to more rigorously. Having noted the trends toward convergence, it is important to point out that important differences remain. First, Mediterranean countries still exhibit important gender differences in the timing of sexual initiation. Men there tend to

initiate sex earlier than they do in other countries, while women tend to initiate sex later than they do in other countries. Second, Iceland, Denmark, and Great Britain continue to have earlier median ages of sexual initiation among both men and women than do other countries, while Norway, Switzerland, Belgium, and the Netherlands have higher median ages of sexual initiation for men and women.

Throughout the changes that have occurred since the 1960s, one aspect of romantic relationships has remained virtually unchanged in all countries: the gender difference in the age of sexual partners has remained large. Women tend to initiate with older men, and men with same-age women (Bozon and Kontula 1998; Bozon 1991). These age differences are consistent with age differences in cohabiting and marital partnerships, which have also changed little.

To sum up the trends in the transitions to first intercourse, there appear to be shifts occurring in the regulation of sexual behavior among youth throughout European countries. Parents are much more tolerant and accepting of children's early romantic and sexual relationships than were their own parents, and perhaps as a cause or consequence of this more accepting attitude, they appear to have lost influence over when and how their children experience the transition to first intercourse. Regardless of whether parents approve or not, the vast majority of youth now initiate within a very narrow window of time. This window is converging both between countries and between genders, within countries. The social regulation of sexual initiation has not weakened over time, but it appears to be increasingly universalistic and peer dictated. Culture still matters; being raised in a country with widely adhered to, clearly demarcated sex roles is associated with large imbalances in the age and circumstances under which youth enter into romantic relationships. Social class also continues to have an effect on timing of sexual initiation in some countries. However, these effects are diminishing rapidly.

The changes in youth normative environments could potentially have large effects on the manner in which youth negotiate and make decisions about their relationships. The narrowing of the window of time within which youth initiate sex suggests that peer socialization and pressure to conform to behavioral norms has increased. On one hand, this may pressure youth to enter their first sexual relationships before or after they are prepared. On the other hand, peer pressure may have beneficial effects, when it dictates healthy and responsible approaches to sex. The very low levels of teen fertility and the tremendous rise in condom use in Europe in the past decade, on which subsequent sections of this article will focus, are suggestive of some positive influences that may be peer initiated, at least in part. The narrowing of the age gap in sexual initiation between sexes suggests that the changes that have occurred in adult gender roles over the past three decades have had an impact on youth as well. This should translate into increased gender egalitarianism within romantic relationships, though this has yet to be proven. Finally, the lengthening of the presexual romantic period means that when they have their first sexual relationships, most youth will have had at least some experience with the emotional aspects of a relationship. Whether this has a beneficial effect on communication with partners is not clear, but the fact that the transition is much slower now, and often evolves slowly "around the bases," does suggest a fundamental change in the transition experience of youth today, compared to those of generations born thirty years earlier.

TRENDS IN EARLY FERTILITY

The last comprehensive account of teenage fertility in Europe dates back to the AGI study, *Teenage Pregnancy in Industrialized Countries* (Jones et al. 1986), which was based on data from the late 1970s and early 1980s. That study is in need of updating, and it focused primarily on cross-sectional comparisons in teen fertility and tried to explain differences in terms of social and economic characteristics of countries. The authors of the study were highly successful at pointing out that the United States was an outlier in terms of teen pregnancy rates, but they were only moderately successful at deciphering the causes of the between-country differences. Among other arguments, they suggested that teen fertility rates in the United States were much higher than in other industrialized countries because of mixed messages youth were receiving from adults. Their hypothesis was that the United States' more puritanical society avoided honest and open discussions about healthy transitions to sexual relationships and that as a consequence, youth entered those transitions ill prepared. While this hypothesis has rarely been countered by academic researchers studying teen fertility or by family planning advocates, it is ignored or rejected outright by policy makers pushing "just say no" approaches to sex education. Their argument is that providing information about sex and contraception to youth will only encourage them to have sex. In fact, there is little evidence in support of either claim. In the United States, most sexually active youth are familiar with different methods of contraception and where they can be obtained, so providing them with more information is unlikely to dramatically lower pregnancies. But there is no evidence, either, that existing programs designed to inform youth about sex or provide them with free contraception increase the likelihood that youth exposed to those programs will be more likely to initiate sex. Another counterargument to the AGI hypothesis is that teen fertility rates in the United States are not higher in more conservative and more puritanical areas of the United States than they are in less conservative and less puritanical urban environments, which is what we would expect to see if openness about sex encouraged more responsible use of contraception. These observations do not negate the argument that cultural differences are at the root of the particularly high levels of teen fertility in the United States, but they question which attributes of American culture are responsible.

By looking at more recent fertility data, and by looking at trends in teen fertility and how they compare with trends in the fertility of older women, we can push the question of where country differences in teen fertility originate. More specifically, we can see to what extent the United States continues to be an outlier, whether other countries also stand out, and how fertility levels of teens relate to adult patterns of family formation.

The data presented in this section are drawn from vital statistic reports from selected Western European and English-speaking countries. Many of these data are now available from Eurostat (see http://europa.eu.int/comm/eurostat/), the statistical office of the European community. Whenever possible, the figures shown in this article were extracted from paper and electronic files published by Eurostat. These data were supplemented with vital statistics reports from individual countries where information was incomplete.

Comparing fertility data across countries does not pose the same types of problems as comparing less well-defined human behaviors. Births are recorded systematically in almost all countries, and birth rates are usually reported. The issue that arises when comparing birth rates or other age-specific fertility measures across countries is that countries differ in when they estimate their populations, which affects the denominator of the fertility measures, and they differ in whether they record the age

FIGURE 3
BIRTH RATE FOR FIFTEEN- TO NINETEEN-YEAR-OLDS, BY YEAR

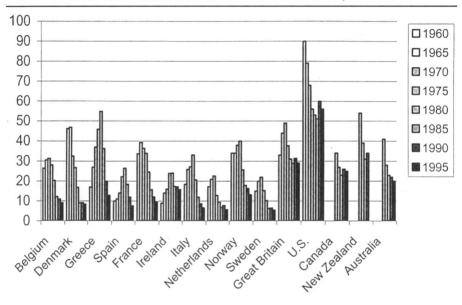

SOURCES: New Cronos Eurostat database and Canadian, Australian, New Zealand, and U.S. vital statistics reports.

of the mother at the time of the birth or the age cohort to which the mother belongs, which affects the numerator. The former is not very consequential, but the latter is, so fertility measures need to be standardized. All of the fertility rates presented in this article are adjusted to the U.S. standard using a method developed by Calot (1984) so that they are comparable.

Figure 3 displays the birth rates of teenagers in fifteen countries, from 1960 to 1995 (left to right). These countries include members of the European Community and additional English-speaking countries; specifically, the United States, Canada, New Zealand, and Australia. The reason for including the latter

countries is to see whether an Anglophone country pattern stands out.

Two clear trends are evident in Figure 3, which graphs the birth rates of fifteen- to nineteen-year-old women in fifteen countries. The first is that most of those countries experienced a very similar pattern of teen fertility between 1960 and 1995. Rates were increasing until the early to mid-1970s, after which they declined precipitously. The pattern of an increase in fertility followed by a decline occurred in all countries. This is not evident for Denmark, Norway, the United States, Canada, New Zealand, or Australia because they reached their peak fertility levels somewhat earlier (around 1960), but the same pattern would be visible if the bar chart went back an additional ten to twenty years. The second observation is that the United States still stands out as an outlier, with teen fertility rates about five times that of most European nations and twice as high as other Anglophone countries.

As with sexual initiation, there is an indication that fertility rates among most European countries are converging. There still remain some across-country differences, but they are smaller than they were twenty or thirty years ago, when Belgium, Denmark, France, and Great Britain all had teen fertility rates at or above 30 per 1,000, about twice the level of Spain, Ireland, the Netherlands, or Switzerland. Now, most western European countries have teen fertility rates below 10 per 1,000, regardless of how high their peak fertility levels were. England is an exception, and fertility in Ireland remains somewhat higher than in continental Europe as well.

From their peak level, usually in the 1970s, the decline in teen fertility rates was spectacular in all non-Anglo countries. The fertility rate of fifteen- to nineteen-year-old women in Greece and Denmark dropped by about 80 percent in two decades. Most other countries saw declines of 60 percent to 70 percent. This is very different from all the English-speaking countries including Ireland, where the decline was much more modest— closer to 30 percent. One result is that the relative magnitude in the difference between the English- and non-English-speaking West has increased. Until the 1980s, England

did not look different from many of the other European countries, nor did Canada, New Zealand, or Australia. Only the United States stood out as dramatically different from all other countries, and at the time, teen fertility rates were only twice the level of many others. The question Figure 3 raises is why the Anglo countries experienced much less of a decline in teen fertility than the non-Anglo countries. This question is slightly different and much more complex than the one usually posed, which is why the United States or Great Britain have higher fertility levels than other western European countries. The shared cultural attributes of all the Anglo countries did not suddenly emerge in the 1970s, when fertility rates in all other countries began to plummet. Whichever shared experiences contributed to the different patterns, they did so by preventing the Anglo countries from experiencing as sharp a reduction in teen fertility rates as did other countries.

To better understand the differential trends in teen fertility, it is useful to compare teen fertility trends with more general fertility trends. Figure 4 shows the total fertility rates (TFRs) for the same countries, over the same years. The graph shows that the TFR decreased in all countries, quite dramatically. Here, too, there is a noticeable convergence between countries. The countries that began the period as outliers, with substantially higher than average fertility (Ireland, the United States, and New Zealand) ended the period more in line with the rest of the countries. The Anglo countries,

FIGURE 4
TOTAL FERTILITY RATE, BY YEAR

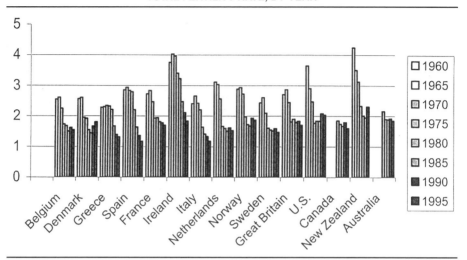

SOURCES: New Cronos Eurostat database and Canadian, Australian, New Zealand, and U.S. vital statistics reports.

particularly the United States and New Zealand, still have slightly higher TFRs, but the difference is less dramatic. There are also a few very low TFR countries along the Mediterranean (Greece, Spain, and Italy), despite their having begun the downward trend later than many other countries. Still, these countries do not stand out as being very different.

The fact that TFRs have converged while teen birth rates, at least between Anglo and non-Anglo countries, have diverged means that the manner in which teen fertility behaviors relate to adult fertility behaviors is variable across countries. Figure 5 illustrates this point more clearly by showing the ratio of teen birth rates to TFRs. The levels of teen fertility relative to overall fertility in Ireland, Great Britain, the United States, and

Canada did not change much since the mid-1970s. During this period, teen fertility followed very much the same pattern as adult fertility (this is not as evident for New Zealand or Australia). In all the other countries, the decline in teen fertility outpaced the decline in overall fertility during the second half of the period. That is, teen fertility declined much more rapidly than did total fertility, even in countries such as Italy that experienced extremely sharp declines in overall fertility.

European countries have varied in their programmatic approaches to sexual education. Some countries, such as the Netherlands and Finland, very actively educate youth about sex, while others, particularly the Mediterranean countries, leave much more of sex education up to youth themselves. However, the

FIGURE 5
RATIO OF BIRTH RATE FOR 15-19 YEAR-OLDS TO TOTAL FERTILITY RATE

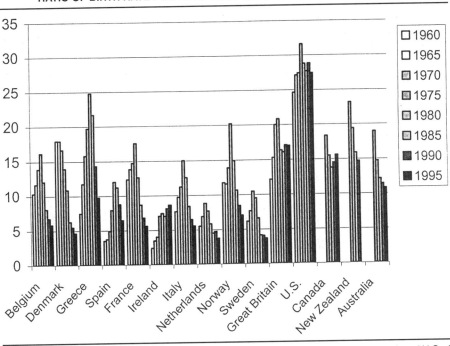

SOURCES: New Cronos Eurostat database and Canadian, Australian, New Zealand, and U.S. vital statistics reports.

decline in teen fertility, in absolute terms and relative to overall fertility, was universal among non-Anglo countries and of similar magnitude. This suggests that the country-specific educational programs probably were not the primary impetus for the changes that occurred in the past couple of decades, and by the same token, developing teen outreach programs in the United States based on European models is unlikely to dramatically reduce teen pregnancy.

If programs do not account for the differences between the Anglo and non-Anglo patterns, what does? Though this question is impossible to answer with any certitude, the relationship between adult and teen fertility trends and changes that have occurred in the family in recent years provides some insights. In the United States, Great Britain, and Ireland, there is a tremendous coupling of teen fertility with overall fertility. The delay in childbearing affected all age groups very similarly— much more so than elsewhere. The implication is, perhaps, that youth in Anglo countries are more affected by, or more a part of, the general normative fertility environment. This would not be surprising given that first births among American and

British women have typically occurred much earlier than in continental western Europe, as has marriage. Among older generations in the United States and Great Britain, it was not uncommon for teenagers, particularly eighteen- and nineteen-year-old women, to be married and have children. In Europe, typical marriage ages dipped into the low twenties for only a brief moment during the 1960s to mid-1970s. During most of the rest of this century, women married later.

Another change that occurred in many European and Anglo countries was the disunion of marriage and births. Increasingly, births are occurring outside of marriage. We can distinguish three different regimes of early fertility and marriage. In the United States and Great Britain, among women, first marriages typically occurred in the early twenties until the mid-1970s (DaVanzo and Rahman 1993). Starting in the early 1970s, the typical age at marriage rose, but at the same time, increasing numbers of births occurred outside of marriage and outside of cohabiting unions, especially among teenagers. As a result, the timing of first births was delayed, but not by as much as changing marriage patterns would have predicted, and teen births continued to be common.

The second pattern is the northern European model including Denmark, Sweden, Finland, Iceland, and Norway. The average age at marriage in these countries was already higher than in many other European countries during the 1970s (around twenty-three to twenty-five), and it has risen further since then, to twenty-six and twenty-seven (Kiernan 1996). These countries also experienced a decoupling of marriage and births. Out of wedlock births now account for about 30 percent of all births in Finland and close to 60 percent of all births in Iceland (Kiernan 1996). The other northern European countries fall somewhere between. However, unlike in the United States, most of these births occur in stable cohabiting unions. The decoupling of marriage and births has not meant a decoupling of romantic partnerships and births. The later age at marriage in the northern countries and the fact that births continue to occur mostly in the context of stable adult relationships meant that teen parenthood was rare to begin with and became more uncommon as modern contraception became more widely available and adult women further delayed having their first child.

The third pattern is exemplified by the Mediterranean countries (Greece, Italy, Portugal, and Spain). Here, marriage typically occurred at younger ages than in the northern European countries and increased after the 1970s, to around twenty-four to twenty-five by 1990, which is very close to ages in the United States and Great Britain. What sets these countries apart from the Anglo countries is their very low rates of out of wedlock births. Fertility and marriage continue to be closely tied. The proportion of nonmarital births in these countries ranges from less than 5 percent (Greece) to around 15 percent (Portugal). Since it is not yet common for births to occur outside of marriage, the rise in the age of marriage had a much greater impact on the fertility rates of teenagers than it did in the Anglo countries.

To conclude this section, the comparisons between adult and teen fertility patterns within the context of trends in cohabitation, marriage, and nonmarital fertility suggest possible explanations for why countries have differed in patters of teen fertility and, more generally, the contexts within which youth enter sexual relationships. Teen fertility in the United States and Great Britain declined since the 1970s, but only to an extent that parallels closely the decline that occurred among all women. Teenagers were and continue to be very close in age to modal ages at first births and, not being constrained to have babies within the context of stable unions, their fertility behavior is very likely to mirror the behavior of slightly older women, irrespective of trends in marriage or cohabitation. In contrast, in European nations, teen births have always been uncommon. Teen fertility rates peaked around 1970 when the age at which women married dipped and then responded extremely rapidly to both overall delays in timing of births and delays in union formation.

The structural explanation advanced above fits the trends in teen fertility better than do explanations that point to morality and society's openness around issues of sexuality. Certainly, these cultural attributes affect how youth communicate with adults about their transitions, but it does not necessarily follow that they would delay having babies if communication about sex,

with adults and between adults, were more frequent and more open. In fact, the trend evidence discussed above suggests that the opposite may be true. Teens in the United States more closely mimic adults around them than do teens in Europe. Their behavior is consistent with that of adults who are a few years older. Whether or not they communicate verbally, they seem to be getting a message, and for some youth that message legitimizes having children early. This explanation also fits variations within the United States better. Fertility among teens is higher in places and among population subgroups where parenthood occurs earlier (even excluding teens). Again, teenagers may perceive that having children is acceptable if it is common among many women just a few years older than them. This does not mean that teens are trying to become parents, but it may translate into more lax attitudes about pregnancy prevention. This brings us to the final section of this article, which looks at changes in contraceptive behavior and abortion.

CONTRACEPTION AND ABORTION

Figures 1 and 2 show that the age at which youth initiate sex in England and the United States is not earlier than in most other European countries. Thus, differences in birth rates are unlikely to be due to differences in exposure to the risk of becoming pregnant. More frequent intercourse could also increase the exposure to risks of pregnancy, but there is no evidence that frequency of intercourse among youth is noticeably higher in the United States and Britain than elsewhere. It is more likely that differences in fertility arise from differences in contraceptive use or in abortions. One would expect that rates of contraception would be substantially higher in non-Anglo countries than in Anglo countries, that the rates would have increased faster in the past several decades, and/or that abortion rates of pregnant teens would be higher. There is some evidence in support of both explanations.

The levels of contraception among teens and the methods they use have changed in all European countries and in the United States. The use of contraception at first intercourse has increased, and there has been a dramatic increase in the use of condoms, by all accounts driven by public awareness campaigns about AIDS and other STDs. First-time use of contraception in France, England, and the Netherlands was 50 percent to 60 percent in the late 1970s (Jones et al. 1986) and 48 percent in the United States in the early 1980s (AGI 1994). By the early 1990s, reported contraceptive use at first intercourse was about 85 percent in Finland, France, and Switzerland (Kontula and Haavio-Mannila 1996; Toulemon and Leridon 1991; Michaud 1997) and 95 percent in Denmark (Knudsen 1997). In Germany, 75 percent of sexually active fifteen- to seventeen-year-old girls reported always using effective contraception (Hellferich 1996). Contraceptive use has also risen in Great Britain and the United States, but not by quite as much. The percentage

using contraception at first intercourse is now about 75 percent in Great Britain (Wellings et al. 1995) and 78 percent in the United States (AGI 1999). The increase in contraceptive use at first intercourse is all the more impressive given the decrease in the median age at first sex. All other factors being equal, the decrease in the age of sexual initiation would have resulted in a decrease in contraceptive use the first time, since the older youth are when they have sex the first time, the more likely they are to contracept.

The initial rapid increase in birth control use among youth can be almost entirely attributed to the increase in the use of birth control pills—by far the most common form of birth control among youth, in most countries, until the late 1980s. Prior to then, condom use as a regular form of protection was rare in most countries. That changed during the 1990s. Now, most youth report having used condoms in all European countries, though a substantial amount of variation exists in the levels of use. Based on the recent European surveys, the proportion of eighteen- to nineteen-year-olds reporting ever having used condoms varies from 54 percent in Greece to 94 percent in Switzerland (Dubois-Arber and Spencer 1998). The variation between countries is somewhat difficult to interpret because of the difference in the timing of the surveys. While the surveys were conducted within a span of only five years (1989 for Greece to 1994 for Switzerland), condom use was greatly increasing during that period, and the ranking of countries by condom use closely follows the timing of the surveys, casting doubt about whether differences between countries are real or reflect period effects. In the United States, condom use at first sex doubled from 1982 to 1988, to half of all teenage women (AGI 1994). Since condom use ever is bound to be higher than first-time use, condom use among teens in the United States falls somewhere within the range for European countries.

Condom use is also related to socioeconomic background in almost all countries. The greater the level of education, the greater the likelihood of ever having used a condom (Dubois-Arber and Spencer 1998; AGI 1994). The exceptions are the Netherlands and Greece, where no relationship seems to exist between education and ever having used a condom. In the case of the Netherlands, however, an educational effect does appear when looking at condom use in the past year.

Overall, trends in contraceptive use are very consistent across western Europe and the United States. Youth appear to be much more cautious about avoiding STDs and pregnancy now than they were just a decade ago. There are no noteworthy exceptions. Not only have rates of usage increased by similar amounts, but the shift from contraceptive pills to condoms has been universal, as have the socioeconomic predictors of various methods of birth control. The United States and England do not stand out as fundamentally different. Before dismissing variations in contraceptive use as a key explanation of Anglo versus non-Anglo

fertility patterns, it is important to point out that measures of use at first sex and at last sex do not capture the consistency with which sexually active teenagers use birth control. Differences in fertility may relate more to how consistent youth are at using contraception each time they have sex, for which few data exist.

In the United States, as sexual activity among teens has increased since the early 1970s, the number of teens who become pregnant has increased. However, increased use of contraception has resulted in a decline in the proportion of sexually active teens becoming pregnant (from about one-forth to one-fifth of all sexually experienced teens). While most of these pregnancies are unintended, slightly more than half of all pregnant teens end up carrying their pregnancies to term (AGI 1994). Abortion rates (among pregnant teens) increased during the early 1970s but then stabilized and started to decrease in the late 1980s and into the 1990s. Among teenagers, abortion rates appear to vary slightly between the United States, other Anglo countries, and northern European countries. In Anglo countries, abortion rates are lower than birth rates, while in all northern European countries except Norway (for which they are about the same) the opposite is true (United Nations 1988). In other words, teen birth rates in Anglo countries are higher than in other European countries in part because pregnancies among teens are more common and in part because when they occur, a greater proportion of teens choose to have the babies.

CONCLUSION

European youth are initiating sex earlier than were previous generations. The trend toward younger ages at sexual initiation is most dramatic in countries where later initiation was more common, which has led to a convergence in sexual behaviors across most developed countries and within countries. The patterns of youth sexual behavior appear to follow increasingly homogeneous and universal norms. Yet the convergence has not been total. Differences between countries remain, and these differences have parallels among the adult population. Countries that have typically been more gender egalitarian in terms of educational attainment and work show smaller gender differences in the timing of sexual initiation.

The linkage between adult norms and youth behavior is also apparent when we look at fertility. Again, there has been a noticeable convergence in teenage fertility between European countries, and the general trend has reflected the trend in adult fertility. Namely, there has been a sharp decrease in fertility rates. But this decrease was more pronounced among the non-English-speaking countries than among English-speaking countries, which resulted in an increasing gap between them. The increasingly transnational norms of sexual behavior appear to relate only to the timing of sexual initiation, not to the approaches youth have toward pregnancy and STD prevention, where a substantial country effect remains.

Since Anglo countries do not differ from other Western countries in the timing of sexual initiation, their higher levels of fertility cannot be explained by differential exposure to the risk of pregnancy. The fertility gap seems to be due in part to differential use of contraception—but without better measures of the consistency of use, it is difficult to know how much is due to this—and some of the gap appears to be due to differences in abortion rates.

What does all of this mean for transition experiences of youth? Mainly, it appears that for at least some segments of the population, the perceived costs of contraceptive failure are lower in Anglo countries than in other developed countries. The acceptability of very early parenthood in Anglo countries is not a recent phenomenon. What is recent is the greater acceptability of nonmarital fertility and, in Anglo countries, fertility outside of stable partnerships. In all developed countries, having sex outside of marriage not only has become acceptable but has become normative. In many countries, so has cohabitation prior to or in place of marriage. In addition, for a sizeable minority of young women in Anglo countries, having a child and raising it without the father is not such a frightening thought.

The fact that adolescents have sex before marrying and are likely to have sexual relations with several partners, over a course of several years, before they settle into a more stable long-term relationship means that the transition to adulthood has become more complex. There now exists a long overlapping period of transitions, during which time youth still reside with their family of origin and are still in school yet establish complex emotional and sexual relationships with peers.

One issue that was not raised in this article because the data were not suited to explore it was that substantial socioeconomic variation exists in teen fertility among Anglo countries. A portion of the Anglo/non-Anglo fertility differential can be accounted for by the especially high teen fertility rates among some subgroups of the population in the United States and Great Britain. The implication is that generalizations between Anglo and non-Anglo fertility trends are perhaps misplaced. Fertility norms may be as variable within country as between country. And social segmentation among youth may itself play a role in explaining differential fertility behaviors. Analyzing trends in sexual, contraceptive, and fertility behaviors by subgroups would allow us to further explore these possibilities. Until we analyze such data, a large part of the explanation of why there is such a large "English-speaking effect" on teen fertility will be missing.

Note

1. These include—in the United States—the Kantner and Zelnick studies in the 1970s and those by Laumann and his colleagues in the early 1990s, the Simon study in France in the early 1970s, and the FINSEX study in Finland.

References

Alan Guttmacher Institute (AGI). 1994. *Sex and America's teenagers.* New York: Alan Guttmacher Institute. Available from www.agi-usa.org

————. 1999. *Facts in brief: Teen sex and pregnancy.* New York: Alan Guttmacher Institute. Available from www.agi-usa.org

Bozon, M. 1991. Women and the age gap between spouses. An accepted domination? *Population: An English Selection* 3:113-48.

Bozon, M., and O. Kontula. 1998. Sexual initiation and gender in Europe. In *Sexual behavior and HIV/AIDS in Europe,* edited by M. Hubert, N. Bajos, and T. Sandfort, 37-67. London: UCL Press.

Calot, G. 1984. *La mésure des taux en démographie.* Cahier numero 104. Paris: Presses Universitaires de France.

DaVanzo, J., and M. Rahman. 1993. *American families: Trends and policy issues.* Santa Monica, CA: RAND.

Dubois-Arber, F., and B. Spencer. 1998. Condom use. In *Sexual behavior and HIV/AIDS in Europe,* edited by M. Hubert, N. Bajos, and T. Sandfort, 266-86. London: UCL Press.

Ermisch, J. 1996. The economic environment for family formation. In *Europe's population in the 1990s,* edited by D. Coleman, 144-62. Oxford, UK: Oxford University Press.

Helfferich, C. 1996. Planification familiale et modes de vie en Allemagne. *Entre Nous* 33:9-10.

Hubert, M., N. Bajos, and T. Sandfort. 1998. *Sexual behavior and HIV/AIDS in Europe.* London: UCL Press.

Jones, E., et al. 1986. *Teenage pregnancy in industrialized countries.* New Haven, CT: Yale University Press.

Kiernan, K. 1996. Partnership behaviour in Europe: Recent trends and issues. In *Europe's population in the 1990s,* edited by D. Coleman, 62-91. Oxford, UK: Oxford University Press.

Knudsen, L. B. 1997. Birth control and pregnancies among teenagers in Denmark. Paper presented at the EAPS international conference, Cracow, Poland, June.

Kontula, O., and E. Haavio-Mannila. 1996. *Sexual pleasures: Enhancement of sex life in Finland, 1971-1992.* Aldershot, UK: Dartmouth.

Lagrange, H. 1998. Le sexe apprivoise où l'invention du flirt. *Revue Francaise de Sociology* 34 (1): 139-75.

Lagrange, H., and B. Lhomond, eds. 1997. *L'entrée dans la sexualité.* Paris: Editions La Découverte.

Michaud, P. 1997. *Adolescents and their sexuality: Context, negociation and choices related to love and sexual life.* Lausanne, Switzerland: IUMSP.

Sandfort, T., M. Hubert, N. Bajos, and H. Bos. 1988. Sexual behaviour and HIV risk: Common patterns and differences between European countries. In *Sexual behavior and HIV/AIDS in Europe,* edited by M. Hubert, N. Bajos, and T. Sandfort, 403-26. London: UCL Press.

Toulemon, L., and H. Leridon. 1991. Vingt années de contraception en France: 1968-1988. *Population* 4:777-812.

United Nations. 1988. *Adolescent reproductive behaviour: Evidence from developed countries.* Vol. 1. New York: United Nations.

Wellings, K., J. Wadsworth, A. Johnson, J. Field, L. Whitaker, and B. Field. 1995. Provision of sex education and early sexual experience: The relation examined. *British Medical Journal* 311:417-20.

Wellings, K., J. Field, A. Johnson, and J. Wadsworth. 1994. *Sexual behavior in Britain.* New York: Penguin.

The Transition to Adulthood:
A Time Use Perspective

By ANNE H. GAUTHIER and FRANK F. FURSTENBERG Jr.

ABSTRACT: This article examines the changes in the patterns of time use of young adults ages eighteen to thirty-four as they make the transition to adulthood. More specifically, it examines the realloca- tion of time associated with the transition from school to work, the transition to partnership, and the transition to parenthood. The em- pirical analysis is based on time use surveys from nine industrialized countries. Results suggest that of the three transitions, it is the tran- sition to parenthood that most significantly alters the pattern of time use of young people, more so for women than for men. The empirical analysis also reveals remarkable similarities across countries in the patterns of time use of young people as they make the transition to adulthood.

Anne H. Gauthier is the Canada Research Chair in comparative public policy at the University of Calgary. She is the author of The State and the Family *(1996).*

Frank F. Furstenberg Jr. is the Zellerbach Family Professor of Sociology and Re- search Associate in the Population Studies Center at the University of Pennsylvania. His interest in the American family began at Columbia University where he received his Ph.D. in 1967. His recent book is Managing to Make It: Urban Families in High-Risk Neighborhoods *with Thomas Cook, Jacquelynne Eccles, Glen Elder, and Arnold Sameroff (1999). His current research projects focus on the family in the context of dis- advantaged urban neighborhoods, adolescent sexual behavior, cross-national research on children's well- being, urban education, and the transition from adolescence to adulthood. He is currently Chair of the MacArthur Foundation Research Network on the Transition to Adulthood.*

NOTE: A first version of this article was presented at the annual meeting of the Population Association of America in Los Angeles in 1998. We are grateful to the discussant for her valuable comments. We would also like to thank our research assistants at the University of Calgary and especially acknowledge the contribution of Cori Pawlak to the data analysis. This article bene- fited from a grant from the Social Sciences and Humanities Research Council of Canada. Data was provided by the Multinational Time Use Study, with additional authorization from Statistics Finland and Statistics Sweden. Address correspondence to Anne H. Gauthier, Department of So- ciology, University of Calgary, 2500 University Dr. NW, Calgary, Alberta, Canada, T2N1N4; fax: (403) 282-9298; e-mail: Gauthier@ucalgary.ca.

THE transition from school to work, the transition to independent living, and the transition to parenthood all result in major changes in lifestyles, responsibilities, and autonomy. Very likely these transitions correspond to different patterns of time use. Yet time use data have rarely been used to examine the transition to adulthood. There are analyses of the patterns of time use of children, teenagers, and the working-age population (Gershuny 2000; Robinson and Godbey 1997), but time use has rarely been used to analyze changes from one status to the other. This article, thus, is a first attempt at using time use data to shed light on the transition to adulthood.

Our approach is mainly descriptive. Using data from nine industrialized countries, we examine changes in the patterns of time use of young adults as they make the transition from school to work, from being single to being partnered, and from childlessness to parenthood. Our emphasis is on the changes in the patterns of time use of young people from one status to the other. In particular, we are interested in possible macro-level regularities in the patterns of time use of young people as they make their transition to adulthood. Results suggest in fact remarkable similarities across countries. As will be seen in this article, the transition to adulthood appears to be associated with similar changes in the patterns of time use of young people across countries.

The article is divided into four main sections. In the first section, we review the relevant literature; in the second, we present our data and methods; and in the third, we present our results. The fourth section concludes the article.

Although the use of time budget data sheds a new light on the transition to adulthood, they are not without limitations. In particular, we should be clear that because of the nature of our data, we are relying on cross-sectional data to study processes that are inherently longitudinal. In doing so, we are assuming that there is no selectivity at work, in that people who make the transition to school, to partnership, and to parenthood are not special subgroups who exhibited a different pattern of time use before the transition, as compared to people who do not make the transition. Considering the decline in young people's propensity to marry and enter parenthood, this assumption may be questionable. In the absence of longitudinal data, however, this assumption is necessary.

LITERATURE

In their analysis of patterns of time use from various countries, Robinson, Converse, and Szalai (1972) concluded that while there were some intercountry differences in patterns of time use among the working-age population, the similarities were overwhelming despite substantial differences in the countries' political organization and cultural traditions:

We have been impressed . . . at the number of points at which the "human design" intrudes to keep relative time allocations remarkably constant across such domains as formal work and housework, travel, and attention to the outer world through the mass media—even in the face of dramatic site [country] differences in industrial development. (P. 144)

On the basis of the same data, Converse (1972) pointed out that differences in patterns of time use by social and economic status (as captured by the combination of gender, labor force status, and the presence of children) overshadowed any cross-national difference. He concluded, "The main lesson . . . is that national differences in time allocation of the kind we have been examining . . . are quite limited when compared to differences in social role within the same site [country]' (p. 169).

Converse's (1972) conclusion was based on data collected in the mid-1960s in twelve countries. In the more recent time use literature, gender, employment status, and the presence of children have also emerged as key determinants (see, e.g., Gershuny 2000). Together, these three variables tend to explain a relatively large fraction of the total variation in time spent on housework, family care, paid work, leisure, and personal activities. In most studies, these variables are included in statistical models to capture the sources of variations in the patterns of time use at one point in time. As such, they are part of a static framework of analysis rather than a dynamic one. This may not be surprising considering that the large majority of time use surveys are cross-sectional. However, even within the constraints imposed by cross-sectional data, time budget surveys have rarely been used in a dynamic framework. Rarely have patterns of time use been linked to life course transitions, for example, the transition from school to work and the transition to independent living. One of the rare exceptions is Cantwell and Sanik's (1993) study of patterns of time use before and after the birth of children.

The near absence of a life course perspective in time use research is in stark contrast with the large number of time use studies on specific subgroups of the population, especially on children (Bianchi and Robinson 1997; Mauldin and Meeks 1990; Robinson and Bianchi 1997; Timmer, Eccles, and O'Brien 1985), teenagers (Alsaker and Flammer 1999; Duncan and Sanik 1991; Flammer, Alsaker, and Noack 1999; Larson and Verma 1999; Robinson 1991), and elderly people (Herzog et al. 1989). This situation also runs counter to the importance currently attached to the life course perspective in sociology and demography (George 1993; Shanahan 2000). As a result, the way young people use their time has not been central to the scholarship on the transition to adulthood. There have been attempts at linking patterns of leisure to teenage careers (Bynner and Ashford 1992), patterns of time use of young adults to deviant behavior (Osgood et al. 1996), and leisure activities to adult roles (Osgood and Lee 1993), but such studies are scarce. Overwhelmingly, the transition to adulthood has instead been studied from the perspective of "objective" demographic markers (such as entry into marriage and parenthood).[1]

Despite the lack of integration between time use research, on one hand, and studies on the transition to adulthood, on the other, there are compelling reasons to expect the transition to adulthood to be reflected by major shifts in the patterns of time use of young adults. The transition to adulthood being associated with an increasing level of autonomy and responsibilities (including financial and familial responsibilities), we can expect these changes to be reflected in distinct patterns of time use. The transition from school to work, the transition to independent living, and the transition to parenthood may all be expected to translate into distinct patterns of time use in view of the related changes in young people's constraints and opportunities. We will test this hypothesis in the empirical section of the article.

To conclude this review of literature, one other issue that we should address concerns the possible confounding effect of age and social roles. The relationships between age, adult status, and the transition to adulthood have been thoroughly discussed in the literature (see, e.g., Marini 1984; Settersen 1998; Settersen and Mayer 1997). On one hand, this literature has pointed to the persistence of age norms and age-related behavior, and on the other, it has also pointed to the increasing individualization and diversity in the paths to adulthood, over time and across countries (Shanahan 2000). With respect to time use, the literature suggests that controlling for adult status only slightly modifies the age profile of patterns of leisure

activities of adults (Osgood and Lee 1993).[2] In this article, we instead focus on the changes in patterns of time use associated with different adult status. Since the timing of the transition to adulthood tends to vary across countries (Corijn 1999; Iacovou 1998), we felt that a focus on age could confound the respective effect of the timing of the transition to adulthood and adult status on patterns of time use and thus would obscure any macro-social regularity. In the following analysis, the variable "age" is therefore not explicitly taken into account (apart from restricting the analysis to the population ages eighteen to thirty-four). Instead, we focus on the patterns of time use of subgroups of young people having achieved different adult statuses.

DATA AND METHOD

The data

In this article, we use time budget surveys to analyze the patterns of time use of young people. Time budget surveys are unusual types of surveys that rely on dairies to collect detailed information on people's daily activities. This means that unlike most other types of surveys, time budget surveys do not only record people's employment status, but they also collect precise information about time spent in school and in paid employment as well as time spent doing other activities such as volunteering, doing unpaid work, attending meetings, and socializing with friends and relatives. A typical time use survey collects information on all activities that took place during a twenty-four-hour period: the time the activity started, the time it ended, the nature of the activity, where it took place, and with whom the activity was carried out. Diaries thus provide information about the time spent on each activity and its context (what? with whom? where?). Diaries have moreover been shown to provide more reliable estimates of time use than stylized questions about time spent on specific activities during a reference period, for example, the past week or past month (Robinson and Godbey 1997; Juster and Stafford 1991).

Since the 1960s, time budget surveys have been carried out in most industrialized countries. They have moreover followed a common methodology established in the 1960s by a multinational study under the direction of A. Szalai (1972). The surveys that we used in this article are all archived at the Multinational Time Use Study (see http://www.iser.essex.ac.uk/mtus/index.php) at the University of Essex in England. They have all been translated into English and have been harmonized into standard variables and standard coding. The harmonized version currently available covers, however, only the population ages twenty to fifty-nine years old even though the original surveys covered a wider age range. For the purpose of this article, we went back to the original surveys and added respondents eighteen and nineteen years old to the harmonized surveys. We also created an additional variable to identify students.

We use data from nine industrialized countries: Austria, Canada, Finland, Germany, Italy, the Netherlands, Sweden, the United Kingdom, and the United States. Details on these surveys appear in Table 1. These surveys represent a small fraction of all extant time budget surveys. The selected surveys were all carried out during the period from 1985 to 1992.[3] As mentioned earlier, all these surveys used the diary as the mode of data collection and a well-established methodology. There are differences between surveys in the actual way by which the dairies were collected (phone, mail back, visit), but the literature suggests that these different modes of data collection do not affect the comparability of the data (Robinson and Godbey 1997). Surveys also differ in terms of their response rate and the coverage of the twelve months of the year. In particular, while most surveys collected data during the twelve months of the year (to capture seasonal variations in patterns of time use), the time use surveys in Austria, Germany, the Netherlands, Sweden, and the United Kingdom collected data over a shorter period. This means that the average time use in these countries will not be fully comparable to the averages in the other countries.

The sample

Our analysis is restricted to young people eighteen to thirty-four years old. Across our nine countries, the corresponding samples vary between less than 500 people in the United Kingdom to more than 10,000 people in Italy. In the empirical part of the article, we distinguish between five main categories of young people:

TABLE 1
TIME USE SURVEYS

Country	Title of Survey	Year of Survey	Age Range	Number of Cases[a]	Response Rate (%)[b]	Type of Diary	Survey period
Austria	*Zeitverwendung*	1992	10 and older	24,901	47	One-day	Two months (March and September)
Canada[c]	Time Use (General Social Survey, Cycle 7)	1992	15 and older	8,996	77	One-day	Twelve months (January to December)
Finland[d]	Time Use Survey	1987-1988	10 and older	15,352	74	Two-day	Twelve months (April 1987 to March 1988)
Germany[e]	Time Budget Survey	1991-1992	12 and older	25,812	Quota	Two-day	Four months (October 1991 and January, April, and July 1992)
Italy[f]	*L'Uso del Tempo in Italia* (The Use of Time in Italy)	1988-1989	All	37,724	75	Two- or three-day	Twelve months (June 1988 to May 1989)
Netherlands[g]	*En Week Tijd* (One Week's Time)	1985	12 and older	3,263	54	Seven-day	One month (October)
Sweden[h]	Time Use Survey	1990-1991	20 to 69	7,140	75	Two-day	Two months (September 1990 and May 1991)
United Kingdom[i]	SCELI Time Use Survey	1987	17 to 74	1,198	70	Seven-day	One month (July)
United States[j]	American's Use of Time Project	1985	18 and older	4,934	55	One-day	Twelve months (January to December)

SOURCE: Fisher (2000).

a. Total number of complete diaries, with the exception of the Netherlands and the United Kingdom, where it refers to the number of respondents. The subsamples used in this article are smaller (see Table 2).

b. Response rate for the total sample.

c. A time use survey was also carried out in 1998. We used the 1992 survey since it was closer in time to the other surveys used in this article.

d. A time use survey was carried out in 1999-2000. The data were not available at the time of writing this article.

e. A new time use survey is currently in the field (2000-2001).

f. A new time use survey is scheduled to take place in 2002-2003.

g. Time use surveys were also carried out in 1990, 1995, and 2000. Data on family status are, however, not available in these more recent surveys. We used the 1985 survey from the harmonized 1975-1995 data set. However, we used the family status data from the old version of the data set.

h. A time use survey was carried out in 2000-2001. The data were not available at the time of writing this article.

i. This is the only survey for which a non–nationally representative sample was used. The sample was drawn from six labor market areas. Time use surveys were carried out also in 1995 and 1999. We used the 1987 survey since it was closer in time to the other surveys used in this article.

j. Time use surveys were carried out also in 1992-1994 and in 1998. At the time of writing this article, data from only the 1992-1994 survey were available. However, the survey does not include data on marital status.

1. Nonpartnered students without children,
2. Nonpartnered employed people without children,
3. Partnered employed people without children,
4. Partnered employed people with children under the age of fifteen, and
5. Nonemployed people (not students) with and without children.

We use the term "partnered" to cover both married and cohabiting couples. In this article, the transition from being single to being married or living as married (cohabiting) is considered as one single transition. These subgroups (apart from the fifth one) follow a traditional life course sequence, starting from still being in school, moving to getting a job, being partnered, and having children. We are not here suggesting that this traditional sequence is the dominant one in our sample. It is simply used as an analytical tool to categorize young adults and to single out specific transitions. More particularly, these subgroups will allow us to examine the transition from school to work, the transition from being single to being partnered, and the transition from childlessness to parenthood. The fifth subgroup (nonemployed, not student) is an exception, as it does not correspond to any specific transition. It was instead added to capture a nonnegligible proportion of young adults. In the analysis, we look at all the nonemployed young adults, regardless of the presence or absence of children, for men, while we restrict the analysis to nonemployed young adults with children

for women. The distribution of our sample across these five subgroups appears in Table 2.

For men, the largest subgroups are the nonpartnered employed people without children (subgroup 2) and the partnered employed people with children (subgroup 4). These two groups represent around 60 percent of all young men eighteen to thirty-four years old in the different countries. For women, the two largest groups are nonpartnered employed people without children (subgroup 2) and nonemployed people with children (subgroup 5). Together these two groups represent around 40 percent of all young women eighteen to thirty-four years old.[4] The residual category represents less than 25 percent of the total sample and encompasses nonpartnered students with children, partnered students with or without children, and employed lone parents. For women, the residual category also encompasses nonemployed people without children. The mean age of these young people varies across subgroups, with nonpartnered students being the youngest subgroup (data not shown). The differences in the mean age across subgroups obviously reflect the timing of the various transitions to adulthood.

Some additional information on the samples is as follows. First, the above subgroups do not explicitly take into account living arrangements. Unfortunately, the harmonized version of the time use survey does not contain a variable that would allow us to distinguish independent living from living with parents. While it may be reasonable to

TABLE 2

**DISTRIBUTION OF CASES BY STATUS, GENDER, AND COUNTRY
(AGES 18 TO 34) (IN PERCENTAGES)**

Status	Country (Year of Survey)								
	Australia (1992)	Canada (1992)	Finland (1987)	Germany (1992)	Italy (1989)	Netherlands (1985)	Sweden (1991)	United Kingdom (1987)	United States (1985)
Men									
Student, nonpartnered, no child[a]	8.5	11.1	11.4	17.2	12.9	13.1	6.8	3.7	6.8
Employed, nonpartnered, no child	40.2	31.5	31.4	35.5	35.4	18.0	36.2	23.2	29.7
Employed, partnered, no child	12.2	13.6	20.5	7.2	10.1	20.6	21.1	13.4	16.8
Employed, partnered, with children[b]	26.8	23.9	25.9	25.1	27.5	25.6	25.3	36.1	25.4
Nonemployed, not a student[c]	3.7	15.7	6.5	2.9	13.8	11.9	5.3	17.5	10.0
Other	8.6	4.1	4.4	12.1	0.4	10.8	5.4	6.1	11.3
Total	100.0	100.0	100.0	100.0	100.0	100.0	100.0	100.0	100.0
Number of cases	3,029	1,653	2,405	3,867	5,133	533	1,193	242	810
Women									
Student, nonpartnered, no child	5.8	7.3	15.2	13.2	12.3	10.3	4.7	2.3	6.4
Employed, nonpartnered, no child	26.7	19.9	21.5	26.7	20.2	16.7	21.7	15.0	23.6
Employed, partnered, no child	11.2	14.2	15.6	7.7	6.5	16.3	18.2	11.1	11.9
Employed, partnered, with children	15.3	15.1	27.1	17.3	18.1	11.5	26.7	17.1	18.6
Nonemployed, not a student, with children	24.7	25.9	8.1	17.0	24.1	29.9	14.6	44.2	17.2
Other	16.3	17.6	12.5	18.1	18.8	15.4	14.2	10.3	22.3
Total	100.0	100.0	100.0	100.0	100.0	100.0	100.0	100.0	100.0
Number of cases	3,392	1,640	2,416	3,787	5,076	514	1,155	237	822

NOTE: All results are based on weighted data. The number of cases refers to the number of complete diaries.

a. In most countries, student status was identified by a question about the main activity during the week prior to the survey. During the school months, full-time students are likely to report that their main activity is to be a student, even though they may also hold a part-time job. Diaries that were filled out during the school vacation are, however, likely to less accurately identify students. Students who filled out their diaries during the vacation may have declared themselves employed if they held a job or unemployed if they did not hold a job. Moreover, during the vacation, students who declared themselves students are likely to have recorded no hours studying or attending classes, thus reducing the overall mean time spent on education in our analysis. One solution would have been to restrict the analysis to nonvacation months. Unfortunately, the month of the survey was not coded in some of the surveys and/or this information is currently not available in the harmonized version of the data set.

b. The presence of children was established by using the variable *famstat* in the harmonized version of the data set. This variable identifies the presence or absence of resident children in the respondents' household. However, it does not specify whether the children are the respondents' own children.

c. The harmonized version of the data set coded respondents who were in the military service as not employed even though they may have reported hours of work during the week prior to the survey. In two countries, Austria and Sweden, we were able to identify these respondents and to recode them as employed if they reported hours of work. In the other countries, we were not able to identify such respondents (either the survey did not code such an employment status or the current version of the survey did not allow access to these data). If respondents who were in the military service were coded as not employed and if they reported some hours of work, their presence in this subgroup of young adults will have the consequence of inflating the mean time devoted to paid work by this subgroup of respondents.

161

assume that young people are living independently when they are partnered and/or have children (subgroups 3 and 4), this may not necessarily be the case for subgroup 2 (nonpartnered, employed, without children) and subgroup 1 (nonpartnered students). Furthermore, major cross-national differences in this respect are also likely (Fernandez Cordon 1997). Finally, we should mention that lone mothers do not appear as a distinct category in our analysis. If they are unemployed, they are part of subgroup 5 alongside partnered housewives. If they are employed, then they are in a residual category not considered in the article. In most surveys, the samples of lone mothers were too small to allow a separate analysis.

The categories of activities

With regard to the coding of the daily activities, most surveys have used variants of the typology developed by the Szalai team in the 1960s (Szalai 1972). In the time use archive, a harmonized forty-activity classification was constructed and applied to all surveys.[5] For the purpose of this article, these forty-activity codes were grouped into four major categories of activities: (1) paid work and education, (2) housework and child care, (3) leisure, and (4) personal activities (including meals, sleep, etc).

The method of analysis

Because most surveys collected a one-day diary, the method of analysis consists of constructing synthetic weeks. This is done by computing the

weekly averages of respondents having filled out their diaries on different days of the week and weighting the data so as to ensure an equal representation of every day of the week (Pentland, Harvey, and Lawton 1999). The assumption is that while data at the individual level may not accurately capture the individuals' average allocation of time, it does so at the aggregate level, when we compare subgroups of people who share similar demographic, social, and economic characteristics (Robinson 1977).[6] Finally, it should be noted that in addition to the day-of-the-week weights (see above), the data were also weighted to correct for undersampling and oversampling.[7]

RESULTS

In what follows, we first describe the overall pattern of time use of young adults as they make the transition to adulthood. We subsequently analyze each of the transitions separately. As explained in the introduction, our aim is to unravel cross-national regularities (if any) in the patterns of time use of young people as they acquire different adult statuses.

Overall patterns of time use

Young people eighteen to thirty-four years old devote, on average, 5.1 hours per day to paid work and education, 3.1 hours per day to housework and child care, 5.5 hours to leisure activities, and 10.2 hours to personal activities.[8] It should be stressed again that these are daily averages across the week and therefore take into account the different patterns of time use observed on weekdays and weekends.

The variation in the number of hours devoted to each of these four main types of activities, by gender, transition status, and country, appears in Figure 1. The cross-national similarities in the patterns of time use across the five subgroups of young adults are remarkable. There are cross-national differences in the levels, that is, in the number of hours devoted to each activity, but the patterns across subgroups are very similar.

Time spent on paid work and education shows a relatively flat pattern as young people make the transition from school to work and from being single to being partnered. Time spent on this category of activity, however, declines significantly for women with the transition to parenthood, while being unaffected for men. Not surprisingly, time spent on work and education is close to zero for the fifth subgroup (nonemployed, not student).

Time spent on housework and child care differs substantially between men and women. For men, the pattern across the five subgroups is relatively flat, with only a small increase associated with the transition to parenthood. For women, time spent on housework increases slightly with the transition to partnership and increases significantly with the transition to parenthood. Time spent on housework and child care is highest for women in the fifth category (nonemployed). Time spent on leisure activities shows a downward trend from the student

subcategory to that of parents for both men and women. Time spent on leisure is substantially higher for the fifth subgroup for men but not for women. Finally, time spent on personal activities is remarkably stable across subgroups. It is only slightly lower for parents with children.

Below, we discuss in more detail the changes in the patterns of time use associated with each transition. This more detailed analysis is based on results broken down by subcategories of activities instead of the four broad categories considered in Figure 1. The detailed tables, however, are not included in the article.

The transition from school to work

The impact of the transition from school to work on patterns of time use is captured in our data by comparing the patterns of time use of nonpartnered students (subgroup 1) with those of nonpartnered employed people (subgroup 2). For some young people, the transition from school to work is also accompanied by the transition to independent living. Unfortunately, and as explained earlier, the data do not allow us to distinguish young people living with their parents from young people living independently.

Not surprisingly, the transition from school to work is associated with a decrease in time spent on education and an increase in time spent on paid work. What is interesting to note, however, is that in all countries and for both genders, time spent on paid work by subgroup 2 exceeds time spent on education by subgroup 1. The difference is on average about

FIGURE 1
TIME SPENT ON VARIOUS ACTIVITIES BY YOUNG ADULTS
AGES 18 TO 34, BY GENDER, TRANSITION STATUS, AND COUNTRY

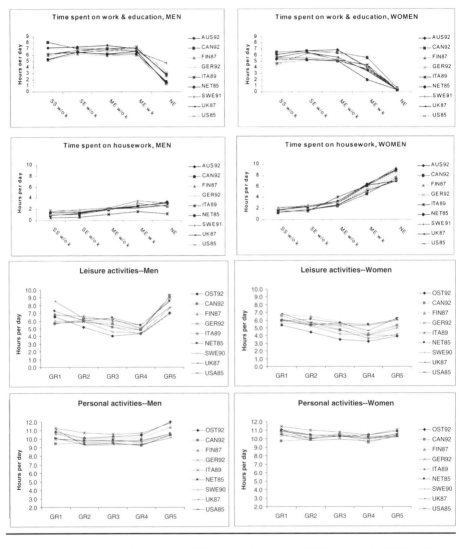

NOTES: OST92 = Austria (1992); CAN92 = Canada (1992); FIN87 = Finland (1987); GER92 = Germany (1992); ITA89 = Italy (1989); NET85 = Netherlands (1985); SWE90 = Sweden (1990); UK87 = United Kingdom (1987); USA85 = United States (1985); GR1 = nonpartnered students without children; GR2 = nonpartnered employed people without children; GR3 = partnered employed people without children; GR4 = partnered employed people with children under age fifteen; GR5 = nonemployed people (and not students) with and without children (for men) and with children (for women). All results based on weighted data.

two hours per day. On the other hand, if we combine both paid work and education, the difference between subgroups 1 and 2 is reduced to about one hour per day. If we define school and work as committed time (as often done in the time use literature), it therefore appears that nonpartnered employed young adults devote more time to this category of activity than their student counterparts do. When both education and paid work are considered, only Canadian men see a reduction in time spent on these combined activities with the transition from school to work.

The transition from school to work is also accompanied by a small increase in time devoted to housework in some countries. This is slightly more so for women (an increase of 0.2 hour) than for men (an increase of 0.1 hour per day). This increase may be capturing the transition to independent living and the corresponding increase in household responsibilities. In most countries, the transition from school to work is also accompanied by a small decrease in the number of hours devoted to personal activities (a decrease of about 0.5 hour per day). Nonpartnered employed young adults also devote less time to leisure activities than their student counterparts do (a decrease of 0.6 hour per day).

The transition from school to work therefore appears to have an impact on the patterns of time use of young adults, but a relatively small one. As will be seen below, other transitions have a larger impact on the allocation of time.

The transition from being single to being partnered

The transition from being single to being partnered is captured in our data by comparing nonpartnered employed people (subgroup 2) and partnered employed people (subgroup 3). We thus restrict the analysis to employed people and do not consider cases of withdrawal from the labor market after partnership. We furthermore consider all employed people, including full-timers and part-timers, to capture the possible impact of partnership on the allocation of time to paid work.

In most surveys, the transition from being single to being partnered does not appear to affect time devoted to paid work, on average, for men. The transition to partnership is, however, associated with a reduction in time devoted to paid work for women in Italy, the United Kingdom, and the United States. Likely, this represents a shift to part-time work for these women. In contrast, the transition to partnership is associated with an increase in time devoted to paid work for men in Germany, Sweden, and the United Kingdom.

The transition to partnership is also associated with a major increase in time devoted to housework by women, especially routine housework (such as cooking and cleaning). For men, the increase is mainly in nonroutine housework (such as do it yourself projects and gardening) (data not shown). Overall, time devoted to housework and child care increases by about 0.9 hour per day for women and 0.5 hour per day for men. For both men and women, the transition to partnership is furthermore associated with a decrease in the overall time devoted to leisure, but especially in time devoted to social leisure. The overall decrease in leisure is 0.5 hour per day for both men and women. Finally, in some countries, the transition to partnership is also accompanied by a slight increase in time devoted to personal activities.

Just like the transition from school to work, the transition from being single to being partnered does not radically alter the patterns of time use of young adults. The impact is, however, larger for women, with a decrease in time devoted to paid work (in some countries) and an increase in time devoted to housework (in all countries). Men's patterns of time use, in contrast, appear to be much less sensitive to changes in adult status (at least before the transition into parenthood).

The transition from
  childlessness to parenthood

The transition to parenthood is captured in our data by comparing partnered employed people without children (subgroup 3) and partnered employed people with children (subgroup 4). Again, we implicitly control for employment status and do not consider cases of withdrawal from the labor market associated with the transition to parenthood.

The transition to parenthood is marked by major changes in the patterns of time use of young adults, especially for women. Time devoted to paid work decreases for women in all countries, thus suggesting a switch to part-time work. The decrease in time devoted to paid

work is particularly large in the Netherlands (with a decrease of 3 hours per day) while being smaller in Canada. Likely, this cross-national difference is explained by cross-national differences in the opportunities for part-time work and in the financial possibility for couples to live on less than two full-time incomes. On the other hand, the transition to parenthood is associated with an increase in time devoted to paid work by men in Finland, Italy, the Netherlands, and the United States. The increase is strongest in the United States, with an increase of 0.8 hour per day.

The transition to parenthood is also associated with a major increase in time devoted to housework for women, especially child care, and only a small increase for men. The increase is about 2.7 hours per day for women (on average) and 0.7 hour per day for men. Conversely, the transition to parenthood is associated with a decrease in time devoted to leisure (around 0.7 hour per day). The decrease is especially noticeable in the social leisure category. The transition to parenthood is also associated with a decrease in the number of hours devoted to personal activities. This decrease is stronger for women than for men and reaches on average 0.3 hour per day.

Of all three transitions, the transition to parenthood is undeniably the one that has the largest impact on the patterns of time use of young adults. The birth (or adoption) of children entails responsibilities that require changes in the allocation of time that are much larger than the changes associated with the transition from school to work and the transition to partnership.

The nonemployed subgroup

As mentioned earlier, we define the nonemployed category differently for men and women. For men, we consider all nonemployed people regardless of family status, while for women, we restrict the analysis to nonemployed people with children. Moreover, unlike the above subgroups, we cannot interpret results for this subgroup in terms of transition. We simply analyze its patterns of time use in comparison with those of other subgroups.

Nonemployed men devote much more time to leisure than do any other subgroups. Time devoted to leisure reaches about eight hours per day, on average, as compared to about five or six hours for the other subgroups. Time spent on personal activities is also higher for this category of men, although just slightly higher than the comparable figure for students.

Nonemployed women spend their time in a very different way, simply because the subgroup is restricted to nonemployed women with children. Time spent on all forms of housework, including child care, is very high compared to the other subgroups. Time spent on housework and child care reaches about eight hours per day, as compared to about two hours per day for childless students. Time spent on leisure is low, although it is slightly higher than for employed women with children. Interestingly, while time freed by not being employed was reallocated to leisure for men, it was reallocated

mainly to housework for women. As mentioned above, the presence of children likely explains part of this difference.

Although time use data have rarely been used to describe the transition to adulthood, it is clear that the acquisition of various adult statuses has a major influence on the ways young adults use their time. These transitions are, however, experienced differently by men and women, with women experiencing larger changes in their patterns of time use as they gradually make their transition to adulthood.

CONCLUSION

From the onset, we expected patterns of time use to be strongly affected by the transition status of young adults. The changes in opportunities and constraints associated with the transition to adulthood could be expected, we argued, to result in distinct patterns of time use. The results turned out, however, to be much more complex than expected. In particular, the transition from school to work is not associated with drastic changes in the patterns of time use of young adults—at least when we combine the number of hours devoted to school and paid work. Employed young adults obviously devote more hours to paid work and less hours to education than their student counterparts do, but when these two categories of activities are combined, the changes are relatively small. In all countries, we found that nonpartnered employed people without children spend only slightly more time on paid work and education combined, as compared to nonpartnered students without children. On the other hand, nonpartnered employed people without children spend slightly less time on leisure activities and slightly less time on personal activities as compared to students—but again, the differences are small.

The transition from being single to being partnered is also not associated with major changes in the patterns of time use for men, with only a small increase in time devoted to housework and a small decrease in time devoted to leisure. For women, however, the transition to partnership is associated with a major increase in time devoted to housework and a decrease in time devoted to paid work in some countries.

Of all three transitions, it is the transition to parenthood that most significantly alters the patterns of time use, again more so for women than for men. Time spent on paid work and leisure decreases for women with the transition to parenthood, while time spent on housework and child care substantially increases. For men, the transition to parenthood is also associated with an increase in time devoted to housework and child care and a decrease in time devoted to leisure, but the changes are much smaller than for women.

From the onset, we also stated that we were interested in whether there were cross-national regularities in the changes in the patterns of time use associated with the transition to adulthood. Studies carried out in the 1960s suggested that the differences in the patterns of time use across social roles were much greater than those observed across countries. Our results suggest a similar conclusion. Across the nine countries analyzed in this article, the similarity in the changes in the patterns of time use associated with the transition to adulthood is striking. As pointed out, there are cross-national differences in levels, that is, in the number of hours devoted to each activity, but the cross-national similarities in the patterns of time use across the transition statuses are remarkable. The transition from school to work, the transition to partnership, and the transition to parenthood all translate into similar reallocation of time in the different countries under analysis. This is all the more remarkable considering the large cross-national differences in the timing of the transition to adulthood and the large cross-national differences in the social and economic context that surrounds the transition to adulthood.

At this point of the article, we have to stress again that our results are based on the comparisons of carefully selected subgroups to mirror some key transitions to adulthood and as such did not exploit the whole complexity and possible permutation of the transitions to adulthood. For instance, by restricting the analysis to employed partnered people when examining the transition to parenthood, we did not allow for withdrawals from the labor market after childbirth, and we did not allow for transition into parenthood for students and single mothers. Considering the numerous trajectories into parenthood (Blossfeld 1995), our analysis centered on the most traditional trajectories. This is an issue that we intend to address in future work.

There are a number of other issues that we also intend to address. First, our analysis is limited in not having taken into account cross-national differences in the timing of the transition to adulthood. By comparing key selected subgroups, and by thus controlling for adult status, we excluded the variable "age" from the analysis and did not examine separately early or late transitions into adulthood. Again, this is an issue that we intend to address in future work, especially considering the wide cross-national differences in timing of the transition to adulthood (Corijn 1999). We intend to examine the extent to which cross-national differences in the timing of key transitions to adulthood translate into different patterns of time use of young adults and the extent to which historical postponements in the transition to adulthood also translate into different patterns of time use of young adults.

Second, we need also to address more systematically other sources of cross-national variations in the patterns of time use of young adults. In our quest for macro-social regularities, we did not fully discuss the cross-national differences in the patterns of time use of young adults. Cross-national differences in the timing of the transition to adulthood and in patterns of time use may result from cross-national differences in opportunities, constraints, norms, and preferences. As such, the transition to adulthood may be affected by numerous macro-level factors such as employment opportunities for young adults, cost of housing, and various public policies. Future analyses should attempt to disentangle these various determinants.

Finally, in our quest for macro-social regularities, we have focused exclusively on country averages and have not examined intracountry variations in patterns of time use, including variations by social class and educational level. Again, this is something that we are planning to examine in the near future.

This article is obviously a first attempt at using time use data to shed light on the transition to adulthood. Time use data are a genuine window onto the everyday life of young adults, and as such, our program of research intends to open further this window to address some of the limitations outlined above.

Notes

1. Subjective and psychological indicators have also been used to study the transition to adulthood but do not include time use–based indicators.

2. The only exception found by Osgood and Lee (1993) is the age pattern of leisure done alone, which substantially differs with and without controls.

3. For comparative purposes, we selected years that were not too far apart. This resulted in surveys' having been carried out in the late 1980s and early 1990s. Note, however, that more recent surveys have been carried out in some of the countries analyzed in this article.

4. In Finland and Sweden, the two largest groups for both men and women are non-partnered employed people without children (subgroup 2) and partnered employed people with children (subgroup 4).

5. Details on the harmonized classification of activities may be found on the Multinational Time Use Study Web site: http://www.iser.essex.ac.uk/mtus/structure.php.

6. It should be noted, however, that such an assumption is not necessary in the case of the Netherlands and the United Kingdom since the results are based on seven-day diaries.

7. In most surveys, we used the weights provided by the statistical institute in charge of administering the survey. However, in the case of Italy and the United Kingdom, no weights were provided. For these two countries, we constructed some post hoc weights by using official data on the structure of the population by age and sex. It should be noted that while the weights ensure an equal representation of every day of the week for the total samples, the weighted distribution is not perfect once the data are broken down by gender and subgroup.

8. These are averages across the nine countries, nonweighted for differences in population size across countries but weighted to reflect the average structure of the population across the five subgroups analyzed in this article.

References

Alsaker, F. D., and A. Flammer. 1999. Time use by adolescents in an international perspective: II—The case of necessary activities. In *The adolescent experience: European and American adolescents in the 1990s*, edited by F. D. Alsaker and A. Flammer, 61-83. Mahwah, NJ: Lawrence Erlbaum.

Bianchi, S. M., and J. Robinson. 1997. What did you do today? Children's use of time, family composition, and the acquisition of social capital. *Journal of Marriage and the Family* 59 (2): 332-44.

Blossfeld, H.-P., ed. 1995. *The new role of women: Family formation in modern societies*. Boulder, CO: Westview.

Bynner, J., and S. Ashford. 1992. Teenage careers and leisure lives: An analysis of lifestyles. *Society and Leisure* 15 (2): 499-520.

Cantwell, M. L., and M. M. Sanik. 1993. Leisure before and after parenthood. *Social Indicators Research* 30:139-47.

Converse, P. E. 1972. Country differences in time use. In *The use of time: Daily activities of urban and suburban populations in twelve countries*, edited by A. Szalai, 145-78. Paris: Mouton.

Corijn, M. 1999. Transitions to adulthood in Europe for the 1950s and 1960s cohorts. Working paper no. 4, Centruum voor Bevolkings–en Gezinsstudie, Brussels, Belgium.

Duncan, K. A., and M. M. Sanik. 1991. Nine-nation typology: Application to adolescent time use. *Journal of Consumer Studies and Home Economics* 15:275-86.

Fernandez Cordon, J. A. 1997. Youth residential independence and autonomy: A comparative study. *Journal of Family Issues* 18:576-607.

Fisher, K. 2000. *Technical details of time use studies*. Release 2. Colchester, UK: Institute for Social and Economic Research, University of Essex. Retrieved from http://www.iser.essex.ac.uk/mtus/technical.php. 30 June.

Flammer, A., F. D. Alsaker, and P. Noack. 1999. Time use by adolescents in an international perspective: I—The case of leisure activities. In *The adolescent experience: European and American adolescents in the 1990s*, edited by F. D. Alsaker and A. Flammer, 33-60. Mahwah, NJ: Lawrence Erlbaum.

George, L. K. 1993. Sociological perspectives on life transitions. *Annual Review of Sociology* 19:353-73.

Gershuny, J. 2000. *Changing times: Work and leisure in postindustrial society*. Oxford, UK: Oxford University Press.

Herzog, A. R., R. L. Kahn, J. N. Morgan, J. S. Jackson, and T. C. Antonucci. 1989. Age differences in productive activities. *Journal of Gerontology: Social Sciences* 44 (4): S129-S138.

Iacovou, M. 1998. Young people in Europe: Two models of household formation. Working paper no. 98-13, Institute for Social and Economic Research, University of Essex,

Colchester, UK. Retrieved from http://www.iser.essex.ac.uk/pubs/workpaps/wp98-13.php

Juster, F. T., and F. P. Stafford. 1991. The allocation of time: Empirical findings, behavioral models, and problems of measurement. *Journal of Economic Literature* XXIX:471-522.

Larson, R. W., and S. Verma. 1999. How children and adolescents spend time across the world: Work, play, and developmental opportunities. *Psychological Bulletin* 125:701-36.

Marini, M. M. 1984. Age and sequencing norms in the transition to adulthood. *Social Forces* 63:229-44.

Mauldin, T., and C. B. Meeks. 1990. Gender differences in children's time use. *Gender Roles* 22 (9/10): 527-54.

Osgood, D. W., and H. Lee. 1993. Leisure activities, age and adult roles across the lifespan. *Society and Leisure* 16 (1): 181-208.

Osgood, D. W., J. K. Wilson, P. M. O'Malley, J. G. Bachman, and L. D. Johnston. 1996. Routine activities and individual deviant behavior. *American Sociological Review* 61:635-55.

Pentland, W. E., A. S. Harvey, and M. P. Lawton, eds. 1999. *Time-Use research in the social sciences.* New York: Plenum.

Robinson, J. 1991. It's 10 o'clock. Do you know where your teenager is? *American Demographics* 13 (10): 8-10.

Robinson, J. P. 1977. *How Americans use time: A social-psychological analysis of everyday behavior.* New York: Praeger.

Robinson, J. P., and S. Bianchi. 1997. The children's hours. *American Demographics* 19 (12): 20-24.

Robinson, J. P., P. E. Converse, and A. Szalai. 1972. Everyday life in twelve countries. In *The use of time: Daily activities of urban and suburban populations in twelve countries,* edited by A. Szalai, 113-44. Paris: Mouton.

Robinson, J. P., and G. Godbey. 1997. *Time for life; The surprising ways Americans use their time.* College Park: Pennsylvania State University Press.

Settersen, R. A. Jr. 1998. A time to leave home and a time never to return? Age constraints around the living arrangements of young adults. *Social Forces* 76:1373-1400.

Settersen, R. A. Jr., and K. U. Mayer. 1997. The measurement of age, age structuring, and the life course. *Annual Review of Sociology* 23:233-61.

Shanahan, M. J. 2000. Pathways to adulthood in changing societies: Variability and mechanisms in life course perspective. *Annual Review of Sociology* 26:667-92.

Szalai, A., ed. 1972. *The use of time: Daily activities of urban and suburban populations in twelve countries.* Paris: Mouton.

Timmer, S. G., J. Eccles, and K. O'Brien. 1985. How children use time. In *Time, goods, and well-being,* edited by F. T. Juster and F. P. Stafford, 353-82. Ann Arbor, MI: Institute for Social Research, University of Michigan.

ANNALS, *AAPSS*, **580**, March 2002

An International Comparison of Adolescent and Young Adult Mortality

By PATRICK HEUVELINE

ABSTRACT: This paper analyzes mortality rates for 3 of the main causes of deaths between the ages of 15 and 34 (motor vehicle injuries, homicide, and suicide) from 1950 to 1996, and across 26 countries. Average sex ratios and age patterns and the trends in age- and sex-standardized mortality rates are analyzed for each cause. Overall, youth violent mortality levels have been remarkably stable since the 1950s. As mortality due to other causes has receded, the contribution of these three causes has increased from 25 to 40 percent between the 1950s and the mid-1970s, and has remained above 40 percent since. Last, a principal component analysis is performed to summarize the variance in age-, sex-, and cause-specific rates over time and across countries. This summary representation of international differences displays regional clusters and emphasizes the "outlying" position of the United States among industrialized nations.

Patrick Heuveline's research interests center on population dynamics and family change. His current research includes a comparative project on the increasing complexity of childhood family experiences across industrialized countries and the impact of these experiences on child well being. Other projects in the developing world focus on how populations, and families in particular, cope with demographic crises. One current project looks at the demographic "recovery" in Cambodia after the Khmers Rouges. Another project under development will study the impact of the HIV epidemic on the reproductive regimes of high-prevalence populations in Eastern Africa.

NOTE: This research was supported in part by a start-up fund allocated by the Population Research Center from its National Institutes of Health grant. The comments and encouragement of Frank F. Furstenberg Jr. from the outset of this project are gratefully acknowledged. I would also like to thank Gail Slap and other participants of the Transition from Adolescence to Early Adulthood Workshop, where this article was first presented, for helpful comments and suggestions. Chi-Young Koh provided skillful assistance during the subsequent revisions.

I N his 1991 presidential address to the Population Association of America, Ronald Rindfuss brought attention to the high "demographic density" of the young adult years (there defined as ages eighteen to thirty). Marriage, fertility, migration, school leaving, and unemployment rates are all highest during these years, which attests "that major decisions and role changes in most areas of life are occurring during a relatively short, overlapping period" (Rindfuss 1991, 498). On the contrary, mortality rates are relatively low, rising only slightly from their minimum during childhood and being still much lower than later in life. In 1995, in the United States, the probability of surviving from age fifteen to age thirty-five was estimated to be 97.7 percent (Anderson, Kochanek, and Murphy 1997). The risk of death may not appear to constitute, on average, a salient aspect of the transition from adolescence to adulthood. Should an issue on the transition from adolescence to adulthood even have an article on mortality during these years? Or differently stated, Can we learn anything about this transition from mortality data?

One of the primary reasons for studying adolescents' and young adults' deaths in public policy circles is their unusual balance of higher than average societal costs and apparently more preventable causes. When productivity losses are added to direct medical care, the societal cost of early deaths rises compared to more frequent deaths at later ages. Deaths between age fifteen and thirty-five also exhibit a distinct set of causes. Again for the United States

in 1995, the top four causes of death at those ages were, in decreasing order, accidents and adverse effects, homicide and legal intervention, HIV infection, and suicide. Together, these four categories represented 70 percent of deaths in this age group compared to 8 percent of all-age deaths. While their overall mortality is low, adolescents and young adults contribute significantly to the societal costs of injury and violence, estimated in the United States at more than $224 billion per year (U.S. Department of Health and Human Services 2000).

That the bulk of adolescent and young adult mortality can be traced to fatal behavior, whether intentional or not, whether one's own or others' behavior, is also of interest to the social scientist. Because of this unique cause-of-death pattern, the social dimension of mortality is probably more transparent in this than in any other age group. Moreover, even if deaths remain fortunately rare, mortality levels are likely to be positively associated with the prevalence of other behaviors of sociological interest, often referred to as "problem behaviors," that are more common but also more difficult to assess. Mortality during these years is perhaps just as revealing of the "major decisions and role changes" taking place during these years as the peaks in fertility, migration, marriage, school leaving, and unemployment rates.

In this article, I review international trends in four major causes of death for adolescents and young adults (defined here as between the ages of fifteen and thirty-five): self-inflicted injuries, injuries intentionally inflicted by others, motor vehicle injuries (the main type of fatal injury at those ages), and HIV infection. I describe the age- and sex-pattern of mortality for each cause, draw temporal and international comparisons, and discuss to what extent these can be taken as markers of the difficulties associated with the transition from adolescence to adulthood.

THE DATA

Most of the data reviewed in this article are readily available from the World Health Organization (WHO) Mortality Database.[1] The database contains information on cause of death originally supplied by countries that have universal registration of deaths in conjunction with a high level of certification of cause of death. The first year of data is 1950, but the number of countries for which data are available gradually increases over time as more countries contribute to the database. The most recent year with data also varies by country. The most recent year is 1996, but for a significant number of countries, the reporting lag is one or a few years longer. Overall, approximately fifty to sixty countries report to WHO regularly, with national time series varying both in range and degree of completeness. In general, there are fairly complete time series for industrialized countries, notably countries in North America and Europe, Australia, New Zealand, and Japan.

For most analyses in this article, I retained all countries that reported at least thirty-five years of usable data on cause-specific mortality

between 1950 and 1996. The purpose of this restriction was to allow more meaningful time series analysis. Countries that contributed fewer years to the WHO Mortality Database typically reported only in more recent years, and these countries are potentially different from those having provided data for a longer period. Temporal comparisons could have been biased by the increasing heterogeneity of the countries in the database over time had such restrictions not been imposed.

The selected countries are shown in Table 1 with their year of available and complete data.[2] As expected, the majority of countries (eighteen) are in Europe. Japan, Australia, New Zealand, Canada, and the United States, but also Chile, Mexico, and Venezuela complete the list for a total of twenty-six countries. The cutoff of thirty-five years is arbitrary but was eventually selected as a threshold below which the number of available years for additional countries drops rapidly. Raising the bar to forty years would have excluded four countries (Greece and Mexico at thirty-six years, Venezuela at thirty-eight years, and Belgium at thirty-nine years), while lowering it to thirty years would have added only one (Uruguay at thirty-one years).

For the purposes of the analyses below, each entry in the database corresponds to a given country in a given year (1,128 observations) and consists of the number of deaths and death rates by sex, age group, and cause of death. Between the ages of fifteen and thirty-five, age is reported in five-year age groups. The cause of death is coded using a three-

TABLE 1

LIST OF COUNTRIES INCLUDED IN THE ANALYSIS WITH AVAILABLE YEARS OF DATA

Region and Country	First Year	Last Year	Years with Full Data	Missing or Incomplete Data
Asia (1)				
Japan	1950	1996	47	
Europe (18)				
Austria	1955	1996	42	
Belgium	1954	1992	39	
Czech Republic[a]	1953	1996	44	
Denmark	1951	1996	46	
Finland	1952	1995	44	
France	1950	1994	45	
Germany[b]	1952	1996	45	
Greece	1956	1996	36	1956-1960
Hungary	1955	1996	42	
Ireland	1950	1994	45	
Italy	1951	1993	43	
Netherlands	1950	1995	46	
Norway	1951	1995	45	
Portugal	1955	1996	42	
Spain	1951	1995	44	1970
Sweden	1951	1995	45	
Switzerland	1951	1994	44	
United Kingdom	1950	1996	47	
Latin America (3)				
Chile	1955	1994	40	
Mexico	1958	1995	36	1977, 1984
Venezuela	1955	1994	38	1984, 1991
North America (2)				
Canada	1950	1995	46	
United States	1950	1995	46	
Oceania (2)				
Australia	1950	1995	46	
New Zealand	1950	1994	45	
Total: Twenty-six countries			1,128	

a. The series for the Czech Republic consist of data reported as Czechoslovakia until 1991 and data reported as the Czech Republic thereafter.

b. The series for Germany consist of data reported as West Germany until 1990 and data reported as Germany thereafter.

character International Classification of Diseases (ICD) code, internally developed and maintained by WHO. The ICD has been revised ten times since its first formulation in the nineteenth century. The database was established after the sixth revision (ICD-6) of 1948. ICD-7 was published in 1955, ICD-8 in 1965, ICD-9 in 1975, and ICD-10 in 1992. Countries did not necessarily all adopt a new revision in the year it appeared, so the switch from one revision to the next is generally staggered.

The degree to which equivalent causes may be tracked from one revision to the next depends on the stability of a label, or for labels that change, it depends on the extent to which the causes subsumed in a label can be distinguished and identified in subsequent revisions. Table 2 shows the categories used in the different classifications to track trends in three causes of death discussed below: suicide, homicide, and motor vehicle injuries. Fortunately, those appear as fairly stable categories across classifications, and tracking these deaths over time is fairly straightforward. Even if mortality data are subject to relatively less variability in definition than most social data, misclassification is a potential issue here. In particular, countries vary in their certification procedures for homicide or suicide (Brooke 1974) and social values toward the latter. International differences in recorded rates might reflect differential reluctance or inefficiency in recording death from specific causes. To provide some data checks (discussed below), I included the "undetermined intent" and "other (than motor vehicle–related) unintentional injury" categories in the database (also shown in Table 2).

Finally, more general concerns about data quality are, as always, in order. The countries described here are believed to have complete death registration systems, and baring serious flaws in the chain of reporting to WHO, these data should be accurate. There was one cause of death though for which data were suspected to be potentially incomplete, namely HIV infection. Countries differ as regards their efforts to identify and report deaths from HIV-related causes. Time trends in reported HIV-related death may reveal more the process of gradual recognition of HIV/AIDS than the actual progression of the epidemic. The analysis of the HIV infection was based instead on the Joint United Nations Programme on HIV/AIDS (UNAIDS) estimates of the cumulative number of HIV-related deaths and adult HIV seroprevalence in each country as of the end of 1997 (UNAIDS 1998).

Because of the different nature of the data, HIV/AIDS data are discussed in a distinct section toward the end of the article. These data are then compared with mortality data from the above-discussed causes. Since the analysis including HIV data is de facto limited to 1980 and thereafter, additional countries could be considered for this part of the analysis only, that is, countries that did not meet the earlier data requirements but had acceptable data for nearly all years after 1980. Of particular interest were countries of eastern Europe because of the economic and social transformations that occurred in the past decade. Among those, only the Czech Republic and Hungary are included in the first analyses, but the satisfactory quality of their post-1980 data allowed the addition of Bulgaria, Poland, the Russian Federation, and Ukraine[3] in the later analyses.

TABLE 2

CAUSES OF DEATH: INTERNATIONAL CLASSIFICATION OF DISEASES (ICD)

	ICD-6 and ICD-7	ICD-8	ICD-9	ICD-10
All causes	B000 or A000	B000 or A000	B00	AAA
Motor vehicle injuries[a]	A000	A138	B471	CAR (car occupant death in traffic accident)
				BUS (occupant—bus—death in traffic accident)
				MCY (motorcycle rider death in traffic accident)
				RWT (all railway-related accident deaths)
				PED (pedestrian death in traffic accident involving a motor vehicle)
				PCY (pedal cyclist death in traffic accident involving motor vehicle)
				TEE (three-wheeled motor vehicle occupant death in traffic accident)
				VAN (occupant—pick-up truck or van—death in traffic accident)
				HTV (occupant—heavy transport vehicle—death in traffic accident)
				OFT (death in other land transport motor vehicle traffic accident)

(continued)

TABLE 2 Continued

	ICD-6 and ICD-7	ICD-8	ICD-9	ICD-10
Other unintentional injuries	A140 (accidental poisoning) A141 (accidental falls) A142 (accident caused by machinery) A143 (accident caused by fire and explosion of combustible material) A144 (accident by hot substance, corrosive liquid, steam, radiation) A145 (accident caused by firearm) A146 (accidental drowning and submersion) A147 (all other accidental causes)	A140 (accidental poisoning) A141 (accidental falls) A142 (injuries caused by fires) A143 (accidental drowning and submersion) A144 (accident caused by firearm missiles) A145 (injuries mainly of industrial types) A146 (all other injuries)	B48 (accidental poisoning) B49 (misadventures during medical care, abnormal reactions, etc.) B50 (accidental falls) B51 (injuries caused by fire and flames) B52 (other injuries: includes A142 in ICD-7; A143 and A144 in ICD-8) B53 (drugs, medicaments causing adverse effects)	ADR (accidental drowning and submersion) AEX (accidental exposure to untabulated causes) ABL (accidental contact with a blunt object) ASH (accidental contact with a sharp object) AFD (accidental firearm discharge) APO (accidental poisoning by noxious substance) AFI (accidental exposure to smoke, fire, and flames) AEL (accidental exposure to electric current) AHO (accidental contact with heat and hot substances) AXP (accidental explosions) AHS (accidental hanging, strangulation, and suffocation) AFA (accidental falls) AGA (accidental exposure to gases and vapors, etc.) AEU (accidental exposure to other specified and unspecified factors)
Suicide (and self-inflicted injury)	A148	A147	B54	SPO (suicide by self-poisoning) SDR (by drowning and submersion) SGS (by hanging, strangulation, and suffocation) SFD (by firearm discharge) SHO (by explosive material; smoke, fire, and flames; etc.) SSH (with a sharp object) SLM (by jumping or lying before a moving object) SMV (by crashing of motor vehicle) SUU (by other specified or unspecified means) SBL (with a blunt object) SGA (by self-poisoning by exposure to gases and vapors, etc.) SFA (by jumping)

Homicide (and injury purposely inflicted by other persons)[b]	A149 (includes death by legal intervention such as by police or execution)	A148 (includes legal intervention such as by police or execution)	B55 (death by legal intervention is excluded)	HFD (by firearm discharge) HHO (by explosive material; smoke, fire, and flames; etc.) HSH (by sharp object) HLM (by pushing or placing the victim before moving object) HFA (by pushing from high place) HDR (by drowning and submersion) HMV (by crashing of motor vehicle) HGA (by gases and vapors) HPO (by noxious substances) HBS (by bodily force, including sexual assault death) HHS (by hanging, strangulation, and suffocation) HBL (by blunt object) HNA (by neglect and abandonment and other maltreatment) HOU (by other specified or unspecified means)
Undetermined intent (whether accidental or purposely inflicted)	No category	A149	B561	UPO (poisoning, exposure to noxious substances, undetermined intent) UGA (exposure to other gases and vapors, undetermined intent) UHS (hanging, strangulation, and suffocation; undetermined intent) UDR (drowning and submersion, undetermined intent) UFD (firearm discharge, undetermined intent) UHO (exposure to explosive material, etc.; undetermined intent) USH (contact with a sharp object, undetermined intent) UBL (contact with a blunt object, undetermined intent) UFA (falling, jumping, or pushing from a high place; undetermined intent) ULM (falling, lying, or running before or into moving object; undetermined intent) UMV (crashing of motor vehicle, undetermined intent) UUU (other specified or unspecified event, undetermined intent)

SOURCES: World Health Organization (WHO), Division of Epidemiological Surveillance and Health Situation and Health Situation and Trend Assessment, WHO Mortality Database (http://www.who.int/whosis/mort/index.html); and WHO (1957).

NOTE: Classification in ICD-10 is drastically different from classification in previous revisions in that ICD-10 has much more detailed classification of "method of death" in each cause. Each cause of death is uniquely entered in three alphabetical characters. Selection and grouping was made according to the "ICD-10 Tabulation List Items Selected or Grouped for Publication of Causes of Death," available in World Health Statistics Annual (1996).

a. Motor vehicle injuries are defined as "any accident (except collision with aircraft) involving a motor vehicle, or happening to a person while entering or leaving a motor vehicle." Motor vehicles are defined as "any mechanically or electrically powered device, not operated on rails, upon which or by which any person or property may be transported or drawn upon a land highway," such as automobile, bus, construction machinery, farm machinery, fire engine, motorcycle, motorized bicycle, tractor, trolley, truck, or van.

b. In ICD-10, "homicide" excludes legal intervention.

TABLE 3
AVERAGE MALE TO FEMALE SEX RATIO, BY CAUSE OF DEATH

| | Age Group | | | | |
	15-34	15-19	20-24	25-29	30-34
All years combined					
All causes	2.1	2.2	2.4	2.0	1.8
Suicide	2.7	2.4	2.8	2.8	2.7
Homicide	4.7	4.1	5.0	5.0	4.7
Motor vehicle injury	4.2	3.3	4.8	4.7	4.4
All other causes	1.6	1.7	1.7	1.5	1.5
1955 to 1964					
All causes	1.7	1.9	1.9	1.6	1.5
Suicide	2.0	1.6	1.9	2.2	2.2
Homicide	4.9	3.6	5.1	5.4	4.9
Motor vehicle injury	5.4	3.9	6.5	6.4	5.6
All other causes	1.3	1.6	1.4	1.3	1.2
1985 to 1994					
All causes	2.7	2.6	3.0	2.7	2.4
Suicide	3.8	3.5	4.3	3.9	3.5
Homicide	5.2	5.4	5.9	5.1	4.7
Motor vehicle injury	3.7	3.0	4.1	4.0	3.8
All other causes	2.1	2.0	2.1	2.1	2.1

THE SEX AND AGE STRUCTURE
OF ADOLESCENT AND YOUNG
ADULT MORTALITY

Sex ratios of mortality by cause

The most salient feature of mortality in those ages is perhaps the high sex ratio of mortality from suicide, homicide, and motor vehicle injuries. The average mortality sex ratio between ages fifteen and thirty-five is 2.7 for suicide, 4.2 for motor vehicle injuries, and 4.7 for homicide (see Table 3). The average mortality sex ratio for all other causes of deaths (after subtracting these three major causes) is 1.6, leading to an all-causes mortality sex ratio of 2.1. For each of the three causes, the average sex ratio increases to a plateau between ages twenty and thirty, after which it declines slightly, whereas

the ratio is nearly constant over age for other causes of death. The distinct pattern of these three behavior-related causes of death is perhaps one of the clearest indications of the social dimension of gender differences. It also suggests that individuals' risk behavior is most gendered during their twenties.

The sex ratios of mortality from behavior-related causes could perhaps be expected to have declined over time with increased female enrollment in higher education institutions or labor force participation. I thus examined these sex ratios over time for the different causes of death. Changes seemed fairly linear over time and are summarized in Table 3 by comparing average ratios for the decade 1955 to 1964 with the most recent decade, 1985 to 1994. The most dramatic change has been indeed the declining sex ratio of mortality from motor vehicle injuries, from 6.5 to 4.1 between ages twenty and thirty. Meanwhile, the sex ratios of mortality from suicide were going in the opposite direction. While between 1955 and 1964, suicide sex ratios averaged between 1.6 and 2.2 across the four five-year age groups, they reached between 3.5 and 4.3 in the most recent decade.[4] Homicide trends are mixed: sex ratios increased between ages fifteen and twenty-five but declined between ages twenty-five and thirty-five.

Overall, sex ratios changed in different directions for each of the three causes of death and did not uniformly decline. In fact, for all causes combined, average mortality sex ratios have increased slightly over time between ages fifteen and thirty-five. Interestingly, the ratios seem to be converging to the extent that the sex ratios that were highest between 1955 and 1964 (motor vehicle injuries and homicide after age twenty-five) declined thereafter, while the other ratios increased. For example, in the earlier decade, the sex ratios between ages twenty-five and thirty ranged from 2.2 for suicide to 6.4 for motor vehicle injuries. In the more recent decade, the sex ratios in the same age group ranged from 3.9 for suicide and motor vehicle injuries to 5.1 for homicide.

Across countries, sex ratios are fairly similar for suicide mortality rates, ranging from 1.8 in Japan and 2.0 in the Netherlands to 4.0 in Chile, 4.1 in Ireland, 4.2 in Norway, and 4.4 in Finland (averages across all available years). No clear regional basis could be detected for these variations. For motor vehicle injuries, sex ratios are lower in the United States (3.6) and Canada (3.8) and were highest in southern Europe (Portugal: 8.1, Italy: 6.4), Japan (6.9), eastern Europe (Hungary: 6.8, the Czech Republic: 6.5), and Latin America (Chile: 6.7, Venezuela: 6.5, and Mexico: 5.9). But regional patterns are most clear for sex ratios of homicide rates. The sex ratios are by far the highest in Latin America (Mexico: 13.1, Venezuela: 11.3, and Chile: 10.2). The only other countries with ratios above four are in southern Europe (Italy: 4.4, Portugal: 4.1, and Spain: 4.0), whereas the ratios are lowest in Denmark (1.0) and Switzerland (1.0). As will be discussed in a section below, the countries with low ratios are also countries with low mortality from homicide, and the low ratios reflect low male mortality from homicide rather than high female mortality.

Age pattern of mortality by cause

The different age patterns by cause are shown in Table 4. For suicide and homicide, mortality is much lower before twenty, especially for males, whose average mortality rates from suicide and homicide roughly double after age twenty. For suicide, average mortality rates continue to increase slightly beyond age twenty and then remain about constant between ages twenty-five and thirty-five. For homicide, the plateau is between ages twenty and thirty, and then average mortality rates begin to decrease. The age pattern for motor vehicle injuries is quite different. For males, the average rates increase

TABLE 4
AVERAGE SEX AND AGE PATTERNS, ALL COUNTRIES AND YEARS

	Age Group				
	15-34	15-19	20-24	25-29	30-34
Male mortality rates (per 100,000)					
All causes	157.68	117.59	163.75	166.23	188.34
Suicide	16.68	9.15	19.03	19.79	19.52
Homicide	11.44	7.16	13.51	13.58	11.82
Motor vehicle injury	37.65	39.33	48.92	34.01	27.13
Female mortality rates (per 100,000)					
All causes	76.36	53.80	69.65	81.73	103.19
Suicide	6.19	3.84	6.85	6.98	7.25
Homicide	2.41	1.74	2.68	2.72	2.53
Motor vehicle injury	8.96	11.82	10.28	7.17	6.22
Population distribution (in percentages)					
Males	50.3	13.5	12.8	12.3	11.6
Females	49.7	13.0	12.7	12.3	11.7
Both sexes	100.0	26.5	25.5	24.6	23.3

after age fifteen to peak in the twenty to twenty-four age group and decline rapidly thereafter, whereas the average rates for females are already highest in the fifteen to nineteen age group. These three age patterns are also quite distinct from most other causes of death whose mortality rates increase at all ages.

The sex and age pattern in Table 4 reflects average rates across years and countries but not necessarily a uniform pattern. Further analyses suggest, however, that the pattern is fairly robust. This is illustrated in Table 5, which tabulates across all observations (country-year), the sex and age group in which mortality rates are highest for different causes of death.

For suicide, mortality rates are highest for males ages thirty to thirty-four in nearly half of the observations, the other half being divided evenly between males ages twenty to twenty-four and males ages twenty-five to twenty-nine. I further investigated whether these age-pattern variations corresponded to different periods. Preston (1984) reported that the age gradient after age twenty-five had become less pronounced in recent years in the United States, and a similar increase of young adult rates relative to older adults has been observed in other countries (Ruzicka 1995). This observation does not apply, however, to most countries in the database. On the contrary, both male and female average mortality rates from suicide peaked in the twenty to twenty-four age group between 1955 and 1964, whereas they increased with age between 1985 and 1994 (results not shown). In absolute terms, female

TABLE 5
**DISTRIBUTION OF PEAK SEX- AND AGE-SPECIFIC MORTALITY,
ACROSS ALL COUNTRIES AND YEARS (IN PERCENTAGES)**

Cause of death	Females, any age group	Males, 15-19	Males, 20-24	Males, 25-29	Males, 30-34
All causes	0.3	0.2	18.9	3.5	77.1
Suicide	0.3	0.1	26.2	26.1	47.4
Homicide	13.8	1.9	21.4	32.9	30.0
Motor vehicle injury	0.0	20.7	63.7	10.4	5.2

NOTE: $N = 1,228$ observations (1,233 for all causes combined).

rates strongly declined at all ages between 1955 and 1964 and between 1985 and 1994, however, whereas male rates increased except for the twenty to twenty-four age group.

Variations in mortality from suicide exhibit a geographical rather than a temporal pattern. Most countries contributing to an early peak are non-European countries. While for European countries, the average male mortality rates from suicide increase with age (from 15.3 per 100,000 between ages twenty and twenty-five to 19.4 between ages thirty and thirty-five), average rates for other countries decrease from the younger to the older age group (from 21.9 to 19.7 per 100,000). The different age gradient of young adult mortality from suicide may be related to a more gradual transition to adulthood in Europe, which is suggested by later median ages for home leaving, first union, or first birth.

Variations in the age pattern are larger for homicide. As shown in Table 5, males ages twenty-five to twenty-nine constitute the peak sex and age group for homicide in about 30 percent of country-year observations, whereas the mortality rates from homicide are highest for males

ages thirty to thirty-four in another 30 percent of the cases. Rates peak with younger males in about 20 percent of the observations but also with females (any of the four age groups) in nearly 14 percent of the cases. The variability of the peak sex- and age-specific rates can be explained in part by fairly low rates, typically on the order of 1 to 3 per 100,000, in all countries except Latin American countries and the United States.

These variations are also due to a visible shift in the male age pattern of homicide mortality. While on average, both male and female rates increased by about 75 percent between the 1955 to 1964 and the 1985 to 1994 decades, female rates increased similarly across all age groups. On the contrary, average male rates increased by about 50 percent after age twenty-five, while rates doubled between the ages of twenty and twenty-five and nearly tripled between the ages of fifteen and twenty (results not shown). Between 1955 and 1964, the average male age pattern exhibits a steep slope from 4.2 per 100,000 between ages fifteen and twenty to a peak at 10.7 per 100,000 between twenty-five and thirty. But between 1985 and

1994, the age slope was reduced to an increase from 11.4 to 16.7 per 100,000 across these two age groups, with the peak shifting earlier to ages twenty to twenty-five (18.1 per 100,000).

Finally, Table 5 shows a relative concentration of peak ages for mortality from motor vehicle injuries. The rates are highest for males ages twenty to twenty-five in nearly two-thirds of the observations, the rest being spread to adjacent male age groups. Latin American countries, Portugal, and Spain often exhibit a late peak. Japan and Nordic countries (Norway, Sweden, and Finland) often exhibit an early peak. Over time, as suggested by trends in sex ratios, average age-specific rates have increased for females in each age group, while they have declined for males except for the fifteen to nineteen age group.

To conclude this section, the average sex and age mortality patterns shown in Table 4 appear fairly robust over time and across countries. To be sure, there are some important deviations such as the decrease in the sex ratio of mortality from motor vehicle injuries, the shift in peak mortality from homicide toward younger ages, or the higher sex ratio of mortality from these two causes in Latin American and south European countries. But overall, Tables 3 through 5 also suggest some important common features across most years and countries, such as high sex ratios for each of the three causes, peak homicide mortality between ages twenty and thirty, and peak mortality from motor vehicle injuries between ages twenty and twenty-five. Because of

these marked sex and age patterns of mortality, the rest of the article addresses temporal and international differences in mortality levels by comparing sex- and age-standardized mortality rates for each cause. The sex and age distribution used as the standard is the average distribution in the population of the database and is also shown in Table 4.

TRENDS IN LEVELS OF ADOLESCENT
AND YOUNG ADULT MORTALITY

For each five-year interval between 1955 and 1994, average standardized mortality rates from each cause are reported in Table 6. To check whether the average trend represents a uniform experience across countries, Table 7 displays the period in which each national time series reaches its maximum and minimum values for each cause of death.

The clearest trend is for mortality rates from motor vehicle injury. The average rates increased rapidly between 1955 and 1964 to reach a maximum between 1965 and 1974 and then declined in the 1980s and 1990s (see Table 6). This trend is fairly uniform across countries since all countries reached their lowest rate either before 1961 or after 1992, while twenty countries out of twenty-six reached their peak year between 1968 and 1978 (see Table 7). Some countries have only recently succeeded in reducing mortality from motor vehicle injury, but with the exception of Greece, recent mortality rates fell significantly below their period peak. Seven countries (Canada, the United States, the Czech Republic, Sweden, Switzerland, the

TABLE 6

MORTALITY TRENDS BY CAUSE, 1955 TO 1994 (STANDARDIZED RATES PER 100,000)

Time Period	Suicide	Homicide	Motor Vehicle Injury	All Causes	Share of the Three Causes (%)
1955-1959	13.00	4.50	20.51	145.02	26.2
1960-1964	10.92	5.85	22.73	133.56	29.6
1965-1969	9.95	5.93	26.86	126.95	33.7
1970-1974	11.03	7.54	28.23	124.69	37.5
1975-1979	12.23	7.33	26.53	110.36	41.8
1980-1984	11.99	7.72	24.80	102.09	43.6
1985-1989	11.44	8.45	22.40	97.31	43.5
1990-1994	10.83	9.93	20.63	96.83	42.7

TABLE 7

PEAK AND TROUGH YEARS IN MORTALITY TIME SERIES, BY CAUSE (NUMBER OF COUNTRY PER PERIOD)

Period	Country-Year of Data	Suicide		Homicide		Motor Vehicle Injury	
		Trough	Peak	Trough	Peak	Trough	Peak
1950-1955	102	8	1	7	1	15	0
1956-1960	123	2	1	6	2	3	0
1961-1965	130	2	1	4	1	1	1
1966-1970	129	3	2	4	2	0	6
1971-1975	130	3	0	1	3	0	11
1976-1980	129	0	3	3	2	0	3
1981-1985	128	0	7	0	3	0	1
1986-1990	130	1	6	0	3	0	3
1991-1996	121	7	5	1	9	7	1

United Kingdom, and Australia) even reached their lowest mortality rates in the 1990s.

A quite different trend is visible for mortality from homicide. Average standardized rates first went up, remained at a plateau during the 1970s and early 1980s, then increased again. Overall, average rates nearly doubled between the late 1950s and the early 1990s. Although not quite as uniform as for motor vehicle injuries, the trend in average rates is applicable to a majority of countries. Every country but one enjoyed its lowest rate before 1977, half of them in the 1950s. Japan is unique for reaching its highest rate in 1955, as well as for reaching its lowest mortality rate in 1995, whereas half the countries reached their highest rate in one of their last ten years of data. The plateau in the average rate is due in part to the fact that some countries did experience an increase in homicide mortality in the 1970s but did not in the 1990s. Their mortality rate thus peaked in the mid- to late 1970s (Canada, Austria, Finland, Portugal, and the United Kingdom).

The trend for suicide is more difficult to characterize. The average standardized rate appeared to decrease in the 1960s, increase in the 1970s, and then decrease in the 1980s and 1990s. There is, however, a lot of variability in country-specific trends. Eighteen countries reach their highest mortality rates after 1982, in a period of average rate decline. But eight countries also reached their lowest mortality rates after 1987: besides Japan, Venezuela, and Portugal, there are five countries in northern and central Europe (the Czech Republic, Hungary, Austria, Germany, and Denmark). By contrast, Canada, the United States, Australia, New Zealand, and six countries in northern and western Europe (France, Belgium, the Netherlands, the United Kingdom, Norway, and Sweden) had their lowest rate in the 1950s.

Again, the mortality trends from these three causes are different from one another but also quite distinct from the other causes of death between ages fifteen and thirty-five. Overall mortality has declined almost linearly since 1950, and the upswings in mortality from motor vehicle injuries, suicide, or homicide only reduced the pace of the decline in one period or another. Between the late 1950s and the early 1990s, average standardized mortality rates from all causes combined declined by a third. Meanwhile, the sum of the mortality rates from the three causes reviewed above—driven by the predominant mortality from motor vehicle injury—increased through the mid-1970s and only slightly decreased thereafter. Overall, the average standardized mortality rate for three causes combined increased by 9 percent, while the corresponding rate for the other causes of death declined by 48 percent. As a result, the contribution of these three causes of death to overall mortality between ages fifteen and thirty-five has risen from 26 percent in the late 1950s to 43 percent from the late 1970s on (see Table 6). When AIDS-related mortality is incorporated (see section below), the increasing contribution over time of behavior-related mortality during the transition to adulthood is even more striking.

INTERNATIONAL VARIATIONS IN
LEVELS OF ADOLESCENT AND
YOUNG ADULT MORTALITY

As in the previous section, international comparisons in mortality levels are drawn from standardized rates to control for differences in the sex and age distribution. In addition, the preceding section has demonstrated some important time trends. To avoid bias due to missing values in early or late years, international comparisons are based on the forty-year average between 1955 and 1994. As shown in Table 1, most countries have data for each year between 1955 and 1994 except Greece (1955 to 1960 missing or incomplete), Mexico (missing 1955 to 1957, 1977, and 1984), Venezuela (missing 1984 and 1991), Belgium (1993 and 1994 not yet available), Spain (missing 1970), and Italy (1994 not yet available).

TABLE 8
**AVERAGE STANDARDIZED MORTALITY RATES,
BY COUNTRY AND BY CAUSE, 1955 TO 1994 (RATES PER 100,000)**

Country	Suicide		Homicide		Motor Vehicle Injury		Three Causes Combined (Rate)
	Rate	Rank	Rate	Rank	Rate	Rank	
Spain	3.66	3	0.81	1	17.46	9	21.93
Chile	8.01	10	4.52	23	10.33	1	22.86
United Kingdom	6.72	8	1.19	8	15.77	5	23.68
Norway	10.47	11	0.95	3	13.18	2	24.6
Netherlands	6.6	7	0.95	3	17.13	8	24.68
Ireland	6.48	6	0.93	2	17.71	12	25.12
Greece	3.13	2	1.12	7	21.2	14	25.45
Italy	4.21	4	2.01	18	21.35	15	27.57
Sweden	15.02	20	1.22	10	15.17	4	31.41
Japan	18.26	22	1.2	9	13.94	3	33.4
Portugal	6.17	5	1.51	16	25.77	17	33.45
Denmark	14.93	19	1.02	5	18.03	13	33.98
Czech Republic	16.44	21	1.42	15	17.54	10	35.4
France	11.77	13	1.32	13	27.61	18	40.7
Belgium	10.86	12	1.26	11	28.74	19	40.86
Switzerland	18.88	24	1.04	6	22.48	16	42.4
Hungary	24.21	26	2.44	20	15.94	6	42.59
Finland	23.91	25	2.88	22	17	7	43.79
Germany	14.82	18	1.31	12	29.08	20	45.21
Canada	13.81	17	2.65	21	29.91	21	46.37
New Zealand	12.26	15	1.94	17	33.49	24	47.69
Australia	13.19	16	2.28	19	33.35	23	48.82
Mexico	3.07	1	30.85	26	17.59	11	51.51
Austria	18.65	23	1.41	14	34.43	25	54.49
United States	12.22	14	14.06	24	33.11	22	59.39
Venezuela	7.83	9	19.39	25	35.03	26	62.25

The average standardized mortality rates for each cause and country are presented in Table 8 (in ascending order of mortality from the three causes combined). The list of countries at the top of the table is somewhat disparate, including southern European countries (Spain, Greece, and Italy), northern European countries (the United Kingdom, Ireland, Norway, and the Netherlands), and Chile. These countries form a heterogeneous group in part because they rank near the top for different causes of death. Southern European countries and Ireland have relatively low mortality rates from suicide, whereas northern European countries and Chile have relatively low mortality rates from motor vehicle injuries.

With the exception of Austria, countries at the bottom of the table are predominantly non-European (Canada, the United States, Australia, New Zealand, Mexico, and Venezuela). For all countries but Mexico, the high combined rate is largely due to high mortality rates from motor vehicle injury, which is the most frequent cause of death of the three included here. High mortality rates from homicide explain the low position of Mexico and, combined with motor vehicle injuries, the bottom positions of the United States and Venezuela. The surprising position of Austria—its combined rate is 20 percent higher than that of Germany, the closest other European country—results from a combination of high mortality from both motor vehicle injuries and suicide.

As often observed and challenged, Catholic countries have the lowest mortality rates from suicide: seven of them (Mexico, Spain, Italy, Portugal, Ireland, Venezuela, and Chile) are here among the ten countries with the lowest rates. Whether this corresponds to lower mortality from suicide or to some lower propensity to report this mortality in the appropriate category remains a contested issue (e.g., Simpson 1998; van Poppel and Day 1996, 1998). In an attempt to detect such inappropriate reporting, I included in the database death rates from causes with undetermined intent and from other unintentional injuries (non–motor vehicle related), two likely candidates for concealed deaths from suicides. Analyses of these two sets of mortality rates do reveal a negative correlation, across sex and age groups, between mortality rates from suicide and both undetermined causes and other unintentional injuries, which is consistent with the suspicion of suicide misreporting in these two sets of causes. The correlation was almost entirely due, however, to the three

Latin American countries. When compared to the other industrialized countries, European Catholic countries (Ireland, Italy, Spain, and Portugal) do not exhibit any significantly different mortality rates from undetermined causes and from other unintentional injuries. Their average mortality rates from the former are actually lower, while their average mortality rates from the latter are higher than those of other European countries but lower than those of the United States and Canada (none of the differences' being significant).

The three Latin American countries do exhibit much higher mortality rates from these two sets of causes. Not having any non-Catholic developing countries in the database, the hypothesis of a Catholic bias cannot be tested. Without inferring any such bias, higher mortality rates from other unintentional injuries are plausible, however, while higher mortality rates from undetermined causes could result from genuine (i.e., nonintentional) differences in death certification procedures. In any event, Latin American mortality rates from suicide should be considered with caution and probably not be interpreted at this stage. But low mortality rates from suicide in European Catholic countries seem to reflect a real difference in the incidence of fatal suicide rather than a statistical artifact. In any event, one finds at the other end of the range of mortality rates from suicide central European countries (Hungary, Austria, Switzerland, and the Czech Republic), northern European countries (Finland, Sweden, and Denmark), and Japan.

The distribution of mortality rates from homicide is much more skewed. At the lower end, Japan and fifteen European countries have average standardized rates ranging from 0.81 and 1.51 per 100,000 (see Table 8). The rates are higher in three European countries (Italy, Hungary, and Finland) and four non-European countries (Canada, Australia, New Zealand, and Chile). Finally, three American countries (the United States, Venezuela, and Mexico) clearly stand out for their mortality rates from homicide, five, seven, and eleven times higher, respectively, than the highest rate in a European country (Finland).

Motor vehicle injuries contribute most to mortality between ages fifteen and thirty-five (except in Mexico), but the international variations are smaller than for mortality rates from suicide (in relative terms) and from homicide (both in relative and absolute terms). Countries with low average rates of mortality from motor vehicle injuries form a disparate group. Except for Spain, European countries are mostly from northern Europe (the United Kingdom, Ireland, the Netherlands, Denmark, Norway, Sweden, and Finland) or from central Europe (the Czech Republic and Hungary), while outside Europe, Japan, Chile, and Mexico also have low average rates. This disparate group seems to be composed of two distinct sets of countries. In the first one, including countries such as Spain, Hungary, and Mexico, rates used to be low but have been increasing in more recent years, perhaps reflecting the trend in motor vehicle density. On the contrary, in other countries such as Sweden, the Netherlands, and the United Kingdom, mortality rates from motor vehicle injuries are declining from high levels in the early 1970s, probably due in part to changes in regulations and safety devices. At the high end of mortality rates, Austria is the only European country, joining Canada, the United States, Australia, New Zealand, and Venezuela. Except for the last two, non-European countries seem to be closing the gap, however, after having led the increasing mortality trend in the late 1960s and early 1970s.

HIV/AIDS MORTALITY

The above database and analytical strategy is not appropriate for the study of HIV/AIDS mortality. Data quality is in general lower for AIDS-related mortality. Because the eventual death of an HIV-infected person results from some additional, opportunistic infection, the certification of death from AIDS-related causes is complex. Although there have been guidelines in classifying causes of deaths as AIDS-related, some international variation likely remains in the certification process. These differences are amplified by the stigma often still attached to the virus, which may lead to avoiding classifying a death as AIDS related, much more than is now the case for suicide, for example.

A second important difference from the standpoint of this study lies in the lag between the incidence of HIV infection and death from AIDS-related causes. Until recently, the median duration from HIV infection to AIDS was about ten years, while the median survival with AIDS was about two years, but recent medical developments have considerably improved the survival of HIV-infected people. The reason to include AIDS-related mortality in this analysis is not simply the sheer mortality impact between ages fifteen and thirty-five, even though in several industrialized countries AIDS-related mortality is ranking among the top causes of death in this age group. The reason is rather that many HIV infections are acquired in this age group so that irrespective of the exact age at death, a premature death can be related to behavior in the age group of interest here. The argument could actually be extended to several other problem behaviors, such as abuse of alcohol, cigarette smoking, or illicit drug consumption, which may result in later life mortality but are often developed in adolescence or early adulthood (see Eisner 2002 [this issue]). The argument remains most convincing for HIV/ AIDS, however, since mortality in the young to middle adult years is low on average so that most HIV infection would end with a premature death from causes directly related to the infection.

HIV incidence in this age group is thus more relevant to this study than is AIDS-related mortality. Unfortunately, data on HIV incidence (new infections) over time is not routinely available for a large number of countries. Recorded trends are often distorted by the fact that they capture the dynamics of the epidemic as well as progress made in tracking and testing HIV-positive people. As a result, the most reliable time series are reconstructed from estimates of the number of currently infected persons and back-calculation of the time of infection (Brookmeyer and Gail 1994).

In this section, I use data from UNAIDS, which regularly estimates the number of HIV-infected persons alive and the cumulative number of deaths from AIDS-related causes for every country in the world. The most recent data at this writing refer to the end of 1997 and are shown in the second two columns of Table 9. The data are not as detailed as the mortality data discussed in previous sections, nor perhaps as one could obtain from national statistical offices from a few of the countries. These estimates have the advantage of originating from a single source, however, and are thus more likely to be comparable across countries.

The estimates of HIV-positive persons are provided for adults and infants, and only the number of HIV-positive adults is reported in Table 9, adults being defined here as between the ages of fifteen and fifty. The numbers of deaths from AIDS-related causes are not available separately for infants and adults. In the countries considered here, however, high sex ratios of HIV infections (typically four males per female), low birth rates, and mother-to-child transmission rates on the order of one in four all contribute to a relatively small number of infant deaths among AIDS-related deaths. The sum of (1) the number of HIV-positive adults alive and (2) the cumulative number of deaths from AIDS-related causes should hence provide a fair

TABLE 9
CUMULATIVE HIV/AIDS STATISTICS, BY COUNTRY, END OF 1997

Country	HIV-Infected Adults	Total AIDS Deaths	Adult HIV-Incidence Ratio (per Thousand)	Annualized Incidence Ratio (per 100,000)	Average Mortality Rates from Three Causes Since 1980
Japan	6,800	1,700	0.14	0.76	25.36
Bulgaria	300	0	0.07	0.40	28.13
United Kingdom	25,000	13,000	1.35	7.48	22.12
Czech Republic	2,000	200	0.41	2.28	27.52
Chile	15,000	2,900	2.31	12.83	20.53
Sweden	3,000	990	0.97	5.37	28.56
Norway	1,300	500	0.83	4.60	29.59
Netherlands	14,000	4,700	2.28	12.69	22.37
Ireland	1,700	360	1.11	6.17	30.47
Poland	12,000	490	0.61	3.39	35.00
Greece	7,500	1,300	1.69	9.36	32.05
Germany	35,000	13,000	1.17	6.50	35.94
Denmark	3,100	1,800	1.88	10.45	32.53
Finland	500	210	0.28	1.54	44.09
Hungary	2,000	200	0.43	2.40	46.46
Italy	90,000	31,000	4.18	23.23	27.74
Australia	11,000	6,000	1.78	9.87	43.91
Belgium	7,200	1,700	1.75	9.71	46.37
Austria	7,500	1,500	2.14	11.90	49.4
Canada	43,000	11,000	3.39	18.84	42.64
New Zealand	1,300	530	0.97	5.40	56.11
Spain	120,000	33,000	7.32	40.68	28.18
Switzerland	12,000	5,100	4.59	25.52	43.45
France	110,000	35,000	4.94	27.45	43.39
Ukraine	110,000	240	4.33	24.05	47.95
Russian Federation	40,000	190	0.52	2.88	74.52
Mexico	180,000	91,000	5.42	30.13	52.79
Portugal	35,000	3,900	7.79	43.28	41.83
Venezuela	81,000	6,600	7.38	41.00	64.16
United States	810,000	410,000	8.69	48.29	59.29

SOURCE: Joint United Nations Programme on HIV/AIDS (1998).

approximation of the total number of adult HIV infection since the onset of the epidemic. On one hand, the total is slightly inflated by the inclusion of child deaths. On the other hand, the total does not include HIV-infected adults who might have died of causes unrelated to their infection.

The next column in Table 9 presents the ratio of the cumulative number of adult HIV infections to the size of the adult population, as of the end of 1997. The term "ratio" is used to emphasize that this quantity does not directly relate occurrences to exposure as opposed to the mortality rates used in previous sections. Yet, in the last two columns of Table 9, I attempted to present adult HIV-infection data and other mortality data in comparable metrics. The adult HIV-infection figure is an annualized ratio; that is, the above ratio divided by eighteen—the number of years between an estimate of the onset of the epidemic (end of the 1970s) and the end of 1997—and expressed in per 100,000 as mortality rates. The denominator is then a crude measure of exposure to HIV infection in the adult population since 1980. On one hand, the annualized ratio uses eighteen times the 1997 adult population instead of person-years of exposure in the adult population between 1980 and 1997, introducing an overestimation bias likely to be small since population growth is slow in most of these countries. On the other hand, the adult (fifteen to fifty) HIV-infection rate likely underestimates the corresponding rate for people ages fifteen to thirty-five.

On balance, the annualized ratio should be reasonably comparable to the HIV-infection rate between ages fifteen and thirty-five, an expectation supported by additional data from the United States. According to UNAIDS data, by the end of 1997, there had been about 1.23 million people infected by the virus in the United States, that is, nearly 70,000 per year between 1980 and 1997. Typically, age at the time of infection is unknown but can be assessed backward from age at the time of death. In 1995, 30,754 out of 43,115 death from AIDS-related causes occurred between the ages of twenty-five and forty-five (Anderson, Kochanek, and Murphy 1997). If we assume a uniform duration from infection to death of ten years, the proportion of all HIV infections that occurred between ages fifteen and thirty-five is about 70 percent. These approximations lead to an estimate of about 49,000

HIV infections between the ages of fifteen and thirty-five between 1980 and 1997, which compares with an estimate from the mortality database of 47,396 deaths from suicide, homicide, and motor vehicle injuries in the United States, on average, between 1980 and 1995. The comparison suggests that in the United States, the average HIV ratio should be about as high as the average mortality rates from the three causes combined. The annualized ratio for the United States is actually 20 percent lower than the three-cause mortality rate (48.29 per 100,00 versus 59.59 per 100,000). For the United States, the annualized ratio appears to be a conservative estimate of average HIV-infection rates since 1980 between ages fifteen and thirty-five but to be reasonably comparable to the average standardized mortality rates.

In Table 9, the annualized ratio is compared with an average standardized mortality rate for the three causes combined (suicide, homicide, and motor vehicle injuries) and computed only for available data after 1980. As mentioned in the Data section above, the restriction of the analysis to those years allows the inclusion of four countries in addition to those presented in Table 1: Bulgaria, Poland, the Russian Federation, and Ukraine. For the three causes of death analyzed so far combined, the post-1980 rate for Bulgaria is low, close in that respect to the Czech Republic, while the rate for Poland is near the average and slightly lower than the rate for Hungary. The rates are quite high for the two countries from the former Soviet Union,

Ukraine, and the Russian Federation. The latter has the highest post-1980 average rate for the three causes combined across the thirty countries included here, and recent data are even more worrisome. The average standardized rates increased for each cause between the 1980s and the early 1990s (1990 to 1995): from 25.9 to 32.3 per 100,000 for suicide (+25 percent), from 22.1 to 32.3 per 100,000 for motor vehicle injuries (+46 percent), and from 13.8 to 29.7 per 100,000 for homicide (+115 percent).

The annualized HIV ratio suggests a high incidence of HIV infection relative to mortality rates from the three causes combined in a number of countries. Besides in the United States, the HIV ratio approaches the three-cause mortality rate in Italy, Switzerland, France, Mexico, and Venezuela; it even surpasses it in Portugal and, foremost, in Spain. Countries in Table 9 were reordered based on the sum of the HIV ratio and mortality rate from the three causes combined. If the HIV ratio was exactly equivalent to the sex- and age-standardized rates, that sum would measure the average sex- and age-standardized rates of HIV infection and death from suicide, homicide, and motor vehicle injuries combined between ages fifteen and thirty-five from 1980 on.

The top third of Table 9 is dominated by northern European countries (the United Kingdom, Ireland, the Netherlands, Norway, and Sweden) but also includes Japan, Bulgaria, the Czech Republic, and Chile. To the extent that we can relate differences in behavior-related mortality to well-being, the presence of these three very different countries seems to indicate that adolescent and young adult well-being can be improved under very different socioeconomic and cultural conditions. This is confirmed by the bottom position of the United States, just below Ukraine, the Russian Federation, Mexico, and Venezuela. As opposed to Table 8, the bottom third of Table 9 now includes southwestern European countries. When the risk of HIV infection is added, Portugal, Spain, France, and Switzerland now fall below non-European countries such as Australia, New Zealand, and Canada.

INTERNATIONAL DIFFERENCES
AND UNDERLYING CAUSES

In the introduction, I underscored that adolescent and young adult mortality was dominated by causes of death related to behavior, whether one's own or not, and whether intentionally fatal or not. To suggest that mortality rates from such causes do reveal something about the transition to adulthood is to assume implicitly that such mortality can be related to some underlying social dimensions. The tables above clearly exhibit marked international differences, but they force comparisons to a monodimensional scale. An alternative way to explore the international differences without preimposing the number of dimensions is to perform a principal components analysis. Each observation in the mortality database (i.e., a country in a given year) is a point in a thirty-two-dimension space, composed of both four age groups for each sex and, for each age-and-sex group, mortality rates from four causes: suicide, homicide, motor vehicle injuries, and other unintentional injuries.[5]

Results shown in the appendix (the first six components only), confirm that there are some strongly invariant elements in age-, sex-, and cause-specific mortality. The thirty-two-dimension space can be reduced to five principal dimensions that account for 95 percent of the database variance. The first component, accounting for 35 percent of the variance, essentially separates suicide rates at all ages and for both sexes from other mortality rates. Mortality from motor vehicle injuries exhibits for each sex a clear age gradient along that component with rates at younger ages closer to mortality rates from suicide and rates at older ages closer to mortality rates from homicide and other unintentional injuries. As young drivers are more frequently involved in motor vehicle accidents, this age effect may reflect a decrease with age of the proportion of motor vehicle fatalities in which the victim was actually driving. Mortality rates at younger ages may then be more closely related to their own behavior (as in the case of suicide), whereas at older ages these rates are more dependent on other drivers' behavior (as in the case of homicide). The first dimension thus seems to capture a distinction between intentional, self-inflicted injuries and unintentional injuries or injuries inflicted by others.

The second dimension appears to represent a weighed sum of the three risk profiles (suicide, homicide, and motor vehicle injuries), as the corresponding mortality rates are separated from other unintentional, arguably more genuinely "accidental" injuries. The second dimension explains another 24 percent of the total variance in youth mortality. The main deviation in age- and sex-group loadings on the second dimension concerns sex differences in mortality rates from homicide. Male rates appear relatively less associated with that dimension than do female rates, and male homicide rates appear closer to mortality rates from unintentional injuries especially at older ages. Although we know that most homicides stem from encounters between a criminal and a victim who know each other, this result may reflect the higher proportion of homicide by strangers that may affect males in high-crime areas.

The next two principal components isolate specific causes of death, motor vehicle injuries and homicide, explaining, respectively, 19 percent and 12 percent of the variance. The fifth component appears to discriminate mostly along gender lines, with male suicide rates being associated with female mortality rates from homicide and motor vehicle injuries at all ages. It is possible that this reflects a higher proportion of female victims of male criminals and female passengers of male drivers. In any event, the fifth component only accounts for 4 percent of the total variance, and subsequent components are even less important.

The principal components analysis allows for parsimonious descriptions of the trends and international patterns in mortality by sex, age, and

FIGURE 1
SUMMARY TRENDS IN ADOLESCENT AND YOUNG ADULT MORTALITY

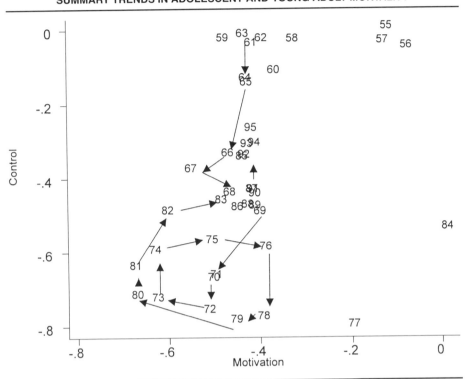

cause of death. Figure 1 summarizes changes over time on the two principal dimensions. The two principal axes have been rotated, and the vertical axis is the second dimension, an aggregate of violent mortality levels, with positive values representing lower mortality. The vertical axis is labeled "control" because variations along this dimension can be thought of as resulting from the various degree of control exerted over potentially harmful behaviors. The horizontal axis, which essentially discriminates between suicide (on the right) and other causes of violent mortality (on the left), is labeled "motivation" because the victim's intentions best discriminate suicide from the other causes of death under consideration. Missing values for Mexico characterize the five years on the right side of the graph (1955, 1956, 1957, 1977, and 1984) because the high homicide rates for Mexico contribute to pull the international average to the left in years Mexican data are available.

Starting in the 1960s, change occurs mostly along the vertical dimension, with a marked decline from 1965 to 1972 and annual average values remaining near their lowest for the rest of the 1970s. The trend is reversed after 1980, and from 1992 on, average values are back to their 1966 level but remain below those of the first decade (1955 to 1965). This analysis is consistent, of course, with the descriptions provided in the sections above and, in particular, with data summarized in Table 6, which suggest that the sum of the three standardized cause-specific mortality rates had increased up to the mid-1970s and declined thereafter. The principal component analysis exhibits, however, a much more coherent average trend than could be detected above.

This representation of past trends does not conform to the common perception of a continued worsening of the social conditions faced by adolescents and young adults. In particular, its timing is inconsistent with the popular argument about increased social disorganization attributed to the recent family changes that have taken place in nearly all the industrialized countries studied here. It is true, however, that the data used in this section do not incorporate the impact of the HIV/AIDS epidemic, which should largely moderate any positive interpretation of the post-1980 trend. With this important reservation, the trend is more consistent with the relative cohort size argument (Easterlin 1980; Ryder 1974), according to which members of a larger cohort experience stiffer competition to access more strained resources. The "worse" years range from 1970 to 1981, years during which the baby boomers entered the fifteen- to thirty-five-year-old age group.[6]

The same representation can be used to summarize international variations (see Figure 2). The most important variations are along the horizontal axis, with the extreme position of Mexico and very high (negative) values for the United States and Venezuela. Japan and northern European countries (Denmark, Sweden, the Netherlands, Norway, and the United Kingdom) are at the other tail of the distribution, but compared with the three American countries above, all other countries seem fairly clustered on the second axis. Noting that the position of Mexico and Venezuela might be rendered more extreme by the suspected underreporting of suicide makes the position of the United States all the more unusual.

On the vertical dimension, low behavior-related mortality countries include Chile, some southern European countries (Spain, Italy, and Greece), and northern European countries (Ireland, the United Kingdom, Norway, and the Netherlands). The United States is again a clear outlier at the other end of this axis, but other non-European English-speaking countries (Australia, New Zealand, and Canada) are also on the negative side. The closest European countries from this group are central European countries (Austria, Germany, Hungary, and Switzerland) and Finland.

Unfortunately, this analytical strategy could not be extended to HIV/AIDS data because there are only thirty observations (countries) as opposed to more than one thousand (country-years) in the above data set. Although a different analytical approach was used, the above results are fairly consistent with those presented in a one-dimensional

FIGURE 2
INTERNATIONAL VARIATIONS IN ADOLESCENT AND YOUNG ADULT MORTALITY

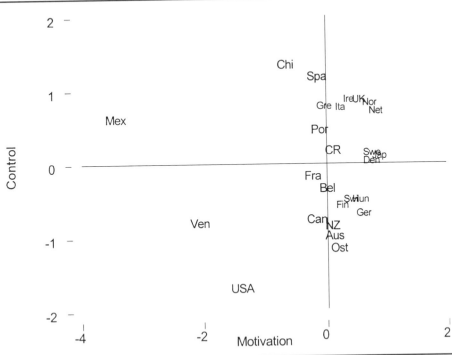

NOTE: Chi = Chile; Spa = Spain; Ire = Ireland; UK = United Kingdom; Gre = Greece; Ita = Italy; Nor = Norway; Net = Netherlands; Mex = Mexico; Por = Portugal; CR = Czech Republic; Swe = Sweden; Jap = Japan; Den = Denmark; Fra = France; Bel = Belgium; Swi = Switzerland; Hun = Hungary; Fin = Finland; Ven = Venezuela; Ger = Germany; Can = Canada; NZ = New Zealand; Aus = Australia; Ost = Austria; USA = United States.

format in Table 8, and I would suggest that a principal components analysis that integrates international variation in HIV infections would also extend and support the results from Table 9. If that leap is valid, countries with high rates of HIV infection, such as the United States, Portugal, Venezuela, Spain, and to a lesser extent, Mexico, France, Switzerland, and Italy should appear lower on the vertical axis. Similarly, Ukraine and the Russian Federation would be expected to be closer to the United States and Venezuela than other European countries.

As a summary of the mortality data between ages fifteen and thirty-five, Figure 2 seems to support the notion that international differences in adolescent and young adult mortality relate to underlying structural differences. First, two of the three less industrialized countries, Mexico and Venezuela, stand out most clearly from the other countries. Then, non-European countries are located at the core of a cluster of European countries. English-speaking non-European countries, Australia, New Zealand, Canada, and foremost, the United States, stand at the low end of one dimension, while Chile stands at the other end of that distribution and Japan stands at the end of the other dimension (opposite Mexico). All European countries are clustered within these extremes, and intra-European differences are more limited. Nevertheless, southern countries (Spain, Greece, and Italy) are closest to Chile, Nordic countries (Denmark and Sweden) are closest to Japan, and central countries (Austria, Germany, Switzerland, and Hungary) are closest to the English-speaking non-European countries. In sum, these clustering patterns provide encouraging prospects for the further investigation of the specific structural factors explaining international variations in adolescent and young adult mortality.

APPENDIX
RESULTS FROM PRINCIPAL COMPONENTS ANALYSIS (FIRST SIX FACTORS): MORTALITY RATES

	Principal Component					
	1	2	3	4	5	6
Suicide						
Males						
15-19	−0.1809	0.6042	0.5979	0.0047	−0.0455	−0.1409
20-24	−0.2323	0.6066	0.6816	0.0161	−0.0251	−0.0698
25-29	−0.2945	0.5815	0.6685	0.0057	−0.1363	−0.2352
30-34	−0.3149	0.5235	0.5795	0.0045	−0.1933	−0.3502
Females						
15-19	−0.0486	0.3461	0.6664	0.1205	0.4186	0.1545
20-24	−0.2301	0.3828	0.6832	0.0857	0.3111	0.3222
25-29	−0.3472	0.5129	0.6214	0.0661	0.1131	0.2104
30-34	−0.4013	0.5257	0.5369	0.0527	−0.0271	0.0446
Homicide						
Males						
15-19	0.7824	0.1360	−0.0049	−0.5122	0.1566	−0.0327
20-24	0.8360	0.0943	0.0249	−0.4756	0.1706	−0.0117
25-29	0.8372	0.0508	0.0535	−0.4682	0.1399	0.0015
30-34	0.8253	0.0280	0.0666	−0.4675	0.1056	0.0051
Females						
15-19	0.5896	0.3529	0.0532	−0.4442	−0.0634	0.0382
20-24	0.6025	0.4423	0.0583	−0.4381	−0.0955	0.0732
25-29	0.6028	0.4414	0.0513	−0.4343	−0.1512	0.0294
30-34	0.5869	0.4247	0.1012	−0.4480	−0.1750	−0.0117
Motor vehicle injury						
Males						
15-19	−0.0671	0.7296	−0.4255	0.2220	−0.0819	0.1517
20-24	0.1280	0.7077	−0.4781	0.3637	0.1301	−0.0033
25-29	0.3694	0.5523	−0.4494	0.3474	0.3759	−0.1853
30-34	0.4366	0.4615	−0.3977	0.3209	0.4296	−0.2225

APPENDIX Continued

	Principal Component					
	1	2	3	4	5	6
Females						
15-19	−0.0517	0.7605	−0.3759	0.1008	−0.3160	0.1969
20-24	0.0668	0.7347	−0.4780	0.1798	−0.2045	0.1125
25-29	0.2079	0.6892	−0.4819	0.1587	−0.0838	0.0017
30-34	0.2617	0.6777	−0.4361	0.1808	−0.0434	−0.0407
Other unintentional injury						
Males						
15-19	0.7851	−0.0999	0.1677	0.4010	0.1007	−0.0228
20-24	0.7816	−0.1516	0.2857	0.4534	−0.0131	0.0058
25-29	0.7843	−0.1905	0.3400	0.3958	−0.0933	−0.0402
30-34	0.7539	−0.1776	0.3769	0.3611	−0.1523	−0.1094
Females						
15-19	0.7476	−0.1424	0.2254	0.4014	−0.0503	0.0786
20-24	0.7510	−0.1770	0.2222	0.3828	−0.1146	0.1179
25-29	0.7664	−0.1620	0.2362	0.3485	−0.1659	0.0723
30-34	0.7366	−0.1280	0.2308	0.2818	−0.1737	0.0239

Factor	Eigenvalue	Difference	Proportion	Cumulative
1	9.85125	3.17560	0.3547	0.3547
2	6.67565	1.32011	0.2404	0.5951
3	5.35554	1.95374	0.1929	0.7880
4	3.40180	2.29099	0.1225	0.9105
5	1.11081	0.52528	0.0400	0.9505
6	0.58553	0.17001	0.0211	0.9716

Notes

1. The short description of the database provided here comes from the database Web page (http://www.who.int/whosis/mort/index.html), where a more comprehensive description can be found.

2. Two relatively small countries (Mauritius, and Trinidad and Tobago) were not included although they would have met these data requirements.

3. Other countries could have been included based on their post-1980 data availability, such as the Baltic Republics or non-European countries. We limited our selection to the larger eastern European countries among which Romania could not be included due to data limitations.

4. Pampel (1998), analyzing trends in eighteen industrialized nations (1953 to 1992), found that trends in suicide sex ratio were not linear but that sex differentials narrowed and then increased on the period. For the age groups considered here (the "young," ages fifteen to thirty-five), however, he reported that the "differentials bottom out early for the young; around 1960, male suicide rates begin to rise faster than female suicide rates" (p. 753). The trend analysis is consistent with ours, while the absolute levels vary because of different sets of countries.

5. Mortality rates from HIV are not available for each observation (i.e., country-year), so to obtain more robust estimated factors, the assessment was conducted on mortality data with suicide, homicide, motor vehicle injuries, and other unintentional injuries. The fourth cause is added to help the interpretation of the principal factors.

6. Results supporting the relative cohort size argument are also reported in a study of persons committing homicide in the United

States between 1960 and 1995 (O'Brien, Stockard, and Isaacson 1999).

References

Anderson, Robert N., Kenneth D. Kochanek, and Sherry Murphy. 1997. *Report of final mortality statistics, 1995*. Hyattsville, MD: National Center for Health Statistics.

Brooke, Eileen M., ed. 1974. *Suicide and attempted suicide*. Geneva, Switzerland: World Health Organization.

Brookmeyer, Ron, and Mitchell H. Gail. 1994. *AIDS epidemiology: A quantitative approach*. New York: Oxford University Press.

Easterlin, Richard A. 1980. *Birth and fortune: The impact of numbers on personal welfare*. New York: Basic Books.

Eisner, Manuel. 2002. Crime, problem drinking, and drug use: Patterns of problem behavior in cross-national perspective. *Annals of the American Academy of Political and Social Science* 580:201-225.

Joint United Nations Programme on HIV/AIDS (UNAIDS). 1998. *Report on the global HIV/AIDS epidemic*. Geneva, Switzerland: World Health Organization.

O'Brien, Robert M., Jean Stockard, and Lynne Isaacson. 1999. The enduring effects of cohort characteristics on age-specific homicide rates, 1960-1995. *American Journal of Sociology* 104:1061-95.

Pampel, Fred C. 1998. National context, social change, and sex differences in suicide rates. *American Sociological Review* 63:744-58.

Preston, Samuel H. 1984. Children and the elderly: Divergent paths for America's dependents. *Demography* 21:435-57.

Rindfuss, Ronald R. 1991. The young adult years: Diversity, structural change, and fertility. *Demography* 28:493-512.

Ruzicka, Lado T. 1995. Suicide mortality in developed countries. In *Adult mortality in developed countries: From description to explanation*, edited by Alan D. Lopez, Graziella Caselli, and Tapani Valkonen, 83-110. Oxford, UK: Clarendon.

Ryder, Norman B. 1974. *Youth: Transition to adulthood report of the Panel on Youth to the President's Science Advisory Committee*. Chicago: University of Chicago Press.

Simpson, Miles. 1998. Suicide and religion: Did Durkheim commit the ecological fallacy, or did van Poppel and Day combine apples and oranges? *American Sociological Review* 63:893-94.

U.S. Department of Health and Human Services. 2000. *Healthy people 2010*. Washington, DC: U.S. Department of Health and Human Services.

van Poppel, Franz, and Lincoln H. Day. 1996. A test of Durkheim's theory of suicide—Without committing the "ecological fallacy." *American Review of Sociology* 61:500-507.

———. 1998. Reply to Simpson. *American Review of Sociology* 63:896-99.

World Health Organization (WHO). 1957. *International classification of diseases*. Vol. 1, Rev. ed., Geneva, Switzerland: World Health Organization.

———. 1996. World health statistics annual. Geneva, Switzerland: World Health Organization.

ANNALS, *AAPSS*, **580**, March 2002

Crime, Problem Drinking, and Drug Use: Patterns of Problem Behavior in Cross-National Perspective

By MANUEL EISNER

ABSTRACT: Previous studies on cross-national patterns of crime and problem behavior have focused primarily on homicide. This article proposes that cross-national research should pay more attention to broadly based measures of various types of problem behavior. By combining different types of sources, I derive measures for four types of problem behavior, namely violent crime, property crime, alcohol abuse, and drug use for a sample of thirty-seven countries. Analysis of these data first shows that, at the level of cross-national comparison, different manifestations of problem behavior do not constitute a single underlying dimension. Rather, a cluster analysis reveals several groups of countries with similar configurations of problem behavior. Many Anglo-American countries, for example, were found to belong to a cluster with a high likelihood of various kinds of problem behavior associated with the transition from adolescence to early adulthood. High levels of violence characterize many Eastern European countries. Further analyses show that distinct types of problem behavior correlate with different contextual variables. Violence is found to be high in countries characterized by great social inequality, low levels of social control, and widespread material poverty. Drug use and alcohol abuse among young people, in contrast, is frequent in highly urbanized, highly affluent contexts where lifestyles are leisure-time oriented.

Manuel Eisner is assistant professor in sociology at the Swiss Federal Institute of Technology and has recently taken up a new position as Lecturer in Criminology at the University of Cambridge. His research interests include the relationship between social change and crime, with a special emphasis on the long-term trajectories of violent crime in Western societies, and the impact of social context on trajectories of problem behavior among youth. Recent publications include "Modernization, Self-Control and Lethal Violence—The Long-Term Dynamics of European Homicide Rates in Theoretical Perspective" (British Journal of Criminology, *2001).*

DURING the past twenty years, there have been a significant number of studies that have examined the determinants of cross-national differences in levels of crime (see, e.g., Bennett 1991; Gartner 1990; Halpern 2001; Krahn, Hartnagel, and Gatrell 1986; LaFree and Kick 1986; Lee and Bankston 1999; Messner 1982; Messner and Rosenfeld 1997). A majority of these studies have focused primarily on the determinants of homicide rates. Only a few studies have attempted to also examine property crime, and even fewer studies have conjointly explored other types of deviant behavior. Those that did primarily focused on comparing, from a Durkheimian viewpoint, the determinants of homicide and suicide (see, e.g., Pampel and Williamson 2001).

However, from a theoretical perspective, the almost exclusive focus on homicide rates appears to be unwarranted. Rather, the arguments of most criminological theories can be used for explaining cross-national differences in many types of problem behavior associated with the transition from adolescence to early adulthood. This raises the empirical issue of whether national levels in various types of problem behavior are determined by the same set of contextual factors or whether each manifestation of problem behavior requires a different explanatory approach.

In view of this question, this article is organized into three main parts. In the first part, I review some arguments for exploring similarities and differences among different types of problem behavior across countries. In the second part, I construct broadly based cross-national measures of four types of problem behavior, namely violent crime, property crime, drug use, and alcohol abuse. These data are then used to explore the possibility of identifying groups of countries with similar configurations of problem behavior. Finally, I examine selected macro-level correlates of problem behavior and discuss the implications for an integrated perspective on cross-national patterns in adolescence-related problem behavior.

AGE AND PROBLEM BEHAVIOR

There are several reasons why cross-national crime research might profit from examining a wider array of problem behaviors simultaneously rather than focusing on a single phenomenon such as homicide rates. Here, I primarily highlight some arguments pertaining to the observation that various kinds of problem behavior are similarly rooted in the transition period from adolescence to early adulthood (Blumstein, Cohen, and Farrington 1988). If a person ever starts with alcohol drinking, cigarette smoking, risky driving, the consumption of illicit drugs, or criminal activity, it is most likely to happen between about ages ten and eighteen. After about age twenty-five, in contrast, the core theme is desistance, a process that has received considerable scientific interest recently (see, e.g., Warr 1998). As a consequence, when observed at the aggregate level of prevalence or incidence rates, different dimensions of problem behavior tend to display similar age curves.

FIGURE 1
HOMICIDE: RECORDED OFFENDERS PER 100,000 PERSONS

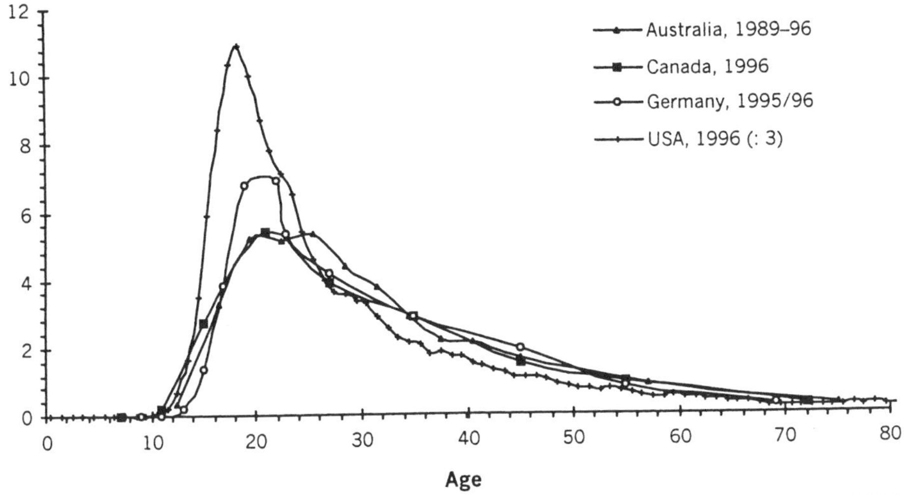

Legend:
- Australia, 1989–96
- Canada, 1996
- Germany, 1995/96
- USA, 1996 (: 3)

Age

SOURCES: Australia—James and Carcach (1997), Canada—Statistics Canada (2001), Germany—Bundeskriminalamt (1998), United States—Bureau of Justice Statistics (2001).

They increase steeply during adolescence and peak between about ages sixteen and twenty-five. From then on, the curves decline, although the slope may differ considerably between specific types of problem behavior.

However, we discover not only great similarity when comparing the age curve of different forms of problem behavior; we also find striking parallels when we examine the same specific problem behavior in a comparison among countries. Figures 1 through 4 illustrate this phenomenon. The figures show, respectively, officially recorded suspects of homicide offences, as an indicator for serious violence; recorded suspects of criminal offences as a whole, as an indicator for conventional mass offences, mainly property crimes;

cannabis consumption within the past year as a general indicator of drug use; and some data on drunkenness and massive consumption of alcohol as an indicator of alcohol abuse. It should be noted that these data cannot be used for comparison of the overall height of the curves. Rather, we are exclusively interested here in illustrating the similarity of the overall age-related patterns.

Figure 1 shows the age curves for rates of suspects on record for homicide offences. These may be used for international comparison, as they are relatively little affected by differences in the gathering of the data. The figure reveals a high similarity among Canada, Australia, and Germany. The data rise steeply from the age of sixteen, reach a maximum between the ages of twenty and

FIGURE 2
ALL CRIMES: RECORDED OFFENDERS PER ONE THOUSAND PERSONS

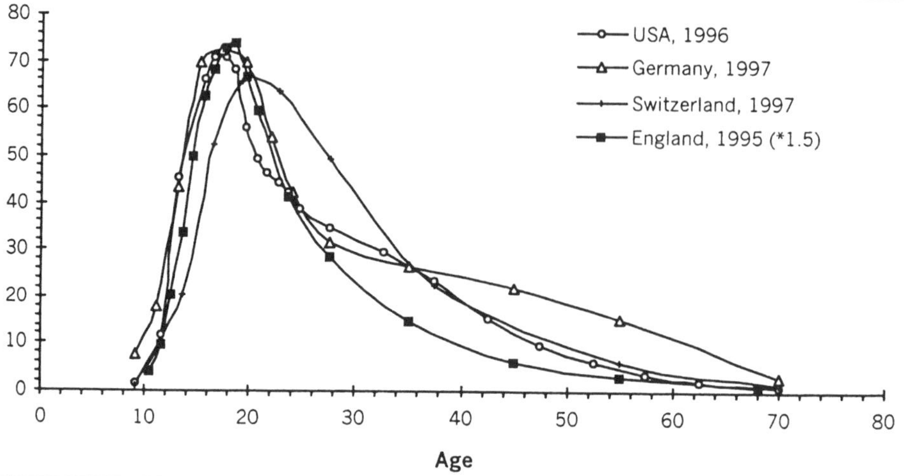

SOURCES: Australia—Ferrante and Loh (1998), United States—U.S. Department of Justice (1996), Switzerland—Kantonspolizei Zürich (1997), Germany—Bundeskriminalamt (1998), England—Home Office (1998).

twenty-five, and then decline steadily with increasing age. The pattern in the United States is slightly different in that the initial rise is steeper, the maximum is reached as early as age eighteen, and the curve declines very sharply with increasing age.

Figure 2 shows data from police statistics for the total number of all suspected offenders in four countries. For better comparability, these are restricted to criminal offences in a narrow sense that excludes drug offences, traffic offences, and minor violations. Except for the slight shift toward older age groups in Switzerland, the graph shows a strikingly similar pattern for all countries. Offender rates rise steeply from about the ages of ten to twelve and peak around age eighteen. In most of the curves, this is followed by a rapid

decline until the age of twenty-five to thirty, and then the rates level off at a slower pace with increasing age. Surveys on self-reported delinquency as a rule show a pattern similar to official crime statistics, although according to survey data, the peak age of offending tends to be one or two years earlier than in official statistics (Junger-Tas, Terlouw, and Klein 1994; Wolfgang, Figlio, and Sellin 1972).

Figure 3 shows age-related data for cannabis consumption within the past twelve months in a number of countries that reveal an astonishing similarity. Cannabis consumption rises rapidly from around the age of twelve. The highest prevalence of consumption is reached between the ages of sixteen and twenty-five. Following a steady decline, consumption virtually disappears by the age of

FIGURE 3
CANNABIS CONSUMPTION WITHIN THE PAST YEAR, ACCORDING TO AGE

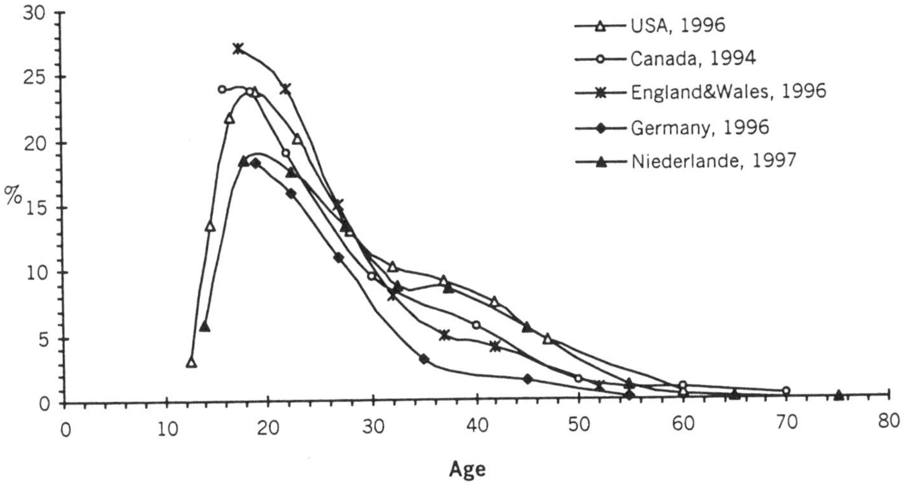

SOURCES: Australia—Makkai and McAllister (1998), the Netherlands—Abraham et al. (1998) (mean from Amsterdam, Tilburg, and Utrecht), United States—Substance Abuse and Mental Health Services Adminstration (1998), Canada—Health Canada (1997), Germany—Kraus and Bauernfeind (1998), England and Wales—Ramsay and Spiller (1997).

fifty. It is noteworthy that there are virtually no discernible indications that ongoing consumption of cannabis has expanded toward older cohorts during the past decades. In comparing survey data referring to the 1980s and 1990s in Holland, Abraham et al. (1998) found that while the age curve for the lifetime prevalence of cannabis consumption has flattened since the 1980s, the age structure of people consuming cannabis at any one time has remained surprisingly stable.

An examination of alcohol consumption, finally, brings two different patterns to light. General prevalence and incidence data for alcohol use as a whole show that consumption starts between the ages of twelve and eighteen and that alcoholic beverages continue to be consumed into old age. However, data on massive alcohol abuse and associated resulting problems (binge drinking; drinking more than five units at a time; regularly occurring drunkenness; driving under the influence) show a pattern with a maximum prevalence between the ages of eighteen and twenty-five and a subsequent decline (see Figure 4).

However, different types of problem behavior are not only interrelated on the macro level of similar age curves. Rather, drug abuse, frequent drunkenness, different kinds of criminal offending, and a multitude of other "vices" are also consistently found to correlate at the level of individuals, in the sense that people who commit any one of them are

FIGURE 4
ALCOHOL ABUSE, VARIOUS INDICATORS

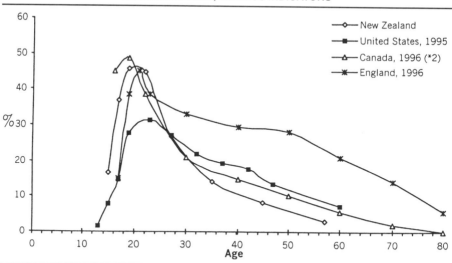

SOURCES: New Zealand—percentage of persons with at least three alcohol-caused problems within the past year (Alcohol and Public Health Research Unit 2001), Canada—percentage of persons who regularly drink five or more alcoholic drinks at a time (Health Canada 1997), England and Wales—consumption of four or more units at a time at least once a month (Prescott-Clarke and Primatesta 1998), United States—binge drinking (at least five or more alcoholic drinks at a time, within the past month) (Substance Abuse and Mental Health Services Administration 1998).

more likely to commit any of the others (Farrington 1994). This tendency for the overlapping of various problem behaviors within the same individual has been demonstrated in all studies around the world (see, for example, Elliott et al. 1985; Moffitt 1994; West and Farrington 1977).

A major theoretical explanation of both the similar age pattern of different kinds of problem behavior and their cumulation within individuals is the general theory of crime proposed by Gottfredson and Hirschi (1990; also see Simons et al. 1998). Essentially, it departs from the presumption that problem behavior is a one-dimensional underlying personality trait (also see, e.g., Farrington

1994). In particular, Gottfredson and Hirschi assume that different manifestations of problem behavior flow from a lack of self-control, acquired during childhood and immune to influences during later phases. Hence, the age-to-problem-behavior pattern is expected to be identical across countries and historical periods (Hirschi 1983). Between countries, age curves may vary in size but not in shape. Second, the latent trait perspective implies that cross-national variation in the average propensity to engage in different types of problem behavior is essentially one-dimensional and depends on the degree to which conditions during childhood promote self-control. Countries should exhibit either larger or smaller average proclivities of their populations to engage in problem behavior. However, Gottfredon and Hirschi emphasize that cross-national differences in manifest problem behavior also depend on the structure of opportunities (e.g., availability of goods or victims). The degree to which countries differ in behavior-specific opportunities such as the availability of drugs or the ease of access to unsupervised material goods is thus assumed to shape the specific configuration of manifest problem behaviors in a given country.

The life-course perspective, in contrast, assumes a higher variability of factors contributing to the formation of different types of problem behaviors. It views the transition from adolescence to early adulthood as a sequence of causal factors that either accentuate or redirect behavioral tendencies (Buchmann 1989; Sampson and Laub 1993). Childhood experiences may thus contribute to shaping generalized propensities. However, cultural and structural circumstances during the transition to adulthood, as well as stressful life events, are assumed to interact with preexisting individual characteristics in molding trajectories of problem behavior. For this reason, the life-course approach expects more variation in problem behavior patterns among countries. For example, the age-graded, social control theory proposed by Sampson and Laub (1993) asserts that social institutions may either accelerate or stabilize delinquent paths during adolescence. As a consequence, criminal

offending may start at a later age in some countries than in others. Also, from a life-course perspective, the propensity to engage in different types of problem behavior is not necessarily one dimensional. Rather, the opportunity structures, control patterns, and strains typical for a given society may result in specific configurations of problem behavior. For example, behavior that involves aggression against others may be motivated by high levels of social inequality, while illicit drug consumption may rather be driven by the availability of respective substances.

CROSS-NATIONAL MEASURES OF
FOUR TYPES OF PROBLEM BEHAVIOR

The main objective of this study is to examine patterns and determinants of four aspects of problem behavior on a cross-national level, namely violent crime, property crime, drug use, and alcohol abuse. In any study of this kind, the choice of data is of pivotal importance. Most prior cross-national studies on crime rates have relied on one single type of source or one single indicator such as, for example, homicide rates derived from the World Health Organization (WHO) vital statistics or theft rates based on the international crime statistics provided by Interpol (International Criminal Police Organization 1977). However, data based on single measures are known to be problematic in at least two respects. First, single measures may not be representative of a wider underlying construct, even if the measurement itself can be assumed to be reliable.

Second, specific data sources such as police statistics may be distorted by national differences in data-gathering procedures and definitions of the respective type of behavior. Therefore, a major concern of this study was to obtain broadly based estimates representing information from different sources and variables. To this aim, I developed a strategy whereby several international sources of data were used and combined. Several base variables were then used for creating an indicator of the underlying construct.

The bulk of the data are taken in the main from four large-scale international comparative data collections.

At present, the most elaborate efforts at internationally collecting officially recorded crime data have gone into the *Fifth United Nations Survey of Crime Trends and Operations of Criminal Justice Systems* (United Nations 1998). At regular intervals, this survey accumulates data on several categories of crime, offenders, and the criminal justice system. Various efforts are made to standardize the data, yet a number of problems pertaining to the comparability of the data (e.g., national differences in definitions of crime, data collection procedures) are only partly resolved (for details, see Kangaspunta, Joutsen, and Ollus 1998, 4ff.). The Fifth United Nations Crime Survey covers the period from 1990 to 1994.

The second source for comparative crime analyses is the International Crime Victim Survey (ICVS), organized by Jan van Dijk and Pat Mayhew (Mayhew and van Dijk

1997; van Dijk, Mayhew, and Killias 1991). Using standardized methodologies and data collection procedures, this survey has gathered data for nineteen industrialized countries. In addition, a large number of surveys have been conducted in mostly urban areas of eastern Europe as well as developing countries (Zvekic 1998). The project thus certainly constitutes the most reliable and encompassing source for comparing levels of criminal victimization in the general population. By definition, these data contain little information about offender characteristics. However, all victimization data used in this article relate to offense categories (assault and threat, vehicle theft), which are mainly committed by young men. All data used in this article refer to victimization during the past five years and are based on average scores if several waves of the survey have been conducted.

My main source for comparing levels of substance use among juveniles in industrialized countries is the European School Survey Project on Alcohol and Other Drugs (ESPAD). It was conducted in twenty-nine countries during 1995 at the initiative of the Pompidou Group of the Council of Europe (Hibell et al. 1997). The survey includes national samples of between 600 (Cyprus) and 17,000 (United States) students ages fifteen to sixteen and covers a wide variety of legal and illegal drugs. Several comparisons with other national and international surveys show a high validity of the ESPAD data (Hibell et al. 1997, 39).

The WHO cross-national study called Health Behaviour in School-

Aged Children (King et al. 1997) was conducted in 1993-1994 and included twenty-four countries. It comprised a variety of questions on health behavior including alcohol consumption but included no items on illicit drug use. Although there is some geographic overlap with the ESPAD survey, many countries have participated in only one of the studies. Representative national samples of children at ages eleven, thirteen, and fifteen were surveyed. However, this study uses the results for the oldest age group only.

Additional sources. The comparative analyses are possible only for those countries for which a full set of information could be obtained. Therefore, care was taken to complement the data set by additional national data sources. With regard to police-recorded crime, for example, the *European Sourcebook of Crime and Criminal Justice Statistics* (European Committee on Crime Problems 1999) was consulted, and respective data were added. In a similar vein, some countries not covered by either the ESPAD study or the WHO study have conducted national student surveys that include questions similar or identical to those used in one of the international surveys.

Utilizing these base data, four indices were constructed. Each index variable is based on several primary variables to obtain the most valid measurement of the constructs (for a similar approach, see Kangaspunta, Joutsen, and Ollus 1998). To compute the indices, each base variable was

first z transformed. In a second step, averages were calculated for each country. Thus, each base variable contributes the same amount of variance to the aggregated variable. Where data were missing in a country for one of the base variables, the mean was based on the variables for which information was available.

Table 1 shows the rank order of countries on each of the four dimensions of problem behavior. The values in parentheses are the standardized scores on the respective dimension.

Estimates for violence rates are based on four variables, namely completed homicide, police-recorded robbery, and past-year victimization rates for robbery and assault. Data on completed homicide and police-recorded robbery are based primarily on the *European Sourcebook of Crime and Criminal Justice Statistics* (European Committee on Crime Problems 1999) as well as the *Fifth United Nations Survey of Crime Trends and Operations of Criminal Justice Systems* (United Nations 1998). Robbery rates were corrected for national differences in the propensity to report crimes to the police as estimated in the ICVS. This correction was deemed important because reporting to the police differs widely between countries. Also, earlier research has shown that the correlation between police-recorded data and results of the ICVS estimates improves significantly after accounting for reporting propensities (van Dijk 1992). Data on victimization rates for robbery and assault are based on the ICVS. All four measures were available for thirty-four nations with a Cronbach's alpha of .77 for the

TABLE 1
RANKING OF COUNTRIES ON FOUR DIMENSIONS OF PROBLEM BEHAVIOR

Quartile	Violent Crime		Property Crime		Alcohol Abuse		Drug Use	
	Country	SS	Country	SS	Country	SS	Country	SS
First	Estonia	2.30	New Zealand	2.24	Denmark	2.61	Scotland	2.76
	Ukraine	2.19	Australia	2.24	Australia	2.22	Australia	2.02
	Russian Republic	1.98	England and Wales	1.85	England and Wales	2.02	United States	1.92
	United States	1.23	United States	1.18	Scotland	1.79	England and Wales	1.74
	Latvia	1.07	Bulgaria	1.08	New Zealand	1.50	New Zealand	1.54
	Bulgaria	1.00	Estonia	1.00	Northern Ireland	1.14	Netherlands	1.18
	Lithuania	0.81	Italy	0.85	Finland	0.83	Canada	1.10
	New Zealand	0.61	Canada	0.79	Austria	0.72	Ireland	1.08
	Romania	0.57	Ukraine	0.70	Ireland	0.57	Northern Ireland	0.70
Second	Poland	0.33	Latvia	0.65	Canada	0.28	Italy	0.33
	Australia	0.30	France	0.58	Czech Republic	0.22	Switzerland	0.22
	Spain	0.12	Czech Republic	0.54	Belgium	0.20	Germany	0.21
	Slovenia	0.12	Denmark	0.49	Netherlands	0.18	Austria	0.00
	Canada	0.11	Scotland	0.37	Germany	0.03	Russian Republic	−0.11
	Finland	−0.02	Spain	0.27	Sweden	0.02	Czech Republic	−0.14
	Slovak Republic	−0.02	Sweden	0.13	Spain	0.01	Belgium	−0.15
	England and Wales	−0.21	Lithuania	0.03	Ukraine	−0.01	Spain	−0.25
	Croatia	−0.31	Slovak Republic	−0.04	Greece	−0.03	France	−0.41

Dimension	SS	Country	SS	Country	SS	Country	SS	Country
Third	−0.32	Czech Republic	−0.04	Poland	−0.05	Slovak Republic	−0.50	Denmark
	−0.33	Netherlands	−0.10	Ireland	−0.10	Malta	−0.50	Cyprus
	−0.41	Denmark	−0.16	Northern Ireland	−0.29	Norway	−0.51	Slovenia
	−0.45	Scotland	−0.17	Hungary	−0.33	Latvia	−0.56	Croatia
	−0.63	Germany	−0.18	Malta	−0.40	Russian Republic	−0.57	Bulgaria
	−0.63	Malta	−0.20	Belgium	−0.42	Poland	−0.60	Slovak Republic
	−0.65	Sweden	−0.29	Russian Republic	−0.44	Hungary	−0.60	Malta
	−0.73	Northern Ireland	−0.39	Netherlands	−0.46	Lithuania	−0.64	Norway
	−0.73	Hungary	−0.54	Portugal	−0.51	Estonia	−0.65	Poland
Fourth	−0.75	France	−0.69	Slovenia	−0.51	United States	−0.71	Ukraine
	−0.78	Greece	−0.78	Germany	−0.53	Italy	−0.75	Portugal
	−0.80	Norway	−1.03	Norway	−0.61	Slovenia	−0.81	Greece
	−0.85	Portugal	−1.05	Romania	−0.65	Bulgaria	−0.82	Estonia
	−0.91	Belgium	−1.14	Greece	−0.74	France	−0.82	Sweden
	−1.00	Switzerland	−1.14	Austria	−0.79	Croatia	−0.89	Finland
	−1.08	Italy	−1.21	Croatia	−1.17	Portugal	−0.90	Latvia
	−1.09	Cyprus	−1.43	Finland	−1.39	Switzerland	−0.91	Hungary
	−1.17	Ireland	−1.45	Switzerland	−1.68	Cyprus	−0.99	Romania
	−1.18	Austria	−1.67	Cyprus	−1.75	Romania	−1.02	Lithuania

NOTE: SS = standardized score on the respective dimension.

aggregate scale. The index scores are presented in Table 1. They show, first, that countries with high levels of violent crime are mostly located in the less prosperous parts of eastern Europe. In particular, countries like the Russian federation, Estonia, and the Ukraine have staggeringly high levels of violent crime according to both police statistics (in particular, homicide rates) and victim surveys. Among Western industrialized countries, only the United States, which has a long historical record of high violent crime, matches these levels. Low levels of violent crime were found in, for example, Switzerland, Italy, Cyprus, Ireland, and Austria.

Property crime was measured by combining four variables. On the level of police-recorded crime, only burglary rates were included. Again, original data were corrected for national differences in the propensity to report crimes to the police as estimated in the ICVS. Also, I included victimization rates of burglary, car theft, and theft from a car according to the ICVS. Thirty-four countries have complete data on all four variables; three countries lacked data on victimization rates. Cronbach's alpha for the overall scale for property crime is .77. It may be noticed that this indicator primarily reflects more serious types of property crime and that no attempt was made to include variables on simple theft. The highest levels of serious property crime were found in New Zealand, Australia, England and Wales, and the United States. Very low property crime rates were found, in contrast, in Cyprus, Switzerland, Finland, Austria, and Croatia.

With few exceptions, data for drug use come from the 1995 ESPAD. Five measures of drug consumption including prevalence rates on cannabis consumption and other illicit substances were used to create an overall measure of drug use among young people. Twenty-nine countries included in this study were covered by the ESPAD data set. For eight countries (i.e., Australia, Austria, Belgium, Canada, Germany, the Netherlands, Switzerland, New Zealand) the data are based on various national surveys among ninth-grade students, which included identical questions on prevalence rates. Cronbach's alpha for the derived scale is .96. All the variables are highly correlated and thus suggest one single underlying dimension. It should be noted, however, that prevalence data do not necessarily reflect the extent of severe addiction problems in a given country. More particularly, school surveys do not adequately cover the marginalized group of heroin or cocaine addicts (see European Monitoring Centre for Drugs and Drug Addiction 1998). The resulting measure shows that all the Anglo-Saxon countries have the highest proportion of juveniles that have consumed illicit substances. Scotland has the highest score with, for example, 46 percent having consumed cannabis products over the past twelve months and 21 percent that have ever consumed LSD or other hallucinogens. The lowest proportion of juveniles having experiences with illicit drugs is found in a rim of countries at the periphery of Europe stretching from Finland and Sweden through eastern European countries like Estonia, Latvia, and Ukraine to Greece and Portugal at the south.

The fourth indicator was constructed as a measure of problem alcohol use among juveniles. It is based on the 1995 ESPAD study and the WHO's Health Behavior in School-Aged Children Project. From these studies, three measures were selected measuring various aspects of serious alcohol consumption among juveniles. Prevalence of drunkenness in the past year and past month and prevalence of drinking five or more drinks in a row represents the consumption of large amounts at once. The proportion of those juveniles who drink alcoholic beverages at least weekly, in contrast, measures regular consumption. Despite the fact that the two surveys used somewhat different wordings in their questionnaires, Hibell et al. (2000, 45) have shown that the two studies yield very similar rankings for those eighteen countries that participated in both studies. Data from either of the studies were available for thirty-five countries with a Cronbach's alpha of .92. For Australia and New Zealand, estimates are based on national surveys. According to the aggregated measure, Denmark, Australia, the British Isles, and New Zealand have the highest levels of problem drinking among juveniles. For example, 61 percent of the Danish juveniles and 52 percent of the Scottish juveniles report having been drunk at least twice during the two months preceding the survey. In contrast, juveniles in Portugal, Cyprus, Switzerland, and Croatia appear to have low levels

of problem drinking. It may be noticed here that this measure is unrelated to overall levels of alcohol consumption in the general population as measured by the quantity of pure alcohol consumed by capita. The variable thus captures a particular drinking culture among juveniles rather than alcohol consumption per se.

A further look at the table reveals that the countries can be characterized by very different configurations of problem behavior. Taking three examples, Estonia shows very high values for violent crime as well as property crime whereas, according to the statistics used, the frequency of alcohol abuse in youth is low and the frequency of drug use very low. In contrast, Australia is characterized by a configuration of consistently high values for all four dimensions. Finally, Switzerland shows a configuration with consistently low values for violent crime, property crime, and alcohol abuse but a relatively high frequency of drug abuse among youth. These examples indicate that countries in international comparison can be assigned to one single latent dimension of "low" to "high" problem behavior only to a very restricted degree. The zero-order correlation matrix among shown in Table 2 further supports this proposition.

It reveals, first, some positive correlation between high alcohol abuse in youth, high frequency of property crime, and drug use. These kinds of problem behavior thus appear to have some common underlying tendency to covary on an international level. Violent crime, in contrast, is

TABLE 2

PRODUCT-MOMENT CORRELATIONS AMONG FOUR MEASURES OF PROBLEM BEHAVIOR

	1	2	3	4
1. Violence	—			
2. Property crime	.42**	—		
3. Alcohol abuse	−.07	.50**	—	
4. Drug use	−.08	.50**	.57**	—

$**p < .01$, two-tailed.

only correlated with property crime and varies independently of drug use and alcohol abuse. Furthermore, it may be noticed that these correlations appear to be rather weak when compared to respective findings at the individual level. The data thus suggest that the common roots of many types of problem behavior at the level of individuals do not translate into a coherent shared pattern of prevalence at the internationally comparative level.

CONFIGURATIONS OF
PROBLEM BEHAVIOR

The most important conclusion to be drawn from these descriptive findings is that different types of problem behavior do not appear to constitute a single vector that distinguishes countries with low and high levels of deviance. Rather, each country seems to be characterized by a distinct configuration of problem behaviors among young people. This result leads us to a further step in examining the issue of the extent to which groups of countries can be found that are characterized by similar configurations of problem behavior. To establish the existence of such groups, I adopted an analytic strategy, which combines a multi-

dimensional scaling approach with results from a cluster analysis. In nontechnical terms, multidimensional scaling is a technique that seeks to spatially represent complex information about the similarity and dissimilarity between objects in a parsimonious way, such that the distances among the points match the proximities among the objects as closely as possible (Kruskal and Wish 1978). Cluster analysis, in turn, is a technique that seeks to identify groups of objects that are similar to each other and dissimilar to other groups of objects (Everitt 1993). Both methods can be usefully combined. Used in conjunction, the two methods yield a graphical visualization of objects that can be interpreted as neighbors in respect of the chosen characteristics. In the present case of four dimensions of problem behavior, therefore, the aim is to identify groups of countries that share similar configurations of problem behavior.

The input for both analyses was the standardized estimates of problem behavior as shown in Table 2. Also, both procedures were run on the basis of Euclidean distance measures between the observations. Multidimensional scaling was performed using the ALSCAL algorithm

TABLE 3

CONFIGURATIONS OF PROBLEM BEHAVIOR IN INTERNATIONAL COMPARISON

| Cluster | Dimension of Problem Behavior | | | | Countries |
	Violent Crime	Property Crime	Drug Use	Alcohol Abuse	
I: High, except violence	0	++	++	++	Australia, Canada, England and Wales, New Zealand, Scotand, United States
II: Alcohol use high	−	0	0	+	Austria, Belgium, Denmark, Finland, Germany, Ireland, Netherlands, Northern Ireland
III: Violence high	++	0	−	0	Bulgaria, Estonia, Latvia, Lithuania, Poland, Russian Republic, Ukraine
IV: Consistently average	−	0	0	0	Czech Republic, France, Hungary, Italy, Malta, Slovak Republic, Slovenia, Spain, Sweden
V: Consistently low	−	−−	−	−	Cyprus, Croatia, Greece, Norway, Portugal, Switzerland

NOTE: Romania not included. ++ indicates that cluster mean > 1; + indicates that cluster mean = 0.5 to 1.0; 0 indicates that cluster mean = −0.5 to 0.5; − indicates that cluster mean = −1.0 to −0.5; −− indicates that cluster mean < −1.0.

provided by SPSS. The results showed that the countries could be represented on a two-dimensional space with a Kruskal's stress value of 0.11. Cluster analysis was performed using agglomerative hierarchical clustering based on the Ward algorithm, which minimizes the sum of squares within a cluster (i.e., between the cluster center and the objects) and maximizes the sum of squares between clusters. The agglomeration schedule was inspected for information about the optimal number of clusters, but the respective scree plot did not suggest an obvious number of clusters. A five-cluster solution was finally accepted for the further analysis since it appeared to be both parsimonious and informative.

The results are summarized in Figure 5 and Table 3. Figure 2 shows the two-dimensional configuration of the thirty-six countries in respect of the four types of problem behavior. The loops indicate the location of the five clusters identified by the cluster analysis. It may be noticed that Romania was excluded from the final cluster analysis since both the multidimensional scaling (MDS) results and prior runs of the cluster analysis suggested that it should be considered an outlier. This may be due to comparatively poor underlying data for this country. In addition, the two-dimensional solution of the MDS yields coordinates for two countries, namely Italy and Finland, which place them outside the boundaries of the respective clusters. This suggests that the two-dimensional solution neglects some information, which would have to be represented in a higher-order solution.

Although our primary aim is to examine groups of countries with similar configurations, a few remarks may be made on the

FIGURE 5
TWO-DIMENSIONAL CONFIGURATION FOR
PROBLEM BEHAVIOR AMONG THIRTY-SIX COUNTRIES.

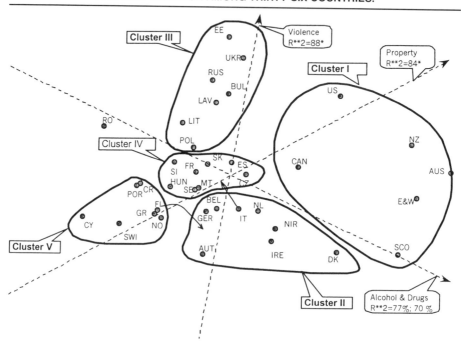

NOTE: The loops drawn are the results of a five-cluster solution of the cluster analysis. Kruskal's Stress = 0.11. R^2 = .95. Abbreviations are defined as follows: In Cluster I, US = United States; NZ = New Zealand; AUS = Australia; CAN = Canada; E&W = England and Wales; SCO = Scotland. In Cluster II, DK = Denmark; IRE = Ireland; NIR = Northern Ireland; NL = Netherlands; BEL = Belgium; AUT = Austria; GER = Germany; FI = Finland. In Cluster III, EE = Estonia; UKR = Ukraine; RUS = Russia; BUL = Bulgaria; LAV = Latvia; LIT = Lithuania; POL = Poland. In Cluster IV, SK = Slovakia; ES = Spain; CZ = Czech Republic; FR = France; MT = Malta; SI = Slovenia; HUN = Hungary; IT = Italy. In Cluster V, CR = Croatia; POR = Portugal; GR = Greece; NO = Norway; SWI = Switzerland; CY = Cyprus.

dimensions of the MDS solution. A good way of interpreting the dimensions of MDS analyses consists of regressing the problem behaviors on the coordinates of the MDS solution (Kruskal and Wish 1978, 36). The derived regression lines can then be interpreted as vectors that distinguish the observations along the respective underlying dimension. They are represented by dotted lines

in Figure 5. They show, first, that countries with low and high levels of violence rates can be distinguished along an axis that is slightly rotated clockwise to the vertical axis. Property crime levels, in turn, are low at the bottom left of the figure and increase toward its upper right corner. Finally, the estimates for drug use and alcohol abuse yielded very close regression slopes and were therefore collapsed into one single line.

Examination of the clusters shows that a first group of countries is characterized by consistently high frequencies on three of the four dimensions of problem behavior examined. This cluster is exclusively composed of Anglo-Saxon countries, all of which share relatively high levels of drug and alcohol use and high levels of property crime. It can also be seen, however, that the United States is somewhat untypical due to its elevated levels of violent crime. The second cluster consists of countries that share high levels of excessive drinking as their most conspicuous trait. Property crime levels and drug use levels, however, are in a middle range, and violent crime tends to be relatively low. Several of these countries are also geographic neighbors (Germany, Austria, Belgium, the Netherlands, and Denmark) and their similar configuration of problem behavior may thus reflect macro-level background conditions. Geographic and historical proximity is also evident for the countries merged in cluster III, which is characterized by very high levels of violent crime on one hand and comparatively low levels in the use of illicit substances on the other. They are all transition countries that were part of the former communist bloc. The main distinctive feature of cluster IV is its consistent configuration of average levels on each of the four dimensions of problem behavior, evidenced by its location in the center of the two-dimensional space. Several of the countries in this group are geographically located in the south of Europe (France, Italy, Malta, Slovenia, and Spain), but the cluster also includes Sweden and Hungary as well as the Czech and the Slovak Republics. Finally, low levels of any type of problem behavior characterize cluster V. It includes Cyprus, Croatia, Greece, Norway, Portugal, and Switzerland. In terms of geographic and historical contiguity, this group is probably the most heterogeneous among the identified clusters.

STRUCTURAL CORRELATES OF PROBLEM BEHAVIOR

These findings suggest that countries with similar profiles of problem behavior tend to also share important historical and cultural properties. Many Anglo-American societies, for example, appear to be characterized by a high likelihood of various kinds of problem behavior associated with the transition from adolescence to early adulthood, and eastern European countries were found to have a distinct pattern of problem behavior characterized by particularly high levels of violent crime. One might therefore conjecture that these societies also share distinct macro-level characteristics, which influence the typical pathways of becoming an adult in a society. However, the typological approach pursued so far yields no systematic information about what these macro-level characteristics might be.

As a next step, I therefore explore some macro-level social and economic correlates of problem behavior. For this purpose, a series of variables was examined, which may be interpreted as measures of important general theories of macro-level differences in deviant behavior.

Strain and relative deprivation theory basically argues that levels of delinquency are the result of frustrations, negative life events, and a sense of injustice originating in the unequal distribution of life chances in a society. Three measures of strain were included in the subsequent analyses. I used the Gini index of income inequality and the relative share of the lowest 20 percent of household incomes as measures of the unequal distribution of economic output. The primary source was the data supplied by the 2000 *World Labour Report* (International Labour Office 2000). Some additional data were taken from the World Bank's (1999) *World Development Indicators 1999*. Most of these data pertain to measurements during the mid-1990s, although some are based on earlier surveys. Income inequality has variously been shown to be a predictor of homicide rates in cross-national analyses. However, much less is known about whether inequality also correlates with a broader measure of violence as well as other types of problem behavior. The third strain-related indicator is the percentage of GDP spent for social security purposes as reported in the 2000 *World Labour Report* (International Labour Office 2000). Relative expenditure on social welfare purposes may be assumed to reflect the degree of a welfare state orientation in a given country. Messner and Rosenfeld (1997) have suggested that social security expenditure can

be interpreted as a proxy measure for protection from market forces as discussed by Esping-Andersen (1990). Also, their research suggests that social welfare expenditures are negatively related to homicide rates in a comparative analysis of forty-five countries.

Both opportunity theory and routine activity theory essentially assume that a major source of cross-national variation in problem behavior is the availability of attractive targets and the exposure to temptations specifically related to the respective problem behavior. In this vein, Felson (1994) argued that increasing affluence and urbanization may be important causes of higher crime in Western societies. I include three general measures of affluence and opportunity structures. One is the overall purchase power–corrected GDP per capita, which can be interpreted as a highly general indicator of affluence-related opportunity structures. The second indicator was the frequency of going out per week in the general population. The main source of these data was figures supplied by Kangaspunta, Joutsen, and Ollus (1998) and based on the ICVS. However, some use was also made of the results of the Health of Youth study (King et al. 1997). This survey included an item on the frequency of going out among juveniles only. Data from both the general population survey (ICVS) and the WHO youth survey were available for seventeen countries and yielded a correlation of $r = .82$. On this basis, both measures were assumed to be measures of the same underlying construct.[1] The third variable was the percentage of newborns who are not expected to survive to age sixty according to the United Nations' *Human Development Report* (United Nations Development Programme, 1999). This measure captures the general quality of life in a society and is influenced by both overall affluence as measured by GDP and the quality of health care and social services.

Finally, social control theory assumes that differences in rates of deviant behavior among juveniles and young adolescents are due to variation in the degree of social control over their behavior. I include three variables, which may be interpreted as measures of informal social control structures at the societal level. The first measure is the proportion of the population living in urban areas according to *World Development Indicators* as provided by the World Bank (1999). Urbanization has often been used in cross-national analyses of crime. Among others, Bennett (1991) assumed that increased urbanization is accompanied by a reduction in the number of lengthy interpersonal ties, a higher level of anonymity, and an increased heterogeneity of the population. All these processes may thwart processes of social control and thus trigger higher levels of problem behavior among juveniles. The second variable is the national divorce rate (United Nations Development Programme 1999). Divorce rates may be interpreted as a proxy for the instability of family arrangements, which in turn encumber the transition from adolescence to early adulthood. Surprisingly, few existing cross-national

studies have examined the relation between divorce rates and deviant behavior. Third, I include the female labor force participation as a measure of the degree to which everyday activities are diverted away from the household and therefore young people may be more likely to be left unsupervised.

Within the exploratory context of this study, I also included the share of the population ages ten to twenty-four, the unemployment rate, and the population size of a country as potentially relevant variables that have often been used in cross-national crime research.

Table 4 shows the bivariate correlations of these variables with the four measures of problem behavior. Due to missing values, the number of valid observations varies between thirty-five and thirty-seven countries. In any statistical analysis with as few as thirty-seven cases, special attention should be paid to influential cases and outliers. This also holds if the analysis is exploratory and descriptive rather than nomothetic and causal. Visual inspection of the scattergrams was therefore used to identify possible problematic observations. However, the results shown below did not appear to be severely affected by single observations.

The results displayed in Table 4 lead us to four conclusions. First, a most noteworthy finding is the complete lack of congruity when we compare the correlation coefficients across different types of problem behavior. Indeed, no single macrosociological variable is consistently correlated with all four sub-

TABLE 4

**PRODUCT-MOMENT CORRELATIONS BETWEEN PROBLEM BEHAVIOR AND SELECTED
MEASURES OF STRAIN, SOCIAL CONTROL, AND OPPORTUNITY STRUCTURES**

	Problem Behavior			
	Violent Crime	Property Crime	Alcohol Abuse	Drug Use
Strain indicators				
Gini index	.50**	.35*	−.08	.30+
Share lowest 20 percent	−.37*	−.37*	.02	−.32+
Percentage welfare expenditures	−.40*	−.07	.34*	.02
Social control				
Urbanization	.04	.47**	.56**	.46**
Divorce rates	.43*	.40*	.40*	.24
Female labour force participation	.65**	.16	−.07	−.31
Affluence and opportunity structures				
GDP per capita	−.56*	.02	.38*	.55**
Going out on weekends	−.33*	.21	.51**	.67**
Percentage not attaining age 60	.75**	.05	−.33*	−.44**
Other variables				
Percentage ages 10-24	.47**	.20	−.10	.02
Percentage unemployed	.17	.10	.02	.19
Population size	.22	.26	.01	.26

NOTE: Ns = 35 to 37.
$*p < .05$, two-tailed. $**p < .01$, two-tailed.

dimensions of problem behavior. Rather, the data suggest that different types of problem behavior combine with national structural conditions in distinct ways. Although based on simple bivariate descriptive statistics, this finding may have two major implications. Empirically, it lends further support to the notion that on a cross-national level, different manifestations of problem behavior do not constitute one single underlying dimension. Theoretically, the finding suggests that any explanation of cross-national differences in a specific type of problem behavior should include explicit arguments about why the supposed causes apply to that specific type of behavior.

Second, violent crime rates show a distinct pattern of correlation with structural variables, which is unique when compared to the other

manifestations of problem behavior. Its distinct feature is its consistent positive correlation with the three measures of social strain and strong negative correlation with all measures of affluence. Also, violence rates are higher in societies with high female labor force participation and a high divorce rate. When entered simultaneously in an exploratory ordinary least squares regression, the Gini index, GDP, and divorce rates have significant effects and explain 59 percent of the variance in the violence measure. It thus appears that violent behavior is particularly high in macro-level contexts, which combine high levels of inequality, low levels of affluence, and low levels of informal social control. However, the results also suggest that this combination of contextual correlates applies only to violence but not to other kinds of problem behavior.

Third, levels of property crime appear to be moderately correlated with high levels of income inequality and somewhat more strongly correlated with high urbanization and elevated divorce rates. Inspection of the scattergrams reveals that the correlation with inequality measures may be due to two influential cases only, while the statistical association with both urbanization and divorce rates is based on a robust, but not very close, relationship. Somewhat surprisingly, however, levels of property crime do not appear to be significantly correlated with measures of affluence. This finding contradicts findings by, for example, Kangaspunta et al. (1999), who found property crime to be high in countries with high levels of affluence.

Fourth, both alcohol abuse and drug use among youth appear to be characterized by a similar profile of correlations with macro-level variables. In particular, both types of problem behavior are more prevalent in countries with a high frequency of going out, a high GDP per capita, and a high level of urbanization. Cross-national levels of juvenile substance use therefore appear to be primarily related to differences in the opportunity structures and patterns of lifestyle that result from the affluence of modern society in general and the structure of everyday life in urban contexts in particular.

CONCLUSIONS

Cross-national comparative studies of crime and deviant behavior are likely to become an increasingly important field of research. This article has explored several patterns and regularities that may be relevant for future research. It has emphasized that cross-national comparative studies should take into account the huge amount of robust findings that have emerged from life-course studies. More particularly, this research shows, among other things, that various manifestations of problem behavior are strongly interrelated at the individual level and that they follow similar developmental patterns throughout the life course—with adolescence found to be the crucial transition phase in all societies. Accordingly, cross-national comparative research should pay greater attention, both theoretically and empirically, to the ways in which macro-level factors intervene in biographical developments during the phase of adolescence and influence the degree to which specific manifestations of problem behavior will be more or less prevalent in a given society. A closer empirical examination of this perspective would require a much more sophisticated data set than could be utilized here, however. It is for this reason that Reiss (1994) in particular pointed out that there is ultimately a need for extremely sophisticated longitudinal studies, designed for international comparison, that include systematic variation at the level of national contexts as a level of investigation.

Second, this article has examined ways by which more broadly based cross-national measures of problem behavior can be obtained than those that have been most often used in past research. In this vein, I have attempted to show that the increasing availability of cross-national survey data may greatly help to overcome some of the limitations of past research. More particularly, by combining different types of data sources, I have attempted to derive measures for four types of problem behavior, namely violent crime, property crime, alcohol abuse, and drug use. Exploratory analysis of these data suggests several findings, which may help to better understand the ways in which macro-level structures influence the transition from adolescence to early adulthood. The analyses reveal, for example, that Anglo-Saxon countries tend to have comparatively high scores on any of the dimensions discussed in this article. Many eastern European countries, in contrast, were found to have high levels of violent crime but low levels of illicit drug consumption. Another group of countries including Cyprus, Greece, Norway, Portugal, and Switzerland was found to have consistently low scores in problem behavior. As yet, there is no conclusive evidence about the factors that can help us to understand the formation of these clusters. However, exploratory examination of some macro-level correlates of different types of problem behavior yields some suggestions. Violence, for instance, appears to be frequent in contexts characterized by great social inequality, low levels of social control, and widespread material poverty. Drug use and alcohol abuse among young people, in contrast, is frequent in highly urbanized, highly affluent contexts where lifestyles are leisure-time oriented. The specific configuration of problem behavior in a country may thus depend on the way in which the transition to early adulthood is molded by the concurrence of opportunities and lifestyles related to general affluence, the intensity of informal social control associated with different family and household patterns, and the strain originating from the degree to which life chances and resources are unequally distributed in a society.

Note

1. To make the data from the Health of Youth study comparable to those given by Kangaspunta, Joutsen, and Ollus (1998), a linear regression was first performed for the seventeen countries with data for both variables. The estimated slope was then used to complement data for four countries (Cyprus, Denmark, Greece, and Portugal) with no data in the International Crime Victim Survey.

References

Abraham, M. D., P.D.A. Cohen, R.-J.v. Til, and M.P.S. Langemeijer. 1998. *Licit and illicit drug use in Amsterdam III: Developments in drug use 1987-1997.* Amsterdam: CEDRO.

Alcohol and Public Health Research Unit. 2001. *Young people and alcohol.* Retrieved 2 February 2001 from http://www.aphru.ac.nz/hot/young.htm.

Bennett, R. B. 1991. Routine activities: A cross-national assessment of a criminological perspective. *Social Forces* 70 (1): 147-63.

Blumstein, A., J. Cohen, and D. Farrington. 1988. Criminal career research: Its value for criminology. *Criminology* 26 (1): 1-35.

Buchmann, M. 1989. *The script of life in modern societies: Entry into adulthood in a changing world.* Chicago: University of Chicago Press.

Bundeskriminalamt. 1998. *Polizeiliche Kriminalstatistik Bundesrepublik Deutschland*. Wiesbaden, Germany: Bundeskriminalamt.

Bureau of Justice Statistics. 2001. *Homicide trends in the United States*. Washington, DC: Bureau of Justice Statistics. Retrieved 2 February 2001 from http://www.ojp.usdoj.gov/bjs/homicide/homtrnd.htm#contents.

Elliott, D. S., D. Huizinga, and S. S. Ageton. 1985. *Explaining delinquency and drug use*. Beverly Hills, CA: Sage.

Esping-Andersen, G. 1990. *The three worlds of welfare capitalism*. Princeton, NJ: Princeton University Press.

European Committee on Crime Problems. 1999. *European sourcebook of crime and criminal justice statistics*. Strasbourg, France: Council of Europe.

European Monitoring Centre for Drugs and Drug Addiction. 1998. *Annual report on the state of the drugs problem in the European Union*. Lisbon, Portugal: European Monitoring Centre for Drugs and Drug Addiction.

Everitt, B. S. 1993. *Cluster analysis*. New York: Edward Arnold.

Farrington, D. P. 1994. Human development and criminal careers. In *The Oxford handbook of criminology*, edited by M. Maguire, R. Morgan, and R. Reiner, 511-84. Oxford, UK: Clarendon.

Felson, M. 1994. *Crime and everyday life: Insight and implications for society*. Thousand Oaks, CA: Pine Forge.

Ferrante, A., and N. Loh. 1998. *Crime and justice statistics for Western Australia: 1997*. Perth: Crime Research Centre, University of Western Australia.

Gartner, R. 1990. The victims of homicide: A temporal and cross-national comparison. *American Sociological Review* 55:92-106.

Gottfredson, M. T., and T. Hirschi. 1990. *A general theory of crime*. Stanford, CA: Stanford University Press.

Halpern, D. 2001. Moral values, social trust, and inequality: Can values explain crime? *British Journal of Criminology* 41 (2): 236-51.

Health Canada. 1997. *Canada's Alcohol and Other Drugs Survey 1994: A discussion of the findings*. Ottawa: Health Canada.

Hibell, B., B. Andersson, S. Ahlström, O. Balakireva, T. Bjarnason, A. Kokkevi, and M. Morgan. 2000. *The 1999 ESPAD report: Alcohol and other drug use among students in 30 European countries*. Stockholm: Swedish Council for Information on Alcohol and Other Drugs.

Hibell, B., B. Andersson, T. Bjarnason, A. Kokkevi, M. Morgan, and A. Narusk. 1997. *The 1995 ESPAD report: Alcohol and other drug use among students in 26 European countries*. Stockholm: Swedish Council for Information on Alcohol and Other Drugs.

Hirschi, T. 1983. Age and the explanation of crime. *American Journal of Sociology* 89 (3): 552-70.

Home Office. 1998. *Criminal statistics, England and Wales*. London: Home Office.

International Criminal Police Organization. 1977. *International crime statistics*. Lyon, France: Interpol.

International Labour Office. 2000. *World labour report: Income security and social protection in a changing world*. Geneva, Switzerland: International Labour Office.

James, M., and C. Carcach. 1997. *Homicide in Australia 1989-96*. Australian Institute of Criminology Research and Public Policy series no. 13. Canberra: Australian Institute of Criminology.

Junger-Tas, J., G. J. Terlouw, and M. W. Klein. 1994. *Delinquent behavior among young people in the Western world: First results of the International Self-Report Delinquency Study*. Amsterdam: Kugler.

Kangaspunta, K., M. Joutsen, and N. Ollus, eds. 1998. *Crime and criminal justice systems in Europe and North America, 1990-1994.* Helsinki, Finland: European Institute for Crime Prevention and Control (HEUNI).

Kangaspunta, K., M. Joutsen, N. Ollus, and S. Nevala. 1999. *Profiles of criminal justice systems in Europe and North America.* HEUNI publication series 33. Helsinki, Finland: European Institute for Crime Prevention and Control (HEUNI).

Kantonspolizei Zürich, ed. 1997. *KRISTA: Kriminalstatistik des Kantons Zürich.* Zürich, Switzerland: Kantonspolizei Zürich.

King, A., B. Wold, C. Tudor-Smith, and Y. Harel. 1997. *The Health of Youth: A cross-national survey.* Geneva, Switzerland: World Health Organization.

Krahn, H., T. F. Hartnagel, and J. W. Gatrell. 1986. Income inequality and homicide rates: Cross national data and criminological theories. *Criminology* 24:269-95.

Kraus, L., and R. Bauernfeind. 1998. *Repräsentativerhebung zum Gebrauch psychoaktiver Substanzen bei Erwachsenen in Deutschland 1997 (Sonderheft 1 der Zeitschrift "Sucht").* Geesthacht, Germany: Neuland.

Kruskal, J. B., and M. Wish. 1978. *Multidimensional scaling.* Beverly Hills, CA: Sage.

LaFree, G. D., and E. L. Kick. 1986. Cross-National effects of development, distributional and demographic variables on crime: A review and analysis. *International Annals of Criminology* 24:213-36.

Lee, M. R., and W. B. Bankston. 1999. Political structure, economic inequality, and homicide: A cross-national analysis. *Deviant Behavior: An Interdisciplinary Journal* 19:27-55.

Loeber, R. 1996. Developmental continuity, change, and pathways in male juvenile problem behaviors and delinquency. In *Delinquency and crime—Current theories,* edited by J. D. Hawkins, 1-27. Cambridge, UK: Cambridge University Press.

Makkai, R., and I. McAllister. 1998. *Patterns of drug use in Australia, 1985-1995.* Canberra: Australian Government Publishing Service.

Mayhew, P., and J.J.M. van Dijk. 1997. *Criminal victimisation in eleven industrialised countries: Key findings from the 1996 International Crime Survey.* The Hague, the Netherlands: Ministry of Justice, WODC.

Messner, S. F., and R. Rosenfeld. 1997. Political restraint of the market and levels of criminal homicide: A cross-national application of institutional-anomie theory. *Social Forces* 75:1393-1416.

Moffitt, T. E. 1994. Natural histories of delinquency. In *Cross-National longitudinal research on human development and criminal behavior,* edited by E.G.M. Weitekamp and H.-J. Kerner, 3-64. Dordrecht, Holland: Kluwer.

Pampel, F. C., and J. B. Williamson. 2001. Age patterns of suicide and homicide mortality rates in high-income nations. *Social Forces* 80 (1): 251-81.

Prescott-Clarke, P., and P. Primatesta, eds. 1998. *Health survey for England '96.* London: HMSO.

Ramsay, M., and J. Spiller. 1997. *Drug misuse declared in 1996: Latest results from the British Crime Survey.* Home Office research study no. 172. London: Home Office.

Reiss, A. J. 1994. Towards comparative societal longitudinal studies. In *Cross-National longitudinal research on human development and criminal behavior,* edited by E.G.M. Weitekamp and H.-J. Kerner, 423-37. Dordrecht, Holland: Kluwer.

Sampson, R. J., and J. H. Laub. 1993. *Crime in the making: Pathways and turning points through life.* Cambridge, MA: Harvard University Press.

Simons, R. L., C. Johnson, R. D. Conger, and G. E. Jr. 1998. A test of latent trait versus life-course perspectives on the stability of adolescent behavior. *Criminology* 36 (2): 217-44.

Statistics Canada. 2001. Homicide victims and suspects, by age and sex. Retrieved 25 January 2001 from http://www.statcan.ca.

Substance Abuse and Mental Health Services Administration. 1998. *National Household Survey on Drug Abuse series H-5: National Household Survey on Drug Abuse main findings 1996.* Rockville, MD: Office of Applied Studies.

United Nations. 1998. *Fifth United Nations survey of crime trends and operations of criminal justice systems.* Vienna: United Nations Office.

United Nations Development Programme. 1999. *Human development report.* New York: United Nations.

U.S. Department of Justice. 1996. *Uniform crime reports for the United States.* Washington, DC: Government Printing Office.

van Dijk, J.J.M. 1992. *Criminal victimization in the industrialized world: Key findings of the 1989 and 1992 International Crime Surveys.* The Hague, the Netherlands: Directorate for Crime Prevention.

van Dijk, J.J.M., P. Mayhew, and M. Killias, eds. 1991. *Experiences of crime across the world: Key findings of the 1989 International Crime Survey.* Deventer, the Netherlands: Kluwer.

Warr, M. 1998. Life-Course transitions and desistance from crime. *Criminology* 36 (2): 183-216.

West, D. J., and D. P. Farrington. 1977. *The delinquent way of life.* London: Heinemann.

Wolfgang, M., R. Figlio, and T. Sellin. 1972. *Delinquency in a birth cohort.* Chicago: University of Chicago Press.

World Bank. 1999. *World development indicators 1999.* Washington, DC: World Bank.

Zvekic, U. 1998. *Criminal victimisation in countries in transition.* Publication no. 61. Rome: UNICRI.

ANNALS, *AAPSS*, **580**, March 2002

Is Youth a Better Predictor of Sociopolitical Values Than Is Nationality?

By JAMES TILLEY

ABSTRACT: Using data from the World Values Survey, this article examines a series of strongly held values and beliefs concerning the political and wider social world, on a cross-nationally comparative basis. Orientations such as political outlook, attitudes toward religion, political participation, social movements, women's roles, and satisfaction with life are examined. Tentative groupings of young people by country are attempted, revealing a commonality of values among the old and young in certain clusters of societies. Within these clusters, the relative magnitude of gender and age differences in attitudinal positioning are analyzed, to show how nationality and youth interact differently when examining different attitudes. It is found that young people do have common values cross-nationally, but only within certain supranational limits.

James Tilley is currently a research fellow at the Department of Political Science, Trinity College Dublin. He studied for his doctorate at Nuffield College, Oxford University, and has published other articles concerning the interaction of political and social values with age.

NOTE: The author gratefully acknowledges the useful suggestions and comments of Anthony Heath, Frank F. Furstenberg Jr., Anne H. Gauthier, and Diego Gambetta on earlier drafts of this article. The World Values Survey data set was supplied by the Data Archive, University of Essex, and was originally assembled and documented by Ronald Inglehart. Neither bears any responsibility for the analysis presented here.

The young always have the same problem—how to rebel and conform at the same time. They have now solved this by defying their parents and copying one another.

—Quentin Crisp
(*The Naked Civil Servant*, 1968)

Postmaterialism and globalization theses have at their heart the idea that national differences between individuals are becoming less important via a generational mechanism. Newer generations of different nationalities have more in common with each other than with their elders in their own countries. Inglehart's theory of increasing postmaterialism postulates a generational process whereby newer cohorts are more postmaterialist in their attitudes than are the old. It is argued that the emergence of advanced industrial society is making particular values of attributes more common among members of those societies (Abramson and Inglehart 1987; Inglehart 1977, 1990; Inglehart and Abramson 1994). Inglehart (1990) stated, "We may be witnessing a broad cultural shift, with one world view replacing another" (p. 424). For this to be the case, one must postulate strong generational processes within countries. Mannheim (1952) characterized generations, those born in close temporal proximity to one another, as being concrete social groups in a similar manner to social classes. Thus, Mannheim argued that cohorts (and hence at any one point in time, age groups) will share similar attitudes.

If these generational theories of increasing differentiation between young and old are correct, then there is potential for an interesting situation in which international differences are of much smaller magnitude than intranational age differences. Inglehart argued that this will be the case with societies increasingly internally divided by the postmaterialist/materialist labels (which are a function of birth cohort). Thus, nationality becomes less important, and supranational organizations, institutions, and movements increase in importance. In particular, young people now will appear quite different to previous generations. Across nations, the young will be more postmaterialist and more likely to be interested in supranational causes such as the ecology and women's movements (Inglehart 1990, 1995). In terms of the future paths taken by international and supranational organizations, such as the European Union and the United Nations, this process is clearly of some importance.

The aim of this article is to assess the degree to which this possible commonality by age group overshadows commonality by nationality. While intranational comparisons between age groups and international comparisons between countries are often made separately, it is rarely considered whether the young are an internationally cohesive group. If Inglehart and colleagues are correct, then this is a very relevant question, for one would expect greater similarity between young people across nations than between people of different ages in the same country.

There is certainly evidence for generational processes' affecting attitudes and values in many differing national contexts. For example, young people have different attitudes toward political parties and political ideologies; both their behavior and their attitudes in the political domain differ from those of their elders. It is a well-documented fact, at least in Britain and the United States, that the young are more left wing in voting behavior and beliefs (Butler and Stokes 1974; Campbell et al. 1960). The same can be said of other fundamental values such as religious beliefs and attitudes toward the family and work. Younger people are often seen as less involved with these institutions. For example, they are less religious in practice and beliefs (Chaves 1989; Stolzenberg 1995).

Although age is thought to be an important predictor of values, cross-national variation in sociopolitical attitudes is also taken for granted. Differences in income, education processes, and historical and religious contexts inevitably mean that attitudes toward various issues will differ. Equally, processes of post-industrialization should be expected to be more advanced in some countries, which will be accordingly more postmaterialist in their outlook. To oversimplify somewhat, one might expect those living in richer countries to exhibit a greater tendency to focus on postmaterialist issues, such as environmental protection, and those in poorer countries to be more concerned about materialist issues such as the control of inflation (Inglehart 1977). The historical

legacies of nations will clearly affect people's attitudes also. Catholicism and communism are likely to mold individuals' beliefs in specific ways.

Allied to this, men and women may well react to the world differently, due to their gender and consequent differences in upbringing and opportunities. The influence of gender on attitudes among young people is also clearly of interest, and this aspect of attitudinal difference will also be referred to when relevant.

Given these two main factors, the operation of nationality and youth on attitudes, which is dominant and to what extent? Is it reasonable to argue that the young are a coherent grouping with a common base of values regardless of nationality, or are age differences swamped by large international differences among youth? The reality is likely to be somewhere in between these two positions. In particular, it is likely that young people in certain sets of countries will exhibit quite similar attitudes due to shared historical experiences, similar institutional arrangements, simple geographical proximity, and correlated levels of economic development. Attempting to compare a large number of separate societies is perhaps not realistic. To try and group these societies and then see how these groupings differ is a much more feasible proposition.

The first aim of this article is an attempt to separate countries into groupings that do have a set of values that young people hold cross-nationally—the assumption being that there are clusters of societies in which people share both similar prescriptive attitudes toward society and similar beliefs about the objective reality of the world. The second and wider-reaching objective is then to see how these groupings differ from one another and whether age or national grouping is a better indicator of attitudinal position.

It is important to be clear which attitudes are amenable to this sort of international generalization. When attempting these comparisons, one must think of fairly fundamental attitudinal stances that one would expect to see manifested in similar ways cross-nationally. A number of factors have been cited as important components of cultural shifts associated with the emergence of advanced industrial society. Work motivations, political outlook, attitudes toward the role of women and religion are all often mentioned. Given this, the focus will be on attitudes in three main areas. First, in the political realm both ideological and participatory values will be analyzed. Second, attitudinal positions toward religion and the role of the family will be explored. Finally, the world of work and general life satisfaction will be examined.

DATA

The data presented in this article are from an age representative survey, the 1990 World Values Survey (WVS). This data set was chosen as its coverage is especially broad; surveys were carried out in forty-three countries in 1990.[1] No other attitudinal survey series can claim this many contributing countries. Not only is the country coverage broad, but so is the question coverage. A large number of questions were asked in all three areas of proposed investigation, and since these questions all come from one survey, comparisons between these areas are made somewhat easier.

Having said this, the sample design for most countries meant that fewer than 2,000 individuals were surveyed. Given that this article is primarily interested in young people, here defined as those younger than thirty-five, the sample sizes are inevitably somewhat small. Nonetheless, samples were typically 500 cases or more even for the younger-than-thirty-five age group.[2] There are particular problems with sampling in certain countries, especially for the Indian and Nigerian samples. The Indian survey concentrated on the literate members of society, only half the actual population; thus, upweighting the small numbers of young illiterates surveyed is liable to produce anomalous results. The Nigerian survey sampled mainly individuals from urban areas, so weighting the rural young is similarly problematic. Given this, both the Indian and Nigerian samples have been excluded from further analysis.

DERIVING INTERNATIONAL GROUPINGS

Before attempting to assess the impact of youth in determining attitudes, it is necessary to try to group similar countries together. A rigorous way of determining clusters of societies is multidimensional scaling (MDS). This involves standardizing a series of measures, then constructing a range of Euclidean distances between countries for each of these variables. By using a two-dimensional solution, one can plot a graph on which each country is represented and see which nationalities tend to group together. This is rather like the more commonly used factor analysis; countries with similar values will cluster together, and those with differing values will not cluster. The more culturally similar the countries are, the closer they cluster together. Moreover, this analysis can then be carried out for those older and younger than thirty-five. This makes it easy to test whether the young cluster differently by country compared with the middle aged and elderly.

As discussed earlier, when trying to build up an attitudinal picture of different nationalities, the focus will have to be on fairly deeply held beliefs. For this reason, the MDS procedure used here only includes measures of political beliefs and involvement, religious beliefs, attitudes toward the role of women, and two measures of satisfaction with the world. These are examined in detail in later sections. The items that were included were the following:

1. the mean score on a religious belief scale,
2. the mean score on a scale measuring traditionalism toward women's roles in society,
3. the mean score on a constructed Left-Right scale,
4. the coherence of Left-Right position (as measured by Cronbach's alpha for the reliability of the Left-Right scale),

5. the mean score on a political action scale,
6. the mean score on a scale indicating approval of new social movements,
7. the mean job satisfaction score, and
8. the mean life satisfaction score.

Since not all countries' surveys asked every one of the attitudinal questions mentioned, young people from some societies cannot be included in this MDS procedure: China, Czechoslovakia, Estonia, Latvia, Lithuania, Poland, Romania, South Africa, South Korea, Switzerland, and Turkey have therefore been excluded.

The two-dimensional scaling plot for young people, Figure 1, shows that there are distinct clusters of countries that appear to group in an intelligible manner. Finland, Norway, and Sweden group rather well in a northern European cluster. Western Europe (Belgium, France, Italy, the Netherlands, and West Germany) forms a central group, with another group consisting of the English-speaking countries of Canada, the United States, and Britain close by. The countries of the Iberian Peninsula and South America form another coherent grouping, with Ireland and Mexico lying between this and the western European group. Belarus, Bulgaria, and Russia form a tight-knit cluster, but Japan appears to be quite singular.

Finally, Austria and Hungary seem quite similar, which, given their very divergent history since the

FIGURE 1
MULTIDIMENSIONAL SCALING (EUCLIDEAN DISTANCE MODEL):
THOSE YOUNGER THAN 35 ONLY

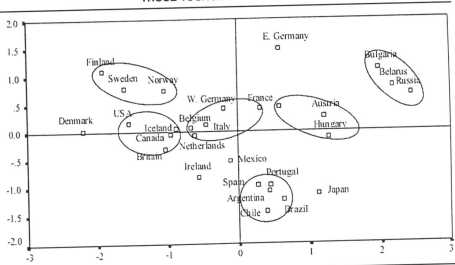

breakup of the Austro-Hungarian empire, is quite surprising. There does, however, appear to be a central European group comprising Austria, Hungary, and Slovenia.[3] With the religious belief scale removed, a series of questions that the Baltic states failed to include in their surveys, another MDS procedure was run. This revealed a similar pattern to the one above, with the Baltic states grouped together quite closely between East Germany and the Russia/Belarus/Bulgaria cluster. In fact, two other East European nations, Romania and Poland, also seem to be fairly close to these other former communist countries.[4]

These groupings seem plausible; young people's attitudes toward a very broad set of issues appear to be consistent across some groups of societies. Moreover, these groups appear to be both cultural and geographical.

Latin American youth attitudes are very close to Iberian youth attitudes, and British young people have more in common with their Canadian peers than with those in the rest of Europe.

Figure 2 shows an identical piece of analysis for those older than thirty-five. As one can see, the picture is not in fact greatly altered, but there are a few differences from the plot for those younger than thirty-five. Northern Europe is somewhat more distinctive and less like the rest of western Europe; also, Britain, Canada, and the United States form a more tightly knit group. In fact, it appears that young people within western Europe, northern Europe, and North America are more homogenous with respect to their attitudes than are their parents' generation. Most clusters seem quite similar though—Russia, Bulgaria, and

FIGURE 2
MULTIDIMENSIONAL SCALING (EUCLIDEAN DISTANCE MODEL):
THOSE OLDER THAN 35 ONLY

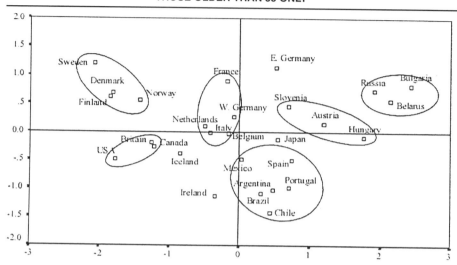

Belarus grouping in a very similar manner, for example.[5]

These two diagrams do not help to establish the relative size of age-related and national-level differences, however. Rather, they show that young and old cluster similarly, and the working hypothesis that there are distinctive groups of societies (which can be condensed to simplify analysis) is largely confirmed. Without examining individual attitudinal measures, it is impossible to say whether there are large age differences within the clusters. Although people within different clusters appear differentiated from one another, it may be that these differences are actually quite small when compared to age differences within the clusters. If the old are substantially more religious than the young, then the young in two different clusters may be more alike than the young and old within one cluster.

These MDS procedures are, however, useful for determining some division into clusters to enable aggregate analyses. The breakdown into groupings, which I will use for further analysis, is based on the results in Figures 1 and 2. The clear similarities that the analyses for those both older than and younger than thirty-five years old share give rise to the groups shown in Table 1. The only country that could be distinguished with the MDS procedure, but that does not fall naturally or easily into a cluster, is Japan. Rather than have a group with only a single member, Japan has been excluded from further analysis.

For the analysis of these groups, mean values of attitudinal variables

TABLE 1
COUNTRIES AND THEIR CLUSTER GROUPS

Group	Country
Anglo-Saxon	Britain, Canada, Ireland, United States
Nordic	Denmark, Finland, Iceland, Norway, Sweden
Western European	Belgium, France, Italy, Netherlands, West Germany
Hispanic	Argentina, Brazil, Chile, Mexico, Portugal, Spain
Central European	Austria, Hungary, Slovenia
Eastern European	Belarus, Bulgaria, East Germany, Estonia, Lithuania, Latvia, Poland, Romania, Russia

have been derived by giving each country equal weight within its cluster.[6] Therefore, the larger sample sizes in some countries will not affect the average for that group. The next step is to establish the extent to which differences between these clusters of countries are overshadowed by age-related differences.

RELIGIOUS AND FAMILY VALUES

Religious beliefs

The sociology of religion often emphasizes the significant age differences in religious beliefs. Work in the United States has demonstrated that disparities in religious practice are often correlated with age and that the young are noticeably less religious than the middle aged (Stolzenberg 1995). Equally, theories of secularization depend to some extent on the idea of generational succession, successive cohorts becoming less religious (Wilson 1982). Inglehart (1990) argued that "the worldview espoused by most of the established religions seems increasingly out of touch with the perceptions and priorities of the younger generation" (p. 187). An intergenerational value shift is argued to be occurring, leading to a secular youth culture as opposed to the more religious set of values that older generations hold. To what extent is this picture of more secular young people replicated across societies? Is it replicated in a way that would incline one to treat youth as a more coherent group than a nation?

The WVS contains a number of questions about adherence to essentially Christian beliefs: belief in the existence of a God, an afterlife, a soul, a heaven, a hell, a devil, and sin. Although these questions were asked in most nominally Christian countries, they were not asked in the Baltic states. Thus, the eastern European grouping includes only Belarus, Bulgaria, East Germany, Poland, Romania, and Russia. Regardless of nationality, answers to these questions cohere extremely well. When constructed, a Likert-type scale[7] had a Cronbach's alpha[8] of around .75 in most countries, and although this is somewhat lower for the younger age groups, it indicates the consistency of these attitudinal positions.

FIGURE 3
MEAN SCORES ON THE RELIGIOUS BELIEFS SCALE

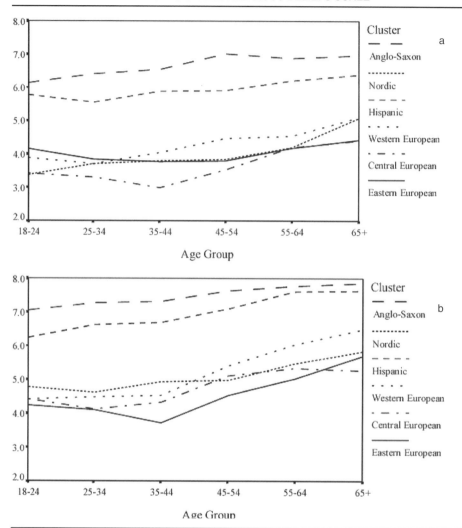

NOTE: Higher scores indicate stronger religious beliefs. a = mean male score on the religious beliefs scale. b = mean female score on the religious beliefs scale.

Figure 3 shows the mean scores on the religious belief scale (0 indicating belief in none of the above pieces of Christian doctrine, 10 indicating belief in all) for each cluster separately by gender and age group. There are therefore four possible factors of interest here: differences by gender, differences by age, differences between clusters, and interactions between age, gender, and country cluster.

Before turning to the question of nationality and age, it is worth noting that women are clearly more religious than are men in every country cluster, an established finding in many studies (Miller and Hoffman 1995; Walter and Davie 1998). Women on average score almost an extra point on the scale compared to men. What is perhaps more interesting is the large disparity in religiosity between different clusters of countries and how this interacts with age-related differences. There is a huge gap between the Anglo-Saxon countries and the rest of the Western industrialized world. Eighteen- to twenty-four-year-olds from western European and Nordic countries have mean scores of around 4, while the score is greater than 6.5 for the corresponding age group in the Anglo-Saxon countries. The enforced secularization of the former communist countries shows in the low scores for the eastern and central European societies,[9] and the practiced Catholicism of the Hispanic nations shows in the high belief scores displayed by this cluster.

There is also an age differential in religious beliefs. The young are noticeably less religious than the old are, and this relationship appears almost linear in some cases. In the Anglo-Saxon grouping, those under twenty-four differ by nearly 1 point from those older than sixty-five. However, what appears a very constant trend in the more religious Hispanic and Anglo-Saxon countries is nonlinear in other societies, this being particularly notable among women. Those younger than thirty-

five in western and Scandinavian Europe are remarkably similar, and it is only among older generations that a noticeable trend to more religious belief is apparent. If this is a generational process of secularization, then it appears to have slowed somewhat in these countries during the past twenty years.

In eastern Europe, there is very little difference between the old and young. Given these provisos, it does seem that national differences are of greater magnitude when considering religious beliefs. Therefore, it seems that youth is not the defining characteristic that determines attitudes toward religion. Instead, it is nationality: specifically the difference between the East and secularized West (western Europe) on one hand and the South (Hispanic cluster) and English-speaking countries on the other. Within these groupings, age does have an effect, but it is less pronounced than any cluster effect.

Women's role in society

Religious beliefs are often linked with attitudes toward the family and the role of women in society. Given the clear differences in religious attitudes between country clusters and the pace of change of these beliefs, is it reasonable to say that there is a coherent set of youth values about family structure? There is a popular perception that "traditional" family structures (with women working in the home) have a tendency to be more strongly supported in religious societies. This intuition has been confirmed by work on the International Social Survey Programme (Harding

1989; Scott, Braun, and Alwin 1993).[10] Country-level differences have also been accounted for by postmaterialist theories, with industrial structure and change proposed as the important factors in explaining national differences. Of course, given the generational nature of the theory, one ought to see age-related differences within countries as well. Indeed, age is certainly a confirmed predictor of traditionalism, the same ISSP studies showing that younger people were more inclined to give liberal responses.

A number of questions about women's employment were included in the WVS. Respondents were asked whether they approved or disapproved of the following statements:

1. A working mother can establish just as warm and secure a relationship with her children as a mother who does not work.

2. A preschool child is likely to suffer if his or her mother works.

3. A job is all right, but what most women really want is a home and children.

4. Being a housewife is just as fulfilling as working for pay.

5. Having a job is the best way for a woman to be an independent person.

6. Both the husband and the wife should contribute to household income.

These items have been combined into a Likert-type scale designed to try to measure the traditionalism of respondents' opinions.[11] The reliability statistics for this scale are not particularly high, at best 0.65 in West Germany, although most Western countries have figures greater than 0.50. The responses from individuals in eastern Europe and less developed countries are generally of lower coherence than this. Therefore, by using this sort of scale, one is sacrificing some detail from the responses. In addition, the first two questions about working mothers are measuring something somewhat different from the last two questions about contributions to household income and independence.[12]

Bearing this in mind, there are still some very interesting disparities in responses, as Figure 4 shows. As might be anticipated, men are generally more traditional in their outlook than are women, and this seems to be true of all age groups in all societies. As might also be expected, the inhabitants of the Nordic countries are the most liberal. However, it is not the Catholic South Americas that are the most traditional but the eastern European cluster.[13] Those younger than twenty-four in these former communist societies are by far the least liberal. The mean for this group is around 1 point higher than that for the same age group in the Nordic countries. Elements of this pattern tend to coincide with findings elsewhere. Despite high female workforce participation rates, eastern Europeans (including the young) remain more traditional in their beliefs about the role of women in society (Scott, Braun, and Alwin 1993; Pilkington 1996). Aside

FIGURE 4
MEAN SCORES ON THE WOMEN'S ROLE SCALE

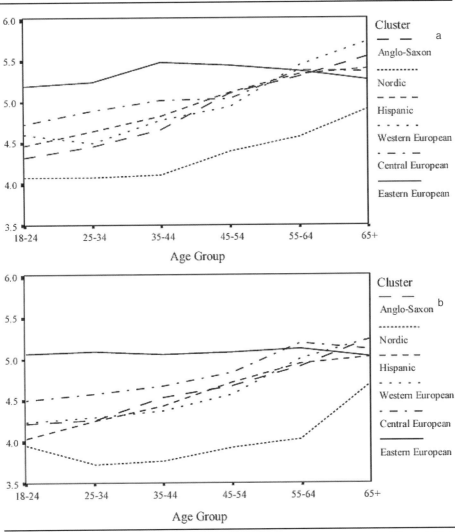

NOTE: Higher scores indicate greater traditionalism. a = mean male scores on the Women's Role Scale. b = mean female scores on the Women's Role Scale.

from the Nordic and eastern European clusters, though, other nationalities appear quite similar.

What is also interesting is the variety of age differences that one can see among the young and the old in attitudes toward women's work. Figure 4 shows that there is really very little difference between the old and young in the eastern European cluster, but elsewhere there is a steady trend for the young to be more liberal than their elders. One obvious explanation is simply that attitudes in the industrialized West have had to accommodate the feminist revolution of the past thirty years. Arguably, the lack of change toward a more advanced postindustrial economy in eastern Europe has meant not only that women's movements have been less successful but that the impetus to postmaterialist values in this form has been much less strong.

When examining attitudes toward social conservatism, as typified by the role of women in society, there is an interesting picture of national difference, age-related divergence, and interaction effects between the two. One sees little attitude change in eastern Europe by generation, the old being indistinguishable from the young, but large intracountry differences by age group exist elsewhere. Thus, youth in eastern Europe is much less important than nationality, but youth in the West supersedes national boundaries to a large extent. By contrast with religious values, in the field of women's roles, the young in Britain and Belgium have much more in common with each other than they do with their respective groups of elders.

POLITICAL VALUES

Young people's positioning on a Left-Right ideological spectrum

The notion that attitudes toward political parties, groups, and issues can be reduced to a single dimension, a socialist–laissez faire economic divide, is a little simplistic. However, it has been shown in numerous Western societies that this is an important underlying dimension to political behavior and more focused political attitudes. Rokeach (1973) put forward a two-value model of political beliefs with core values of "equality versus inequality" and "freedom versus authoritarianism" forming people's attitudes. He argued that these values underlie popular political ideologies, and he proceeded to fit systems to value combinations; that is, capitalism would be unequal but free, and communism equal but authoritarian. Thus, his value of equality is analogous to a Left-Right dimension in political belief, and many have used this as a starting point to analyze behavior on Left-Right scales (Feldman 1988; Heath, Evans, and Martin 1994; Evans, Heath, and Lalljee 1996).

Moreover, this dimension has often been shown to be age related. In many Western societies, the young tend to be more left wing than are the middle aged and elderly (Butler and Stokes 1974; Jennings and Niemi 1981). Given this, it seems reasonable to ask about the extent to which these differences are replicated across societies. Is this age dimension more important than cross-national dispersion?

This article will attempt to answer that question using a Likert-type scale constructed from a series of six

TABLE 2
LEFT-RIGHT RELIABILITY (CRONBACH'S ALPHA AND CORRELATION
BETWEEN SELF-PLACEMENT AND LEFT-RIGHT SCALE SCORE)

Cluster	Cronbach's Alpha	Correlation
Anglo-Saxon	.67	.23*
Nordic	.67	.47*
Western European	.63	.33*
Hispanic	.49	.18*
Central European	.48	.12*
Eastern European	.46	.06*

*Significant at the .01 level.

questions in the WVS that tap into this economic liberalism versus state interventionism divide. Respondents were asked to place themselves on a scale of 1 to 10, with the responses below representing the two extremes.

a. Incomes should be made more equal.
   There should be greater incentives for individual effort.

b. Private ownership of business and industry should be increased.
   Government ownership of business and industry should be increased.

c. Individuals should take more responsibility for providing for themselves.
   The state should take more responsibility to ensure that everyone is provided for.

d. People who are unemployed should have to take any job available or lose their unemployment benefits.

People who are unemployed should have the right to refuse a job they do not want.

e. Competition is good. It stimulates people to work hard and develop new ideas.
   Competition is harmful. It brings out the worst in people.

f. In the long run, hard work usually brings a better life.
   Hard work does not generally bring success—it is more a matter of luck and connections.

This sort of scale, comprising similar questions, has been used previously in research in Britain and has been found to be fairly robust (Heath, Evans, and Martin 1994; Evans, Heath, and Lalljee 1996). However, it is reasonable to ask whether this robust scale reliability can be maintained when looking at such a diverse range of countries. What emerges from examining scale reliabilities for these items, as measured by Cronbach's alpha, is that intercountry differences in scale reliability are of a fairly large magnitude. A Cronbach's alpha of .7 is generally taken to indicate a relatively coherent scale. As Table 2 shows, in some countries, one can expect a much more coherent set of answers to questions involving Left-Right economic matters than in others. The countries in the Nordic, Anglo-Saxon, and western European groups score much more highly than countries in the other three groups (and are in fact quite close to the .7 boundary).

These groupings are supported by another piece of evidence. If individuals do have a political worldview predicated on a Left-Right dimension, one would expect their subjective view of their own Left-Right position to correlate in some way with the more objective scale measure. As Table 2 shows, this is only really the case in the Nordic and western European clusters.

The correlations in the Anglo-Saxon cluster are almost as weak as those in the Hispanic countries. This is due to the lack of any correlation in North America, which may be an artifact of asking about "Left" and "Right," when "liberal" and "conservative" might be more appropriate synonyms in Canada and the United States.[14] It seems clear that the inhabitants of the Anglo-Saxon, Nordic, and western European clusters have attitudes that conform most consistently to the Left-Right dimension. This is perhaps not very surprising given that politics in these countries can be easily caricatured as operating mainly on a Left-Right

axis and that issues are often articulated in these terms.

As Figure 5 shows, even given problems of comparability, some patterns can be discerned. There is some tendency for women to be marginally more left wing than their male counterparts, but this is certainly not as obvious as international differences. The Hispanic cluster of countries is clearly the most left wing, while the Nordic and Anglo-Saxon countries are the most right wing. These differences at the maximum are around 1 point; for example, the Nordic eighteen- to twenty-four-year-olds have a mean score of around 4.4 compared to the mean score of greater than 5.5 for their Hispanic equivalents. Of the three clusters for which the scale proved most reliable, western Europe seems the most left wing, and the Anglo-Saxon and Nordic clusters more right wing.

If nationality seems a reasonable predictor of political positioning, so does age. The clearest trend is that the young, outside eastern and central Europe, are more left wing than are their elders. Outside the former communist countries, the mean score for those older than sixty-five in most clusters is around 0.4 less than that for those younger than twenty-four. This scale of difference means that (within the three clusters with most scale reliability) it is age differences that are most prominent.

When examining all nationalities, it seems that it is international differences that predominate, however. It is only in the Nordic, western European, and Anglo-Saxon clusters that

FIGURE 5
MEAN SCORE ON THE LEFT-RIGHT SCALE

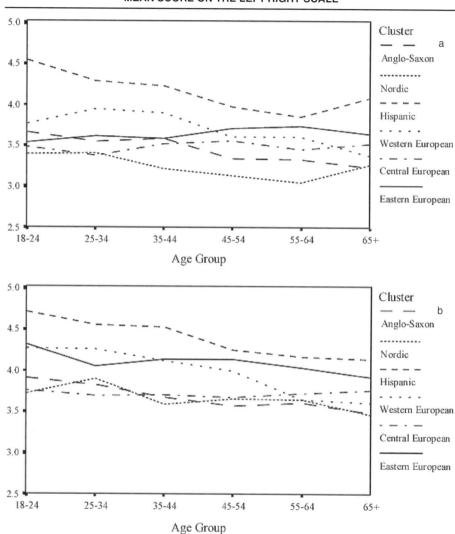

NOTE: Higher scores indicate a more left wing position. a = mean male score on the Left-Right Scale. b = mean female score on the Left-Right Scale.

age effects outweigh national differences. In looking for more obviously coherent youth attitudes, perhaps those toward the political process, rather than prescriptive political positions, will prove more fruitful.

Young people's political activism

Young people in the West are often pictured as simultaneously politically apathetic and, paradoxically, also activist and radical (see, e.g., Wilkinson and Mulgan 1995). There is also plenty of evidence to suggest that institutional and cultural arrangements affect levels of participation and attitudes to involvement. Almond and Verba's (1963) *The Civic Culture* shows quite clearly that attitudes toward the political arena differ markedly from society to society. Thus, it is of interest to ask not only whether young people's attitudes toward politics can be characterized as indifferent or radical but also how large the magnitude of age differences are when compared with cross-national differences.

One way of approaching this question is to attempt a comparison of levels of willingness to perform political actions.[15] A series of questions in the WVS focused on whether people had, would, or would never perform certain acts. These were signing a petition, joining a boycott, attending a lawful demonstration, joining an unofficial strike, and occupying a building or factory.

Opportunities to take part in these activities obviously vary across societies, and comparing these responses will inevitably confuse predispositions with opportunities. Thus, only those saying that they would never perform an act have been included. "Never" responses for each of the actions were aggregated into a 0 to 10 scale, 0 indicating that the respondent would never perform any of the listed actions, and 10 that he or she would perform all of them.[16]

The lower the score, the more willing individuals are to engage in political action.

As Figure 6 shows, there is a clear sex differential, with men showing more political activism than do women. This does not seem to interact with cluster membership or age. Women—regardless of country or age group—score lower on this scale. This is a common finding across societies. Women tend to be less interested in national politics and related political activities (Hayes and Bean 1993; Verba et al. 1993; Verba, Burns, and Schlozman 1997).

The Hispanic and central European groups appear to be the least willing to engage in political activity, and the Nordic nations are the most willing. Eastern European scores are quite mixed and do not cohere very well for this measure. In fact, the groups of countries with the least politically active young people are essentially South America and parts of the formerly communist eastern Europe. What characterizes these societies is that in 1990, or somewhat before that, they had fairly repressive political regimes. Protest was (at the least) not encouraged and in places actively discouraged. These are countries with essentially weak civil societies. There is no culture of protest, and there are few mechanisms by which protest can take place.

This is perhaps to be expected, and international differences are probably not as illuminating as age differences within these countries. Young people are certainly distinct from their elders. As age increases, people are less likely to agree to political

FIGURE 6
MEAN SCORES ON THE POLITICAL ACTION SCALE

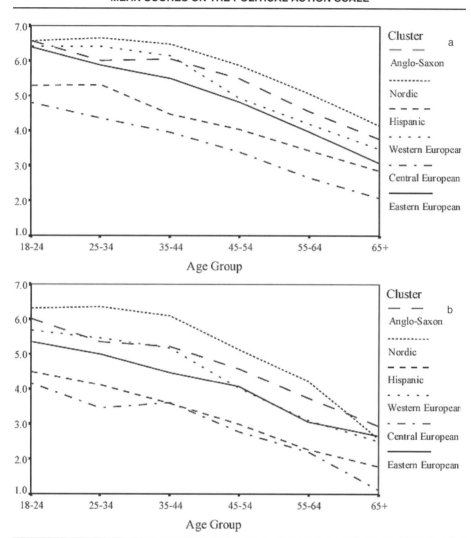

NOTE: Higher scores indicate greater political activity. a = mean male scores on the Political Action Scale. b = mean female scores on the Political Action Scale.

activism, and this seems to be a trend regardless of country cluster. To highlight these large age differences, the mean score for the Anglo-Saxon eighteen- to twenty-four-year-olds is greater than 6, yet for those older than sixty-five, it is less than 4. This magnitude of difference is apparent in all six clusters. Clearly, age differences are of much greater size than any national-level disparities. It is youth and not nationality that is the better predictor of political activism in this sense.

APPROVAL OF NEW SOCIAL MOVEMENTS

New social movements are often thought to have a special resonance for the young. It is also suggested that they may be a more important outlet for political action than the conventional array of political parties and interest groups (Ganzeboom and Flap 1989; Abramson and Inglehart 1987). Thus, one might expect to find greater support among the young for the women's movement, the peace movement, and the ecology movement than among the elderly. Equally, theories of postmaterialism might predict greater social movement support in wealthier countries. Given that new social movements embody many postmaterialist attitudinal positions, from increased concern for the environment to increased legal rights for citizens, one might expect to see more favorable attitudes toward such movements in materially wealthy and secure societies (Inglehart 1977, 1990). To what extent then are any age (or generational) differences overshadowed by these international differences?

To examine this question, a Likert-type scale was constructed using questions on respondents' approval or disapproval of various new social movements: the ecological movement, the disarmament movement, various human rights movements, the women's movement, and the antinuclear movement.[17] The reliability of this scale is very good in all countries. Young people approved or disapproved in similar ways of all five movements.[18] One could therefore argue that approval is linked to approval of the typology of political discourse embodied by movements as well as the issues underlying their formation. Figure 7 shows the mean cluster scores for this scale. Women are somewhat more approving of these movements in general. Unsurprisingly, this difference is accounted for by their higher level of support for the women's movement. There are somewhat larger discrepancies between male and female support for movements in the Nordic and Anglo-Saxon clusters.

However, the differences between cluster groups seem more significant. Mean approval ratings generally follow the same pattern, with wealthier societies being the most hostile and poorer societies, that is, eastern Europe[19] and South America, being more approving. This may seem surprising though. Why is it that in more developed countries in which, following Inglehart, one would expect to find high levels of support from younger generations for postmaterialist organizations, that support is actually lowest? Moreover, if one examines which particular rich countries have young people exhibiting hostility, it is those with well-developed and long-standing movements. It is the Anglo-Saxon and Nordic countries that have the lowest ratings and

FIGURE 7
MEAN SCORE ON THE NEW SOCIAL MOVEMENTS SCALE

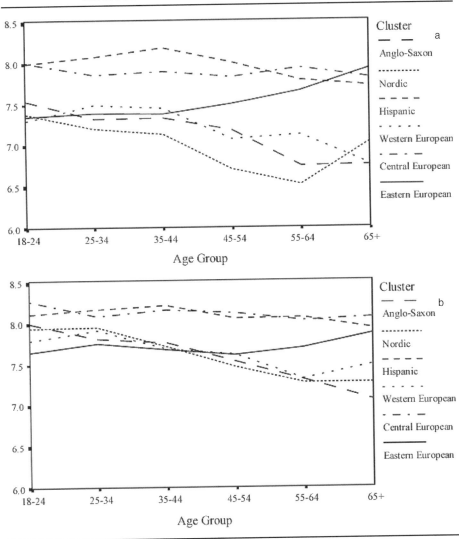

NOTE: Higher scores indicate greater approval. a = mean male score on the New Social Movement Scale. b = mean female score on the New Social Movement Scale.

yet have the most active and visible movements.

Although this initially appears difficult to explain, it is perhaps less surprising than one might think, for the simple reason that individuals are not making choices informed by the same experiences. This again ties in with the idea of weaker civil societies within certain countries. In the abstract, movements dedicated to the improvement of women's position in society or protection of the environment may sound uncontroversially admirable. However, in countries with fewer outlets for political activity (including social movements), people are essentially forced to answer about what is for them an abstraction. In most countries in the Hispanic cluster, there are simply not large visible ecology movements. Thus, there may be an approval of vague gestures toward a better environment, but this is different from concrete approval for, say, higher taxes on fuel, which may be a well-known objective of the environmental movement in western Europe.

Compared to this, age differences show a much less surprising picture. The old appear somewhat less approving of these new political movements in most countries. There are, however, some significant interaction effects between age and cluster, for the greatest disparity by age is clearly in the Anglo-Saxon, Nordic, and western European clusters. These are, of course, the countries in which much new social movement activity developed, and they are thus more likely to have generational differences.

The young in these developed Western societies have much more in common with each other than they do with their own elderly countrymen. The important effect in the West is of age and not of nationality. Young people in the West are thus more left wing, more likely to protest, and more approving of new social movements than are their elders. The same pattern cannot be discerned in the Hispanic and eastern European/central European clusters, where not only do most people have fairly incoherent Left-Right attitudes, display more approval of social movements, and less inclination to protest, but the existence of age disparities is also much more debatable. The reasons behind these cluster characteristics seem to depend on the nature of economic change and civic society within each cluster. Economic change has manifested itself in generational differences in the industrialized West. The lack of postmaterialist change in the Hispanic and eastern European societies and the additional lack of an established civil society within which movements, protest groups, and political parties can operate has meant that generational differences are few, and participation and knowledge are generally lower.

JOB AND LIFE SATISFACTION

This final section examines young people's satisfaction with their work and their life more generally. Why do people work, what level of satisfaction does it give them, and how does this relate to their life satisfaction more generally? International differences might be expected, with people deriving different benefits and looking for different rewards from work cross-nationally. There may also be an expectation that young people approach work differently than do their elders. As individuals pass through the life cycle, their priorities probably change; the stereotype of

FIGURE 8
MEAN SCORE FOR JOB SATISFACTION

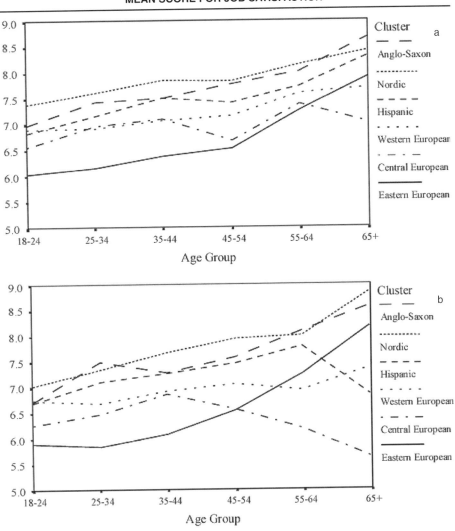

NOTE: Higher scores indicate greater satisfaction. a = mean male score for job satisfaction. b = mean female score for job satisfaction.

the ambitious youth and more passive, security-seeking older individual appears to have some basis in fact (Hagstrom and Gamberale 1995).

Standard 1 to 10–scale questions were asked on job satisfaction and general life satisfaction. The WVS asked the employed, "How satisfied

TABLE 3
PERCENTAGES OF YOUNG PEOPLE (YOUNGER THAN 35)
TAKING PRIDE IN THEIR WORK

Country Cluster	Great Deal of Pride	Some Pride	Little or No Pride
Anglo-Saxon	75.8	20.5	3.7
Nordic	63.4	30.1	6.4
Hispanic	52.1	33.8	14.2
Western European	22.4	51.3	26.3
Central European	29.2	44.2	26.6
Eastern European	14.2	44.5	41.2

or dissatisfied are you with your job?" and sought a figure between 1 and 10 in response. Mean values for this score, as before adjusted to a 0 to 10 scale to make comparability between all attitudes across countries easier, are shown in Figure 8.

The most obvious pattern is that young people in poorer countries tend to be less satisfied with their jobs than are those in richer societies. The Nordic and Anglo-Saxon clusters rank quite high, and the eastern European young people are at the bottom of the rankings. Low job satisfaction ratings in the former communist countries have been found before, work on the ISSP showing that Hungarian workers were noticeably more dissatisfied than their Western counterparts (Curtice 1993).

This finding is further corroborated by Table 3. This shows the extent to which young people from different countries gave differing responses to the question, "How much pride do you take in your work?" The eastern European cluster consistently scores in a manner indicating a lack of pride on this scale. Again, the Anglo-Saxon countries

are much more positive. More than 75 percent of working young people report that they take a great deal of pride in their work.

Older people appear to be considerably happier with their work on the measure of satisfaction.[20] The differences for job satisfaction are quite large, men ages fifty-five to sixty-four in the Anglo-Saxon grouping having a mean score of more than 1 point more than those younger than twenty-four. This is typical of age differences across clusters. Some authors (e.g., see Blanchflower and Oswald 1997) have found a U-shaped pattern to age-related differences in job satisfaction. However, the mean values in Figure 8 show that satisfaction with work rises at a fairly uniform rate in all clusters apart from the central European grouping where the old appear no more satisfied than do the young.

In the main, for those younger than sixty-five, differences by gender are not large. However, since the number of women working after the age of sixty-five is so strongly self-selected, there are apparent differences between the men and women in this age group. It is quite clear,

FIGURE 9
YOUNG PEOPLE'S MEAN SCORES FOR JOB AND LIFE SATISFACTION, BY COUNTRY

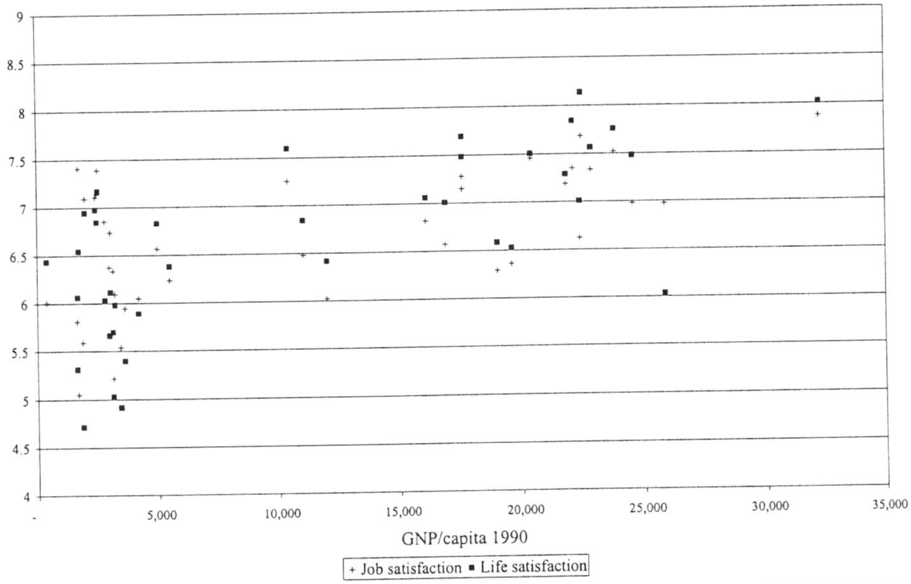

GNP/capita 1990

+ Job satisfaction ■ Life satisfaction

though, that it is age and intercluster differences that are of most importance in describing attitudes toward job satisfaction. As Figure 8 shows, these are effects of a comparable magnitude to each other in most cases. Since a large proportion of life is spent in work, one would expect some correlation between job and life satisfaction; when one is satisfied at work, one is satisfied in life. At the individual level, there is a relatively strong level of correspondence between the two ratings, and correlations are relatively high in most countries. (Virtually all are greater than .3, and most are considerably higher.)

Figure 9 plots GNP per capita[21] against the mean country scores for the job and life satisfaction of those younger than thirty-five in all surveyed countries. This confirms the correlation between job and life satisfaction on the aggregate level but also suggests that there may be a relationship between GNP and job satisfaction/life satisfaction. As national wealth increases, young people give responses that indicate that they are happier in their jobs and in their lives. Other authors have found differing results. Easterlin (1974) concluded that individual happiness appeared to be similar across poor and rich countries. Subsequent work on time series has shown that GNP differences between nations may have an effect on happiness/satisfaction (Veenhoven 1991). This supports the trend shown in Figure 9, which is virtually linear. If it were not for some of the Hispanic nations with fairly low GNP per

FIGURE 10
MEAN SCORE FOR LIFE SATISFACTION

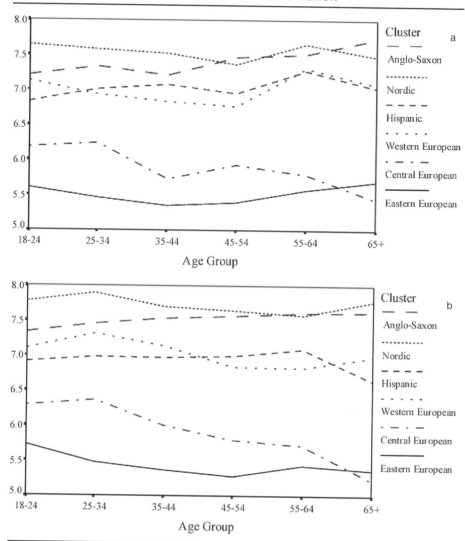

NOTE: Higher scores indicate greater satisfaction. a = mean male score for life satisfaction. b = mean female score for life satisfaction.

capita ratings but also relatively satisfied inhabitants, the fit for a simple linear relationship would be remarkably good.

Due to the apparent linkage between national wealth and job satisfaction/life satisfaction, cluster patterns for life satisfaction are similar to those for job satisfaction. As Figure 10 shows, the eastern and central Europeans are the most dissatisfied, and the Nordic and Anglo-Saxon countries the most satisfied. However, these clear international differences are not matched by clear age differences. In fact, unlike the increased job satisfaction older people show, there is little difference between the young and old in terms of how satisfied they are with life. The differences are clearly between cluster membership and attitudes and not between age and attitudes. Youth is not a helpful factor when attempting to explain differences in the life satisfaction of individuals. In summary, the old seem no happier than the young in life, but in work there is an age gradient that seems of somewhat less importance than cluster membership differences.

CONCLUSION

The aim of this article was twofold: first, to try to group young people from different countries into clusters of societies that are similar with regard to attitudes and beliefs and, second, to determine whether young people had more in common with other young people from different clusters of societies or with their elders from the same country cluster.

Groupings of societies do seem to exist. Individuals in different countries with shared histories and languages and similar levels of economic development (and to some extent geographical proximity) do have beliefs that often coincide. These groupings appear quite distinct, but

are they more distinct than cross-national age groups?

As the previous sections have shown, the level of age-related differences and cluster-level differences vary to some degree, as one might expect, across the range of attitudes. While political activity appeared to be predicated mainly on age/cohort, life satisfaction appears not to be linked to age/cohort at all. To test all these attitudes together and to see whether youth or country is more important in determining young people's values, one can use a MANOVA procedure.

The factor variables of cluster, age, and sex divide the population into groups. Using a general linear modeling procedure, it is possible to test for the effects of these three variables on the means of various groupings for a joint distribution in the attitudinal dependent variables. Table 4 shows the results of a MANOVA run with the three explanatory variables and an interaction term between cluster and age group. Interactions between gender and cluster and gender and age group were also tested but not found to be significant. All the attitudinal measures examined previously have been included, apart from job satisfaction. The latter was excluded to try to keep the sample numbers fairly high. Since job satisfaction was asked of only those in work, this question has the most missing responses of any of the attitudinal questions used in this article and thus is not included in the MANOVA. For the items that were included, the F value indicates the explanatory power of the fixed effect, cluster, and so forth. The higher this value, the

TABLE 4
**MANOVA: ATTITUDES AS DEPENDENT VARIABLES AND CLUSTER,
AGE, AND GENDER AS FIXED EFFECTS**

Source	Attitudinal Variable	F Value
Intercept	Religious beliefs	39737.8*
	Women's Roles	142867.8*
	Left-Right placement	68328.4*
	Political action	36731.7*
	New social movements	261391.9*
	Life satisfaction	122590.2*
Cluster	Religious beliefs	709.2*
	Women's roles	159.2*
	Left-Right placement	96.4*
	Political action	176.2*
	New social movements	80.9*
	Life satisfaction	359.2*
Age group	Religious beliefs	37.1*
	Women's roles	82.0*
	Left-Right placement	16.8*
	Political action	290.8*
	New social movements	16.5*
	Life satisfaction	2.0
Gender	Religious beliefs	227.2*
	Women's roles	229.5*
	Left-Right placement	164.8*
	Political action	248.6*
	New social movements	109.0*
	Life satisfaction	0.6
Cluster × Age Group	Religious beliefs	3.7*
	Women's roles	8.0*
	Left-Right placement	4.0*
	Political action	2.9*
	New social movements	4.6*
	Life satisfaction	3.2*

*Significant at the .01 level.

better that effect is at explaining values of the attitudinal variable.

Table 4 shows that apart from political activity, cluster membership has a greater effect than does age group. A young person's being from a particular national grouping is a better predictor of his or her attitudes, aside from willingness to participate in political activities, than is his or her youth. Some of these differences are more striking than others, but it is only really the effect of youth

on attitudes toward women's roles that comes close in magnitude to the national grouping effects. Although all age-group effects are significant (apart from life satisfaction), they are generally dwarfed by the much larger effects of nationality.[22] The young worldwide do not appear to be a coherent grouping with a common base of values.

Table 4 also shows that gender is clearly an important determinant of attitudes. While gender differences are not the core focus of this article, it is clear that this divergence of attitudes by gender outweighs differences by age quite substantially. Equally, aside from life satisfaction and religious beliefs (which are dominated by cluster effects), gender differences are of comparable magnitude to international effects.

Interaction effects between cluster and age group are significant for all attitudes, suggesting that youth does not have a uniform effect globally. These interactions were seen clearly in earlier sections. The large interaction effect for attitude toward women's roles is unsurprising given that eastern European mean values were virtually unchanged by age, but the young were noticeably more liberal then their elders in most Western countries. The presence of these interaction effects between age and cluster are helpful in showing that while a coherent, fully international view of youth is not tenable, a more limited position is not unreasonable.

Some clusters are actually rather similar. The main divide is in fact between the East, the West, and to a lesser extent, Hispanic clusters. Often, the mean scores for the Anglo-Saxons, Nordic, and western European citizens are relatively similar.[23] Moreover, age differences are generally much more pronounced in these countries. Whether concerning attitudes toward women's work or approval of new social movements, the old tend to differ from the young to a greater degree in Western societies than in the Eastern and Southern nations.

This clearly ties in with the postmaterialism thesis, for Inglehart and his colleagues would predict that only in countries where advanced industrial society is emerging, that is, in the Western world, would large generational differences exist. As one can see in the case of political attitudes, without the foundation of a politicized society enabled by postmodernization and the changes caused by economic growth and increased security, newer generations do not appear distinctive. Although the previous analysis has shown the predominance of nationality as a predictor of attitude, it is important to note that within more limited groups of countries, young people appear to hold quite similar values. Hence, young people do have common values cross-nationally, but within prescribed supranational limits. It is difficult to argue that there is a recognizable global youth view of the world, for differences in values by age are generally overshadowed by national effects. Within clusters of societies, and more broadly within the industrialized West, young people are distinct from their elders, however, and have more in common internationally with their own age group than nationally with people of their parents and grandparents' age.

Notes

1. Most of the surveys were carried out in 1990, but two (in Switzerland and Poland) were carried out the year before. Two surveys (those in Russia and Turkey) were completed in early 1991, while another (in Slovenia) was carried out during 1992. The Romanian survey was carried out in early 1993.

2. Due to low sample size, Northern Ireland has been dropped from this analysis.

3. Slovenia was part of the Austro-Hungarian Empire until the end of the First

World War and gained independence only in 1918.

4. To include Romania and Poland, the item concerning women's role in society had to be excluded from the multidimensional scaling (MDS) procedure.

5. Again, when this MDS analysis was repeated for other eastern European countries, they appeared to lie between East Germany and the Russian cluster.

6. All figures are weighted within countries to account for the oversampling of certain sectors of society in each country.

7. *Don't knows* were given a score of 1, compared to 2 for belief and 0 for disbelief. *Don't knows* in this context presumably indicate agnosticism, which it is desirable to capture. The responses to these questions have been aggregated and scaled to produce a 0 to 10 scale.

8. The reliability of an indicator made up of a number of measured items is often assessed using Cronbach's alpha. This is calculated as a function of the mean interitem correlation and the number of items: $\alpha = N\rho / (1 + \rho (N-1))$, where ρ is the mean interitem correlation, and N the number of items. Conventionally, scores greater than .70 are taken to mean the scale is extremely coherent (Nunnally 1978).

9. In fact, the former would be even lower were it not for the inclusion of Poland and its continued history of Catholicism under communist rule.

10. Both studies examined only a small number of countries, but religiosity did appear to be one of the factors in explaining traditional family attitudes.

11. Question 3 was not asked in Sweden, and thus for this country, the scale uses only the other five questions weighted accordingly. All questions 1 through 6 were not asked in Poland and Romania; hence, the eastern European cluster does not contain these countries. *Strong approval* scored 0; *moderate approval*, 1; *moderate disapproval*, 2; and *strong disapproval*, 3. The answers to questions 2, 3, and 4 were reversed so the higher the score, the more traditional was the scale score. The scale again runs from 0 to 10.

12. Factor analysis on these questions reveals that in some countries there are potentially two dimensions to responses. The first scores more highly with the four questions that mention children and housework explicitly, whereas the second is more heavily loaded to the last two questions, which concentrate more on income and pay. Removing either dimension's questions from the scale does not significantly improve the reliability of the scale.

13. It should be noted that the young people of Spain and Portugal are among the most liberal, which brings down the average of the Hispanic cluster.

14. To test the reliability of the scale further, a factor analysis was run using the six items. This used maximum likelihood as the estimation method with a varimax rotation and was repeated independently for each country. If there is a coherent notion that these questions address, one would expect to find a single major dimension, the Left-Right dimension, to individuals' responses. Outside northern Europe, parts of western Europe, and North America, this was not the case.

15. While questions were asked directly concerning political interest, these are not necessarily the best proxy for attitudinal involvement, as answers are often closely linked to national events, such as elections and the fall of governments.

16. Reliability for this scale is very high, with alpha values greater than .7 in most countries. Individuals, both young and old, tend to have an attitude of either action or inaction.

17. A score of 1 indicated *approving strongly*; 2, *approving somewhat*; 3, *disapproving somewhat*; and 4, *disapproving strongly*. The answers to each movement question were then averaged and up-rated to make a 10-point scale.

18. For all respondents in the youth category, the alpha statistic is .71. Somewhat lower figures were recorded in eastern Europe and South America, but none fell below .60. The responses of those older than thirty-five were marginally more coherent than those in the younger age group.

19. The three Baltic states are much more disapproving than the rest of eastern Europe, all age groups scoring less than 7 on the scale. The main driving force behind these low scores is the very widespread disapproval of the disarmament movement. This is hardly surprising given that there was, in fact, a widespread movement for rearmament in the Baltic

states. As former communist countries that directly border Russia and moreover contain sizeable Russian minorities, there is a widespread fear of potential Russian imperialism. Without these countries in the eastern European cluster, this grouping would appear the most approving of new social movement activity.

20. Those older than sixty-five are generally the happiest in most countries, but given that retirement ages are around sixty to sixty-five in most societies, this group may be somewhat self-selected, with those who enjoy their jobs continuing to work after retirement age. Given this, the high satisfaction ratings from this group might usefully be disregarded. The pattern of age-related increase in job satisfaction remains, however.

21. These are 1990 per capita GNP figures, as provided in the World Bank's *World Development Report 1993*.

22. If an ANOVA is run with job satisfaction as the dependent variable, then the same pattern appears to prevail. Cluster is more important than age, although both are significant at the .01 level.

23. The MDS procedure showed that although the Nordic, Anglo, and western European clusters were distinct, the greatest distance was between East, West, and South.

References

Abramson, P. R., and R. Inglehart. 1987. Generational replacement and the future of post-materialist values. *Journal of Politics* 49:231-41.

Almond, G. A., and S. Verba. 1963. *The civic culture*. Princeton, NJ: Princeton University Press.

Blanchflower, D. G., and A. G. Oswald. 1997. The rising well-being of the young. Labour Market Consequences of Technical and Structural Change discussion paper series 16. London: Centre for Economic Performance.

Butler, D., and D. Stokes. 1974. *Political change in Britain*. 2d ed. London: Macmillan.

Campbell, A., P. E. Converse, W. E. Miller, and D. Stokes. 1960. *The American voter*. New York: Wiley.

Chaves, M. 1989. Secularization and religious revival: Evidence from US church attendance rates 1972-1986. *Journal for the Scientific Study of Religion* 28:464-77.

Curtice, J. 1993. Satisfying work: If you can get it. In *International social attitudes: The 10th BSA report*, edited by R. Jowell, L. Brook, and L. Dowds, 103-21. Aldershot, UK: Dartmouth.

Easterlin, R. 1974. Does economic growth improve the human lot? Some empirical evidence. In *Nations and households in economic growth: Essays in honour of Moses Abramowitz*, edited by P. A. David and M. W. Reder, 89-125. New York: Academic Press.

Evans, G., A. F. Heath, and M. G. Lalljee. 1996. Measuring left-right and libertarian-authoritarian values in the British electorate. *British Journal of Sociology* 47:93-112.

Feldman, S. 1988. Structure and consistency in public opinion: The role of core beliefs and values. *American Journal of Political Science* 32:416-40.

Ganzeboom, H. B., and H. Flap, eds. 1989. *New social movements and value change: Theoretical developments and empirical analysis*. Amsterdam, the Netherlands: SISWO.

Hagstrom, T., and F. Gamberale. 1995. Young people's work motivation and value orientations. *Journal of Adolescence* 18:475-90.

Harding, S. 1989. Interim report: The changing family. In *British social attitudes: International report*, 6th report, edited by R. Jowell, S. Witherspoon, and L. Brook, 143-55. Aldershot, UK: Gower.

Hayes, B. C., and C. S. Bean. 1993. Gender and local political interest: Some international comparisons. *Political Studies* 41:672-82.

Heath, A. F., G. A. Evans, and J. Martin. 1994. The measurement of core beliefs and values: The development of balanced socialist/laissez-faire and libertarian/authoritarian scales. *British Journal of Political Science* 24:115-32.

Inglehart, R. 1977. *The silent revolution: Changing values and political styles among Western publics*. Princeton, NJ: Princeton University Press.

———. 1990. *Culture shift in advanced industrial society*. Princeton, NJ: Princeton University Press.

———. 1995. Changing values, economic development and political change. *International Social Science Journal* 47:379-403.

Inglehart, R., and P. R. Abramson. 1994. Economic security and value change. *American Political Science Review* 88:336-54.

Jennings, M. K., and R. G. Niemi. 1981. *Generations and politics: A panel study of young adults and their parents*. Princeton, NJ: Princeton University Press.

Mannheim, K. 1952. The problem of generations. In *Essays on the sociology of knowledge*, edited by P. Kecskemeti. New York: Oxford University Press.

Miller, A. S., and J. P. Hoffman. 1995. Risk and religion: An explanation of gender differences in religiosity. *Journal for the Scientific Study of Religion* 34:63-75.

Nunnally, J. 1978. *Psychometric theory*. New York: McGraw-Hill.

Pilkington, H., ed. 1996. *Gender, generation and identity in contemporary Russia*. London: Routledge.

Rokeach, M. 1973. *The nature of human values*. New York: Free Press.

Scott, J., M. Braun, and D. Alwin. 1993. The family way. In *International social attitudes: the 10th BSA Report*, edited by R. Jowell, L. Brook, and L. Dowds, 23-47. Aldershot, UK: Dartmouth.

Stolzenberg, R. M. 1995. Religious participation in early adulthood. *American Sociological Review* 60:84-103.

Veenhoven, R. 1991. Is happiness relative? *Social Indicators Research* 24:1-34.

Verba, S., N. Burns, and K. L. Schlozman. 1997. Knowing and caring about politics: Gender and political engagement. *Journal of Politics* 59:1051-72.

Verba, S., K. L. Schlozman, H. Brady, and N. H. Nie. 1993. Citizen activity: Who participates? What do they say? *American Political Science Review* 87:303-18.

Walter, T., and G. Davie. 1998. The religiosity of women in the modern West. *British Journal of Sociology* 49:640-60.

Wilkinson, H., and G. Mulgan. 1995. *Freedom's children*. Demos paper 17. London: Demos.

Wilson, B. R. 1982. *Religion in sociological perspective*. Oxford, UK: Oxford University Press.

World Bank. 1993. *World development report 1993: Investing in health*. New York: World Bank.

ANNALS, *AAPSS*, **580**, March 2002

Explaining Aspects of the Transition to Adulthood in Italy, Sweden, Germany, and the United States: A Cross-Disciplinary, Case Synthesis Approach

By THOMAS D. COOK and FRANK F. FURSTENBERG JR.

ABSTRACT: This paper synthesizes essays on Italy, Sweden, Germany, and the United States that were presented at a conference seeking to explain the school, work, and family findings outlined in these foregoing chapters. Three essays were written per country—by a social historian, by a developmental scientist, and by someone in social policy. This paper synthesizes these country-specific accounts. For Italy, the synthesis constructed stresses the accommodations the Italian family has to make because of the protracted period during which adult children live at home. For Sweden, the synthesis emphasizes the willingness of many formal and informal institutions to support youthful experimentation, so long as it does not go over into the early twenties. For Germany, the synthesis stresses the strains the apprenticeship system is under because of the increasing strength of market-oriented labor policies in German business. And for the United States, the synthesis emphasizes how race and poverty create particularly difficult transitions in a nation that stresses individual initiative, and where second or third chances are available but are not easily attainable.

NOTE: The authors would like to acknowledge the financial support of the Johan Jacobs Foundation and the William T. Grant Foundation; the stimulation offered to both authors by the Center for Advanced Study in the Behavioral Sciences supported by a grant from the Carnegie Foundation and to the first author by the Max Planck Institute for Human Development in Berlin; the intellectual support of Richard Breen, Marlis Buchmann, Robert Sampson, and Gail Slap; and the support of all those scholars who presented at a conference titled International Perspectives on the Transition to Adulthood held at Marbach Castle, Switzerland, in October 1999. Christopher Jencks's insightful commentary on a prior draft of this article is especially appreciated.

T HIS article is the first of two that seeks to explain the results presented in earlier articles. The prior articles contain many discrete findings for many countries, and it is therefore impossible to explain everything. Instead, we restrict our focus to three western European nations and the United States and then consider only the findings about school, family, and work relationships. The relevant descriptive findings are most comprehensively outlined in Iacovou's article, but others are elaborated on in several of the other articles.

The findings are simple in a gross overview. In nation after nation, young people younger than sixteen live in their family of origin, attend school full-time, are not employed, are unmarried, and are childless. After about age thirty-five, national variation is again minimal. Few

mature adults are still in school or live in their family of origin. Instead, most work full-time, have their own household, are married, and have at least one child. In contrast, between ages sixteen and thirty-five, nations differ markedly in how and when transitions occur in the school, family, and work domains and in how the domains intersect with each other as individuals pass into full adult status. So this article describes and explains national differences in the paths from adolescence to mature adulthood.

It does this for Italy, Sweden, Germany, and the United States. These nations were chosen because they are all highly developed economically; because they differ strikingly in how school, work, and family factors are normatively structured and individually negotiated; and because they represent the major welfare

Thomas D. Cook is professor of sociology, psychology, and education and social policy at Northwestern University. His bachelor's degree is from Oxford and his Ph.D. is from Stanford. He also did graduate work at the University of Saarbruecken and has been an academic visitor at the London School of Economics, the Russell Sage Foundation, and the Center for Advanced Studies in the Behavioral Sciences. He has published widely in methodology and in substantive areas in psychology, human development and education. His current research is on evaluation theory and practice, on improving methods for making causal inferences, on educational reform in the United States, and on the community-building aspects of club drugs in the United States and elsewhere. He is a member of the American Academy of Arts and Sciences and is a Trustee of the Russell Sage Foundation.

Frank F. Furstenberg is the Zellerbach Family Professor of Sociology and Research Associate in the Population Studies Center at the University of Pennsylvania. His interest in the American family began at Columbia University where he received his Ph.D. in 1967. His recent book is Managing to Make It: Urban Families in High-Risk Neighborhoods *with Thomas Cook, Jacquelynne Eccles, Glen Elder, and Arnold Sameroff (1999). His current research projects focus on the family in the context of disadvantaged urban neighborhoods, adolescent sexual behavior, cross-national research on children's wellbeing, urban education, and the transition from adolescence to adulthood. He is currently Chair of the MacArthur Foundation Research Network on the Transition to Adulthood.*

state types most often discussed by macro-level theorists. The next article, by Breen and Buchmann, explicitly uses such macro-level theory to understand national differences in the transition to adulthood, largely from an institutional perspective but also weaving in cultural and other factors. This article's goal is more case dependent. For each of the four countries, we provide a data-informed multidisciplinary understanding of how the various transitions take place and are interrelated and how they relate to unique cultural realities within each nation, most of them deeply historically embedded but nonetheless always subject to some renegotiation and redefinition.

Our account of the transition to adulthood comes primarily from papers prepared for a conference in Marbach Castle, Germany, funded by the Jacob Foundation. The conference required experts on each of our four nations to read drafts of this issue's descriptive articles and then do two things: first, to outline in which ways the transition to adulthood is unique in their nation and, second, to explain why the transition in their country is distinctive in the ways noted. Most essay writers focused on explaining the interface between school, work, and family in their country, and so we will do the same. Three essays were written about each country—one by a social historian, another by a student of social policy, and the third by a professor of developmental science. These disciplines were chosen because each deals with youth and early adulthood. Taken together,

they illuminate the tricky concept of explanation better than any single disciplinary perspective could. However, in the country-specific accounts that follow, we interweave the three Marbach explanations for each country to avoid redundancy. Thus, we present our own synthesis of three different disciplinary accounts.

Several disclaimers are needed before proceeding with these nation-specific multidisciplinary syntheses. First, the national differences we discuss are occurring against a backdrop of generally similar historical changes across all western European and North American nations. One of these changes is the expansion of secondary and higher education. Young people are staying in education for longer, prompted by changes in school-leaving laws, expanding opportunities in higher education, increasing equality for women, and higher unemployment rates among youth than adults. Full-time jobs for young people are also on the decline, particularly in domestic service, agriculture, and manufacturing. In every country, young people now enter the labor force later, they work more often at temporary or part-time jobs, and they increasingly work and go to school at the same time. Also noteworthy are changes in household arrangements. Cohabitation is on the increase, marriages are occurring later, children are born later, and the birth rate is lower. Yet as common as these changes are, they occur at different rates, from different levels, with different timing, and with different codependency patterns. Even so, there are generally similar time trends across all the nations we analyze.

Second, between ages sixteen and thirty-five, pathways to adulthood vary within nations as well as between them. Indeed, each nation we discuss pursues some social policies designed to help certain subpopulations more than others, often under the assumption that the transition to adulthood is especially problematic for some population groups. The groups in question vary by nation. Sometimes, within-country race, class, or regional status is emphasized, as sometimes is immigrant, employment, or health status. But this article only deals with within-country variation, when ignoring it we would critically distort the cross-national account.

Third, we use terms such as *path* or *pathway*. These should not be understood as those roads on a nation's cultural map that indicate how to move effortlessly from birth to successful adulthood. No cultural maps exist that clearly specify what is required to reach the interim destinations of successful infancy, successful early childhood, and so on. Such maps could be constructed for each nation. But many details on them would not be clear, the details would vary by historical time period, and the contemporary map would be very complex, containing some paths that are circuitous rather than direct and others that fit the experiences of some population groups more than others. To avoid premature theoretical specificity, we use the pathway notion only as a loose metaphor, not as a more literal construct.

Finally, while demographic, structural, and institutional terms are necessary for understanding national variation in work, school, and family interfaces, cultural factors are also at play. This is not the place to explicate "culture." We understand it here in the weak sense that stresses explanatory concepts that are traditionally treated as neither structural, institutional, nor demographic. Behavioral norms, ways of thinking and feeling, and ways of shared self-expression play central roles in such theories of culture, as do contemporaneous forces that transmit messages about what to expect and value and historical factors that describe how the cultural meanings evolved. Norms, beliefs, meanings, and feelings are linked in complex ways, not just to each other, but also to demography, institutions, and structures. So, culture can never be totally separated from these other social forces. Nonetheless, we use it in the weak sense above to help in the constructions we make to explain national differences in the transition to adulthood.

ITALY: WHERE STRAINED BUT
RESILIENT NUCLEAR FAMILIES
HAVE TO TAKE UP THE SLACK

Egle Becchi, Alessandro Cavalli, and Giovanni Sgritta wrote the conference reports on work, family, and school in Italy. We rely on them for the basic facts and some interpretation. The facts are these. Between the ages of eighteen and thirty, Italians have recently been going into higher education at a more rapid rate than in other countries, albeit from a lower baseline. On the average, undergraduate training lasts longer than in most other countries—seven years—and university students are particularly likely to live at home and study locally rather than to go to another region where they would live in lodgings to study.

Nonstudents are mostly employed. But their unemployment rate is still among the highest in Europe. In 1999, the official Organization for Economic Cooperation and Development rate was 32 percent for all nonstudents between twenty and thirty-four. Whether employed or not, young adults in Italy live with their parents for longer than in other nations. Veneto has the lowest unemployment in Italy, but even so, more than 60 percent of the employed twenty-five- to thirty-five-year-olds living there in 1999 were residing with their parents. The rate of living with parents is presumably even higher among the unemployed who are even more dependent on parents for food and lodging.

Italians leave their family of origin and start their own households later than elsewhere. But when they do so, it is more often for marriage rather than to live alone or to cohabit. So Italy has one of the lowest rates of out of wedlock birth in Europe. But since marriage occurs at a later age than elsewhere, Italy has fewer children per woman than any other country we examine.[1]

Italy is not the only nation with this pattern of protracted reliance on the family of origin, the long-term postponement of personal independence, the relative avoidance of cohabitation, and the small size of the independent family eventually achieved. Data in this issue reveal the same pattern in Greece and Spain. It is thus a Mediterranean phenomenon. However, it also occurs in attenuated form in Ireland, implying a possible Catholic influence as well. Yet church attendance in Italy and Spain is strikingly low, and Greeks are not Roman Catholics. So if Church influences operate, they probably do so indirectly through a cultural heritage mechanism rather than directly through current religious beliefs and practices.

The Italian transition to adulthood is related to several unique structural elements in that nation. The diffusion of mass university education took place later there than elsewhere—in the late 1970s and 1980s. The university system is centralized, and the rapid expansion required systemwide reforms that unfortunately did not take place. In frustration, existing faculty raised their requirements and curricular standards, leading both to a longer period of study and to more dropouts. Although many new universities were started in all regions, *numerus clausus* restrictions were instituted in very few fields. Thus, few students had to travel to another region to study in their field of choice. Outside of the rural south, nearly all students can live at home, commute to a nearby university, and still study what they want. In some ways, this is a boon, given the paucity of university scholarships. It is also a boon, though, in that it preserves familial and regional ties, increases university attendance, holds down annual costs per family, underwrites the long undergraduate study period, and keeps young Italians out of a labor market that cannot readily absorb them because of higher unemployment rates than elsewhere. The downside, though, is that Italian universities tend to be undercapitalized, overcrowded, and poorly administered, with too many long-term students who would rather be working than studying. One Marbach presenter described them as "parking lots for young people."

The vicissitudes of the labor market for young Italian adults are striking. As Cavalli noted, "in Italy, . . . more than half of all unemployed are young people, aged 14 to 24, in search of their first job and more than 70% of all unemployed are aged below 29." Unemployment is much lower in mature adult groups, and this is no accident. In Italy, employment and retirement policies favor household heads who currently work in the legitimate labor market or who used to. In Italy, there is rhetoric about youth unemployment, but analysis of central government expenditures indicates that an atypically high priority is given to protecting high-paying jobs and to ensuring comfortable pensions from an unusually early retirement age. While strong unions and electoral politics are behind this cozy relationship, it also reflects the cultural expectation that Italian fathers should be household authority figures. Yet whatever the origins, the reality is that young Italians are left to pick up seasonal or part-time jobs that do not constitute a vocational training and are disproportionately in the large Italian informal economy. Individuals in

their teens and twenties find it very difficult to earn a family wage or even to gain the experience needed to enter the competition for "good" jobs.

Young Italians are also disadvantaged because vocational training is more limited there than elsewhere. Vocational secondary schools exist, as do some work-study arrangements with larger firms. But the Italian political system does not spend heavily on job training and retraining, and the economy has many small firms that are not easily organized to provide formal training of high quality. These difficulties are not restricted to the lower end of the job market. One of the reasons undergraduate study takes longer in Italy is that employment-based incentives for on-time graduation are few.

In Italy and other parts of Southern Europe, there have been profound changes in the gender-linked primary and secondary education that used to channel women's expectations into marriage and motherhood. Rates of university study are comparable to those of males. In 1974 and 1978, respectively, laws were passed allowing divorce and abortion, each symbolizing greater independence for Italian women in a nation where traditional Catholic conceptions of gender and birth control had been dominant. These changes may be responsible for Italian women's delaying marriage and childbirth more than in other nations and also for reducing the number of children they eventually have.

The delays are not associated with lesser sexual activity, though. The cultural link between first intercourse and marriage ended with the demise of fascism, and the link between intercourse and childbirth ended with acceptance of contraception and abortion. However, delaying marriage means that young Italian women now have time to fill between ending school and getting married. They fill this time with paid work if it is available or with more study. More than elsewhere, Italian women stop working when they get married or have a child, each of which comes later than elsewhere. Young Italian women have much more discretion over their lives than their mothers did at a comparable age. Even so, the female role is probably still more fluid in Italy today than in any of the other countries we consider.

Thanks to mass media, international travel, and the European Union, all Italy is now in the European cultural mainstream. It is difficult to believe that young Italians expect to consume at different levels from their cohorts in northern Europe. Yet individual wages are still somewhat lower in Italy than elsewhere, possibly even after correcting for cost of living differences. Thus, to enjoy even a modest lifestyle, young adults have to cut back on something. One way to avoid "unnecessary" expenditures is by continuing to live at home without contributing very much to room and board. The loss here is in personal autonomy, for by living with parents a young person has not attained one of the most visible symbols of adulthood—having one's own household.

Both the consumption and autonomy ends could be reached by other means than living at home with parents. Individuals could cohabit with a lover, thus sharing expenses and pooling wages. But in Italy, cohabitation is still rare outside of large cities. Another option would be nonfamilial, nonamorous roommates. But that too is rare. If unmarried Italians have to live outside of the home, it is usually with an extended family member or a mature adult cochosen with parents. In this cultural context, independence from the parental home usually entails marriage. But more so than elsewhere, marriage in Italy means women's leaving paid work and having a baby, both factors that prejudice personal consumption in a nation where, generally, neither the central state nor businesses provide quality daycare or generous child allowances, though some regional governments do. In any event, to enjoy a lifestyle with consumption levels equal to north and west European models entails young Italians' feeling they have to live at home with their parents. Cultural factors probably contribute to making this a more attractive option in Italy than elsewhere, but these same factors also close off the cohabitation and roommate options that other countries use.

The prolonged presence of adult children in the parental home has led to adjustments within the Italian family. Historically, Italians lived in large nuclear families that were patriarchal in some clearly demarcated domains and matriarchal in others. Children living at home were subject to this gender- and generation-based family stratification system. But it seems to be breaking down, in part because more adult children live at home and they are generally more educated than are their parents. Their education gives them a special form of capital that parents generally respect. It allows them to express what they need and want and also to negotiate to meet their needs in direct and indirect ways. Adult parents and adult children living together report to interviewers that they eventually reach a more egalitarian modus vivendi. It is characterized by mutual affective dependency, each generation having its own space, each generation using communal space when needed, each agreeing to tolerate the other's unique cultural productions, and the older generation swallowing large doses of "don't ask, don't tell." As a result, members of the younger generation are to a considerable degree socially and personally independent. They often have a room of their own, can invite in friends of both sexes, listen to music and watch TV as they want, and can even use the family car until they get one of their own. Of course, this picture is more middle class and hence also, in the Italian context, regional. It is also more relevant for families with fewer children. However, if middle-class families are the carriers of the dominant family model in Italy, then the current younger generation has modeled a unique future mix for less-favored families. The mix entails delaying economic self-sufficiency and household independence in exchange for continuing to live at home in circumstances where there is not much loss of a unique generational voice, of personal independence, and of a comfortable material life.

Other structural changes occurring in Italian society facilitate this culturally negotiated increase in equality between generations. For instance, the low national birth rates and the high levels of rural migration mean that more Italian families can afford a home in the country. When adult children have newer relationships that are romantically expressed in ways that might offend or discomfort their parents, where better to go than to the family country place? Young adults in Italy are as sexually active as elsewhere, and this would not be possible unless there were some complicity between the generations.

Since traditional parental dominance will not work well with adult children, this raises the possibility that future changes will take place in Italian family relationships. When people now in their early thirties begin their own families, will they prefer the hierarchical relationships that characterized how they related to their parents as children, or will they instead prefer the more egalitarian relationships that characterize how they related to their parents when they became adults? Italians now in their thirties will probably have few children. Will this also contribute to a new adult generation that is more egalitarian with its own children, adoring the little prince or princess of which there will modally be but one? The reality of two nonelderly adult generations sharing the same household requires intergenerational accommodations that may cause future nuclear families to be more egalitarian than their predecessors were.

Italian tradition associates independence with three *M*s to be achieved in the late teens or early twenties: *mestiere, matrimonio, e macchina* (a steady job, marriage, and a car). The employment situation makes it difficult to attain a good job by the early twenties. And early matrimony prevents buying a car because a baby is likely, and relatively few wives work. Since the old cultural model cannot work within the age span specified, the three *M*s are now linked to marriage from the late twenties to the mid-thirties. Only by delaying marriage can most individuals cobble together the material resources required to attain nationally (and increasingly, internationally) validated consumption packages plus whatever social identities go with these consumption styles. In a society where roommates and cohabitation are rare, few legitimate paths to independence exist other than through marriage, and marriage itself depends on parents' subsidizing their adult children at home during the premarriage years. According to surveys, young people who live at home do not give their parents much, and most of their income goes to personal consumption rather than savings. So we might assume that Italians can eventually afford to marry primarily because of the higher wages age brings and only secondarily because of capital accumulation in the form of a car or modest savings.

In Italy, young people and their parents are trapped, but in a partly gilded cage. It is a cage that the young people have themselves codesigned so that it continues their economic subsidy for room, board, and even pocket money without infringing much on their personal and social freedoms. Their parents are also trapped, but not totally unhappily so. They get to see their children regularly and have some first-hand knowledge of what their offspring are doing. Moreover, the prolonged stay may mean that the children's obligations to their parents are now even deeper. These obligations are particularly important in families where the parents have had less work in the legitimate workforce and so receive meager pension benefits. Do adult children who have lived at home contribute more to their parents' underfinanced retirement years? We do not know yet. But it is important to note that the new Italian family system implies mutual gains, not just one generation's being a parasite on the other. This is not to deny the tensions that arise when two nonelderly generations live together for longer. But mutual affective regard may mute these tensions in Italy more than in countries with less strong familistic traditions.

Historically, Italian families had to be so strong because government did so little for individuals once their formal education was finished. This is still true compared to other European nations. Regional differences aside, Italy enjoys relatively little job training, few income supports for the young unemployed, and little support for young children. Families are expected to be the first line of support for individuals in need, and nongovernmental welfare agencies (often associated with the Catholic Church) come second. City, regional, and national governments usually come last. Tax collection is also less developed in Italy than elsewhere, adding to the low level of expectation about what the state can provide other than to those family heads who worked in the legitimate labor market before becoming unemployed or retiring. In a nation organized along these lines, little remains in government budgets for young families. So for the support they need, they have to turn to family or to the informal economy.

However, we should not surmise from this account that there is little state support for young people. There is considerable support, but it is indirect. This is because the Italian parent generation transfers resources to their children for longer than in other nations, and those older parents who have a history of legitimate work disproportionately benefit from Italian state tax resources. So some of the state benefits to parents trickle down to their adult children who live with them. It is impossible to know how much this transfer involves, and it is almost certainly less well targeted than would be the case with policies aimed exclusively at young adults. But nonetheless, some transfer from the state to adult children living at home does occur.

The Italian story is about international structural changes that are influencing the nation, but not all in the same way as elsewhere. In general, the changes have come more recently to Italy and have bit more deeply, especially as concerns the longer undergraduate study period, how much longer young adults live at home, the later age at which marriage occurs, and the small number of children. But Italian culture affects how these structural changes are experienced and buffers their impacts. Cultural factors curtail cohabitation and living with stranger roommates as ways to leave the family home. More so than in other nations, it links marriage to childbirth and female withdrawal from the labor market, thus delaying marriage for those not willing to see their standard of living compromised. And it builds on the already strong affective ties that characterize Italian family life, in some ways renewing them by making them more egalitarian and by ensuring that the younger generation's economic dependence does not diminish its personal or social independence. The family has become less unequal in its internal power relations. Young women have gained dramatically more control over their lives. And young men and women have learned that their parents are willing to be complicit in their children's sexual and cultural lives even when they do not agree with the choices being made. Structural changes are modifying cultural forms, and cultural traditions are modifying the influences of structure. Intimately connected, structure and culture mirror the dance between two mutually accommodating nonelderly adult generations that coexist in the same home and create a new equality without diminishing traditional affective ties. All very Italian—and the adult children get to stay home longer to enjoy Mother's cooking.

SWEDEN: WHERE NATIONALLY SPONSORED INDIVIDUAL EXPERIMENTATION PROMOTES EARLY SELF-RELIANCE

Sweden is the country least like Italy in the transition to adulthood, though it shares the same generic goals—getting a good job, enjoying material satisfaction, and creating a stable home in which to raise children. Moreover, both countries are exposed to many of the same international structural changes. For instance, despite a recent upturn, it is increasingly more difficult for Swedes younger than twenty-five to obtain steady and career-building work. Marriage is being ever more delayed. University enrollments are increasing, but many young people attend university only because they cannot find jobs they consider suitable.

However, it is striking how the school, work, and family transitions are compressed in Sweden as compared to Italy, resulting in full autonomy at an earlier age. Differences also exist in the value accorded to formal marriage, cohabitation, and out of wedlock births, with Sweden being more prone to dissociate marriage from both childbirth and new household formation.

The family and state also play different roles. In Sweden, the state (and corporations) actively supports the transition to adulthood to develop a productive and financially self-reliant citizenry and to increase the odds that young people will voluntarily carry out the obligations of citizenship. If personal autonomy is central to adulthood, then most Swedes are adult by about age twenty-five. They have moved out of the parental home and have started their own home. Indeed, most leave home soon after high school, mostly to live alone or cohabit, often alternating between the two and only returning to their parents' home for brief interludes. By age twenty-five, most Swedes have been in stable cohabiting relationships that are in some respects like experiments in marriage, though marriage itself occurs on average at age thirty for women and at age thirty-two for men. Marriage is not considered necessary for parenthood, and more than half of all births are to unmarried women, with the first birth occurring at age 28.5 on the average.

By age twenty-five, most Swedes who have not attended a university have settled into a steady job in the legitimate labor market despite some earlier "job churning" that labor economists view as experiments in identifying personally suitable long-term employment. Swedish unemployment rates for young people are consistently lower than in the other countries we explore. Entering university students tend to be older in Sweden because many young people take several years off after high school to travel or be employed. As a result, only about half of the university students have graduated by age twenty-five. But the age of university admission is now going down, and the age of graduation may sink also. Most Swedish students are confident that on graduation, they will get a job with responsibility and financial potential, and so they do not feel the same crisis that many Italian and French students do.

To summarize the descriptive findings, by age twenty-five, the vast majority of native Swedes have left their parents' home, are or have been in stable cohabiting relationships, and are well established in the labor market or are completing their university studies and face good job prospects. There are some exceptions to this general pattern, especially among Sweden's non-Scandinavian immigrants. Yet the picture is accurate on the whole. By age twenty-five, most young Swedes can see they are already largely autonomous, although children and marriage do not come for five more years.

We need to explore the system that produces these results, to examine how it works, and to understand what pressures it currently faces. Staffan Eklund, Ann-Sofie Ohlander, and Margaret Weir and Hakan Stattin wrote the Marbach conference reports we used for understanding the Swedish story. It is not exclusive to Sweden, though. It more or less applies to each of the other Nordic countries. Thus, the Italy/Sweden contrast is also a Mediterranean/Nordic contrast.

In 1991, Sweden reformed its three-year high schools that are attended by 97 percent of those who complete their compulsory earlier education. The new high schools aim to provide a broad basic education and to prepare individuals for further education, mostly in national study programs. These same dual goals hold even for students in the high school vocational training program, though they are especially likely to leave high school for paid work rather than further study.

Firms throughout Sweden are encouraged to participate in work-study programs, this being promoted as an informal duty of firms and as a chance for young people to be noticed by possible future employers. Across all forms of high school, only 10 percent of young people drop out—a very high completion rate.

Even so, Swedish high schools do not accomplish all the state expects of them. The standards set for them place a high value on helping students acquire the independent problem-solving and responsible-citizenship skills that are central to a participatory democracy. These skills are supposed to be developed and modeled in the student-teacher relationship, but apparently teachers find it difficult to incorporate these complex values into their relationships, and their teaching styles still tend to be autocratic, leaving students with little voice. Still, it is interesting to note how clear and broad is the state's interest in high schools. It wants them not only to prepare individuals for work or university study but also to foster their citizenship and self-reliance, helping them to recognize their obligations to others and to participate in local decision-making and agenda-setting activities.

Of Swedes ages nineteen to twenty-two, slightly more than 40 percent are in full-time higher education. Study grants and loans are available to everyone, with loans composing about 72 percent of the total. Over the years, these loans can entail significant personal debt, particularly since the stipend levels are set assuming summer work.

Moreover, until a revival in the late 1990s, the labor market had not been what it formerly was for students seeking to reduce their debt by combining study and work, whether in summer or during the academic year. Obviously, the way higher education is funded favors young people from more affluent families who need fewer loans. But university study is still possible for every high school graduate willing to take on loans and summer work.

Progress through university is better regulated in Sweden than in Italy, and so graduation takes less time. Although graduates tend to be younger in Sweden, this is not by much since many Swedes wait some years before attending university. However, delayed entry has recently become less prevalent, and the university graduation age is actually falling. In any event, the relatively compressed course of university study in Sweden may be one reason why there are fewer quasi-professional students there than in Italy or France, say. (These are students critical of a bourgeois society that they cannot or will not fully join. They need a long-term shelter against an impending bourgeois fate, and prolonged study allows this.)

The vast majority of Swedish students live in dormitories or lodgings, reflecting the high national value placed on being independent and leaving home. This implies the availability of relatively cheap rental housing, perhaps a legacy of housing policies dating back to the 1930s. Inexpensive housing is also available in Italy, but much of it is in the countryside and not in the cities where universities tend to be located. Young Swedes have a less marked preference for local universities compared to what one finds in Italy. Swedes are socialized to be proud of their own locality, but they are also socialized to be nationally and internationally cosmopolitan. So studying away from home is like an adventure, whereas for regionally chauvinistic Italians it is more like a burden. And since the *numerus clausus* system is widespread in Sweden, students wanting to matriculate in a particular field have to go wherever a suitable place is available. Whether planned or not, the Swedish university system promotes personal autonomy in young people while also providing a relatively clear and generally dependable path to quality employment. Italy is not like this, given its less structured university system, its apparently tighter urban housing market, its regionalism, and its weaker legitimate labor market.

Almost 60 percent of Swedes do not go to university, preferring to work instead. Historically, the work situation for young Swedes (ages sixteen to twenty-four) has been much better than elsewhere. In the recession of the early 1990s, their unemployment rose to 19 percent, a level that was seen as a crisis in Sweden but would have been labeled a policy victory in Italy. (However, Sweden's "off the books" economy is much smaller than Italy's.) By 1999, the recession had ended, and the youth unemployment rate fell to 8 percent, a figure most countries would envy. There is no separate youth labor market in the sense that young adults are grossly overrepresented in some economic sectors and not others. What is striking, though, is the high fraction of young Swedes now in temporary or part-time employment. In 1987, 71 percent of the twenty to twenty-four group had a job classified as steady; in 1998, when the recession was already over by several years, it had dropped to 54 percent. And the disposable income available to young people had also dropped by about 25 percent. The Swedish youth labor market seems to be getting worse, even if it is better than elsewhere.

In Sweden, both the state and corporations acknowledge responsibility for training young people. This is to invest in both their productivity and their independence. The state and industry fund many training schemes, both individually and jointly. In the recession of the early 1990s, the state mounted even more of them. What makes state-business training partnerships easier is that business ownership is more concentrated in Sweden than in Italy, making it easier for the state to interact with business. Also important is the success of Swedish business in exporting high value–added goods, making salient the need for quality workers and thus for investment in their training. And finally, Swedes in general acknowledge that the state has a responsibility to help people of all ages maximize their personal independence. So state and business support for job training reflects deep cultural and economic values in Sweden. However, since so much of the training involves state partnerships with business, market realities are always heeded in training activities.

The state only trains for jobs employers feel they truly need.

The state provides benefits to young persons who are unemployed. There is general unemployment insurance (*Akassan*) for everyone with even a modest history in the labor market. This pays up to 80 percent of the salary earned immediately before becoming unemployed. Young people are eligible for it. There is also a basic unemployment benefit for those with little employment history. This has been reduced several times during the 1990s and now pays about $3,500 per year. This is not enough to live on, and by reducing the benefit level, the state is reinforcing the message that work will pay and that nonwork will not. Unfortunately, the fraction of young people receiving basic rather than general unemployment insurance rose strongly during the 1990s. For those who cannot live off basic insurance and cannot get help from parents, the state pays a supplementary benefit designed to meet basic living standards for an individual. Among persons ages twenty to twenty-four, the take-up rate for supplementary benefits doubled from 10 percent to almost 20 percent during the 1990s, while it hardly changed for other age groups. For those who do not go to university, the youth labor market is increasingly more difficult, and the unemployment benefits less generous.

The Swedish state actively promotes the autonomy of its young citizens. It values the life-long self-reliance and civic engagement that are thought to follow from individuals' making a positive entry into early adulthood. However, its attempts to help position youth for the labor market through education, training, partnerships with industry, and subsidies to industry are running into problems. In economic hard times, young workers are the first to be fired since they are not as immediately productive as experienced workers, and international competition is probably forcing businesses to be leaner. It requires investments in the next generation to be justified economically and not as contributions to maintaining the civic life of the state. Jobs do not last a lifetime anymore, and to be apprenticed in one trade is no guarantee that the same trade will exist when one is fifty-five. The central dilemma of the Swedish system is retaining and developing quality jobs with good prospects for those who do not go to university. As temporary and part-time jobs proliferate, things are getting worse, especially for immigrants from non-Scandinavian countries. Even so, the state of affairs is generally better than elsewhere. Most twenty- to twenty-four-year-old Swedish nonstudents are in steady jobs, and to judge by the 8 percent unemployment rate, nearly all the remainder have access to temporary and part-time work that allows them to experiment with what they would like to do on a more permanent basis.

Swedes place a very high value on personal autonomy and self-reliance. By age twenty, most Swedes are out of the family home for all or most of the year, whether they study at a university or not. However, the rate of those still in their parents' home in their early twenties is increasing, albeit from a low base rate. When young Swedes first leave home, 70 percent of those between ages sixteen and twenty-four go to live alone in a small rented apartment. Most of the others are in cohabiting relationships, especially in their twenties rather than late teens. Moving back to live with parents occurs infrequently. The expectation and reality is that most individuals will live independently and will responsibly experiment with new partners until they eventually settle down and marry the latest partner. Swedes do not encourage early marriage as much as they encourage marriages where each partner knows the other's strengths and idiosyncrasies.

Despite the prevalence of cohabitation, marriages still tend to take place slightly earlier in Sweden than in Italy, being thirty-two for men and thirty for women. However, marriage is much less strongly associated with childbirth. Sweden has one of the highest rates of out of wedlock births in western Europe, though the father and mother often marry later. Even so, the average age of women when their first child is born is lower than the average age at which they marry (28.5 versus 30). Out of wedlock births still carry stigma in Italy, but rarely in Sweden. Moreover, Swedish women tend to have among the largest families in Europe—2.1 children compared to Italy's 1.3—and the state is quite active in supporting families and especially children. While the hope is that individual adults will earn enough to support a family, the modern reality is that a comfortable lifestyle in Sweden requires two incomes. So in addition to the university scholarships, job training, and unemployment provisions already mentioned, the state and business have developed systems for maternity (and paternity) leave, child allowances, and daycare.

The Swedish story is one of individuals' being supported after high school to study at a university or to learn to work, with the clear expectation that this support is for promoting self-reliant individuals and active citizens. As they grow older, young persons are expected to help themselves more and more, and reliance on parents is minimal. Frank recognition is made that young people in their late teens and early twenties do not always know what they want. They might want to see the world, to experiment with whether to go to university, to experiment with different kinds of jobs, to experiment with living alone or with another person, and even to experiment with several partners to learn mutual intimacy and responsibility. The state actively sponsors such experimentation and also acts to support rather than undermine individual initiative. So study grants are provided, but a loan or parental help is also needed, as is some paid work. When unemployment occurs, past work will be rewarded but prolonged inactivity will not, though enough is provided to keep life and limb together. When children are born, couples are not left alone to struggle. Child supports are in place that allow each parent to stay in the workforce and so contribute to family and personal independence.

But the system is threatened, particularly for those who do not attend university. International competition and the growth of non-Swedish multinational corporations mean that market principles are gaining ground. These are associated with lower levels of collaboration between businesses and the state and perhaps with lower total tax revenues, each of which could hurt young workers and parents more than others. Moreover, the changing structure of work means that individuals can no longer be trained for a specific job in the expectation they will hold it for their entire working life or even half of it. And finally, new immigrant groups constitute the hardest-hit segment in Swedish society. Over the long term, and in economic recessions, public opinion might turn against them and the support system that helps them. Even so, Sweden is unique among the nations we consider in encouraging early adult experimentation in many areas of personal life and in fostering a relatively orderly transition to adulthood. By age twenty-five, most Swedes live as autonomous individuals in their own household supported by steady work or scholarships and loans. They have future prospects and a developed sense of social citizenship, though they are not yet parents nor are they married.

GERMANY: WHERE ROLES ARE
CLEAR EARLY BUT THE CROWN
JEWELS ARE IN PERIL

Rainer Silbereisen and Walter Heinz wrote the conference papers on the transition to adulthood in Germany, and Karl-Ulrich Mayer provided some commentary on their accounts. Most aspects of the transition are not distinctive for Germany, whether we refer to high school graduation rates, the average age of leaving home, age of marriage, marriage rates, the incidence of cohabitation, the number of births, mother's age at first birth, or youth unemployment.

Three differences do stand out, though. One concerns the early age at which important schooling decisions are made that influence individual life chances. Another is related to changes underway in the higher-education system to process greater numbers of students, to reduce their graduation time, to absorb East German institutions of higher education, and to clarify the respective roles of research centers, universities, and polytechnics. The third issue concerns those who do not enter higher education but instead seek apprenticeships. Despite its international fame, the German apprenticeship system is currently experiencing considerable shocks from which it might not recover in its current form, thus implying new problems for German nongraduates in how they make the transition to adulthood. The German story has a lot in common with the story in Austria and Switzerland, and much of the following discussion applies to German-speaking countries, plus West Switzerland, Ticino, and the Engadine valley.

In Germany, the transition to adulthood depends partly on the secondary school one attends. Usually after fourth grade (but sometimes after sixth), young people enter a *Hauptschule, Realschule,* or *Gymnasium* that they then leave, if on track, after a total of nine, ten, or thirteen years of schooling, respectively. These three school types constitute the stratified system that channels young people either into vocational preparation and then work (the first two) or into a course of study designed to prepare them for postsecondary education in a polytechnic or university (the last). So at a very early age, important life decisions are made in Germany based on parent requests, fallible tests, and teacher testimonials.

These school decisions have occupational consequences. For instance, in the late 1990s, one-third of all apprenticeships went to students from *Hauptschulen,* and these students mainly entered craft and blue-collar occupations. Two-fifths went to students from *Realschulen,* and most of them were trained for occupations in commerce and technology. Only one-fifth went to *Gymnasium* graduates, and they tended to enter careers in business, commerce, and public service. It is difficult to believe that this correspondence between a school's prestige and the occupational stratification of its graduates is entirely due to true fourth-grade merit differences. That is, no causal role should be ascribed to regional differences in the availability of various tracks or to social class, race, and religious factors in knowing how to manipulate the educational system so as to increase the chances of a favorable track placement for one's child.

In this connection, the contrast with other countries is striking. In Sweden, everyone attends the same kind of school until the last three years, when vocational and university track choices are made. The same is basically true in Italy. And in American public high schools, tracking generally occurs within schools rather than between them. One implication of such early school tracking is that the German educational system may ignore many students whose clear cognitive interests and gifts emerge only after sixth grade. Another is that the school system is likely to reproduce existing class differences in the next generation. And another is that federal states differ in their commitment to quality education. In Hamburg, a state with a long egalitarian history, 34 percent of students enter the *Gymnasium* and so have a chance to go to university. In Bavaria, only 19 percent do.

German universities are organized by states, and students clearly prefer to study close to home. But the preference is weaker than in Italy. Moreover, many fields of study are governed by *numerus clausus* restrictions that encourage migration to other parts of the country. So does the old tradition of attending several different universities before completing one's higher education. German undergraduate study has traditionally not been highly structured, and individual variation in the number of years it takes to graduate is considerable. Some students spend longer because they want to explore life options in academics and elsewhere. Others see continuous study as a means to avoid becoming bourgeois. Some students fall through the administrative cracks because it is widely assumed that those with

enough ability to get into a university are able to manage their own course progression while there. And some students take longer because they are apprehensive about whether the jobs university graduates traditionally fill will be available, given Germany's changing job structure and the increased competition from other students in the expanding university and even polytechnic systems.

Serious attempts have recently been made to get undergraduates to finish within five years, even if this means more graduates holding jobs inferior to what they expect. Things could also deteriorate if student numbers continue to increase without a corresponding increase in funds. University faculty members generally resent being required to teach more, and this could lead to watering down the curriculum or even tightening it so that only better students complete their studies. German professors also resent having less time and resources for research, since this is increasingly being conducted by national and international centers or by temporary university-based centers like *Sonderforschungsbereiche* or *Schwerpunktsprogramme*. Competitive grants to individual researchers are rarer than in the United States. However much university and polytechnic students might be hurt by shorter graduation periods and creeping changes in the professorial role, they still symbolize superiority in the skill mix thought to be required for executive and professional jobs. Whatever the actual skill levels of future German graduates, their comparative advantage within their own nation is quite clear.

The centerpiece of the German transition to adulthood for those who do not attend university is the apprenticeship system. Every country has a large group of young people who want to go straight from high school to paid work, and the apprenticeship system is designed for them. It consists partly of on the job training and partly of school-based vocational instruction, and so it is called the dual system. The apprenticeship lasts for at least three years, and certificates are usually gained at age eighteen, though that is creeping up also. The dual system is buttressed by agreements between government, unions, and employers and incorporated into a vocational training act that is supported by a federal agency that develops, reforms, and evaluates training ordinances for 360 occupations in the craft, technical, commercial, and service areas. The hope of all young Germans, and the expectation of most, is that they will be offered a job in the trade and even in the business where they did their training. Additional training is often asked for, and it can be provided on the job, in a special technical school, or more likely, in some combination of both. Thus, the apprenticeship system is for a minimum of three years. It can last longer, depending on the complexity of the skills involved.

This dual system is widespread. Almost 80 percent of recent German school leavers obtain either an occupational certificate or an undergraduate degree, whereas less than 50 percent of all Americans reach these same standards. Given these numbers and the institutional commitment of government, unions, and employers, the German apprenticeship system is often held to be the most successful of all the national school-to-work models. For teens who find traditional school work punitive, it provides an alternative that links school and work in practical ways. It also provides young people with a clear path to a secure economic and social future, thus avoiding the uncertainties plaguing many young Italians and Americans in particular. It may also reduce the level of juvenile behavior problems and sow the seeds for a later family life based on just one wage, thus avoiding some of the child care complications that arise when both parents need to work. It also sows the seeds for occupational advancement. Anyone who already has a certificate can work in his or her occupation for five years, and then over the next three years and with a government subsidy, he or she can learn how to become a self-employed master whose own business can then train the next generation of apprentices.

The apprenticeship system helps the nation at large, not just the apprentices and their employers. It produces a large group of young Germans in 360 different occupations who have a certified level of performance in clearly specified occupation-specific tasks. This has helped create a work force that produces export-worthy goods with a high value–added component for which most citizens hold the trainers partly responsible. The latter then feel justifiably proud of their accomplishments. The apprenticeship system also provides another potent symbol—about the possibility and benefits of cooperative relationships between government, unions, and businesses. In Germany, these entities seem less antagonistic to each other than in, say, France, Italy, or the United States. Thus, the apprenticeship system also helps symbolize a cooperative industrial policy.

However, the apprenticeship system is under considerable strain and probably cannot survive in its current form. The strains are many. While each might be surmountable individually—some more readily than others—the cumulative weight of so many sources of strain is striking. However, the system has shown itself to be adaptable in the past, and maybe it will show the same resiliency in the future. Who knows?

In the past, there was a marked bias toward jobs traditionally filled by men. Apprenticeships are now more equal by gender, though young women still tend to be steered toward traditionally female roles that are also associated with lesser pay during training. But other long-standing tensions have not been dealt with even this well, for instance the ethnic/religious bias against offering apprenticeships to non-Germans. It affects not just new immigrants from eastern Europe, Africa, and Asia but also those young Turks who are third generation in Germany. Indeed, only 37 percent of all eligible Turks make it into the dual system, and those who do so are trained for more menial positions than the office and technical jobs that disproportionately go to Germans.

In recent years, the percentage of persons offering to train apprentices has been going down relative to the demand. It is increasingly common to see official signs imploring local small business owners or independent craftsmen to take on apprentices. This has to be seen against the reality that city busses and trains are flooded with signs by private-sector companies offering temporary or part-time employment and many different forms of training. All this suggests that the apprenticeship system is not producing people who can readily fit into the existing job structure. Otherwise, why would private sector firms advertise for labor and why would temporary employment firms advertise their ability to provide part-time work and to train in basic skills? Exacerbating the slowdown in demand for apprentices has been the faster rate of growth in small firms relative to large ones. In general, smaller firms are less organized to recruit and train apprentices and perhaps also to employ them subsequently. Indeed, some smaller businesses are more interested in apprenticeships as subsidized labor for current production than for training the next generation. Thus, they are less willing (and able) to rotate young people through a broad array of trade-specific tasks on each of which they are thoroughly trained by a master craftsman.

Outmoded trainers are everywhere, especially in East Germany where so many cannot perform at the standards required nationally. Inspectors are supposed to detect inadequate training. But the bureaucracy is keen to keep the numbers of apprenticeships up, and this adds to the inevitable slowness in identifying lax firms. There is also slowness in updating job descriptions so that each job can reflect the changing skill demand. It is not a surprise, therefore, to note that 20 percent of those who begin an apprenticeship leave it within the first year, either because they do not like the job or work site or because they want to go into other work or back to school. Of those who complete their apprenticeship, 40 percent cannot subsequently find a job in the occupation in which they were trained. In some years, fewer than 45 percent of those who do manage to get a job do so in the firm where they trained. It is understandable that some young people lose interest in their occupation. But some train with masters who are not very accomplished and others are trained for skills that are hardly needed in the emergent labor market.

The growing skill mismatch is evidenced by two things. One is the flourishing private sector firms that specialize in employment and training, and the other is the current paucity of German workers in certain fields—for example, information technologies and business administration at intermediate levels. (Germany has recently had to recruit workers in information technology from India, even creating special immigration status for them.) Those running the apprenticeship system were either not able to foresee the newly emerging needs or not able to do anything about them in the time available. The private sector now seems willing to provide the flexibility in training and employment that

the public sector is increasingly less able to generate.

The greatest threats to the apprenticeship system come from structural changes in the labor market, especially for youth. In an economy that is increasingly global and service oriented, more of the jobs for young people are part-time or temporary. Yet a flourishing guild-based apprenticeship system assumes greater job stability than now seems promised. It also requires better prediction of the number and kinds of jobs that will be needed twenty or even ten years from now. Some traditional occupations are now becoming obsolete, others have radically and speedily changed their content, and new occupations are continually emerging. A largely centralized guild model based on complex government, business, and union interdependencies may not be able to adjust well to the fast pace of labor market change.

What are some of the new employment realities? While soft skills were never neglected in the apprenticeship system, they may now be even more important than job-specific skills. How one learns has become as important as what one knows. Yet social scientists see the ability to learn resulting more from general education than from specific job training. The growth of private sector employment firms reflects the desire of German employers for greater freedom from regulation of all kinds and especially for greater freedom to hire, train, and fire. Businesses also increasingly value last-minute assembly processes using internationally generated components. They want the training and availability of labor to mirror the changing ebbs and flows in the volume of work as well as to reflect the changing nature of the products and services being assembled. Flexibility is the employers' slogan. It is difficult to manage a large apprenticeship system that meets the needs of business when the occupational world is characterized by speedy obsolescence and unpredictable creation.

Adding to this difficulty is that more of the businesses operating in Germany are foreign owned or co-owned, while native German businesses are experiencing ever stiffer international competition. Have these factors reduced business commitment to the German apprenticeship system? Will recruitment be based even more on temporary staff so as to weather market fluctuations and to employ only the skill mixes currently needed? Will training become oriented more to learning one or two production-specific tasks for the short-term as opposed to learning a complex set of tasks presumed to be relevant for a lifetime? Will the German labor market for young people move toward the more market-oriented Anglo-American model where occupation and occupational pride are less relevant than flexible hiring and firing and on-site training in highly specific skills? Will future demand be more for people who are educated rather than people who are trained? For those who attend a *Hauptschule* or *Realschule*, the German educational system is about training, and education is only a priority for those attending a *Gymnasium*.

The transition to adulthood in Germany is not very special with respect to the age at which individuals leave home, get married, and have children or with respect to the numbers attending higher education or the time such education takes. Even so, Germany has considerable emergent problems. Its school system is stratified so early and is based on a model of training versus education that may not reflect well industry's changing need for people who are well educated rather than well trained. Moreover, its universities are experiencing considerable pressure and some role confusion, largely because of the increase in student numbers without a corresponding rise in expenditures, the competition from more occupationally oriented *Fachhochschulen*, and the growing political interest in universities as sites for teaching rather than research. And the world-famous apprenticeship system may have been a better solution for the former world of work than for the world now emerging. There may be less need today for acquiring the set of skills historically associated with a given occupation and more need to learn specific skills that can be taught on site for jobs that last much less than a lifetime.

Unfortunately, no obviously effective solutions are under discussion for the problems associated with the inflexible school structure, the expanding and strained university system, and the apprenticeship system's inability to mirror changing labor force and work realities. Any proposed solution has to take account of the fact that businesses increasingly favor flexibility and decision independence over involvement in complex training schemes with government and unions. Can the current apprenticeship system be redesigned?

THE UNITED STATES: WHERE
EXPECTATIONS ABOUT INDIVIDUAL
SELF-HELP PROMOTE A SINK-OR-SWIM
TRANSITION TO ADULTHOOD

The Marbach papers on the United States were written by Jacquelynne Eccles, David Ellwood, and John Modell, and Christopher Jencks commented on them. We depend on these accounts for many of the facts and interpretations presented here. However, the current authors know more about the transition to adulthood in the United States than elsewhere and use this extraconference knowledge in what follows. In most respects, the transition is similar in America, Canada, and the United Kingdom, and so it is probably warranted to talk of an Anglo-American model to complement the Mediterranean, Nordic, and German-speaking models considered earlier.

The United States is distinct in several ways. Its secondary school system has more private schools than elsewhere, the majority Catholic. Its public schools are not stratified by presumed ability as in Italy, Sweden, or Germany. Instead, tracking generally takes place within these all-purpose schools, especially at the high school level. The percentage of eighteen-year-olds still in high school is lowest in the United States, reflecting a higher dropout rate.

The higher-education system is structurally similar to other countries, with vocational colleges, undergraduate colleges, and universities, plus some postgraduate facilities. There are some functional differences, though. Two-year colleges in America have both a vocational mission and a mission to prepare students for a four-year college, and it is not always clear for a given institution which mission is paramount, leading to some confusion for faculty and students. Undergraduate institutions have mostly an educational mission, and they vary in quality to a degree probably not found in Sweden and Germany. Indeed, the American stratification system is opposite to the German where secondary schools are more stratified than universities. Americans seek to delay institutional stratification so as to provide individuals with second and third chances should their motivation to get ahead come late or should they stumble at earlier points. The pinnacle of the American higher-education system is its graduate schools that have educational, research, and professional training missions. They cater to a higher percentage of young people in a given cohort than in other countries, though the numbers are still not high.

When they leave home to attend university or work full-time, young Americans are the most likely to have roommates of the same sex. They are also the most likely to be incarcerated or otherwise involved with the legal system. Although there is nothing exceptional about American rates and ages of cohabitation and marriage, the average childbearing pattern is more like Sweden's than Italy's—about 2.1 children per women, with births beginning in the late twenties on the average. However, there is considerable dispersion by age, and births to women younger than twenty are much more prevalent in the United States than elsewhere, though they are a small fraction of all births. Compared to other nations, teenage Americans do not seem to be as sophisticated about using birth control.

In the United States, there is extensive part-time and temporary employment after age sixteen and considerable mixing of school and work. Full merit scholarships to attend a university are rare, except in nonprofessional graduate fields. As a result, most students without affluent parents need work or loans or some combination of the two. For those who do not attend university, the United States has relatively high levels of unemployment before age twenty-five and the highest levels of churning around different jobs. Most businesses are reluctant to collaborate with unions and government, and so vocational training is not well established. Firms prefer to do their own training and want maximal flexibility in hiring, training, and firing. So finding jobs is more a matter of individual initiative and social networks than of third-party placement. Indeed, agencies counseling the young unemployed now emphasize how to search for jobs and provide incentives to do so, but they do not go out of their way to locate jobs or to teach task-specific skills.

In every country we have considered, some groups make an effortless transition to successful adulthood while others do not. One recipe for success is clear everywhere—work hard in secondary school, graduate from university, do not get involved with the law, do not have children before the late twenties, and marry or cohabit with someone at least as well educated as yourself. For those who do not go to college, the recipe is somewhat different. It stresses graduating from high school, getting a job with prospects, acquiring both soft and hard job skills, developing a broad network of job contacts, avoiding repeated contact with the law, marrying a partner in the mid-twenties with a good job, and avoiding children before roughly the same age.

Each nation also has groups that make poorer transitions to adulthood. Physical and mental health can play a role here, as can learning skills. So can race and ethnicity, particularly as they intersect with class (and sometimes immigrant status). Although people of color in every nation are overrepresented among those experiencing a difficult transition, our impression is that the situation is most acute in the United States. Striking is the high percentage of less-educated African Americans and Puerto Ricans who experience unemployment, incarceration, homelessness, poverty, childbearing before twenty, and single parenthood. While very few of them experience all or most of these complications, many experience several of them. The United States probably has more variation than elsewhere in the quality of the transition its citizens make to adulthood.

Normatively, the United States offers second and third chances to young people, especially in education. Those who have not done well in high school or who dropped out can nonetheless attend a community college and make up the shortfall. If they meet the necessary standards, they can then transfer to a university; and if they do well there they can even attend graduate school. If they go to a lesser-known university, perhaps because their high school grades were weak, they can still go on to a quality graduate school if their undergraduate performance is very good. Second chances are also evident in the employment domain. Prospective employers do not seem reluctant to hire young people with a poor work history, provided it occurred before their mid-twenties and was not attributable to incarceration. Some employers encourage their young workers to attend evening classes, and some employees do this even without encouragement. Individuals who have had disorderly lives in their teens and early twenties and do not want further education can sometimes get into the military and thereby signal their trustworthiness and dependability to prospective employers. Alternatively, they can take whatever jobs there are to demonstrate their reliability, motivation, and even job performance. Important is signaling one's personal commitment to work. In contrast, the German school-to-work system lets potential employees know that they will be looked after if they play the game, and it

signals to employers that a dependable labor force with appropriate skills will be on hand when needed. The German and Swedish systems are suffused with well-tested and culturally respected institutional collaborations that are quite different from what we find in the United States with its more individualistic culture and more widespread business and citizen distrust of government.

Second chances are not restricted to schooling and early employment. It is also the case in the personal domain. Stigma about cohabitation and divorce in the early twenties is on the wane in the United States, and divorce and remarriage are more common than in the other nations. Very young women who have had a child usually get formal and informal support not to have another, whether in school or through the welfare system. Thus, very few mothers who have a child before eighteen have another before they are twenty, giving them a chance to get more firmly established in the world of work or study.

Other nations also seek to promote both catching up by those who are temporarily off track and self-improvement on the part of those who discover they originally aimed too low. Thus, a German can use an apprenticeship as a stepping stone to further education in a polytechnic or evening school. But no national system is as fluid as the American one with respect to the number of opportunities that individuals have to get back on track. And no nation leaves so late the fundamental choices that have to be made about the quality of educational institution to attend. The American system seeks to provide individuals with opportunities they can utilize when their abilities, interests, and needs have crystallized. Contrast this with Germany where the secondary school transition has such lifelong consequences and occurs almost ten years before the corresponding formal choices occur in America—about whether to attend some form of college and then what kind of college. But in the American system, individuals have to want these opportunities, and it is tougher to take advantage of them the older one is and the more one has already slipped behind. To have a system of second chances does not mean that those who most need such chances know of them and have the freedom to avail themselves of them without considerable moral effort and personal sacrifice. For instance, the voluntary military system provides an important institution for self-renewal and access to a good job after a period shielded from street dangers. But it is now well nigh impossible to be accepted into the American military without high school graduation, and recruiters do not appreciate involvement with the criminal justice system other than for minor adolescent infringements. The military is a second-chance option, but it is not open to all.

America does not afford the same cultural sponsorship of youthful experimentation that one finds in Sweden, at least not for its less privileged young people. For the most part, cohabitation is not normatively encouraged, though it is increasingly practiced. Single mothers in America do not get child support services that are as generous or as free of stigma as in Sweden. State and business support to young adults for education and job training are not as generous in the United States as in Sweden or Germany. Maternity and paternity leaves are not as widespread nor as generous when they are available, and civic obligations to hire young workers are not as deeply entrenched in the United States as in Sweden or even Germany. America is also the most prone to incarcerate young repeat offenders and to do so in ways that do not seriously aim at rehabilitation. The young adult prisoner profile is disproportionately race based, with African Americans, particularly those from poorer urban neighborhoods, being heavily overrepresented. This "lock them up and throw away the key" policy would probably find less acceptance in other countries and certainly affects the lives of a greater percentage of young Americans than young Italians, Germans, or Swedes.

In Sweden, the state wants to support individuals without undermining their individual initiative. There seems to be widespread agreement that many young people are not sure what they want to do and that in experimenting with their private and work lives, they will inevitably make some mistakes that have nontrivial consequences. In the United States, the main assumption is that individuals should get ahead by themselves by virtue of their own willpower and initiative, provided that the institutions are in place from which they can benefit, primarily schools and colleges. It is up to each young person to take advantage of the existing opportunities, relying for this on his or her own general cultural knowledge and on supportive others who know of the opportunities available and of any dangers that young people might confront. Such knowledge and networks may be more unequally distributed in the United States than elsewhere, and second-chance opportunities may therefore not be as universally available or as practically accessible as many Americans would like to think. Is this why incarceration rates seem to be so much higher for young male adults from disadvantaged American neighborhoods than from poverty settings elsewhere? Do such Americans experiment with their lives as part of natural human development but without as much sponsorship and understanding from mature adults and national institutions as occurs elsewhere, instead relying for guidance on peers experimenting in the same ways? We need to learn how mature adults in different nations understand repeated youthful indiscretions and to document which policies deal with this.

In the United States, practical family support for the transition to adulthood is less available than in Italy. Self-reliance being such a salient national goal, relatively few young American adults live primarily with their parents, and of those who do, few want to. Even parents expect their children to leave home by their early twenties. But realities of the housing market often make autonomous living difficult prior to marriage. So compared to other nations, more Americans live with nonfamilial roommates to share housing expenses and maintain autonomy. Also, a relatively high percentage of young unmarried mothers live in households with other family members who contribute to living expenses and help with child care. Even here, though, it is unlikely that the total level of family support matches Italy's. Lower-class families in the United States are rarely in a strong position to help a young unmarried mother with shelter, food, and money. And it is obviously easier for two generations to live together without a small child (as in Italy) than when a child is present (as in the United States). Extensive child care is needed if young women from poor backgrounds are to work, and generating this within the household or extended family burdens the older generation or siblings who provide the care while possibly adding to the anxieties of working women with a child but no long-term partner.

Until very recently, wages for poorly educated young Americans have stagnated and, for some subgroups, have even declined in real money terms. The federal government has tried to counter this growing income disparity and the income decline by attempting, like the Swedes, to make work pay, especially via the Earned Income Tax Credit (EITC). This supplements wages (but not unemployment) for low-wage workers, who are disproportionately young adults. Daycare provisions are improving for three- and four-year-olds with less affluent mothers, largely because Head Start has been expanding through both Republican and Democratic administrations.

Businesses want female workers to feel comfortable about their child care arrangements but do not want to pay for them directly, while liberals see quality daycare as a chance for small children from straightened circumstances to learn middle-class relationship skills and to prepare for school. By now, slighter more than 50 percent of the families eligible for Head Start are in the program, and many of the remainder take part in other state or local subsidized daycare programs that vary considerably in structure and quality. Implicit in EITC and Head Start (as well as sporadic calls to increase the minimum wage) is both the philosophy that work should be supported and the reality that government has to do something about the stagnant wages paid to less-educated workers. Indeed, the gap separating the top part of the income distribution from the bottom part is growing faster in the United States than in other countries, especially when the top and bottom deciles are contrasted. Paid work is essential for those young Americans not in higher education, in part because it is necessary for EITC.

Yet in the late teens and twenties, official unemployment is higher in the United States than in Sweden, though not Italy or Germany. Unemployed persons are not eligible for EITC. Even more striking than the unemployment rate, though, is the pattern whereby less well-educated Americans experience more periods of unemployment, hold more jobs, work part-time more often, and receive stagnant or declining wages. Yet despite such employment

instability and restricted access to good jobs, young Americans are expected to be heavy consumers, and the advertising industry targets them as such. So if they are to live a material lifestyle they find acceptable, their expenditure needs are likely to outstrip their legitimate income. Where can such money come from if families or steady work cannot often provide it?

Part of the answer is "hustling" in some form or another. The American underground economy is most prevalent among those who cannot or will not get attached to the legitimate labor market before their late twenties. Given recent changes in judicial sentencing practices, crime now entails an even greater likelihood of eventual incarceration, especially for young males. Most Americans seem willing to accept these increasing incarceration rates and the expenditures they entail because less crime is thought to result. However, the families of those incarcerated also bear costs. They now lack a partner and source of income, and poorer communities become even poorer and depleted of adult males in their twenties and thirties. The criminals themselves are probably affected long term since they are taken out of circulation at an age when they might be accumulating long-lasting social and cultural capital. In prison, they mostly generate life histories that make most potential employers suspicious of them. No nation is as draconian as the United States with respect to the incarceration of young offenders. Given the national philosophy of second chances, young people are rarely incarcerated for a first offense. But they are in deep trouble by the third recorded offense. Then they are treated as though they had failed a national test of personal character, as having refused to take advantage of the institutional first and second chances offered them, and as having willfully rejected the personal self-improvement philosophy of the United States.

Notice the informal and formal context in which such a poor transition to adulthood takes place. Informal support is supposed to come primarily from families, and in all social classes in all countries, nearly all families provide some support. However, the level is lower in the United States than in Italy, the other country where weak school, government, and business support forces greater dependence on the family. Formal support is less generous in the United States than in Sweden or Germany. Thus, the United States has some of the lowest achieving high schools, and school links to quality jobs seem to be more tenuous there than in Germany. Moreover, American business has no taste for training young workers through partnerships with unions and government. Nor is there a normative structure in the United States such as that in Sweden that sees experimentation as an inevitable part of human development between ages sixteen and twenty-five. Most Americans do make a successful transition, some through the conventional route via higher education, others through the conventional route of early stable employment thanks to network and union connections or to luck and character. And some young

Americans make it by utilizing second chances after having earlier gotten off track. But it is worthwhile designing future research to document whether the wastage really is greater in the United States than elsewhere, given what seem to be poorer family and institutional supports and a greater presumption of individual will and initiative in the teens and early twenties.

The United States is the most individualistic laissez-faire nation we consider and the most market dominated even at these young adult ages. Most individuals swim in the tides created, thanks to careful parenting and family willingness to co-invest in higher education. The prevailing ethos is one of individuals who must negotiate markets for education, jobs, and life partners, and in these markets, they are free both to make whatever decisions they want and to live with their consequences, though some second chances are possible. Young people in America are expected to make the transition using cultural knowledge they have picked up in their family and school. A greater fraction in the United States than elsewhere seems to sink, especially among the poor and racial minorities, given that the adequacy and relevance of their knowledge of the dominant culture leaves a lot to be desired. Especially hard knocks await all those young Americans who deviate from any one of the safe paths to successful adulthood.

CONCLUSIONS

This article has been about differences between four nations. But the similarities are striking also. They include the expansion of higher education, the growing difficulties in the youth labor market, and increases in cohabitation, later marriage, and fewer children. We should not forget the increasing percentages of those who simultaneously study and work or the variation within each nation. Also not to be forgotten are the many young people who make it through the conventional pathways of attending a university or getting a good job early. But there are always those who flounder significantly, disproportionately poorer people whose race, ethnicity, or religion makes them different from national demographic norms. The international factors creating such similarity in cross-national trends need to be explored. But that was not our concern here. Our story concerned national differences.

Italy, a country with a weaker state and smaller businesses than elsewhere, relies on its family heritage to cushion young people. In so doing, family relationships become more egalitarian as the better-educated younger generation negotiates with its parent generation to retain social and personal independence while surrendering a little economic independence and also postponing the creation of an independent household and the marriage and childbearing that this household implies.

Sweden promotes individual self-reliance but does so through its tolerance of early experimentation and the support that state, industry, and union sponsorship. By age twenty-five, most Swedes have made a successful transition to autonomous living and a steady job or tertiary education with good employment prospects. Marriage and children are still to come, but most have cohabited by then, learning mature relationship attitudes and skills. The main problem is that Swedish businesses want more control over hiring, firing, and training, thus threatening the national partnership model.

A somewhat similar model pertains in Germany. However, Germany forces much earlier occupation-relevant schooling decisions on behalf of children. For those not on a university track, it seeks to inculcate hope and direction by training students for one of 360 occupations that suit a wide range of talents. But this apprenticeship system probably cannot continue in its current form. Increasingly, firms want to make their own decisions about hiring and training, and the job structure is changing in a way that a traditional guild model cannot match. Temporary and part-time work is more prevalent now, new occupations are emerging that require skills not yet in the system, and businesses seek workers who can learn new skills quickly rather than those who know a prescribed set of skills. Yet if an education model were to replace the current training model for Germans not on a university track, this could well exacerbate the problems German higher education already faces.

The United States is the most individualistic of the nations we consider. Family support is generally lower than in Italy and government and business support less than in Germany or Sweden. So young people who do not go to university flounder more than elsewhere, and these flounderers are disproportionately poor and of color. They have significant problems with schooling, living arrangements, incarceration, early childbearing, overstressed families, and a labor market in which, until very recently, real wages were stagnating and in some cases even declining. The United States prides itself on giving all individuals a second and sometimes third chance when they deviate from the most common paths to successful adulthood. Such opportunities are indeed available, though knowledge of them and the ability to access them are not equally distributed.

What do such national differences matter, though, if Americans, Swedes, Germans, and Italians all look demographically similar by about age thirty-five? That is, most work full-time, have their own home, are married, have children, and are no longer in full-time education. However different the national pathways to adulthood, the end result still seems to be the same. So, do national differences in pathways through youth and early adulthood really matter?

From age sixteen to thirty-five is almost twenty years, about a quarter of a lifetime. Thus, how these years are spent is important in its own right. As Rabbi Hillel said, all the rest is commentary.

But academics thrive on commentary, and we are academics. To begin that commentary, it is worth noting that marriage may not mean the same thing in all these nations and that the variation may in part be due to national differences in cohabitation patterns or the strength of the cultural links between marriage and childbearing. Commitments to work may also not be similar in practice, perhaps due to experiences such as being churned through many jobs in the United States as opposed to spending longer in the same job or trade, as in Germany. Commitments to family size and all the consequences of this might also vary, depending on how old one is at marriage, this being older in Italy than, say, the United States. We can go on and on. The point is that our demographic indicators of a successful transition have to do with demographic milestones, such as marriage and moving away from home. But these milestones do not unpack the meanings nationally attached to such events and the consequences that arise because the event was arrived at one way versus another. It is surely an important research agenda for the future to explore if the manner in which the transition to adulthood takes place affects important outcomes like how marriage is experienced, how parent- ing takes place, how much political participation occurs, and how young adults forge a personal identity.

Note

1. Some of these between-nation differences run counter to temporal changes occurring within Italy. For instance, more and more Italians are leaving home to cohabit, especially if they live in industrialized northern nations. But even so, cohabitation is still less prevalent in Italy, and marriage is more common. We mention within-country changes only when the rate of change is unique in the nation under consideration or when the mention corrects what might otherwise be a misinterpretation.

ANNALS, *AAPSS*, **580**, March 2002

Institutional Variation and the Position of Young People: A Comparative Perspective

By RICHARD BREEN and MARLIS BUCHMANN

ABSTRACT: The articles in this issue report on a variety of young people's behaviors and attitudes, drawn from a wide range of countries. An obvious challenge to which these findings give rise is to explain the differences between countries in these attitudes and behaviors. In this article, we look to institutional variation to supply an answer. Institutions establish a set of opportunities and constraints to which young people respond, but they also reflect, and help to establish, normatively appropriate ways of behaving. We conceptualize institutional variation in terms of welfare regime types, labor market regulation, and educational systems, and we try to sketch some of the ways in which variations in these might explain some national differences in some aspects of the position of young people and the transition from youth to adulthood.

Richard Breen is an official fellow of Nuffield College, Oxford. He is a member of the Royal Irish Academy and a fellow of the British Academy. His research interests are social stratification and rational choice models. His most recent publications are Ireland North and South, Perspectives from Social Science: Proceedings of the British Academy 98, *which he coedited with Anthony Heath and Christopher T. Whelan (1999, Oxford University Press); "Class Inequality and Social Mobility in Northern Ireland, 1973-1996" in* American Sociological Review *(June 2000); and (with Jan O. Jonsson) "A Multinomial Transition Model for Analyzing Educational Careers" in* American Sociological Review *(October 2000).*

Marlis Buchmann is professor of sociology both at the University of Zurich and the Swiss Federal Institute of Technology in Zurich. Her research interests include patterns of intragenerational social mobility, gender inequality in the labor market, life course issues, and social change. Her work has been published in American and European scholarly journals. A book, The Script of Life in Modern Society, *has been published by The University of Chicago Press. Currently, she is studying the interplay between occupational qualifications, skill demands, and their joint effects on career outcomes in Switzerland. Another current research project explores shifts in the imagery of the self over the twentieth century in Switzerland (with Manuel Eisner).*

T HE articles in this issue report on a variety of young people's behaviors and attitudes drawn from a wide range of countries. In this article, we pose a more general question: how might we explain the differences between countries in these attitudes and behaviors? We suggest that for at least some of them, institutional variation supplies a partial answer. That is to say, differences between countries in many aspects of the transition to adulthood are, to an extent, the product of institutional variations that shape the context in which this transition takes place.

But to apply such an approach to accounting for national variation would require us to identify the specific institutional arrangements that are relevant for each of the behaviors and attitudes that are discussed in the articles in this issue. And our task is further complicated because each of the substantive articles deals with a different, though overlapping, set of countries. So, to make things more tractable, we limit ourselves in two respects. We will deal only with the countries of western Europe and the English-speaking non-European countries, and we will consider only some of the range of youth behaviors and attitudes described throughout this issue. We will focus on the economic position and residential and familial arrangements of young people in the transition to adulthood, and we will also look at their value orientations, their problem behavior, and the timing of their sexual initiation.

The institutional differences on which we focus concern the welfare state: differences in welfare state arrangements will play a crucial role in accounting for such variation, and we capture the variety of welfare state arrangements by using the typology of welfare regimes derived originally from the work of Esping-Andersen (1990). In discussing labor market outcomes, we also take account of differences in educational systems and in the regulation of labor markets, but these—particularly the latter—are in any case highly correlated with welfare regimes. Thus, our approach in this article might be summarized as an attempt to account for national differences in the situation of young people according to institutional differences in the welfare state and in closely related areas.

HOW INSTITUTIONS
MATTER

Cross-national variation in the age at which young people leave the parental home provides a simple example of one way in which institutions shape youth transitions. Three factors (among a number of others) are likely to be important in determining the age at which young people leave home. First, since young people seldom, if ever, leave the parental home before they have completed secondary education, the median or normal age of leaving secondary school will set a lower bound on the age of leaving home. Second, in

NOTE: In drafting this article, we have drawn heavily on ideas outlined by Karl Ulrich Mayer (1997, 2001).

many countries, young people first leave home to attend tertiary education, and so the organization of tertiary education will be an important factor in shaping the age at which this transition occurs. Three aspects of this will play a role: the normal age of entry to third-level education; the proportion of each age cohort that enters; and whether tertiary education is provided locally (so allowing students to live at home) or not, and whether grants and other forms of subsidy are available to allow students to live away from home. And the third important factor has to do with the functioning of the youth labor market and its links with the educational system: how easily and how quickly do young people find a stable job after leaving school or college? Of course, within any given set of institutional arrangements, there will exist a good deal of individual variation in behavior, and indeed, some arrangements will be less constraining, and will permit greater variation in behavior, than others. Nevertheless, if we want to compare societies in terms of their average patterns of behavior or in their distributions of particular behavior, institutional differences will be relevant. As a example, consider two societies, A and B. In society A, the normal age of completing full-time education is low, the tertiary education system encourages people to attend universities and colleges some distance from their family home, and jobs are relatively easy for young people to acquire. Conversely, in society B, education is prolonged, tertiary education is provided locally and there are no incentives to travel farther afield,

and it is difficult to get a foothold in the labor market. It would be surprising indeed if the average age of leaving the parental home were lower in society B than in A.

INSTITUTIONAL ARRANGEMENTS THAT INFLUENCE LABOR MARKET AND FAMILY TRANSITIONS

Three areas of institutional variation are relevant in explaining national differences in young people's labor market position and living arrangements. These are the overall welfare regime; the nature of the educational system, particularly the link between it and the system of economic production; and the regulation of the labor market. We now outline the major variation in each of these among the advanced societies, and then we will show how they interact to shape young people's labor market status and living arrangements.

Welfare regimes

The seminal work on welfare regimes is Esping-Andersen (1990). Drawing on earlier distinctions made by Titmuss (1974), Esping-Andersen proposed "three worlds of welfare capitalism." Conservative welfare regimes attempt to preserve status differentials and social policies and are thus often divided into occupational- or status-based programs that differ in their benefit level. Thus, status distinctions based on labor market position are carried over to the programs of the welfare state. The German- and French-speaking countries of continental Europe exemplify conservative welfare regimes. Liberal welfare regimes, typical of the Anglo-Saxon countries, are guided by a belief in the central role of the market. Minimal interference with the market leads to means-tested benefits, which are often stigmatized, and are applicable only in cases of market failure. Socialist or social democratic welfare regimes, usually associated with the Scandinavian countries, tend to favor universalistic, individual entitlements and benefit levels set at average or middle-class levels. Later authors have extended this typology by separating the welfare regimes of the southern European countries—notably Italy and Spain—from the conservative cluster to form a southern European variant. Like the conservative welfare regimes, the welfare arrangements here subscribe to the principle of subsidiarity with respect to the family; that is, welfare benefits tend to be channeled to individuals through the head of the household, who holds the direct entitlement to them. But in this case, this is coupled with an overall low level of provision of welfare by the state, except to the (usually male) head of the household who, once in a job, enjoys almost complete security of tenure and receives a generous pension. There is therefore a strong reliance on the family to provide welfare for its members.

Educational systems

Following the work of Allmendinger (1989), there has been a good deal of interest in characterizing educational systems according to dimensions relevant for how young people make the transition to the labor market. Allmendinger proposed that the two important aspects are the degree of standardization of educational provision and the stratification of the educational system. The former refers to the degree to which schools and other institutions adhere to common rules and standards, the latter to the extent of educational tracking. So in Germany, for example, stratification is marked because pupils begin to follow different tracks at a very early age. Allmendinger argued that the link between occupation and education is most specific in societies in which both standardization and stratification are high, because it is in such cases that "credentials provide detailed signals about the educational achievements of job applicants . . . [and] employers can rely on credentials to represent skill content reliably" (Müller and Shavit 1998, 7).

Later authors (notably Hannan, Raffe, and Smyth 1996) have presented revised versions of this typology, but the grouping of countries that usually emerges is closely related to the distinction made by Maurice, Sellier, and Silvestre (1982, 1986) between national systems characterized as "organizational spaces" and "qualification spaces." This is meant to capture the difference between a labor market in which qualifications have general currency (a qualification space), such as in Germany, and one in which they do not; rather, skills tend to be more organization specific (France is the case to which Maurice, Sellier, and Silvestre refered).

The essential distinction that all these categorizations make might be said to be between societies in which educational qualifications provide a very clear signal to employers of the potential productivity of a young person, with respect to the particular job that the employer is offering, and those in which this is not the case. This is also likely to be highly correlated with the balance between training for a particular job, which occurs within the educational system and within the firm itself, with the tendency for within-firm training to be relatively more important in cases where the educational system sends weak signals. A slightly more differentiated categorization results if we separate those systems wherein pupils in the educational system receive their vocational training both in schools and at the workplace (the so-called dual system) as found in Germany, Austria, and Switzerland; those where it takes place in vocational schools (Sweden and the other Scandinavian countries, Belgium, the Netherlands); and the remaining countries where vocational skills tend not to be taught, or to be taught only at a very low level, within the formal educational system.

Labor market regulation

The crucial issue, as far as the position of young people is concerned, concerns the degree of security of tenure that is enjoyed by occupants of jobs. It is well known that this can vary widely between different occupations and sectors in the same country, but it is also true that countries vary considerably in the extent of legal, and other, obstacles to the firing of workers. The Organization for

TABLE 1
EMPLOYMENT PROTECTION LEGISLATION

Country	Employment Protection Index	Youth/Adult Unemployment Rate Ratio, 1996
Netherlands	3.1	2.20
Germany	2.8	1.19
Sweden	2.8	2.59
Italy	2.8	3.67
Austria	2.6	1.35
Norway	2.4	3.18
Finland	2.4	2.04
France	2.3	2.39
New Zealand	1.7	2.41
Denmark	1.6	1.77
Ireland	1.6	1.65
Belgium	1.5	2.38
Switzerland	1.2	1.27
Australia	1.0	2.18
Canada	0.9	1.87
United Kingdom	0.8	2.10
United States	0.2	2.79

SOURCE: Organization for Economic Cooperation and Development (1999) (unemployment rate ratios calculated from pp. 228-30).

Economic Cooperation and Development (OECD) publishes an index of the restrictiveness of hiring and firing due to legislation and collective agreements, which is reproduced here in the second column of Table 1. As can be seen, employment protection legislation is strongest in some of the social democratic and conservative welfare regimes and weakest in the liberal, Anglo-Saxon countries. In the conservative and social democratic welfare states, high levels of employee protection can be seen as part of the normal corporatist trade-off between labor and capital, but in the southern European welfare states, a secure economic position for the head of the household is an essential component of a system in which the provision of welfare rests with the family rather than the state.

Although there is a good deal of literature arguing that institutionalized employment protection of the type found in Germany, for example, mitigates against economic performance, Estevez-Abe, Iversen and Soskice (2001) argued that "social protection aids the market by helping economic actors overcome market failures in skill formation." (p. 1). Furthermore, variations in employment protection can be explained as the consequence of the different functional necessities of the typical production systems found in different countries. So, Estevez-Abe, Iversen and Soskice argued, security of tenure and generous unemployment compensation in Germany provide the insurance that workers require to persuade them to invest in firm-specific and sector-specific, rather than general, skills. Conversely, in Britain and the United States, where general skills are in demand, there can be little functional justification for security of tenure or generous unemployment compensation. Nevertheless, our argument is that strong employment protection will lead to worse outcomes for young people in the labor market, most markedly so at times of high uncertainty about the future or when the economic outlook for firms is poor. This is simply because at such times, employers will be reluctant to hire new workers when they know that it will be difficult to get rid of them should the need arise (Bertola 1990).

To conclude this review of three institutional areas relevant to understanding the position of young people, three comments might be made. First, these are ideal types: they characterize national systems, but in the details of their welfare or educational arrangements, real national systems are always some mixture of types. Second, as with any typology, within-category variation is ignored. On closer examination, many differences exist among countries in the same regime cluster. A good example is the difference in the level of employment protection in Denmark, Finland, and Sweden, which is shown in Table 1. Another is provided by the differences in the nature of youth unemployment in Italy and Spain. While the Italian and Spanish labor markets and welfare regimes are remarkably similar in many respects, including the high degree of employment protection for mainly male adult workers, in the former, unemployed young people are overwhelmingly first job seekers, while in Spain, they have mainly had at least one job (Soro-Bonmati 2001). This difference is due to the introduction of temporary employment contracts for young people during the late 1980s and early 1990s on a much greater scale in Spain than in Italy. Last, there is a strong correlation between the three sets of arrangements that we have outlined—or, at any rate, there are some clear clusters. For instance, and most noticeably, liberal welfare regimes tend to have labor markets that operate in qualification space (educational outputs are not closely tailored to job demands) and in which employment security of tenure is low. In the German-speaking nations, which are a subset of the conservative welfare regimes, the opposite is true: educational outputs are closely linked to specific jobs, and security of tenure is high.

YOUTH UNEMPLOYMENT

To see how these three sets of institutional factors interact to influence young people, we consider first youth unemployment. On one hand, we should expect that all else equal, high levels of worker protection will reduce the chances of young people's acquiring a job, for reasons discussed above. But on the other hand, this effect will be offset in cases where there is a very close link between the educational system and particular jobs. Here education will carry very specific signals about the young person's suitability for and potential productivity in the job, and thus employers will be more confident that they are hiring the right kind of job seeker. Of course, the rate of youth unemployment will also be sensitive to a number of factors other than the kind of institutional arrangements we have described: not least, macro-economic conditions will probably be the most important determinant of its rate, and if different countries are at different points of the business cycle, this will lead to cross-national variation. Given our interest in institutions, this and similar differences can be seen as confounding factors. We can, however, control for some of these by looking not at the rate or level of youth

unemployment but at the ratio of the youth to the adult rate. This ratio is shown in the third column of Table 1 where, following OECD, we define youth to be men and women ages fifteen to twenty-four; the adult rate is the rate of unemployment for men and women twenty-five to fifty-four years of age. A quick glance at the figures shows that Germany, Austria, and Switzerland have very low ratios of youth to adult unemployment, while the ratio is particularly high in Italy and Greece. The correlation between this ratio and employment protection, shown in column 2, is only .1. But this is due both to the fact that the ratio is low in Austria and Germany where employment protection is high and to the fact that the ratio is high in the United States where employment protection is weak. If, however, we omit the United States and regress the youth/adult ratio on the measure of employment protection and also a dummy variable that distinguishes the German-speaking countries (Germany, Austria, and Switzerland), we obtain a coefficient of 0.319 (SE = .161) for employment protection, a coefficient of −1.162 (SE = .306) for being a German-speaking country, and an R^2 of .56. Thus, slightly more than half the national variation in the ratio of youth to adult unemployment rates can be explained by these two factors. That is to say, among the countries listed in Table 1, strong employment protection is associated with more severe problems of youth unemployment except where this tendency is offset by the existence of very close links between the educational system and employers and in which educational qualifications function as a very clear signal of a young person's productivity. The exception to this pattern is the United States where, despite low levels of employment protection, the youth/adult unemployment rate ratio is high, though within the context of very low absolute levels of unemployment.

AGE AT
LEAVING SCHOOL

Age-specific enrollment rates in secondary education tend to cluster according to the four types of welfare regimes discussed earlier. Table 1 of Fussell's (2002 [this issue]) article shows that rates of enrollment at age seventeen are highest in countries that fall into the social democratic or continental types and lowest in the liberal (or Anglo-Saxon) and southern European variants. But that table also shows that secondary education is prolonged to later ages in countries that have a well-developed system of vocational training, either through the dual system (in Germany and Switzerland; data for Austria are not reported in her table) or within school (notably in the Netherlands, Denmark, Norway, and Finland). The other side of this picture is then that entry into tertiary education tends to occur at younger ages in the Anglo-Saxon regimes and, to a less marked extent, the southern European countries (see Table 2 of Fussell's article). Attendance at university is often prolonged in southern Europe (see Cook and Furstenberg's [2002 (this issue)] article for the Italian case), and so it is in the liberal regimes that we find the earliest

conclusion to tertiary education. At age twenty-three, around or more than 20 percent of Danes, Finns, and Norwegians are still enrolled in tertiary education, compared with 12 percent of Americans and less than 10 percent of twenty-three-year-olds in the United Kingdom, Ireland, Australia, and New Zealand. In southern Europe, with the exception of Greece, enrollment rates in tertiary education tend to be quite high because access to some form of tertiary education is relatively easy. Overall, the picture that emerges is one of early completion of education in liberal welfare regimes and later completion elsewhere, particularly in the conservative and southern European regimes. These differences are evident in the data reported in the article by Smeeding and Phillips (2002 [this issue]). Drawing on a smaller set of countries, they show (see their Figure 1) that below the age of about twenty-five, the proportion of young men of a given age who are working full-year, full-time is markedly higher in the United Kingdom and United States than in Germany or Italy.

FAMILY FORMATION

One hypothesis about the kind of differences in the age of leaving home reported in Maria Iacovou's (2002 [this issue]) article is that they are substantially due to the interplay of the age of completion of full-time education and the likelihood of acquiring a job. An early age of completion of education will tend to reduce the age of leaving home, while high rates of youth unemployment will operate in the opposite direction. Thus, we should expect to see earlier home leaving in the liberal Anglo-Saxon welfare regimes (early completion of education, low youth unemployment) and the latest age of home leaving in the southern European countries (prolonged education and high youth unemployment).[1] The conservative and social democratic states should be intermediate. In the Germanic nations, the two factors operate in different directions: age of completing education is rather late, but youth unemployment is not a severe problem. This is also true of Denmark, though for a different reason (the high level of flexibility in the Danish labor market keeps youth unemployment low). In the case of France, education continues to quite a late age, and youth unemployment is high, but many young people leave the family home to attend university (Jurado Guerrero 1999).

By and large, this is the pattern we observe. Among the ten countries shown in Figure 4 of Iacovou's (2002) article, residence with parents is most prolonged in Italy, Greece, Spain, and Portugal (and also Ireland) and least prolonged in (in ascending order) Denmark, the United Kingdom, the Netherlands, France, and Belgium. The position of Ireland is somewhat anomalous: according to our hypothesis, it should display an early age of home leaving because education is completed at an early age and rates of youth unemployment are quite low, whereas in fact, it shows a relatively late age. What separates the Irish case from Italy and Spain, however, is that in the latter, unlike the former, the age at leaving home has increased in the recent past as the economic position of young people has worsened. This suggests that different explanatory factors may be at work in the Irish case.

In broad terms, then, we can discern the following patterns in young people's economic and residential transitions. At one extreme are the countries considered to have liberal welfare regimes. Here, early completion of education leads to rapid entry into the labor force and leaving of the parental home. This makes possible the formation of unions at an early age and early childbearing. Less regulated labor markets provide for relatively ready access to jobs but do not provide security of employment. Thus, we find relatively high rates of poverty among young people. Finally, given independence at an early age, we should expect that as well as significant life transitions occurring at a low mean age, they should also display, in their timing, greater variation around these means than we observe in other types of welfare regimes.

At the other extreme lie the southern European countries, characterized by a prolonged period in education, a very delayed transition into a regular full-time job, and a late age of home leaving. In essence, young people must become insiders in the labor market before they can embark on marriage and childbearing, and the time taken to achieve this is considerable; but once this hurdle has been passed, these life events follow rapidly.

PATTERNS OF CROSS-NATIONAL DIFFERENCES IN JUVENILE ATTITUDES AND BEHAVIORS

So far, we have gathered some evidence that the three sets of institutional factors considered here interact to influence the timing of major status changes in young people's transition to adulthood. We now extend our analysis to include various areas of juvenile attitudes and behaviors. The question we ask is whether the same sets of institutional characteristics are salient for structuring the contexts in which young people's attitudes and behaviors are molded. If distinct patterns of cross-national differences in juvenile attitudes and behaviors emerge, we can be somewhat confident that structural and cultural circumstances experienced during the transition to adulthood affect young people's preferences and styles of behavior. We will focus on some of those attitudinal and behavioral areas that are considered to be most constitutive of the youth life stage and the transition to adulthood. These include the formation of young people's value orientations, the development of behavior problems, and the timing of their sexual initiation. For the respective information, we will draw on several contributions to this issue.

The institutional approach emphasized in this article suggests that the structural and cultural properties associated with the institutional arrangements of the overall welfare regime, the nature of the educational system, and the system of labor market regulation are conducive to particular styles of behavior.

That is to say, a wide array of young people's attitudes and behaviors are expressions or manifestations of an underlying behavioral style that varies with the country-specific sets of institutional characteristics. With this assumption, we can now proceed to identify the styles of behavior that are related to particular institutional arrangements. In doing so, we will give preference to the institutional factor of the overall welfare regime. Our major argument is that clusters of welfare regimes are associated with basic patterns of everyday life in which young people's behavior is intrinsically enmeshed.

WELFARE REGIMES AND STYLES OF BEHAVIOR

To specify the associations between welfare regimes and styles of behavior, we refer to the four types of welfare arrangements outlined earlier in this article. Conservative welfare regimes are family oriented such that the state provides many services only in case of "family failures." In these instances, it is the head of the household who holds the direct entitlement to the welfare benefits, which are then channeled to the individual family members. This type of welfare arrangement embodies a family culture that is male dominated and hierarchical, including the cultural notion of wives and children as dependents. Although marriage has been considerably redefined in favor of more egalitarian relationships between husbands and wives during the recent past, the deep-rooted cultural imagery of men's role as breadwinners is still widely accepted (Pfau-Effinger 1999). This cultural stereotype helps to reinforce hierarchical, authoritarian relationships between husbands and wives as well as between the generations. The dependent status attributed to the younger generation within the family and, by extension, in the society at large constitutes a context in which there is, first, a relatively high level of social control over the young and, second, a rather strong dissociation between youth and adult cultures. That is to say, the cultural expressions preferred by the young greatly differ from those chosen by adults (Buchmann 2002).

Against this background, we expect relatively strong differences between young people's value orientations and those of adults. Likewise, young people are expected to engage relatively often in behaviors with which they can easily express the cultural distance to the adult world (e.g., illicit drug consumption). However, the relatively high level of social control over the young should attenuate the extent to which they engage in behavior problems. This is expected to hold especially in the Germanic nations of Austria, Germany, and Switzerland. The rather clearly demarcated, orderly pathways to adulthood, provided by the nature of the educational system with its tight links to the labor market and by the especially low levels of youth unemployment (see above), leave little room for uncertainties and normatively ill-defined, in-between situations in the transition to adulthood. As the age of completing education is rather late and youth unemployment is not a problem, the forces likely to promote higher levels of behavior problems, such as a strong dissociation between youth and adult culture, are attenuated.

The southern European variant of the conservative cluster of welfare arrangements referred to above shares the principle of subsidiarity with respect to the family. However, the overall level of provision of welfare in countries such as Italy and Spain is so poor that there is an extremely strong reliance on the family to provide welfare for its members (Esping-Andersen 1999; Millar 1996). Since little can be expected of the state, this institutional arrangement was traditionally associated with a male-dominated family structure, headed by fathers as strong household authority figures. The strong gender- and generation-based family stratification system goes hand in hand with high levels of parental control and surveillance of the young. As argued above, the strong inequality between generations fosters the dissociation between youth and adult culture. This is only the case, however, when there are many structural opportunities for engaging in juvenile subcultural activities. In Italy or Spain, these opportunities are not abundant. This is so mainly because the great majority of the young—the large group of the unemployed; those in institutions of higher education; and those holding precarious, temporary jobs—are sheltered by the family. They are forced to rely on the family for financial reasons and practical support, such as prolonged residence with the parents. Moreover, as Cook and Furstenberg (2002) convincingly argue in their contribution to this issue, the mounting difficulties of young people in Italy and Spain in finding secure economic positions and in successfully integrating themselves in the adult world have changed the family relationships. With the extremely prolonged common residence of the parent generation and the grown-up children generation, family relationships have been negotiated to become more egalitarian. The grown-up children have gained more autonomy and independence within their family of origin, thus loosening the former tight grip of social control while at the same time attenuating the desire to culturally distance themselves from the adult world.

Against this background, we expect a style of behavior to prevail in these countries that is—all in all—similar to the behavioral patterns characteristic of nations belonging to the main cluster of conservative welfare arrangements. In the absence of clearly demarcated pathways to adulthood due to the lack of vocational training opportunities and the high youth unemployment rate, we expect the level of behavior problems to be generally higher as larger groups of young people will encounter major difficulties in the transition to adulthood.

The socialist or social democratic welfare regimes, associated with the Scandinavian countries, are characterized by universal access to welfare benefits. Entitlements are to the individual and not to the head of the household. Welfare support covers a wide array of life circumstances, and benefit levels are generous (Mayer 2001). The cultural prevalence of universalistic principles in providing welfare benefits encourages egalitarian relationships between the sexes and the generations. Consequently, within the family and in society at large, young people are not primarily conceived as dependents (as in the conservative welfare regimes); rather, they are regarded as individuals with rights and obligations. The cultural incentives to become independent, autonomous, self-reliant, and responsible individuals are thus particularly strong. In their attempts to attain this goal, young people are not left alone, nor are they solely left in the hands of the family (as in the southern European variant of the conservative welfare regime). Rather, by actively supporting young people with, for example, study grants and loans, affordable housing, vocational training (together with private industry), or unemployment insurance, the state assumes responsibility in helping young people to successfully manage the transition to adulthood. As an active player in promoting young people's self-reliance, personal autonomy, and (financial) independence from their parents, the state also sends the cultural message to the young that they should aim at becoming active, responsible citizens. In this context, the dissociation between youth and adult culture is much weaker compared to countries in the conservative welfare cluster. In general, the high collective responsibility for the welfare of the individual creates a cultural climate that may be characterized as risk adverse.

Against this background, we expect relatively small differences between young people's value orientations and those of adults. Given the cultural sponsorship for early self-reliance and independence (see Cook and Furstenberg 2002), the incentives for engaging in subcultural activities to symbolically express the cultural distance to the adult world are not particularly strong. Likewise, the level of problem behavior is expected to be moderate as welfare benefits help to integrate young people into the society or help them to cope with adverse life circumstances. Engagement in risky behavior (e.g., risky driving and early pregnancy) tends to be low in the context of a risk-adverse cultural climate.

Finally, liberal welfare regimes, typical of the Anglo-Saxon countries, are market-driven. The credo of minimal interference with the market leads to state interventions only in cases of "market failures." Benefit eligibility is thus primarily based on economic need (Mayer 2001). The individual in need holds the direct entitlement to the welfare benefit. The market model embodies the fundamental idea that individuals can get ahead by themselves thanks to their own initiative and will power. More than any other welfare regime, the liberal model celebrates self-reliance in that it is up to each individual to take advantage of the opportunities that she or he may encounter. In contrast to the social democratic welfare arrangements, the collective responsibility for (young) individuals to attain this central cultural goal is minimal. Success or failure in attaining self-

reliance is thus culturally coded as personal failure. The salient role attributed to the individual's initiative and capacity for decision making is reflected in the highly competitive, risk-prone, and individualistic cultural climate prevalent in Anglo-Saxon nations. Within this cultural context, young people are primarily regarded as individuals. Accordingly, the family is characterized by relatively egalitarian relationships between the generations and the sexes. As argued before, egalitarian family structures constrain the dissociation between youth and adult culture.

Against this background, we expect relatively small differences between young people's value orientations and those of adults. With regard to juvenile behavior problems, we expect to find the highest level in the liberal nations for several reasons. First, when competition and risk taking is an important part of the cultural repertoire, young people are more likely to engage in risky behaviors than elsewhere. Second, a highly individualistic and competitive context may exert more pressure to engage in problem behavior to attain some highly valued goals. Third, the laissez-faire culture of liberal nations is likely to produce a larger share of young people who encounter difficulties in making the transition to adulthood for which it then provides little support. Finally, the cultural coding of missed opportunities as individual failure enhances the likelihood of engaging in deviant behavior to experience some kind of success and thus to keep up young people's self-esteem.

VALUE ORIENTATIONS

To test our expectations about patterns of cross-national differences in young people's value orientations, we draw on the information provided by James Tilley's (2002 [this issue]) contribution to this issue. With one exception, the country clusters on which his analyses are based serve our purposes. There is no cluster for the southern European variant of the conservative welfare regime.[2]

Compared to the liberal and the social democratic welfare regimes, the country cluster of conservative nations exhibits, in general, the largest age differences in attitudes. This is especially true for religious beliefs, to a lesser extent for attitudes toward women's role in society, for Left-Right political attitudes and attitudes toward political activities (if we discount the steeper age gradient for the older than fifty-five-year-olds in the social democratic country cluster), and for overall life satisfaction. It does not hold, however, for the attitudes toward new social movements. Overall, Tilley's (2002) findings lend some support to our expectation that the dissociation between youth and adult culture is most pronounced in the country cluster of the conservative welfare regime.

In the country cluster of the social democratic welfare regime, we further note the most gender-egalitarian attitudes toward women's role in society and the greatest willingness to engage in political activities. These findings correspond with the normative structure of a culture strongly based on universalistic principles and of promoting responsible citizens. Compared to their counterparts growing up in liberal or conservative welfare regimes, young people living in countries characterized by social democratic welfare arrangements also show the highest life satisfaction. Apparently, the collective support for early self-reliance and personal autonomy provided by the social democratic welfare regime translates into a high level of life satisfaction among the young.

BEHAVIOR PROBLEMS

The contributions by Manuel Eisner (2002 [this issue]) and Patrick Heuveline (2002 [this issue]) provide the information we can draw on to compare patterns of cross-national differences in young people's behavior problems and behavior-related mortality. The analyses presented in Eisner's and Heuveline's articles are based on much larger country samples than is of immediate interest here. For each behavioral dimension considered here (i.e., suicide, violent crime, property crime, illicit drug consumption, problem drinking, and death from motor vehicle injuries), we therefore computed the rank ordering of the subset of countries included in our comparison of welfare regimes.[3]

With the partial exception of the United Kingdom and especially Ireland, young people living in countries characterized by liberal welfare arrangements score highest on almost all dimensions of behavior problems considered here. It is only the consistently moderate suicide rate that deviates from the general pattern of high involvement in behavior problems.[4] This is consistent with our expectation that young people exposed to a highly competitive, risk-prone culture providing little collective support for the transition to adulthood are more likely to get involved in risky behavior (e.g., risky driving), sensation-seeking behavior (i.e., illicit drug consumption), and other forms of deviant activities.

The opposite pattern of generally low involvement in problem behavior applies to the country cluster of the social democratic welfare regime. Denmark, however, is the big country exception to the rule, where high levels of problem drinking and property crime prevail. And contrary to the expectation of low involvement in behavior problems is the high death rate from suicide, which does not apply to Norway, however. Many findings are in line with our expectations, namely that the collective sponsorship for early self-reliance and personal autonomy prevalent in the social democratic welfare regimes is likely to attenuate juvenile behavioral problems. The findings that deviate from our expectations remind us, however, that monocausal explanations do not do justice to the highly complex processes involved in the development of juvenile behavior problems (for this argument, see Eisner 2002).

The country clusters of the conservative welfare regime and its southern European variant exhibit levels of young people's engagement in behavior problems that are intermediate when compared to the high level characteristic of the liberal nations and to the low level observed in countries within the social democratic welfare cluster. Within the conservative country cluster, we find a clear distinction between the French-speaking countries (Belgium and France) and the German-speaking countries (Austria, Germany, and Switzerland) on some dimensions (e.g., suicide, substance abuse) but not on others (e.g., problem drinking, death rate caused by motor vehicle injuries). The country cluster of the southern European variant of the conservative welfare regime, which includes Italy and Spain, holds consistently moderate levels of involvement across all dimensions of behavior problems. The only exception is the low suicide rate. As discussed above, a complex mix of structural and cultural factors that mold young people's behaviors characterizes the two types of welfare regime. Factors such as strong dissociation between youth and adult culture, strong parental control and surveillance, and well-demarcated pathways to adulthood in the Germanic countries are likely to simultaneously reinforce and attenuate engagement in deviant behavior, so that a relatively complex picture of young people's engagement in problem behavior emerges.

TIMING OF
SEXUAL INITIATION

For information on differences in patterns of sexual initiation and teenage fertility, we refer to the contribution written by Julien Teitler (2002 [this issue]). In the 1970s, the last decade for which Teitler provides data, some cross-national differences in timing of sexual initiation still exist, but they have dramatically declined.[5] Hence, the overall trend observed is one of between-country convergence in the timing of sexual initiation. This trend is accompanied by considerable between-gender convergence. Against the general trend of convergence, some country differences nonetheless stick out. Early sexual initiation for both young men and young women still apply to countries of the liberal welfare regime. In the country cluster of the social democratic welfare regime, we observe very early initiation for women and—with the exception of Denmark—somewhat later initiation for men. Relatively late initiation for both men and women is characteristic of the nations included in the cluster of conservative welfare regimes. Finally, the country cluster of the southern European variant of the conservative welfare regime shows tremendous gender differences with very early initiation for men and very late initiation for women. Overall, the findings reported here suggest a relationship between the degree of dissociation between youth and adult culture associated with welfare regimes and the timing of sexual initiation: early initiation for countries characterized by weak dissociation and later initiation for countries characterized by strong dissociation.

CONCLUDING COMMENTS

In this article, we have sought to sketch some of the ways in which institutional variation might explain some national differences in some aspects of the position of young people in society and in their transition from youth to adulthood. Institutions affect these things because they establish a set of opportunities and constraints to which young people and other relevant parties (such as employers) respond. But institutional arrangements also reflect, and in other cases help to establish, what counts as normatively appropriate behavior. We conceptualized institutional variation in terms of the four major welfare regime types that have been prominent in the literature for the past decade—liberal, social democratic, conservative, and southern European—together with labor market regulation and educational systems.

The use of a typology such as this is admittedly a rather blunt instrument with which to explain differences between countries in very specific patterns of behavior; not least, it implies that a given outcome will be the same in all countries of the same type. To understand differences within clusters we need to posit other cross-cutting typologies—such as the distinction between kinds of educational system and education–labor market linkages that make the Germanic countries distinctive within the conservative type. And ultimately, of course, a fuller understanding of cross-national variation within types would draw on nationally specific factors of culture and history. Having said that, however, it is clear to us that for some of the behaviors discussed in this issue, the institutional differences that we have invoked provide at least some—

and in certain instances, a good deal of—explanatory leverage.

Notes

1. Prolonged education may itself be a response to the difficulties of obtaining a job.

2. The countries labeled Anglo-Saxon in Tilley's (2002) article (Britain, Canada, Ireland, the United States) correspond to nations characterized by liberal welfare regimes. The Nordic country group (Denmark, Finland, Iceland, Norway, and Sweden) refers to the country cluster we labeled social democratic welfare arrangements. Finally, the western European country cluster (Belgium, France, Italy, Ireland, West Germany) greatly corresponds to what we have labeled the conservative welfare regimes.

3. The country cluster of the liberal welfare regime includes Australia, Canada, Ireland, New Zealand, the United Kingdom, and the United States. Social democratic welfare arrangements characterize the following countries: Denmark, Finland, Norway, and Sweden. We include Austria, Germany, and Switzerland as well as Belgium, France, and the Netherlands into the country cluster of the conservative welfare regime. Finally, Italy and Spain make up the southern European variant of the conservative welfare arrangements.

4. The low problem drinking observed for the United States is another, albeit singular, country-specific deviation to the general pattern.

5. Again, the set of countries considered in Teitler's (2002) analyses differs somewhat from the ones described before. The country cluster of the liberal welfare regime includes Great Britain and the United States. The social democratic welfare regime refers to Denmark, Finland, Iceland, and Norway. Conservative welfare arrangements apply to Belgium, France, Germany, the Netherlands, and Switzerland. Finally, Greece and Portugal stand for the southern European variant of the conservative welfare regime.

References

Allmendinger, Jutta. 1989. Educational systems and labor market outcomes. *European Sociological Review* 5:231-50.

Bertola, Giuseppe. 1990. Job security, employment and wages. *European Economic Review* 34:851-79.

Buchmann, Marlis. 2002 (forthcoming). The sociology of youth culture. In *International encyclopedia of the social and behavioral sciences*, edited by Neil J. Smelser and Paul B. Baltes. Oxford, UK: Elsevier Science.

Cook, Thomas D., and Frank F. Furstenberg Jr. 2002. Explaining aspects of the transition to adulthood in Italy, Sweden, Germany, and the United States: A cross-disciplinary, case synthesis approach. *Annals of the American Academy of Political and Social Science* 580:257-87.

Eisner, Manuel. 2002. Crime, problem drinking, and drug use: Patterns of problem behavior in cross-national perspective. *Annals of the American Academy of Political and Social Science* 580:201-25.

Esping-Andersen, Gøsta. 1990. *The three worlds of welfare capitalism*. Cambridge, MA: Polity.

———. 1999. *Social foundations of postindustrial economies*. Oxford, UK: Oxford University Press.

Estevez-Abe, Margarita, Torben Iversen, and David Soskice. 2001. Social protection and the formation of skills: A reinterpretation of the welfare state. In *Varieties of capitalism: The challenges facing contemporary political economies*, edited by Peter Hall and David Soskice. Oxford, UK: Oxford University Press.

Fussell, Elizabeth. 2002. The transition to adulthood in aging societies. *Annals of the American Academy of Political and Social Science* 580:16-39.

Hannan, D. F., David Raffe, and Emer Smyth. 1996. Cross national research on school to work transitions: An analytical framework. Unpublished paper.

Heuveline, Patrick. 2002. An international comparison of adolescent and young adult mortality. *Annals of the American Academy of Political and Social Science* 580:172-200.

Iacovou, Maria. 2002. Regional differences in the transitions to adulthood. *Annals of the American Academy of Political and Social Science* 580:40-69.

Jurado Guerrero, Teresa. 1999. Why do Spanish young people stay longer at home than the French? The role of employment, housing and social policies. Ph.D. thesis, European University Institute, Florence, Italy.

Maurice, Marc, François Sellier, and Jean-Jaques Silvestre. 1982. *Politique d'éducation et organisation industrielle en France et en Allemagne: Essay d'analyse sociétal*. Paris: Presses Universitaire de France.

——. 1986. *The social foundations of industrial power*. Cambridge, MA: MIT Press.

Mayer, Karl Ulrich. 1997. Notes on a comparative political economy of life courses. *Comparative Social Research* 16:203-26.

——. 2001. The paradox of global social change and national path dependencies. In *Inclusions and exclusions in European societies*, edited by Alison Woodward and Martin Kohli, 89-110. New York: Routledge.

Millar, J. 1996. Family obligations in Europe: Patterns and policy trends. Paper prepared for the seminar of the European Observatory on National Family Policies, El Escorial, Madrid.

Müller, Walter, and Yossi Shavit. 1998. The institutional embeddedness of the stratification process: A comparative study of qualifications and occupations in thirteen countries. In *From school to work: A comparative study of educational qualifications and occupational destinations*, edited by Yossi Shavit and Walter Müller, 1-48. Oxford, UK: Oxford University Press.

Organization for Economic Cooperation and Development (OECD). 1999. *Employment outlook 1999*. Paris: OECD.

Pfau-Effinger, Birgit. 1999. Welfare regimes and the gendered division of labour in cross-national perspective—Theoretical framework and empirical results. In *Working Europe: Reshaping European employment system*, edited by Jens Christiansen, Anna Kovalainen, and Pertti Koistinen, 69-96. Aldershot, UK: Ashgate.

Smeeding, Timothy M., and Katherin Ross Phillips. 2002. Cross-National differences in employment and economic sufficiency. *Annals of the American Academy of Political and Social Science* 580:103-33.

Soro-Bonmati, Asuncion. 2001. From school to work: A comparison of labour market transitions and leaving home decisions of young people in Germany, Italy and Spain. Ph.D. thesis, European University Institute, Florence, Italy.

Teitler, Julien O. 2002. Trends in youth sexual initiation and fertility in developed countries: 1960-1995. *Annals of the American Academy of Political and Social Science* 580:134-52.

Tilley, James. 2002. Is youth a better predictor of sociopolitical values than is nationality? *Annals of the American Academy of Political and Social Science* 580:226-56.

Titmuss, Richard M. 1974. *Social policy*. London: Allen and Unwin.

VISIT SAGE ONLINE AT: WWW.SAGEPUB.COM

Find what you are looking for faster!

Our advanced search engine allows you to find what you are looking for quickly and easily. Searches can be conducted by:

- Author/Editor
- Keyword/Discipline
- Product Type
- ISSN/ISBN
- Title

Payment online is secure and confidential!

Rest assured that all Web site transactions are completed on a secured server. Only you and Sage Customer Service have access to ordering information. Using your Visa, MasterCard, Discover,
or American Express card, you can complete your order in just minutes.

Placing your order is easier than ever before!

Ordering online is simple using the Sage shopping cart feature. Just click on the "Buy Now!" logo next to the product, and it is automatically added to your shopping cart. When you are ready to check out, a listing of all selected products appears for confirmation before your order is completed.

WE'RE ONLINE!

Visit our Web site at: http://www.sagepub.com

BUY RECYCLED.

AND SAVE.

Thanks to you, all sorts of everyday products are being made from materials you've recycled. But to keep recycling working to help the environment, you need to buy those products.

So look for products made from recycled materials, and buy them. It would mean the world to all of us. For a free brochure, please write *Buy Recycled*, Environmental Defense Fund, 257 Park Ave. South, New York, NY 10010, or call 1-800-CALL-EDF.

Ad Council A Public Service of This Publication

EPA

ENVIRONMENTAL DEFENSE FUND EDF

You aren't looking at
a future pilot.

You're looking at YOUR
future pilot.

Higher academic standards are good for everyone.
What a child learns today could have a major effect tomorrow. Not just on him or her, but on the rest of
the world. Your world. Since 1992, we've worked to raise academic standards. Because quite simply,
smarter kids make smarter adults. For more information, call 1-800-38-BE-SMART or visit www.edex.org.

The Business Roundtable • U.S. Department of Education • Achieve
American Federation of Teachers • National Alliance of Business
National Education Association • National Governors Association   Education / Excellence Partnership